BI 0724637 4

KT-579-267

26

BIRMINGHAM CITY
UNIVERSITY
DISCARDED

OPTION VALUATION
Analyzing and Pricing Standardized Option Contracts

McGraw-Hill Series in Finance

Consulting Editor
Charles A. D'Ambrosio, *University of Washington*

Archer and Kerr: *Readings and Cases in Corporate Finance*
Brealey and Myers: *Principles of Corporate Finance*
Doherty: *Corporate Risk Management: A Financial Exposition*
Edmister: *Financial Institutions: Markets and Management*
Francis: *Investments: Analysis and Management*
Francis: *Management of Investments*
Fuller and Farrell: *Modern Investments and Security Analysis*
Garbade: *Securities Markets*
Gibson: *Option Valuation: Analyzing and Pricing Standardized Option Contracts*
Johnson and Slottje: *Case Studies in Finance Using Lotus 1-2-3®*
Johnson and Slottje: *Case Studies in Finance Using Microsoft® Excel*
Lang: *Strategy for Personal Finance*
Levi: *International Finance: The Markets and Financial Management of Multinational Business*
Maness: *Introduction to Corporate Finance*
Martin, Petty, and Klock: *Personal Financial Management*
Schall and Haley: *Introduction to Financial Management*
Sharpe: *Portfolio Theory and Capital Markets*
Smith: *Case Problems and Readings: A Supplement for Investments and Portfolio Management*
Smith: *The Modern Theory of Corporate Finance*
Stevenson: *Fundamentals of Finance*

OPTION VALUATION
Analyzing and Pricing Standardized Option Contracts

Rajna Gibson

Assistant Professor of Finance
Groupe H.E.C.
(Hautes Études Commerciales)
Paris, France

McGraw-Hill, Inc.

New York   St. Louis   San Francisco   Auckland   Bogotá   Caracas   Hamburg
Lisbon   London   Madrid   Mexico   Milan   Montreal   New Delhi   Panama
Paris   San Juan   São Paulo   Singapore   Sydney   Tokyo   Toronto

Generous financial support for writing this book was provided by the Geneva Stock Exchange.

OPTION VALUATION
Analyzing and Pricing Standardized Option Contracts

Original edition published by Georg Editeur, Geneva, Switzerland.

Copyright © 1991 by McGraw-Hill, Inc. All rights reserved.
Printed in the United States of America. Except as permitted under the
United States Copyright Act of 1976, no part of this publication may be
reproduced or distributed in any form or by any means, or stored in a data
base or retrieval system, without the prior written permission of the
publisher.

2 3 4 5 6 7 8 9 0 DOC DOC 9 5 4 3 2 1

ISBN 0-07-023447-7

This book was set in Times Roman by Publication Services.
The editor was Kenneth A. MacLeod;
the production supervisor was Kathryn Porzio.
The cover was designed by Rafael Hernandez.
Project supervision was done by Publication Services.
R. R. Donnelley & Sons Company was printer and binder.

UNIVERSITY OF
CENTRAL ENGLAND

Book no. 07246374

Subject no. 332.63222 Gib

INFORMATION SERVICES

Library of Congress Cataloging-in-Publication Data

Gibson, Rajna.
   Option valuation: analyzing and pricing standardized option
contracts / Rajna Gibson.
       p.   cm.—(McGraw-Hill series in finance)
Includes bibliographical references (p.   ) and index.
ISBN 0-07-023447-7
1. Options (Finance)—Prices—Mathematical models.   I.   Title.
II. Series
HG6024.A3G53   1991   90-6625
332.63′ 228—dc20

ABOUT THE AUTHOR

Rajna Gibson is Assistant Professor of Finance at Groupe H.E.C., Paris, France. She was previously visiting scholar at New York University and at the University of California, Los Angeles. She received her Ph.D. in Finance from the University of Geneva, Switzerland. Her research is concerned with the valuation of—real and financial—derivative securities. She has also written *Bonds and Bond Optional Features: Valuation Principles*, to be published in French by Presses Universitaires de France, Paris, France, in 1990.

TO MICHAEL

CONTENTS

Foreword   xi

Preface   xiii

1 An Introduction to the General Characteristics of Options   1

1 Introduction   1
2 What Is an Option?   3
3 Basic Properties of an Option's Price   8
4 Analyzing Option Strategies   13
5 Why Standardized Option Markets?   21
6 Conclusion   22

2 Rational Boundaries to Option Pricing   25

1 Introduction   25
2 General Restrictions on European and American Option Prices   26
3 Impact of Dividends on Option Price Boundaries   32
4 Put-Call Parity Relations   38
   A Put-Call Parity Relationship for European Options on
      Nondividend-Paying Stocks   38
   B Put-Call Parity Relationship for European Options on
      Dividend-Paying Stocks   41
   C Put-Call Relationship for American Options on
      Nondividend-Paying Stocks   42
   D Put-Call Relationship for American Options on
      Dividend-Paying Stocks   44
5 Conclusion   46

**3 The Pricing of a European Option on a
     Nondividend-Paying Stock**   49

1 Introduction   49
2 The Replicating Portfolio   50
3 Assumptions Underlying the Binomial Approach   51
4 The Binomial Option Pricing Formula   55

5   Applying the Binomial Approach: An Example   61
    A   The Recursive Approach   61
    B   The Binomial Pricing Formula   64
6   A Closer Look at the Binomial Option Pricing Formula   66
7   Conclusion   71

4   The Black and Scholes Option Pricing Formula   **73**

1   Introduction   73
2   The Black and Scholes Formula Viewed as the Limiting Case of
    the Binomial Option Pricing Formula   74
3   An Example   81
4   Some Insights into the Black and Scholes
    Option Pricing Model   83
5   The Determinants of an Option's Price   88
    A   The Striking Price   89
    B   The Time to Maturity   89
    C   The Interest Rate   91
    D   The Stock Price   92
    E   The Standard Deviation of Stock Returns   97
6   Illustrating European Option Prices, Behavior   98
7   Conclusion   100

    Appendix 4.1   **102**

    Appendix 4.2   **105**

**5   The Black and Scholes Formula as an Investment
    Decision-Making Tool**   **107**

1   Introduction   107
2   How to Compute the Black and Scholes Formula:
    Some Technical Considerations   108
    A   The Stock price: S 109
    B   The Exercise Price: K 109
    C   The Time to Maturity: τ 111
    D   The Riskless Interest Rate: τ 112
    E   The Variance of Stock Returns: σ^2 113
    F   A Numerical Example   120
3   Extending the Black and Scholes Formula to the Pricing of
    Dividend Paying Stock Options   122
    A   Introducing the Dividends in the Black and Scholes
        Option Pricing Model   122
    B   The Black and Scholes Formula and the Pricing of
        American Options   127
4   Measuring the Risk Exposure of Option Positions   133
    A   Defining and Using Option Price Sensitivity Measures   133
    B   A Numerical Example   136
    C   The Concept of an Option's Price Elasticity   139
5   Conclusion   143

6 **Improving and Extending the Single Factor Option Pricing Model**   145

1 Introduction   145
2 Relaxing the Constant Risk-Free Interest Rate Assumption   146
3 The Early Exercise Feature of American Options Revisited   150
   A The Binomial Approach   150
   B Other Solutions to the Pricing of American Options   156
4 A Closer Look at the Distributional Properties of the Stock Price   161
   A Nonstationarity of the Stock Returns' Variance   163
   B Discontinuities in the Stock Price Sample Path   168
5 Conclusion   176

7 **Generalizing the Arbitrage-Free Pricing Approach to Stock Index and Stock Index Futures Written Options**   181

1 Introduction   181
2 General Characteristics of Stock Indexes: An Overview   183
   A Equally-Weighted Stock Indexes   184
   B Price-Weighted Stock Indexes   185
   C Market-Weighted Stock Indexes   187
3 Analyzing Options Written on Stock Indexes   188
   A Description of a Stock Index Option Contract   188
   B Stock Index Options and Portfolio Management Strategies   190
   C Valuing European Stock Index Options   192
   D The Valuation of American Stock Index Options   196
   E General Problems Related to the Pricing of Stock Index Options   198
4 General Characteristics of Forward Contracts, Futures Contracts, and Stock Index Futures   202
   A Forward Contracts: Basic Properties   202
   B Financial Futures Contracts: Basic Properties   211
   C Stock Index Futures Contracts: Basic Properties   215
   D Valuing Stock Index Futures Contracts   219
5 Analyzing Options Written on Stock Index Futures   224
   A The Pricing of European Options Written on Stock Index Futures Contracts   226
   B The Pricing of American Options Written on Stock Index Futures Contracts   232
6 Options on the Spot Index, Options on the Futures Index, and Market Integration: Concluding Remarks   241

8 **Analyzing and Pricing Foreign Currency Options**   245

1 Introduction   245
2 General Characteristics of a Foreign Currency Option   248
3 General Arbitrage Restrictions Applying to Foreign Currency Option Prices   252
4 The Pricing of European Foreign Currency Options   264
5 The Pricing of American Foreign Currency Options   273

6   Analyzing the Problems Related to the Pricing of Foreign Currency Options   276
    A   The Distributional Properties of the Exchange Rate
        and the Pricing of Foreign Currency Options   276
    B   Some Other Issues Related to the Pricing of Foreign Currency Options   282
7   Conclusion   285

9   Conclusion   289

    References and Further Reading   293
    Index   297

FOREWORD

As a student of Myron Scholes in the late 1960s, I was privileged to have been present at the birth of the option pricing paradigm. The labor was long, for although the central ideas were in place when I graduated in 1970, it was not until 1973 that the *Journal of Political Economy* published the seminal paper of Black and Scholes. This was the same year that trading in listed options contracts began in Chicago, a coincidence that epitomizes the symbiotic relation that has persisted between the academic theory of option pricing on the one hand and its practical application on the other.

Although the original markets in stock option contracts were highly successful, they have since been surpassed by more generic, less specific option contracts: contracts based on stock market indexes, interest rates, and exchange rates. This development is not surprising, for the behavior of interest rates or currencies, or stock indices such as the Standard and Poor's 500, is of considerably greater importance for the well-being of most investors than is the behavior of any individual stock, such as IBM. Thus investors are interested in contracts that allow them to hedge away part of the risk associated with holding a portfolio of stocks, such as that represented by the S&P 500, or a portfolio of bonds or foreign assets.

As the markets for option contracts increase in sophistication and scope, it becomes more important for the individual who trades in these markets to be familiar with the relevant theory that underlies the pricing of these contracts. For example, the increasing popularity of customized contracts, which are traded over the counter rather than on organized exchanges, increases the need for purchasers to beware lest the price they pay be too high relative to what they are receiving. At the same time the institution selling such options must be familiar with the techniques available not only to price but also to hedge the liability arising from such contracts.

This book provides the student an introduction to option pricing theory and simultaneously an extension of its application to those standardized option contracts that are most often used for risk monitoring purposes. It also develops the student's critical judgment by emphasizing strengths and weaknesses of the different option pricing models in light of the empirical evidence and the theoretical assumptions on which they rely.

Although the theory of option pricing can be daunting to the novice, Professor Gibson presents the major concepts in a simple and intuitive way without sacrificing rigor. A particular strength of this book is the careful attention it gives to futures contracts and options on stock index futures and foreign currencies.

Michael Brennan
University of California, Los Angeles

PREFACE

The development of option markets represents a most striking financial innovation that has over the past decade transformed the process of managing asset portfolios. From an academic viewpoint, the mere existence of standardized option contracts has challenged the establishment of the classical theory of finance by introducing the contingent claims valuation approach. Indeed, the concept of "optional contract" extends—implicitly or explicitly—far beyond the standardized contracts traded on exchanges since it can be embedded in many other real or financial assets as well as in the investment and financing decision-making process of the firm.

This textbook focuses primarily on the valuation of options and more specifically of standardized option contracts. Its main intention is to present the option pricing theory not only as a rather complex set of valuation formulae but also as a pedagogical instrument that can be used to assess the basic factors affecting option prices, their risk-return trade-off, and their trading mechanisms. The approach therefore aims at being rigorous as well as at providing the intuition and the practical applications underlying each valuation model.

One of the original features of the book lies in its structure, which is set in two main parts: a general one, focusing on the common stock option as the illustrative example. The first part is intended to present the basic concepts, the methodology as well as the economic rationale of the most commonly known option pricing models. This part encompasses Chapters 1 to 5.

The second part, Chapters 6 to 8, gradually broadens the topic along two different dimensions. First relaxing some of the disturbing hypotheses of the standard single factor option pricing model (Chapter 6), we are progressively driven to the current frontiers of option pricing theory while getting an insight into its major extensions over the past decade. We are thus led in Chapters 7 and 8 to analyze in detail the pricing mechanism of two other important types of standardized options, namely those written on a basket of stocks and those written on a currency. In discussing the properties of stock index options, stock index futures options (Chapter 7), and foreign currency options (Chapter 8), we acknowledge that the option pricing theory plays a key function in the currency- and market-risk exposure monitoring process. This provides an important economic justification to the mere existence of these derivative securities. In parallel, we reconsider the strengths and limits of the most commonly used option pricing models as applied to those option categories. This leads us to emphasize some interesting problems arising when the underlying asset is not traded, when the contract involves some specific provisions (such as the cash settlement of stock index options, for example), and when the trading structure is inefficient.

An overview of the structure of the book is provided in the table of contents and is further detailed at the end of Chapter 1. As can be seen from its definition, *Option Valuation* is primarily suited as the core reading for an elective course on "Options" intended for graduate and advanced undergraduate students in finance or economics. However, the chapters are sufficiently self-contained to recommend this textbook as supplementary reading material for a large variety of elective courses focusing on options. More specifically, it can be recommended for:

> a graduate course on "Futures and Options" for which Chapters 1 to 7 are well suited
>
> an "Introductory Course on Options" for which Chapters 1 to 5 are recommended
>
> a graduate course on "Portfolio Management" (based on Chapters 5 to 7 if the student already has a prior knowledge of option pricing theory, the whole book excluding Chapter 8 otherwise)
>
> a graduate course on "International Portfolio Management," for which Chapters 7 and 8 provide a valuable support

Thus, even though the book's main audience consists of MBA program students specializing in finance, it can be very useful to students in business economics or economics interested in the applications of the contingent claims pricing methodology to economic modeling.

The prerequisites to understanding *Option Valuation* are introductory courses in investments and in corporate finance as well as a first-level course in probability and statistics.

Finally, I wish to emphasize that one advantage of this textbook lies in its intuitive yet detailed analysis of the valuation of options, a feature that extends its audience to any practitioner dealing in options or actively managing option portfolios' risk exposure. The reading of the second part of the book is particularly suited to any practioner who feels the need to understand what is behind the "black box" when using standardized options for market timing or domestic and international hedging purposes.

ACKNOWLEDGMENTS

Before entering more deeply into the subject, I would like to express my gratitude and my deep acknowledgments to the Geneva Stock Exchange for financially supporting the realization of this book.

I would further like to thank Professor André Bender of the University of Geneva, Switzerland, for initiating the whole project and for defending the choice of this subject proposal. I am also very grateful to Professor Pierre-André Dumont and Nils Tuchschmid of the above-mentioned university as well as to my husband, Michael Gibson, for their precious contribution in reading the preliminary drafts of the book and providing meaningful comments and insights to improve its final version.

This book has benefited greatly from the insightful discussions I had with Professors Michael Brennan, Julian Franks, and Eduardo Schwartz during my stay at the University of California at Los Angeles. My thanks to them all and especially to Michael Brennan for agreeing to write the foreword.

I am further indebted to Suzanne Be Dell and Kenneth MacLeod of McGraw-Hill, in New York for their helpful assistance and contribution to the publication of *Option Valuation*.

I must also mention Alan E. Grunewald, Michigan State University and C. Thomas Howard, University of Denver for their suggestions during early review of the manuscript.

The last word goes to my husband and my mother, Michael and Mila, to thank them for providing through their moral support and affection a (paradoxically) invaluable contribution to the completion of *Option Valuation*.

Rajna Gibson

CHAPTER
1

AN INTRODUCTION TO THE GENERAL CHARACTERISTICS OF OPTIONS

1 INTRODUCTION

Historically, the first type of option contract to be traded consisted of put options on tulip bulbs that Dutch growers would purchase to protect the price of their crops. This example, dating back to the seventeenth century, has been followed by an erratic development, including common stock written options trade in Great Britain during the eighteenth century and in the United States since the beginning of the nineteenth century. During those days, however, option contracts were not standardized. The markets were not regulated and were often manipulated, leading on several occasions to suspensions of option trading.

The major breakthrough in the development of option markets happened in April 1973, when the Chicago Board of Options Exchange began trading standardized call option contracts on 16 common stocks and thereby offered the first regulated structure capable of providing the volume, the liquidity, and the solvability necessary to create efficient option markets. Since then, the Chicago Board of Options Exchange has also developed transactions in put options, and several other exchanges in the United States, such as the American Stock Exchange, the Philadelphia Stock Exchange, the Pacific Stock Exchange, and the New York Stock Exchange, have begun trading standardized call and put contracts written on common stocks. In terms of volume, the success of these instruments has been tremendous, as can be observed through the fact that the number of options contracts traded since the early 1980s exceeds—in terms of their underlying stock equivalent—the number of shares traded on the New York Stock Exchange.

Furthermore, standardized option markets experienced in parallel a geographical expansion whereby we can nowadays engage in a stock option transaction in London, Montreal, Paris, Sydney, Amsterdam, Stockholm, or Geneva—in other words, from almost any major financial center around the world.

However, the most remarkable feature of the recent development of standardized option contracts has to be its expansion in the variety of option contracts written on different types of underlying instruments that have been introduced in different exchanges since the beginning of the 1980s.

Indeed, stock written options are now just one type of option contract among a large population consisting of stock index options, stock index futures options, fixed-income securities written options, foreign currency written options, commodity options, and so on. The success of some of these newest option contracts, such as the stock indexes written options, the Treasury bond and the Treasury bond futures written options, and the oil futures written options, sets them currently among the leading and most actively traded financial instruments. In fact, the introduction of standardized option contracts, the geographical expansion, the increasing volume of trading, and the variety of innovative—newly created—option contracts jointly represent the most spectacular phenomenon in the evolution of financial markets over the last century.

The success of standardized option contracts can be explained by the negotiability, the liquidity, and the smaller transactions costs their centralized, regulated, and standardized trading has been able to offer market participants. But to an even greater extent, this success has to be found in the very nature of an option and thereby in the "original" payoff structure and various risk-monitoring strategies this financial instrument can provide to its potential buyer or seller.

Finally, it should be noted that although options have indeed gained interest among the academic community since the introduction of standardized option contracts—with the pioneering development of the Black and Scholes option pricing formula in 1973—the analysis of options and the development of pricing models to assess their "fair," or theoretical, value extend far beyond the concept of standardized option contracts. Indeed, options can be found "everywhere"; they can be standardized or not, traded or not traded—such as the option embedded in a callable bond. Some securities or financial decisions that do not even look like options at first sight can easily be analyzed and priced in the general setting of option pricing theory.

Indisputably, the importance of the concept of an option can be ignored neither by the academic involved in research topics focusing on the financial markets nor by any other professional actively involved in the portfolio management process. From the latter profession's perspective we can say that options have and still are inducing noticeable transformations in the "traditional" asset allocation and asset management approaches. Options have a lot to offer owing to their specific payoff structure and their ability to hedge—or speculate with—various sources of investment risk, but they simultaneously put pressure on every professional who has to understand those rather complex financial instruments in order to value them and manage them efficiently.

It is therefore the purpose of this study to provide the reader with (1) a general understanding of the essential features of an option contract, (2) an in-depth analysis of the main option pricing models—some of which are very simple, others more complex in their formulation—which are useful in pricing or managing option positions, and (3) a well-informed, hopefully objective, attitude toward the main achievements and main weaknesses of the option pricing theory.

Ultimately, whether for the sake of integrating options in an existing asset allocation plan, for hedging purposes, or for the specification and valuation of new financial instruments embedding "option-type" features, everybody would agree that the pedagogical effort is worth the potential rewards one may expect from a thorough understanding of the concept of an option.

However, before entering more deeply into the analysis of option contracts, one must first become familiar with the features of an option, with its qualitative definition, with its contractual specifications, and with all the necessary vocabulary that surrounds the description, trading, and management of this financial instrument. This introductory chapter shall therefore be concerned with the general description of an option contract, and for that purpose we shall begin with the most common type of standardized option, namely a stock written option contract. This will enable us to simplify the presentation while leaving us with enough generality because the contractual specification, the basic strategies, and the vocabulary applying to the different option contracts are similar (once we abstract from the institutional features that may vary from one option contract to the other or from one exchange to the other).

2   WHAT IS AN OPTION?

Broadly speaking, an option is a contract that entitles its owner with the right to buy or sell a specific quantity of the underlying instrument—here the stock—at a specific price and during a specific time period. The first part of this general definition of an option contract is related to the fact that this instrument conveys a "right," not an obligation, to its owner; in other words, the choice of buying or selling the underlying instrument is "optional" and cannot be imposed on the option owner. This is very different from a futures contract or a forward contract since these financial instruments "oblige" both parties—the buyer and the seller—to meet their obligations at the contract's expiration date.

However, the preceding definition of an option is still too vague at this stage since it doesn't explicitly emphasize that there are two types of options, namely call and put options. The former type of option conveys to its owner the right to buy, and the latter gives its owner the right to sell the underlying instrument. We can now use this distinction to define the call option and the put option more precisely:

A *call option* is a contract that gives its owner the right to buy the underlying instrument at a predetermined price and during a specific time period.

A *put option* is a contract that gives its owner the right to sell the underlying instrument at a predetermined price and during a specific time period.

When the owner of a call or put option decides to use the right to buy or sell the underlying instrument, we say that he is *exercising* his option. The owner has the choice of deciding whether or not to exercise that right, but note that the counterpart to the call or the put contract is *obliged* to sell (in the case of an exercised call) or to buy (in the case of an exercised put) the underlying instrument.

Hence, we can already see that the structure of the payoffs an option provides to its owner and to its seller—the counterpart is generally called the option writer—are not the same since the former bears a right while the latter has the resulting obligation to eventually—if the owner exercises the option—buy or sell the underlying security.

Since the option writer provides a "valuable" financial instrument to the option owners, he will have to be compensated by a cash amount equal to the market price of the option, also called the *option premium*. This price should represent the "fair" compensation to the option writer for bearing the counterpart's obligation of eventually having to buy or to sell the underlying instrument.

However, we should at this stage also distinguish between (1) those options that enable the owner to exercise his right at any time during the contract's lifetime and (2) those that only enable him to exercise the option at the expiration date of the contract. In the earlier definitions of a call and a put option, we were explicitly assuming that they belong to the first category, or that they were of the *American* type. The second category contains options that can only be exercised at expiration and that are generally referred to as European options. This geographical distinction is somewhat artificial nowadays since most standardized option contracts trading in and outside the United States are of the American type. European option contracts are more typically found among over-the-counter–traded stock options and among interbank-traded foreign currency options. However, recently some standardized option contracts written on stock indexes—such as the Institutional Index option contract traded on the American Stock Exchange—were also designed to allow for exercise only at the expiration date of the contract. Since American puts and calls clearly provide additional rights—in terms of allowing the owner to exercise the option over its entire lifetime—with respect to their European counterparts, they should always sell for at least the same price as otherwise identical European puts and calls.[1]

We shall now examine the main parameters that define and distinguish one option contract from the other. As we already mentioned, options can be of the

---

[1] However, we shall see that due to their early exercise possibilities, American options generally require a more complex pricing methodology than do otherwise identical European options written on the same underlying instrument.

American or of the European type and they can allow us to buy or sell the underlying instrument in which case we shall refer to a call or a put option respectively. However option contracts must also be distinguished through the nature of the "underlying instrument" their owner may buy or sell.

In the case of a stock written call or put option, the "underlying instrument" is a common stock. This suggests that when we exercise this call (put) we are in fact buying (selling) a specific number of stock shares at the conditions specified in the contract. Similarly, we can trade options written on Treasury bond securities, foreign currencies, gold, or oil futures, thereby acquiring the right—as the option owner—to buy or sell a specific quantity of Treasury bonds, foreign currencies, gold, or oil futures contracts that are the respective underlying instruments of the preceding designated option contracts.

To simplify and preserve the homogeneity of this presentation, we shall describe the main parameters and features of an option contract by referring exclusively to the category of options whose underlying instrument is a common stock. When necessary, we shall illustrate our comments by reference to common stock options trading on the Chicago Board of Options Exchange.[2] Since these contracts are standardized, they will conform to a uniform specification regardless of the underlying stock on which they are based.

In particular, a call or a put option written on a stock is characterized by the following:

1. The size of the contract is the number of shares of stock a single option contract allows you to buy or sell. Generally, a single contract enables its owner to buy or sell 100 shares of the underlying stock. In cases of stock splits or stock dividends this number can be adjusted.

2. The striking price or exercise price of an option represents the fixed-price the owner of the call (put) will have to pay (receive) for one share of stock when he exercises his option.

   Depending on the level of the stock price, options are issued over a wide range of exercise prices that span its current level and are generally integer numbers. For example, the SEC (Security and Exchange Commission) authorizes all exchanges in the United States to design stock options with striking prices evenly divisible by five, and defined over 5-point intervals for striking prices up to $100 and over 10-point intervals for striking prices greater than $100.[3] Obviously, this integer rule can be violated in the case of adjustments for stock splits or stock dividends.

---

[2] Obviously, the contractual features of a common stock written option trading on another exchange will be defined similarly although the figures that are associated with each individual parameter's value (for example, the number of shares of stock underlying one option contract) and the trading regulations (regarding, for example, position limits or margin deposits) may differ across exchanges or countries.

[3] For some stocks, an exchange may choose to use larger striking price intervals as long as they remain approved by the SEC.

3. The time to maturity of an option contract is also standardized, so we usually observe that each stock has options with three different maturities that trade at the same time and belong to one of the following expiration cycles:

January/April/July/October
February/May/August/November
March/June/September/December

Hence, at any time, options are available with the nearest three terms to the present, so their time to maturity shall never exceed nine months.[4] Furthermore, standardized option contracts have a last trading date that is the third Friday of the expiration month and they effectively expire on the following Saturday.

4. The payout-protection rule indicates whether the terms of the contract are adjusted for some type of events that can dilute the stock price. Typically, standardized option contracts are protected against stock splits and stock dividends,[5] but they are not adjusted for cash dividends.[6] Note that the latter statement doesn't apply to over-the-counter traded stock options that are generally protected against cash dividends paid during their time to maturity.

5. The underlying stock must be identified through its name and must also meet certain requirements in order to serve as the underlying instrument of listed options. Typically, exchanges will impose limits on the minimum volume of outstanding shares, the liquidity of the stock, the profit capacity of the firm, the solvability of the firm, and so on before they would issue options on a specific stock.

6. Finally, we should note that standardized stock options can be exercised at any time since they are almost always of the American type. This is true for standardized options regardless of the country where they are actually traded.

While these features characterize the option as a contract bearing static rights and characteristics, we still need to complete its description by examining the dynamics of this financial instrument and hence its daily transaction reports. For that purpose, let us look at the price quotes reported from *The Wall Street Journal* for some stock options traded on the Chicago Board of Options Exchange: As we can see in Table 1.1, options are quoted with respect to their underlying stock. By reading the quotes from left to right we see that the first available information is the closing price of the underlying stock as of the previous day. Then, if we read

---

[4] Note that since 1985, each option belonging to an expiration cycle can trade an additional near-term contract so some stock options now have four expiration dates available simultaneously.

[5] The adjustment procedure will be discussed in detail in Chapter 5, Section 2.

[6] The existence of the dividends can therefore induce the owner of an American call option to exercise his call prior to expiration as we shall see in Chapter 2.

TABLE 1.1
Stock option price quotes, Tuesday, May 17, 1988

Option & Strike NY Close Price		Calls–Last			Puts–Last		
		May	Jun	Sep	May	Jun	Sep
Apache	7½	r	r	1¼	r	r	r
7⅞	10	r	r	¼	r	r	r
BrisMy	35	r	r	r	r	r	11/16
39½	40	⅜	1¼	2½	¾	1⅜	2¼
39½	45	1/16	3/16	⅞	5⅜	r	r
39½	50	r	1/16	¼	r	r	r
Bruns	10	s	12⅞	s	s	r	s
22⅛	20	2¾	3	4¼	r	r	r
22⅛	22½	5/16	⅞	2¼	1/16	1	1⅜
22⅛	25	1/16	⅜	1 1/16	r	r	r
Chamin	30	r	3¾	r	r	r	r
33¼	35	1/16	½	1⅝	1⅝	2	r
CompSc	40	1¼	r	r	⅛	r	r
41	45	r	r	1¾	4	r	5⅜
DowCh	65	s	r	s	s	1/16	s
82⅛	75	r	9	r	1/16	⅜	1¾
82⅛	80	2½	4¾	7½	¼	1½	3½
82⅛	85	3/16	1⅞	4½	2¼	4	r
82⅛	90	1/16	7/16	2½	7	7¼	r
82⅛	95	r	⅛	1½	r	r	r
FBost	25	r	r	5½	r	½	⅞
29	30	⅝	1¼	2¾	¾	r	r
29	35	s	⅜	r	s	r	r
Ford	40	9⅛	8⅜	9⅝	r	1/16	½
48¼	42½	s	6¼	s	s	⅛	s
48¼	45	3⅛	3⅞	5⅛	1/16	7/16	1½
48¼	47½	s	2 1/16	s	s	1	s
48¼	50	⅛	⅞	2 7/16	1⅜	2⅝	3⅝
Gap	17½	r	6⅜	r	r	r	r
23½	20	3¾	3⅝	r	r	¼	r
23½	22½	⅞	2	3⅝	⅛	¾	1⅞
23½	25	⅛	⅞	2	r	2⅝	r
23½	30	r	¼	r	r	6	r
Gencp	15	r	3½	r	r	r	r
18⅛	17½	¾	r	r	r	r	r
18⅛	20	r	¾	r	r	r	r

CHICAGO BOARD

Total call vol	283,077	Call open int	3,003,967
Total put vol	190,719	Put open int	1,283,303

r-Not Traded. s-No Option.

Source: The Wall Street Journal, May 18, 1988. Reprinted by permission of *The Wall Street Journal*, ©Dow Jones and Company, Inc., 1988. All rights reserved.

horizontally, we have for each series containing options with the same striking price and with different expiration dates—in the case, May–June–September— the closing prices of the calls and then of the puts. Each successive row contains the same information for options written on the same stock, but lists a different exercise price until we exhaust the whole exercise price range of a given category of stock options, and thus reach a new stock that has its own option contracts quoting.

Note that the price quoted for each option is the price per underlying share of stock, that is, the value of one contract is obtained by multiplying the quoted price by 100 (the size of each option contract). Also note that option contracts that have prices under $3 trade in sixteenths of a point, while those with a price exceeding $3 trade in eights of a point. For example, by using Table 1.1 to compute the price of one Ford 45 call expiring in June, we find that it is equal to

$$3\,\tfrac{7}{8} \times 100 = \$387.50$$

In addition, observe in Table 1.1 that the letters "r" and "s" are sometimes used instead of a reported price. The letter "r" indicates that this specific put or call didn't trade, while the letter "s" indicates that this specific put or call has not been opened by the exchange.

Finally, each exchange also reports summary statistics about the trading activity in all its stock option contracts. The first of these statistics reports the total volume of call contracts—here 283,077—and of put contracts—here 190,719— and thereby measures the total number of call and put contracts respectively that were traded on a specific day. The open interest, the second of these statistics, measures the number of outstanding call (here 3,003,967) and put contracts (here 1,283,303) still available—because they have not been exercised or closed—at the end of the day.

3   BASIC PROPERTIES OF AN OPTION'S PRICE

There are four basic strategies associated to the trading of an option:

- An individual can buy a call or a put and it is then common to say that he enters into an "opening" long position in the call or in the put. The buyer pays the price of the option to the writer, and in exchange acquires the right to buy or sell the underlying stock at a future time.
- An individual can sell a call or a put and it is then common to say that he enters into an "opening" short position in the call or in the put. The seller receives the premium or market price of the option but must be prepared to buy or to sell the underlying stock whenever his short call or put is exercised. The individual who sells the option is generally called the option writer.

Note that buying or selling an option may actually result in a closing transaction if the individual had previously undertaken an opposite transaction by respectively selling or buying the same option. Closing purchases or sales of options are also called offsetting transactions when their resulting effect is to cancel the long or the short put or call position previously opened.

- An individual can exercise his option at any time (if it is an American option) or at its expiration date (if it is a European option) by buying or selling a certain number of shares of the underlying stock at a price per share equal to the striking price specified in the contract. When exercising a call, he receives the shares and pays the exercise price times the number of shares specified in the contract. By exercising a put, he delivers the shares and receives a cash amount equal to the exercise price times the number of shares.
- An individual has another possibility if he already owns a call or a put that is doing nothing, and thereby letting his right expire worthless at expiration.

To understand the basic mechanisms underlying an option's price let us first examine the possible transactions and the resulting payoffs associated respectively with a call and a put option at their expiration date. At the expiration date—denoted by T—the owner of the call compares the current value of the stock price S^* with the exercise price (K) of the call to determine what optimal action should be taken. If the stock price is greater than the exercise price of the call, it is optimal for the owner to exercise the option, hence paying \$$K$ for a share that is worth S^* on the market. Alternatively, if the owner doesn't want to exercise the option, he can sell his call. In both cases the value of the call at expiration—denoted by C^*—must be equal to the difference between the stock price and the exercise price. Therefore it must be true that

$$C^* = S^* - K \qquad \text{if } S^* > K \qquad (1.1a)$$

If the call price were smaller than $S^* - K$ everybody would buy it, exercise it, and immediately make an arbitrage profit equal to $S^* - K - C^*$. Hence, the presence of arbitrageurs would bid the call price up. Similarly, if the call price were greater than $S^* - K$, arbitrageurs would sell the call and buy the underlying security simultaneously. When the call is exercised the arbitrageurs would receive the striking price in exchange for the stock, and the transaction would give them a riskless profit of $C^* - S^* + K$ which is exactly equal to the amount by which the call trades above its "fair value" $S^* - K$. Everybody would like to engage in such a transaction, thereby creating a selling pressure on the call's price, driving it down to its only possible equilibrium value, namely $S^* - K$.

If on the expiration date T^*, the striking price is greater than the observed stock price, then of course nobody would be willing to pay \$$K$ for a stock that is worth less ($S^* < K$) on the market. Thus, the call will expire unexercised and worthless.

When the exercise price is equal to the stock price at expiration, however, everybody is indifferent to deciding between exercising the call—paying $K = S^*$ for the stock—or letting it expire worthless since the price of the stock on the market is as good a deal as it is exercising the option.

It must therefore be true that the price of the call at expiration satisfies

$$C^* = 0 \qquad \text{if } S^* \le K \qquad (1.1b)$$

Combining (1.1a) and (1.1b), we can state that the price of the call at expiration must be worth

$$C^* = \begin{cases} S^* - K & \text{if } S^* > K \\ 0 & \text{if } S^* \le K \end{cases}$$

or in other words

$$C^* = \max[0, S^* - K] \qquad (1.2)$$

We can now illustrate graphically the call price as a function of its underlying stock price at expiration. Figure 1.1 shows the "unusual" payoff structure of a call option. Contrary to a forward or futures contract owner, the option holder has no "obligation" and can therefore throw the option away—letting it expire worthless— whenever it is unfavorable to use the right inherent in this contract. Therefore, the call's price at expiration has an unlimited upward potential whenever the stock price increases above the striking price and has a limited—to zero since it has limited liability—downward potential whenever the stock price is less than the exercise price.

By analogy, we can also show that the owner of a put option will exercise his right to sell the stock at K if the stock price (S^*) is lower than the exercise price at maturity. The presence of arbitrageurs will assure that in this case

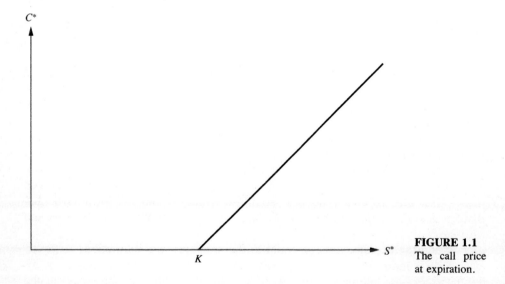

FIGURE 1.1
The call price at expiration.

the put must sell for exactly its "exercise value" $K - S^*$, the difference between the striking price of the put and the stock price. Hence, at the expiration date, the price P^* of the put option must satisfy

$$P^* = K - S^* \qquad \text{if } K > S^* \qquad (1.3a)$$

If the stock price at that time happens to be higher than the exercise price, there is no incentive for the put owner to exercise the right to sell the stock for $\$K$ if he can sell it directly in the market at a higher price S^*. The owner will therefore let the put expire worthless. Similarly, if the striking price of the put is exactly equal to the stock price at expiration, there is no advantage for the owner between exercising his right to sell the stock and letting it expire worthless.

Thus whenever the striking price of the put is less than or equal to the stock price at the expiration date, the put expires worthless:

$$P^* = 0 \qquad \text{if } K \leq S^* \qquad (1.3b)$$

Combining Equations 1.3a and 1.3b, we obtain the general equation defining a put option's price at its expiration date:

$$P^* = \max[0, K - S^*] \qquad (1.4)$$

Graphically the put price at expiration can be represented as shown in Fig. 1.2. This simple diagram illustrates that the put price reaches its maximum value at expiration—-equal to the exercise price—when the stock price is worthless. Its value then gradually declines as the stock price increases, reaching zero when the

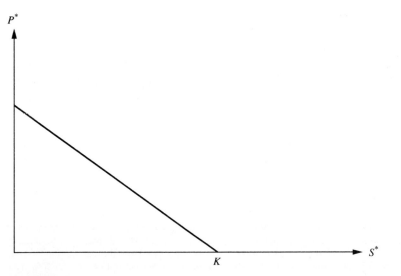

FIGURE 1.2
The put price at expiration.

stock price is equal to the exercise price. Thereafter, even though the stock price continues to increase, the put's value is always equal to zero since its owner has no obligation to exercise his option when it is unfavorable to do so.

Note that the terms max[O, $S*-K$] max[O, $K-S*$] defining the call and put prices at expiration are also called the exercise values of the call and put options at maturity. At any given date $t(t < T)$ before expiration, the terms max[O, $S - K$] and max[O, $K - S$] also give the prevailing exercise values[7] of the call and the put.

Whenever the current value of the stock price (S) is greater than the exercise price, we say that the call is in-the-money; whenever the current value of the stock price is equal to the exercise price, the call is at-the-money; and finally, whenever the current stock price is smaller that the exercise price, the call is out-of-the money. By a symmetric argument, we can say that a put option is trading in-, at-, or out-of-the money, respectively, whenever its striking price is greater than, equal to, or smaller than the currently prevailing stock price.

At their expiration dates, the call and the put trade exactly at their exercise or "intrinsic" values. However, at any time prior to expiration, their market price should be at least equal[8] to or greater than their intrinsic value. The difference between the market price of a call option and its exercise value ($C -$ max $[O, S - K]$) or between the market price of a put option and its exercise value ($P -$ max $[O, K - S]$) is defined as the "time value" of the option. The time value explains why, for example, out-of-the money options that have no intrinsic value still have a strictly positive market price before their expiration date. Hence, we can define the current price of an option before its expiration date as equal to its exercise value plus its time value.

The time value of an option contains the factors that provide it with additional value. Due to the volatility of the underlying stock, the longer the option's time to maturity, the more chances there are to observe it expire in-the-money. The time value of an option is a rather complex component of its price that is a function of the time to maturity of the option, the underlying stock's degree of volatility, and the level of interest rates. We shall discuss the concept of time value in more detail when we will come to the central topic of this study—the analysis and the pricing of options.

Now that we have defined some basic properties of the option's price and we know exactly how to compute the latter at its expiration date, it will be easier to analyze some simple option strategies and compare their outcomes with those obtained by investing in more "traditional" securities.

---

[7] Strictly speaking this is only true for American call and put options since they can be exercised at any time prior to maturity. For European options, the exercise value at a given time prior to maturity is simply the stock price less the present value of the exercise price for the call option and the present value of the exercise price less the current stock price for the put option. We shall analyse this specific feature of European options in Section 2 of Chapter 2.

[8] Strictly speaking this relationship applies only to American options that can be exercised prior to their expiration date. Further explanations on this subject will be provided in Chapters 2, 5, and 6.

4 ANALYZING OPTION STRATEGIES

Let us first focus on the simplest two types of strategies one can undertake with options, namely buying or selling a call or a put option and holding that long or short position until the expiration date of the option.[9]

For the call option, this will lead to the following payoffs shown in Fig. 1.3 at the expiration date. When observing these profit and loss diagrams, it immediately appears that the call owner's position is perfectly symmetric to that of its writer. In fact, by paying the initial price $(-C)$ of the call, the owner has "de facto" protected himself against any downside movement in the stock price—below the exercise price—that could occur at the expiration date of the contract. Clearly, this has a cost[10] equal to the initial value of the call $(-C)$ that

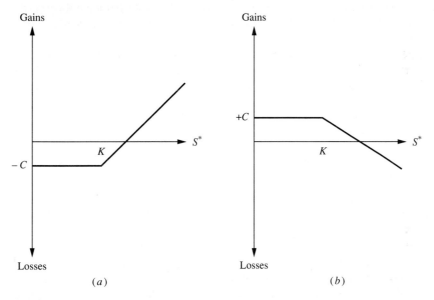

FIGURE 1.3
Payoffs at expiration date: (*a*) long call; (*b*) short call.

---

[9] We shall abstract from the early exercise feature of American options, and therefore, we can think about the strategies presented in this section as being undertaken with European call and put options or with American options held until expiration. The early exercise feature of American options can alter the outcome of a given strategy especially when we are talking about short positions. Hence, the discussion of when and why the early exercise of an American option may actually occur and of its impact on option strategies will be discussed in the next chapters.

[10] Since the initial price of the option is paid before the expiration date, the "true" gains and losses diagrams should also take into account the foregone (earned) interest on the call premium over the period lasting between the call's original purchase (sale) date and its expiration date. To simplify, we shall assume that this period is very small and this interest rate component can be neglected. This is a pedagogical simplification that we must rectify in practice if we want to assess the true gains or losses associated with a particular strategy.

the writer of the call will in fact receive $(+C)$ as a compensation for taking the opposite part of the transaction and hence bearing "exercise risk". Thus, the buyer of a call knows that his maximum loss is equal to the cost of the option $(-C)$ but that he has unlimited upside potential if the stock ends up in-the-money at expiration. Clearly such a strategy suggests that the buyer of a call option has "bullish" views about the stock's price evolution. Contrarily, the call writer has a limited profit that can never be greater than the initial price of the call but can bear an unlimited loss if the stock expires deeply in-the-money. Obviously, to take such a risky position the writer of a call must expect the stock to remain fairly stable over time or to have a slight downward trend.

In other words, the buyer and the seller of a call option actually participate in a zero-sum game in which one party always loses exactly what the other gains. We can also see that the buyer and the seller have in fact split between themselves or "redistributed" part of the payoffs that are otherwise obtained by having a long and a short position in the stock.

Indeed, the buyer and the seller of a share of stock have the potential to realize the following gains and losses at the expiration date of the option[11] given that they have initially bought and sold the stock for a price equal to $\hat{S}$ (see Fig. 1.4). If we compare Figs. 1.3a and 1.4a, we see that the owner of the

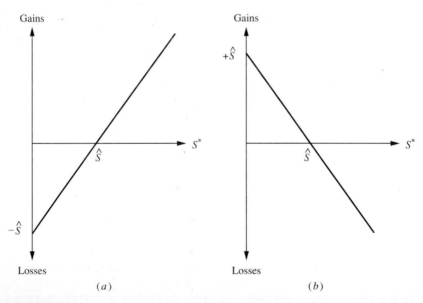

FIGURE 1.4
Payoffs from (a) a long stock and (b) a short stock position.

---

[11] We can think of the time period between the stock purchase (sale) and the expiration date of the option as the investment horizon over which we shall compare the payoffs of the option to those of the stock.

call has bought protection against the potential stock price decline by paying "an insurance" premium that limits the maximal loss to the call's price instead of the initial stock price. For a whole range of terminal stock prices ($S^* < K$), the call owner will always face a constant loss that is equal to the call's purchase price.

Contrarily, if we compare the position of the call writer in Fig. 1.3*b* with the position of the stock short seller in Fig. 1.4*b*, we see that the former has de facto engaged in a more risky position by selling the call and collecting the premium. Indeed, this premium represents the call writer's maximal expected profit while he participates—like the short seller of the stock—in the unlimited loss potential that might occur if the stock price increases. We see that the call option writer only has an advantage over the stock short seller if the stock price remains fairly stable since in the latter case the premium he receives represents a better deal than the zero net profit on the short stock position.

Finally, Fig. 1.5 illustrates the gains and losses the buyer and seller of a put option will actually incur by holding their positions until expiration. By looking at the payoffs to the put owner, we see that he has a position similar to that of the short seller of the stock except that he has bought "insurance" against any increase in the stock price greater than the striking price. Hence, he gains if the stock price at expiration is less than the exercise price by an amount sufficient to cover the initial purchase price of the put. Note that unlike the buyer of a call, the buyer of the put has a "limited" profit potential since his gain can never exceed the difference between the put's striking price and its purchase price ($K - P$), which represents the maximal proceeds earned if the underlying stock is worthless at expiration.

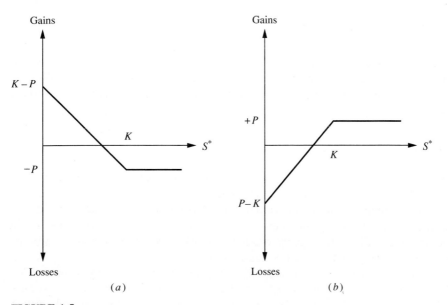

FIGURE 1.5
Payoffs for a put option at its expiration date: (*a*) long put; (*b*) short put.

Further, observe that like the buyer of the call, the put owner has insured himself by limiting his maximal loss to the purchase price of the put $(-P)$. In other words, a long position in the put corresponds to a short position in the stock plus an "insurance" policy against any increase in the stock price above the striking price. Obviously, a bearish view about the expected value of the stock at the expiration date is associated with this position.

Since the put writer is willing to accept any losses stemming from a potential stock price decline, he receives, in exchange for the premium—or the put's price, payoffs "symmetric" to those of the put option owner. The risk transferred by the put owner to the put writer is, however, limited since the stock price can never fall below zero. Hence the put writer's maximal loss—the premium less the exercise price $(P - K)$—is bounded while the call writer's loss is theoretically unbounded (if the stock price goes to infinity). Moreover, the put writer has a maximal gain equal to the premium he initially receives $(+P)$, indicating that his payoff structure is comparable to one resulting from a truncated long-stock position. Indeed, by collecting the "put price," the put writer is willing to take the risk of a decline in the stock price but simultaneously renounces any gains should the stock price rise above the exercise price. By limiting ex ante his maximal profit to the amount of the premium, he only has an advantage over the owner of a stock if the stock price remains fairly stable or rises very slightly. Hence, the writer of a put expects a stable stock price at expiration and can be viewed as slightly bullish.

In summary, this description of the basic buy- and sell-strategies available with put and call options emphasizes several features of these financial instruments:

- The buyer and the seller of an option play a fair "zero-sum game" (as do the buyer and the seller of any other security such as a stock, for example).
- By using "insurance" against the undesirable part of the stock price payoffs, the buyers and the sellers of put and call options actually "allocate" or "split" the payoffs of a long and a short position in the underlying stock among themselves.
- While the payoffs to the owner or writer of put and call options are contingent upon the evolution of the underlying stock price, they are nonlinear and therefore unlike the latter asset's payoffs.

This nonlinear payoff structure is very important in explaining the success of options as financial instruments that provide investors and managers with profit and loss functions unattainable by individually purchasing or selling other securities—like common stocks, bonds, or futures contracts. Indeed, options positions enable the buying and selling of a "right" whereas a stock or a futures position commits both its owner and seller with obligations.

So far, we have analyzed "naked" positions that involve buying or selling a single financial instrument or security. However, calls and puts will generally be used in more complex strategies involving more than one option and serving various portfolio management purposes.

The first of these more sophisticated strategies involves a put or a call and the underlying stock and is usually referred to as a "hedge." Hedging is a very useful risk-monitoring strategy that aims at offsetting the gains (losses) on one asset by the losses (gains) on another asset, and thereby reducing—even eliminating in a "perfect hedge"—the global risk exposure of the resulting position. Typically, any position in a stock or in a stock written option will be sensitive to unexpected stock price shifts, and this uncertainty can be modified by combining the stock with either a call or a put position.

If we are long in a share of stock, we can hedge it either by writing call options or by buying put options. In both cases, the options are sold and bought respectively to create a potential selling obligation or right that has to offset the long position in the stock.

We shall talk about hedging strategies and the way they are implemented in the next chapters. To illustrate their possible payoffs, however, we shall illustrate graphically two of the most common ones. The first hedge aims at offsetting a long position in the stock[12] by one written call and is often called a "covered call" position shown in Fig. 1.6. This payoff looks familiar since its shape can also be achieved by shorting a put option (see Fig. 1.5b). This suggests that we can easily replicate the structure of one option, such as a put, by taking adequate positions in the underlying stock and in the call option.[13]

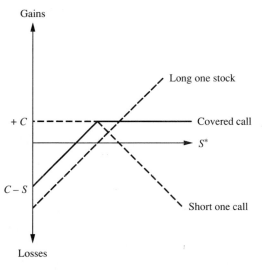

FIGURE 1.6
Covered call position

---

[12] For simplicity we assume that the purchase price of the stock (S) is equal to the striking price of the call option (K).

[13] More precisely using the so-called "put-call parity" relationship it can be shown that a short put can be replicated by selling the call, buying the stock and lending the present value of the exercise price. The put-call parity relationship will be discussed in detail in Chapter 2, section 4.

How such a replicating strategy may be accomplished—by creating "synthetic" put or call positions—is discussed more thoroughly in Chapter 2.

Note that this covered call strategy doesn't offer much protection compared to what we would traditionally expect from a "perfect" hedge. In fact, to create a perfectly hedged position involving one written call, we shall generally need less than one share of stock, and the precise number of stock shares required— usually called the "hedge ratio"—is computed from some theoretical option pricing model–derived sensitivity measure of the call's price with respect to the underlying stock price. In the next chapters, we shall be particularly interested in analyzing the properties of this hedge ratio that enables us to combine the written call with "the relevant" fraction of stock shares held long in such a way as to obtain a perfectly riskless or hedged position. Any gains (or losses) on the written call will then be exactly offset by equal dollar losses (or gains) on the long-stock position.

The second type of hedge also involves a long position in one share of stock. The offsetting position, however, is now taken by buying one put on this underlying stock. At expiration, this so-called "protective put" strategy leads to the payoffs shown in Fig. 1.7.[14]

A protective put hedge really involves "buying" insurance against any decline in the stock price below its initial level ($S = K$) at a cost equal to the purchase price of the put ($-P$). With this strategy we limit our downside risk but still maintain the benefits related to any increase in the stock price exceeding the

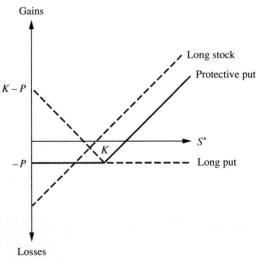

FIGURE 1.7
Protective put hedge.

---

[14] We assume as before that the purchase price of the stock (S) is equal to the exercise price of the put (K).

level $(K + P)$. The payoff diagram of the protective put strategy looks familiar since it's exactly the same shape as the one associated to a long position in a call option. This leads us back to our previous comment since we can again show that the payoff structure of one option (here the call option) can in fact be replicated—relying on the put-call parity relationship—with an appropriate combination of the other option (here the put option) the stock and riskless bonds. Hence, provided that there is only one class of options—either calls or puts— trading in the market, we could still achieve the payoff patterns associated to the missing option by simply implementing different strategies combining the traded option, the underlying stock, and riskless bonds. [15]

Finally, note that the counterparts or symmetric strategies to hedges are called "reverse hedges." They typically involve a short position in the stock that is either offset by a long-call position or a short-put position. The term "reverse hedge" is used to distinguish situations in which we are de facto "protecting" a short position in the underlying stock from those requiring the protection of a long position in the underlying stock, which are commonly referred to as "hedges."

The third group of "elaborated" option strategies attempts to achieve new payoff structures by combining either options within the same class or options from two distinct classes. In the first case, we form positions involving only call options or only put options written on the same underlying stock. The resulting combinations are called "spread" positions, which typically have two main variants called the vertical spreads and the horizontal spreads both belonging within "option class" strategies. In a horizontal call spread we buy one call and sell another call written on the same security, and while both options have the same exercise price, they have different expiration dates. Similarly, a horizontal put spread involves buying one put and selling another put on the same underlying security that has the same exercise price but a different expiration date. Vertical spreads involve the purchase of one option and the sale of another option belonging to the same class (either puts or calls) where both are written on the same security and expire on the same date, but have different exercise prices.

Typically, a spread can be bullish or bearish[16] depending on whether it induces gains or losses with an increase in the stock price. In a bullish horizontal spread we would typically buy the longer-term option and sell the one with a shorter maturity, and vice versa in a bearish horizontal spread. In a bullish vertical spread the option with the lower striking price is purchased and the one with the higher striking price is sold, while the reverse is true for a bearish vertical spread.

---

[15] Such asset replicating strategies will be discussed in Chapter 2 when we will discuss the put-call parity relationship as well as in Chapters 3 and 4 when we will present the binomial option pricing model and the Black and Scholes option pricing model respectively.

[16] While this relationship always holds in the case of vertical "spreads," it is not necessarily true for horizontal spreads as has been pointed out by Cox and Rubinstein (1985). This is because the passage of time can affect long-term and short-term options differently. This phenomenon will be discussed in more detail in Chapters 4 and 5.

We illustrate the payoff structure at expiration of a bullish put vertical spread in Fig. 1.8. In this strategy, the put with the lower striking price (K^-) is bought while the put with the higher striking price (K^+) is sold. By combining options from the same class in this vertical spread, we can achieve new nonlinear payoff structures. In this case, the maximal gain and loss potentials are limited. The spread is indeed "bullish" since the profit area lies in the region of terminal stock prices greater than the initial stock price (S) that prevailed at the date this strategy was implemented.

There are more sophisticated versions of spread strategies. For example, the "diagonal" spread involves buying and selling options from the same class and written on the same underlying security, but where both options have different exercise prices and different expiration dates. Diagonal spreads therefore combine the properties of both horizontal and vertical spreads.

The last type of strategy involving options from the same class consists of combining two—horizontal or vertical—"spreads" together. This is accomplished by buying (writing) two calls with an intermediate exercise price or time to maturity and simultaneously selling (buying) two calls that have respectively a smaller exercise price or time to maturity and a higher exercise price or time to maturity. The resulting strategy is then called a vertical or horizontal "butterfly spread." Similarly, butterfly spreads can be implemented using put options.

Finally, a second type of strategy involving options "only" exists, and it relies on the combination of options belonging to different classes. Typically, such option combinations are implemented by simultaneously buying (or selling) a call and a put option written on the same underlying stock. When both options have

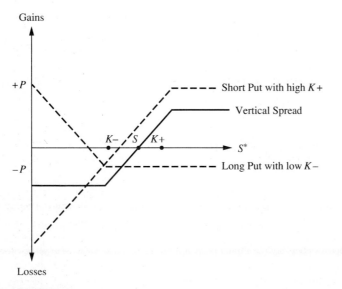

FIGURE 1.8
Bullish vertical spread.

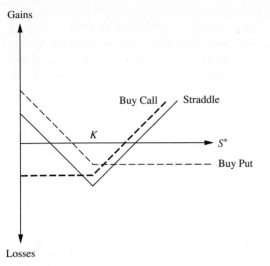

FIGURE 1.9
A long straddle.

the same expiration date and exercise prices, the combination is called a "straddle." For example, in a "long straddle" we buy both a call and a put written on the same stock, each of which has the same exercise price and expiration date.[17] Graphically, the payoff structure of a long straddle at its expiration date can be represented as shown in Fig. 1.9.

The long straddle strategy, which is also called bottom straddle, will only be rewarding if the stock is highly volatile and makes either a large upward or downward movement at the option's expiration date. Of course, there are many other combinations involving the purchase or sale of a put and a call that can be created by selecting both options' that have different exercise prices and/or expiration dates. While the payoff structures created by these sophisticated option strategies are very appealing, they have the disadvantage of requiring a greater degree of monitoring from the portfolio manager to prevent or reduce the considerable losses that could result if the stock price's evolution or the stock return's volatility are not accurately predicted.

5   WHY STANDARDIZED OPTION MARKETS?

Options undoubtedly provide investors with simple ways to achieve nonlinear payoff structures that provide them with an important risk monitoring tool. Indeed, options enable investors to hedge a given position, to speculate, the undertake arbitrages, and to "delay" a given investment decision until another time.

---

[17] Conversely, in a short or "top" straddle we would sell the put and the call written on the same underlying instrument and having identical contractual specifications.

Although options aren't new financial instruments, the recent development of standardized option markets has substantially contributed to their increased trading activity and popularity as investment vehicles. Indeed, contrary to the over-the-counter trading system, option markets have simultaneously reunified and centralized all trades on individual exchanges, and provided a regulated environment that fulfills the following functions:

- Guarantees the solvability of each party to the contract through the existence of a corporation—called the Option Clearing Corporation in the United States—that interacts between the buyer and the seller of the option and de facto warrants the execution of each trade and controls whether the individual parties meet their obligations (for example, in the case of early exercise).

- Creates a true secondary market for trading in options. Nobody is obliged to hold a long or a short position until its expiration date since a closing transaction can be initiated at any time during the option's lifetime. In this secondary market the buyer and the seller do not know each other, since the real counterpart to every transaction is the Clearing Corporation. The credit risk of the individual buyer in an over-the-counter market has been transferred to the central authority that regulates the exchange.

- Provides liquidity through the standardization of the contracts.

- Reduces transaction costs by centralizing the trading activity. Moreover, the standardization and the liquidity of these contracts have also narrowed the bid and ask spreads of option contracts.

- Prevents market manipulation by imposing several constraints on the trading activity. For example, position limits preclude each agent from owning more than a specified number of option positions on the same underlying instrument and on the same side (buying or the selling) of the market. Margin deposits for option writers also prevent individuals from taking large short positions in an attempt to "corner" the market. These margins have also been implemented to maintain a sufficient "solvability" pressure on every option writer. Finally, under some special circumstances each exchange can also impose trading suspensions or price limits if there are concerns that the liquidity of the whole system is in danger and/or if the market has been manipulated.

Indisputably, the centralization of option trades and the standardization of option contracts have been beneficial institutional innovations. They have contributed to the structure, discipline, and liquidity of options markets. They have allowed options to become an attractive alternative in an investor's investment opportunity set.

6   CONCLUSION

Options should no longer be compared to gambling or horse racing games. Options are traded all around the world on regulated exchanges, on different underlying instruments, and in standardized contracts providing a generally accepted and effective tool for investors, producers, farmers, and consumers to transfer and monitor various sources of uncertainties. By paying a "premium," the option owner acquires "insurance" that essentially eliminates an undesirable portion of the underlying instrument's potential payoff structure. In exchange for the premium, the option writer essentially "accepts" to "insure" the option owner while hoping the evolution of the underlying instrument will go in the opposite direction, and thereby impose no further obligation for him to buy or to sell the underlying instrument.

Option markets therefore provide an essential risk-shifting function among individuals of different beliefs, preferences, investment objectives, and risk-tolerance levels. The distinguishing feature of options is that the buyer of the option contract "pays" for a "right" to flexibility and hence generates the highly nonlinear payoff structure of these "optional" claims that give them such attractive properties. Since this study is essentially concerned with financial options, we will focus on understanding and analyzing these properties as they relate to that specific category of options.

In the first part of this book we concentrate on the most common and frequently researched single option contract, the stock option. We will use the stock option as *the* illustrative contract and analyze common valuation problems that arise first irrespective of and then related to the underlying asset's nature.

Chapters 2 to 4 address these common valuation problems in detail. In Chapter 2, we state and prove some general restrictions that apply to the rational pricing of any option. In Chapter 3, we present the binomial option pricing model and show how appealing its underlying framework is for both pricing of an option and understanding option pricing theory. In Chapter 4, we then present the well-known Black and Scholes option pricing model and show that it can be derived as a limiting case of the binomial option pricing model. Some essential properties of the Black and Scholes option pricing model are also discussed in this chapter.

The features of the stock option become central to the discussion presented in the next two chapters since we ask ourselves which properties of this financial claim and its underlying instrument deserve more thorough attention in existing option pricing models. In Chapter 5 we discuss some modifications of the Black and Scholes model—for example, when the underlying stock pays dividends—that can improve both its pricing accuracy and efficiency when used in portfolio management strategies. In Chapter 6, however, some major theoretical and practical weaknesses of this model are analyzed. A presentation of the academic research since 1973 developed to improve and extend the option pricing theory follows.

In the second part of this study we attempt to broaden our analysis by extending to other standardized traded options that can be particularly useful as portfolio management or risk-monitoring tools. For that purpose, we have concentrated on three categories of standardized options: stock index options, stock index futures options, and foreign currency options. In Chapter 7, we examine the first two categories of options in detail and emphasize how they should be priced and used to hedge the market risk exposure of an equity portfolio. We also analyze stock index futures contracts to see how they compete with stock index options and stock index futures options at providing various market risk-monitoring strategies to the investor. This however required that we first define the properties of a futures contract and assess how to price such a financial instrument. The last part of Chapter 7 addresses the practical and theoretical problems associated with the valuation of stock index written options and stock index futures written options.

Since most portfolios are nowadays diversified internationally, currency risk exposure is an investment risk component that portfolio managers or investors can no more ignore. Therefore Chapter 8 presents and analyzes foreign currency options. In particular, we describe the features and economic functions of these options, and examine several pricing models that are currently used to value and—to a lesser extent due to their recent development or mathematical complexity—to manage foreign currency options. We finally point out some important factors related to the international dimension of these options that have been neglected in the foreign currency option pricing models presented so far.

Chapter 9 concludes this study on a more philosophical note, attempting to summarize the main contributions of the option pricing theory from both an academic and a practitioner's perspective. It emphasizes how the analytical tools developed in this book can be extended to price other types of options and to build investment decisions with optional features. Finally, it suggests interesting and challenging research topics for which the option pricing theory provides a useful, tractable, and powerful modeling framework and hence proves to be worth studying.

CHAPTER 2

RATIONAL BOUNDARIES TO OPTION PRICING

1 INTRODUCTION

In this chapter we study some fundamental "restrictions" or boundaries that option prices must satisfy to preclude riskless arbitrage opportunities in the market. That is, even though we have not yet developed an option pricing theory to determine what "fair" option prices should be, we can nevertheless assess reliable limits or "bounds" to their market values. Underlying the establishment of these "rational" boundaries is the concept of "nondominance" among financial assets: *An asset A is said to be dominant if its return is greater than the return on asset B in some states of nature and is at least equal to the return on asset B in all possible states of nature*.

Since dominated and/or dominating assets would immediately lead to riskless arbitrage opportunities in the market, it is important to assess how traded options should be priced to avoid such a situation. To determine the restrictions on option pricing we first look at European and American options on securities that do not pay dividends. Then we analyze the impact of the dividends on these boundary values for both European and American options. Finally, we examine whether there are similar restrictions that guarantee for put and call options to be fairly priced relative to each other. (The answer to that question will be provided by the "put-call parity" relationships.)

Definitions of the mathematical symbols used in the presentation are provided below. We will use the same symbols throughout the book, and alter them only if more precision is needed to define certain parameters. Additional symbols will be introduced when needed.

Let us define the following symbols:

S = Current price of the underlying asset (the stock)

K = Striking price of the option

C = Current price of a European call

C' = Current price of an American call

P = Current price of a European put

P' = Current price of an American put

T = Expiration date of the option

$\tau = (T - t)$ = Time to maturity of the put and call options as determined at t (current time) and expressed in years unless otherwise stated

S^* = Price of the underlying asset (the stock) on the expiration date (T) of the option

$B(r)$ = Current price of a zero-coupon riskless bond that pays \$1 at time T and whose time to maturity is τ

R = One plus the interest rate on a default-free discount bond for a given period. R is also defined as the compounding factor corresponding to an arbitrary unit of time (a day, week, or more frequently, year.)

2   GENERAL RESTRICTIONS ON EUROPEAN AND AMERICAN OPTION PRICES

An option is a security that has limited liability. That is, an option doesn't oblige its owner to commit any additional funds over the call's purchase price if its exercise privilege is unattractive. Therefore, the value of an option can never become negative. Restriction 1 formally states the nonnegativity condition that applies to the price of any kind[1] of option.

Restriction 1

$$C \geq 0, C' \geq 0, P \geq 0, \text{ and } P' \geq 0 \qquad (2.1)$$

A second restriction addresses the value of options at their expiration date. To illustrate their payoff structure at maturity, let us first consider a European call option and see what it will be worth under the two possible subdivisions of the states of nature at expiration date T:

States of nature
at expiration date
$$S^* > K \quad S^* \le K$$

Value of a European call $\quad S^* - K \quad\quad 0$

In other words, if at maturity the stock price S^* is greater than the exercise price K, the option will be exercised, and it is therefore worth $S^* - K$. On the other hand, if at time T the stock price is equal to or less than the striking price, the call will expire worthless.

We can therefore express the value of a European call at maturity ($\tau = 0$) as a function of its underlying stock price (S^*) and its exercise price (K):

$$C(S^*, 0, K) = \max[0, S^* - K]$$

Since European and American options are identical at maturity we can also write

$$C'(S^*, 0, K) = C(S^*, 0, K) = \max[0, S^* - K]$$

Using the same methodology we can show that put options will expire worthless if the stock price at maturity is equal to or greater than their exercise price, and that they will be exercised if the stock price is less than their striking price:

States of nature
at expiration date
$$S^* \ge K \quad S^* < K$$

Value of a European put $\quad\quad 0 \quad\quad K - S^*$

More formally, since European and American puts have the same rights and therefore should have the same value at maturity, we obtain

$$P'(S^*, 0, K) = P(S^*, 0, K) = \max[0, K - S^*]$$

Therefore, Restriction 2, which precludes riskless arbitrage between stocks and options at the latter's expiration date, simply says that an option at time T should be worth the higher of its intrinsic values (($S^* - K$) for a call option and ($K - S^*$) for a put option) and zero. Restriction 2 states:

Restriction 2

$$C'(S^*, 0, K) = C(S^*, 0, K) = \max[0, S^* - K] \quad\quad (2.2)$$

$$P'(S^*, 0, K) = P(S^*, 0, K) = \max[0, K - S^*] \quad\quad (2.3)$$

For American put and call options we can even go further in assessing their limiting values through time. Since an American option can be exercised at any time, it must always be worth at least its intrinsic value, otherwise arbitrage profits could be made by buying the option and exercising it immediately. Therefore, Restriction 3 states:

Restriction 3

$$C'(S, \tau, K) \geq S - K \qquad (2.4)$$

$$P'(S, \tau, K) \geq K - S \qquad (2.5)$$

Note that this condition need not be valid for European options since they cannot be exercised before maturity, and therefore cannot lead to this type of arbitrage except at time T.

The next restriction is concerned with the relationship between option prices and their exercise prices. American and European calls are nonincreasing functions of their exercise prices while American and European puts are nondecreasing functions of their exercise prices. This is because the striking price represents the cash outflow associated with exercising call options, while it is the cash inflow associated with exercising put options. In the first case, a higher striking price lowers the call's expected profit; in the second case, a higher expected profit is precisely induced by a higher cash inflow or striking price. Therefore, Restriction 4 states the relationship between option prices and their striking prices as follows:

Restriction 4

$$C(S, \tau, K_1) \leq C(S, \tau, K_2) \qquad (2.6)$$
$$\text{for } K_1 > K_2$$
$$C'(S, \tau, K_1) \leq C'(S, \tau, K_2) \qquad (2.7)$$

and

$$P(S, \tau, K_1) \geq P(S, \tau, K_2) \qquad (2.8)$$
$$\text{for } K_1 > K_2$$
$$P'(S, \tau, K_1) \geq P'(S, \tau, K_2) \qquad (2.9)$$

We can also infer some general ranking among American calls and puts that differ only through their remaining time to maturity. Since the right to exercise at any time during an additional period can certainly do no harm and may even provide more chances to meet favorable opportunities, it should be true that if two calls (or puts) differ solely by their time to maturity, the longer maturity call (or put) will have a value equal to or greater than the shorter call (or put). We have Restriction 5 that states:

Restriction 5

$$C'(S, \tau_1, K) \geq C'(S, \tau_2, K) \qquad \tau_1 > \tau_2 \qquad (2.10)$$

$$P'(S, \tau_1, K) \geq P'(S, \tau_2, K) \qquad \tau_1 > \tau_2 \qquad (2.11)$$

If this were not true, a riskless arbitrage could be easily formed by purchasing the longer maturity American call and simultaneously selling the other American call short.[1] This would provide an immediate profit of $C'(S, \tau_2, K) - C'(S, \tau_1, K)$, and no matter what happened in the future, the result would at least equal this initial profit. To see why this assertion holds, consider your position at the time the shorter maturity option expires or is exercised, you actually own[2]

$$C'(S', \tau_1', K) - \max[0, S' - K]$$

If this amount is positive, you should sell the call and use the money to close out the short position, and you still end up with an additional profit to the one initially made at time t. If this amount is negative, you should exercise the call, get the amount $\max[0, S' - K]$ to close your short position, and you end up with no additional gains or losses (to the initial profit made at time t). Therefore longer-lived American options should sell for a price at least as high as shorter-term options written on the same stock and having the same exercise price since otherwise riskless arbitrage is not precluded.

Note that Restriction 5 doesn't necessarily hold for European puts and calls since these options do not allow us to set up such arbitrage strategies. More precisely, in the example, we wouldn't be able to close out the position by exercising the longer-lived call option $C(S, \tau_1, K)$ before its maturity date T_1. As we shall see in the following chapters, there are even stronger reasons that preclude the validity of Restriction 5 for European put options.

Since an American option offers more flexibility than a European option by allowing its owner to exercise the option at any time before its expiration date, an American option written on the same stock and with the same striking price as its European counterpart will sell for at least the same price. This is simply a consequence of the fact that additional rights cannot have a negative value, and it enables us to state Restriction 6 as the general relationship between American and European options prices.

Restriction 6

$$C'(S, \tau, K) \geq C(S, \tau, K) \qquad (2.12)$$

$$P'(S, \tau, K) \geq P(S, \tau, K) \qquad (2.13)$$

The stock price itself can be viewed as an American call option of infinite maturity with a striking price equal to zero. But we already know from Restrictions 4 and 5 that the longer the maturity and the lower the striking price, the more valu-

---

[1] A similar argument can be held for American put options.

[2] The symbols S' and τ' are used to emphasize that we are now at another time between date t and date T_2 (the expiration date of the shorter maturity call option).

able a call option will be. It follows that the stock price must always be at least as high as the price of an American call option written on the same stock. And since the American call's price is always at least as high as its European counterpart, we can say that the stock's price is the upper boundary to call option prices. More formally, Restriction 7 states:

Restriction 7

$$S = C(S, \infty, 0) \geq C'(S, \tau, K) \geq C(S, \tau, K) \qquad (2.14)$$

By combining Restrictions 7 and 1, we can say that if the stock's price is equal to zero, American and European call option prices will also be equal to zero because they are limited liability contracts. We can state this proposition as Restriction 8.

Restriction 8

$$C'(0, \tau, K) = C(0, \tau, K) = 0 \qquad (2.15)$$

The fact that the stock is also an asset with limited liability tells us that American put option values have an upper boundary equal to their striking prices. This means that American put options reach their maximal values (equal to K) whenever the underlying stock is worthless. Combining this statement with Restriction 6 implies Restriction 9 that states:[3]

Restriction 9

$$K \geq P'(S, \tau, K) \geq P(S, \tau, K) \qquad (2.16)$$

For a European call on a nondividend paying stock, we can now go even further in assessing a boundary to its price across time and not only at its expiration date (see Restriction 2). In fact, a European call's price should always be at least equal to the value of the stock minus the present value of its exercise price K, which is stated in Restriction 10 as follows:

---

[3] In fact since a European put cannot be exercised before its expiration date, its maximum value will be given by the present value of the exercise price, namely:

$$KB(\tau) \geq P(0, \tau, K)$$

when the stock price is equal to zero.

Restriction 10

$$C(S, \tau, K) \geq S - KB(\tau) \qquad (2.17)$$

To prove this assertion, let us compare the value of two portfolios, A and B, formed at time t. Portfolio A consists of one European call option $C(S, r, K)$ held long and of an amount K of riskless zero coupon bonds maturing at time T. Portfolio B consists of one share of stock bought at the current price S. Now, what will these two investments be worth at the expiration date T of the option?

	Value at time t	Value at time T	
		$S^* \leq K$	$S^* > K$
Portfolio A:	$C(S, \tau, K) + KB(\tau)$	$0 + K$	$(S^* - K) + K$
Portfolio B:	S	S^*	S^*
Result		$A > B$	$A = B$

Since the terminal value of Portfolio A is in every state of nature at least as high as that of Portfolio B, it follows from the nondominance criterion, that Portfolio A must also have an initial value (at time t) at least equal to that of Portfolio B. That means

$$C(S, \tau, K) + KB(\tau) \geq S \iff C(S, \tau, K) \geq S - KB(\tau)$$

Therefore, Restriction 10 must hold for European call options on nondividend paying stocks.

By combining Restrictions 5 and 10, we obtain our most important assertion concerning the price of an American call option on a nondividend paying stock.

$$C'(S, \tau, K) \geq C(S, \tau, K) \geq S - KB(\tau)$$

We will now show that this superior position collapses for American call options written on nondividend paying stocks. First, note that the term $S - KB(\tau)$ represents the minimal value of a European call that has a remaining time to maturity equal to τ. However, the American call option price must also satisfy Restriction 3, by which its price should be at least equal to its exercise value $S - K$. But the latter term is smaller than $S - KB(\tau)$, which is shown as follows:

$$S - K < S - KB(\tau) \text{ since}^4 \ B(\tau) < 1$$

---

[4] The price $B(\tau)$ of a zero-coupon riskless bond that matures at date T (and has a remaining time to maturity of τ) is equivalent to the discount factor used to discount riskless future cash flows accruing at date T. Since a discount factor is always inferior to one providing that the interest rate is strictly positive and that $\tau \neq 0$, the above result follows. When $\tau = 0$, $B = 1$ since the price of the bond is then equal to its face value of $1.

This means that the exercise value of an American call option on a nondividend paying stock is always (except at expiration) smaller than its unexercised value. Hence, the American call on a nondividend paying stock is always worth more "alive" than exercised. It then follows that its additional right stemming for the continuous exercise possibility has no value and that such a call should therefore sell for the same price as an otherwise identical European call option.

Restriction 11

For call options on nondividend paying stocks, the following relationship must always hold:

$$C'(S, \tau, K) = C(S, \tau, K) \tag{2.18}$$

Note that we cannot draw the same kind of conclusions for the prices of American put options since these options may be exercised prior to their expiration date even when the underlying stock pays no dividends. Therefore, Restriction 6 is valid for the comparison of American and European put option prices.

3 IMPACT OF DIVIDENDS ON OPTION PRICE BOUNDARIES

Until now we have analyzed rational boundaries for option prices on nondividend paying stocks. This means that the conclusions we derived are valid for very few traded stock options, essentially short-term options for which we can assume that no dividend will be paid until their final maturity date.[5] To allow for more generality and realism, it is now necessary to show how those boundaries may change when we explicitly introduce the fact that the underlying stock pays dividends. However, in order to simplify the following demonstrations, we will assume that the amount of the dividends as well as their payment dates are known.[6]

Since the owner of a European call is not entitled to receive the dividends paid on the stock during its remaining time to maturity, a call on a dividend paying

---

[5] Note that this condition is not necessarily true for all countries. In Switzerland, for example, companies pay a dividend only once a year and hence the no-dividend assumption can therefore be accepted even for medium-term options.

[6] This assumption is not unrealistic since over a short time period (less than one year) corresponding to the typical maturity of an option, the dividend policy of a company will generally not be subject to major changes. This latter assumption is also consistent for most Swiss companies, which tend to follow a very stable (and therefore predictable) dividend policy. The results will not change very much if we introduce unknown dividends in the discussion, essentially by introducing the concept of minimum and maximum expected dividend payments over the option's remaining time to maturity. For more information, refer to Cox and Rubinstein (1985).

stock is worth less than if the underlying stock were not paying any dividends. Hence, we can say that the value of a European call on a dividend-paying stock must be at least equal to the value of the stock minus the present value of the striking price and minus the present value of all dividends to be paid during the option's remaining time to maturity. Let us use the symbol D to represent the present value of all known dividends to be paid between the current date and the option's expiration date T. We can then state Restriction 12 as follows:

Restriction 12

$$C(S, D, \tau, K) \geq S - KB(\tau) - D \qquad (2.19)$$

If this were not true we could set up the following arbitrage strategy: sell the stock short, buy the European call option, and buy a quantity of $D + KB(\tau)$ riskless zero-coupon bonds. More formally, the initial investment (profit) would be equal to

$$S - C(S, D, \tau, K) - KB(\tau) - D > 0$$

At the expiration date of the option, we would liquidate the amount D invested in bonds, which would exactly match the value of the dividends we owe on the short position in the stock. Moreover, we would liquidate the rest of our position by buying back the stock, selling or exercising our call, and receiving \$K from our initial riskless bond investment:

$$-S^* + C(S^*, D, O, K) + K$$

Depending on which state of nature is prevailing at time T, we would end up with the following payoff:

	Do not exercise $S^* \leq K$	Exercise $S^* > K$
	$-S^* + (0) + K$	$-S^* + (S^* - K) + K$
Result	$K - S^*$	0

That is, no matter what happens at maturity, we know that we cannot make a loss, and therefore the initial gain we made when constructing our position is our minimal "sure" profit. This is clearly a riskless arbitrage opportunity that cannot exist, and therefore implies that Restriction 12 must hold in an efficient market.

When comparing Restriction 12 to Restriction 10 we can immediately observe

$$S - KB(\tau) - D < S - KB(\tau)$$

Hence, it must be true that, all other thing being equal, a European call on a nondividend-paying stock should be worth more than a European call on a dividend paying stock:

$$C(S, \tau, K) > C(S, D, \tau, K) \qquad (2.20)$$

For American options, the existence of dividends has much stronger consequences since they create the incentive to exercise the option prior to its maturity date. Referring to Restriction 3 for an American call option, we find

$$C'(S, \tau, K) \geq S - K$$

We know that for American options on nondividend-paying stocks, a strong inequality must hold at all times prior to the expiration date of the option, since we have proven that such an option is always worth more "alive" than exercised.

However, for call options on dividend paying stocks, there are some other points in time where Restriction 3 can degenerate into an equality. In fact, it may be optimal to exercise an American call option an instant before each ex-dividend date and hence to observe at these dates that the call is selling for its exercise value $(S - K)$. To see why this is the case, suppose you make the following investment an instant before the ex-dividend date t_1: buy the call, sell the stock short, and invest $K in riskless bonds. Your initial investment equals

$$S - C - K$$

Now, if you close your position at the ex-dividend date (or after) you would not only have to buy the stock back but also make the dividend payment on that stock. Since it is not certain that the interest earned on the $K is sufficient to cover the dividend payment, you may actually lose money when you liquidate the whole position. Therefore, the fact that the call may sell for its exercise price $(S - K)$ prior to an ex-dividend date t_1 doesn't lead to an arbitrage opportunity since (with the above aforementioned strategy) you would be investing $S - (S - K) - K$ or $0 at t_1 without having the possibility to earn a sure profit at liquidation. The instants prior to each ex-dividend date are the only times when early exercise of American call options should ever be considered because at all other moments between two ex-dividend dates Restriction 3 tells us that the American call is worth more "alive" than exercised.

There is, however, one more point we need to clarify and it concerns identifying the relevant factors that lead to the premature exercise of an American call option. Intuitively, we can think of an early exercise opportunity as a positive tradeoff between the dividend received through exercising prematurely the call option and the foregone interest that could have otherwise been earned on the invested striking price.

Basically, we can say that if at all points in time the present value of the dividends to be paid on the stock until the option's expiration date is less than the present value of the interest that can be earned on the striking price of the call during its remaining time to maturity, then the American call on a dividend-paying stock will never be exercised prior to its expiration date. To see why this is true, let us consider Restriction 12 which we previously stated for a European call on a dividend paying stock:

$$C(S, D, \tau, K) \geq S - KB(\tau) - D$$

Since by Restriction 6 an American call option is always worth at least as much as its European counterpart, it must be true that:

$$C'(S, D, \tau, K) \geq C(S, D, \tau, K) \geq S - KB(\tau) - D$$

However, we also know that an American call option can never sell for less than its exercise value $(S - K)$ and since

$$S - KB(\tau) - D > S - K \qquad (2.21)$$

$$\text{for} \qquad K(1 - B(\tau)) > D \qquad (2.22)$$

we see that an American call option on a dividend-paying stock will never be exercised prior to its maturity date if the present value of the interest earned on the striking price $K(1 - B(\tau))$ is greater than the present value of the dividends D. If the opposite were true, the American call's exercise value could be greater than its unexercised lower boundary:

$$S - K > S - KB(\tau) - D$$

$$\Longleftrightarrow S - K > C'(S, D, \tau, K)$$

could occur and hence contradict Restriction 3. In other words, whenever the present value of the dividends is greater than the interest we can earn on the striking price:

$$D > K(1 - B(\tau))$$

the early exercise of the call option prior to maturity cannot be ruled out. Since we saw that these situations can only be optimal at some specific points in time, namely just before ex-dividend dates, we can therefore state Restriction 13 as follows:

Restriction 13

   If at all ex-dividend dates during an option's time to maturity, the relationship:

$$K(1 - B(\tau)) > D \qquad (2.23)$$

is verified, then an American call on a dividend-paying stock will never be exercised prior to its expiration date, and hence it will have the same price as its European counterpart.

However, if this relationship doesn't hold, it might be optimal to exercise the American call prior to its expiration date, which according to Restriction 6 would then imply that it is worth more than its European counterpart.

   Dividends are shown to have a negative impact on the prices of call options, however the opposite is true for put options. Since the owner of a put always gains from declines in the stock market price, the same positive impact must arise from stock price declines due to dividend payments. It follows that the owner of a put has a position that is even better than that of the short seller of the stock since the former doesn't have to make restitution for the dividend payments and can therefore fully benefit from the positive impact of any dividend distributions. We can say that the value of a European put option must always be at least equal to the present value of its striking price plus the present value of the dividends and minus the stock price. More formally, Restriction 14 states:

Restriction 14

$$P \geq -S + D + KB(\tau) \qquad (2.24)$$

If this relationship were not true, we could lock in a sure profit by constructing the following arbitrage position: buy the put option, buy the stock, sell an amount equal to the present value of the dividends, and borrow an amount equal to the present value of the striking price. At the expiration date of the option, we would first of all be using the dividends paid by the stock to restitute those initially sold, and we would liquidate the rest of the position by selling the stock, selling the put, and paying back \$K for the loan we originally made at time t, that is, our payoff at maturity would be the following:

	Expiration date	
	$S^* < K$	$S^* \geq K$
Sell the put	$K - S^*$	—
Sell the stock	S^*	S^*
Reimburse the loan	$-K$	$-K$
Total result	0	$S^* - K$

No matter what state of nature prevails at maturity, we know that we will end up with at least the profit initially realized at time t and with an even greater profit if the stock's price at time T is higher than the striking price. Therefore, Restriction 14 must hold to prevent riskless arbitrage opportunities arising from European put options mispricing.

Since an American put offers the same amount as a European put—and even more by allowing for early exercise, Restriction 14 must hold for an American put, too. By combining Restriction 14 and 6, we have Restriction 15 that states:

Restriction 15

$$P'(S, D, \tau, K) \geq P(S, D, \tau, K) \geq -S + D + KB(\tau) \qquad (2.25)$$

However, the early exercise possibilities for put options are much more frequent and less predictable than they were for call options. First, put options on nondividend-paying stocks may be exercised before maturity. To see why this may happen, consider the case in which the stock price is very low at some point in time. Then it may be that early exercise at an immediate net gain of $K - S$ clearly compensates for even the present value of the maximum gain available (when $S^* = 0$) by exercising the put at maturity. That is if:

$$K - S > KB(\tau) - 0$$

then it may be optimal to exercise a put immediately.[7] Hence it isn't true that an American put on a nondividend-paying stock is always worth more "alive" than exercised as was previously stated for American call options.

With American puts on dividend-paying stocks, the early exercise feature is even more difficult to assess. On one hand, a sufficiently low current stock price could lead to early exercise (as seen above) while, on the other hand, early exercise would in this case have a negative impact since it precludes the owner of the put to fully benefit from the positive influence of the future dividends that will be paid on the stock. However, if the present value of all the dividends to be received during an American put's time to maturity compensates for the present value of the interest that could have been earned on the exercise price during the remainder of the period, then we know that the put will not be exercised until at least the last dividend date T^* ($T^* < T$). That is, if we combine Restrictions 15 and 3, we find that a sufficient condition for no-early exercise of a put option until date T^* is

$$-S + D + KB(\tau) > K - S$$

$$\Longleftrightarrow \qquad D > K(1 - B(\tau)) \tag{2.26}$$

However, this is a much weaker condition than the one previously stated for the no-early exercise of an American call option on a dividend paying stock, since here we can only guarantee that it will hold until the last dividend date T^*. After that date, we are again subject to uncertainty since the price of the put now behaves like that of an American put on a nondividend paying stock, and can hence be exercised at any time if the stock's price happens to trade at a sufficiently low level.[8] Therefore, we must remember that all put options (whether written on dividend- or on nondividend-paying stocks) may be exercised at any point in time and not just at some specific dates. It is therefore much more difficult, to price an American put than an American call. We will analyze the problem of early exercise for American puts in more detail when we discuss option pricing models. However, it is important to remember that for American put options, the early exercise feature

---

[7] Note that since this comparison involves only the lower bounds of American and European put options prices when $s^* = 0$, it still doesn't represent a necessary condition for the optimal timing of early exercise.

[8] The latter fact may even be reinforced or simply induced by a very high interest rate level.

- applies to puts written on both dividend- and nondividend-paying stocks,
- can happen at any point in time and not just at some specific dates, and
- is, at best, under control until the last dividend date during the put option's time to maturity if the present value of the dividend is higher than the present value of the interest that can be earned on the striking price until maturity.

Considering that dividend cash flows, dividend dates, and interest rates cannot be fully predicted, we will generally have to check for a put option's early exercise possibility at each point in time if we want to value this asset consistently.

It should be noted that when Restriction 13 and Eq. (2.26) are not fulfilled it *may be*—but is not necessarily—optimal to exercise the American call or put before expiration. The optimal timing or early exercise policy is then given by Restriction 3, namely by comparing the lower bound of the American option— that is, its intrinsic value ($S - K$ for the call and $K - S$ for the put)—to its unexercised value.[9]

4 PUT-CALL PARITY RELATIONSHIPS

Until now we have addressed restrictions on call and put options that guarantee no riskless arbitrage opportunities for strategies including the stock, a riskless bond (sometimes), and either a put or a call option. Ruling out those types of strategies in an efficient market we have been able to derive consistent boundaries for both put and call options prices that take into account the underlying stock price, its dividend, the riskless bond's price, the time to maturity, and the striking price of these options. However, it would also be useful to analyze the call versus put option pricing restrictions that guarantee no riskless profit opportunities when trading these two types of assets simultaneously. In other words, we are now going to impose some constraints on the prices of put and call options written on the same stock with the same striking prices and expiration dates.

A Put-Call Parity Relationship for European Options on Nondividend-Paying Stocks

The value of a European put on a nondividend-paying stock must be equal to the price of an identical call minus the price of the underlying stock and plus the present value of the striking price. That is, the first put-call parity relationship is as follows:

Put-Call Parity Relationship I:

$$P(S, \tau, K) = C(S, \tau, K) - S + KB(\tau). \qquad (2.27)$$

---

[9] Note that this statement holds for American calls on dividend paying stocks and for American puts on dividend as well as nondividend-paying stocks.

To see why this identity must hold we have to show that a long position in the put option is identical to a long position in Portfolio B, which consists of one call option held long, one share of stock sold short, and the present lending value of $K. If these two portfolios are identical, their payoffs at the expiration date of both options must be equal whichever state of nature prevails. We shall observe the following at date T:

	$S^* < K$	$S^* \geq K$
A: Sell the put	$K - S^*$	—
B: Liquidate portfolio B, sell the call, buy back the stock, and get restitution of K dollars originally lent	$0 - S^* + K$	$(S^* - K) - S^* + K$
Result	$A = B$	$A = B$

We see that no matter which state of nature is prevailing at expiration date T, the long position in the put will have exactly the same payoff as Portfolio B, hence they must initially sell for the same price to avoid arbitrage opportunities.

The put-call parity relationship is also interesting from another point of view since it allows us to price a put (a call) once we know the current price of the stock, the current price of the call (the put), the striking price, and the interest rate. This means that if we are able to derive an option pricing formula for a European call (put) on a nondividend-paying stock, we can then simply use the put-call parity relationship to compute the current price of the put (call) option.[10]

Basically, the put-call parity relationship can also be used to show that if only a single type of option exists, let us say a call (or a put), we can still duplicate the payoff structure of the put (or the call). We could replicate or create a put option simply by buying the call, selling the stock short, and lending the present value of the exercise price. Intuitively, we can see that this is true since a put is like a "limited" short selling position in the stock whose immediate cash inflow has been partially spent on lending and on buying a call.[11] This latter fact precisely insures that the short position is "limited" to the extent that by exercising the call the owner will never have to pay more than $K for the stock to close out the "implicit" short position in the stock, and $K will be offset by recovering the amount originally lent. A similar argument could be followed to explain how to replicate the payoff structure of a call option, and the fundamental issue here is that since you can always replicate each of these two options by using the other, the stock and the riskless bond their market prices should definitely reflect the put-call parity relationship to avoid arbitrage opportunities.

---

[10] We will see in Chapter 4 that this is precisely what we do with the Black-Scholes option pricing formula for European call options. We then simply use the formula's theoretical call price and apply the put-call parity relationship to derive the put's theoretical price.

[11] This point has already been emphasized in Section 4 of Chapter 1.

Let us take the following example regarding two European put and call options written on stock Delta:

Current stock price	$S_0 = 100$
Time to maturity of the put and the call	$\tau = 0.50$ (6 months)
Exercise price of the put and the call	$K = 90$
Current market price of the call	$C_0 = 15.00$
Current market price of the put	$P_0 = 1.25$
Current price of a 6-month T-Bill[12]	$B(0.5) = 0.9535$

Applying the put-call parity relationship, we find the put's price equals

$$P = 15.00 - 100 + (90 \times 0.9535)$$

$$= \$0.815$$

Clearly its current market price of $1.25 indicates that the put is overpriced relative to the call and that we can make a riskless profit of $0.435 by selling the put, buying the call, selling the stock, and lending $K for six months. The following table illustrates the payoff of this strategy.

	Expiration date	
	$S^* > 90$	$S^* \leq 90$
Liquidate the position		
Buy back the put	0	$(90 - S^*)$
Sell or exercise the call	$S^* - 90$	0
Buy back the stock	(S^*)	(S^*)
Receive proceeds on the amount lent for 6 months	90	90
A) Value of portfolio at liquidation	0	0
B) Initial investment at time t $P_0 + S_0 - KB(\tau) - C$	0.435	0.435
C) Net result	$+\$0.435$	$+\$0.435$

This is a sure profit since no matter what happens at maturity, there is no loss potential associated with the liquidation of this position.

Note that when the put-call parity is applied to the given market price of an option to infer the value of the other option, it cannot tell us which of the two options (the call or the put) is incorrectly priced in the market. It can only indicate a relative mispricing of the call with respect to the put (or vice versa) and that therefore an arbitrage opportunity exists.

---

[12] Since we assume that τ is expressed in terms of years, we use $B(0.5)$ to denote the current price of a 6-month riskless bond.

B Put-Call Parity Relationship for European Options on Dividend-Paying Stocks

The relationship is very similar to the one derived under the no dividend case if we again assume that the present value of the dividends to be paid over the option's time to maturity is known. When explaining the put's (call's) price as a function of the call's (put's) price—the stock's price and the bond's price—we must take into consideration that cash dividends increase the value of a put option while they decrease the value of an identical call option.

We can therefore say that the value of a European put on a dividend-paying stock must be equal to the value of an identical call minus the value of the stock plus the present value of the dividends and plus the present value of the striking price. That is, we can state the second put-call parity relationship as follows:

Put-Call Parity Relationship II:

$$P(S, D, \tau, K) = C(S, D, \tau, K) - S + D + KB(\tau) \qquad (2.28)$$

We will briefly state why this relationship must hold to avoid sure profit strategies. Suppose that the put is overpriced relative to the call, that is

$$P(S, D, \tau, K) > C(S, D, \tau, K) - S + D + KB(\tau)$$

We could then make the following investment: sell the put, buy the call, sell the stock, buy an amount equal to the present value of the dividends, and buy K riskless bonds. The initial investment would result in a net profit. At the expiration date of both options, we would first have to pay back the dividends due on the short position in the stock by using the money and the interest earned on the $\$D$ initially bought. Our remaining position would be liquidated as follows:

	Expiration date	
	$S^* < K$	$S^* \geq K$
Buy the put	$-(K - S^*)$	—
Sell the call	—	$S^* - K$
Buy the stock	$-S^*$	$-S^*$
Sell K bonds	K	K
Total profit	0	0

Since we definitely end up with a zero net profit in all states of nature, it must be that our initial position was riskless and that clearly Put-Call Parity Relationship II must hold to preclude such a riskless arbitrage opportunity.

C   Put-Call Relationship for American Options
on Nondividend-Paying Stocks

First, we know that American call options on nondividend-paying stocks are never exercised prior to their expiration date, while this may happen to otherwise identical put options. We will therefore not be able to obtain a parity relationship in the sense of an equality between a call's (put's) price and the price of an identical put (call), the price of the stock, and the present value of the exercise price. Here the term "identical" option is inaccurate. On one side we have an American call that bears no additional value stemming from its early exercise feature, and therefore is priced like a European call. On the other side we have an American put option whose early exercise possibility is positively priced. It is therefore intuitively simple to understand that by using an American call, a stock, and a bond, we cannot exactly replicate the American put option since we do not have the early exercise positively valued feature that the put's price reflects. This is why we can only derive upper and lower bounds for the value of an American call (put) option relative to the values of the "identical" put (call), of the stock and of the riskless bond.

Therefore, we will state the put-call relationship for American options on nondividend-paying stocks as follows: the put's price should never exceed the value of an "identical" call plus the striking price and minus the value of the stock, that is

$$P'(S, \tau, K) \leq C'(S, \tau, K) + K - S$$

And the value of the put should never be less than the value of the call, plus the present value of the striking price, and minus the current stock price; that is

$$P'(S, \tau, K) \geq C'(S, \tau, K) + KB(\tau) - S$$

Combining these two boundaries we can state the third put-call relationship that applies to American nondividend-paying stock options as follows:

Put-Call Relationship III

$$C'(S, \tau, K) + K - S \geq P'(S, \tau, K) \geq C'(S, \tau, K) + KB(\tau) - S \qquad (2.29)$$

We will first prove the upper boundary limit for the put's price by contradiction. That is suppose $P'(S, \tau, K) > C'(S, \tau, K) + K - S$. We could then form a riskless arbitrage position by selling the put, buying the call, selling the stock short, and buying K bonds, and realize an immediate profit on our initial position. If the put isn't exercised before maturity we can liquidate our position on that day in the following way:

	$S^* < K$	$S* \geq K$
Buy the put	$-(K - S^*)$	0
Sell the call	0	$S^* - K$
Buy the stock	$-S^*$	$-S^*$
Withdraw the K invested	$K/B(\tau)$	$K/B(\tau)$
Result	$[K/B(\tau)] - K$	$[K/B(\tau)] - K$

No matter what happens at maturity, we end up with a profit[13] equal to the interest earned on the striking price, that is $K((1/B(\tau)) - 1)$. So it cannot be possible that our initial investment was a positive cash inflow, too.

If the put is exercised before maturity, we would have to use the K initially invested to buy back the stock from the option's owner and then use that stock to close out our initial short position. Hence, we would still end up with a profit stemming from the interest earned on the K originally invested and from the nonnegative value of the long position in the call that we still hold. So whatever the final outcome, the following equation

$$C'(S, \tau, K) + K - S \geq P'(S, \tau, K)$$

must hold to avoid a "sure profit" opportunity.

We can now prove in the same way that the lower boundary to the put's price must hold to avoid "free lunches" in the market. If this weren't true, that is, if

$$P'(S, \tau, K) < C'(S, \tau, K) + KB(\tau) - S$$

then we could make a sure profit initially by buying the put, selling the call, buying the stock, and borrowing an amount equal to the present value of the striking price. Now, since we wouldn't be exercised on the call until maturity,[14] we would then liquidate our position at the expiration date as follows:

	$S^* < K$	$S^* \geq K$
Sell the put	$K - S^*$	—
Buy the call	—	$-(S^* - K)$
Sell the stock	S^*	S^*
Reimburse the loan	$-K$	$-K$
Total	0	0

---

[13] Since $B(\tau) < 1$ for $\tau \neq 0$, it must be that $1/B(\tau) > 1$ if the interest rate prevailing in the market is strictly positive.

[14] Since it is an American call on a nondividend-paying stock.

Obviously, we end up making neither a gain nor a loss whichever state of nature prevails at expiration, and it is therefore clear that the initial positive cash inflow (profit) resulting from the assumption:

$$P'(S, \tau, K) < C'(S, \tau, K) + KB(\tau) - S$$

violates the non-arbitrage opportunity condition. This proves by contradiction that the lower boundary of the put-call relationship III must hold.

We can now use an example to see how we can set limits on call (put) prices by applying this relationship. Suppose that we observe the following data on both a 3-month American call and a 3-month American put written on the stock of company X:

Current stock price	S	$= 41.250$
Current put market price	P'	$= 2.625$
Current call market price	C'	$= 4.125$
Striking price	K	$= 40$
Price of a 3-month T-bill	$B(0.25)$	$= 0.9742$

Let us see if the put's market price is consistent with the put-call relationship III. The lower boundary for the put's price equals

$$4.125 + (40 \times 0.9742) - 41.25 = \$1.843$$

The upper boundary for the put's price equals

$$4.125 + 40 - 41.25 = \$2.875$$

Now we observe that the put's market price of $2.625 violates neither the lower nor the upper boundary since:

$$2.875 > 2.625 > 1.843$$

The market is therefore showing a consistent relative pricing relationship between the call and the put written on stock X.

D Put-Call Relationship for American Options on Dividend-Paying Stocks

Since most traded options are written on dividend paying stocks, it is interesting to see how these cash inflows affect the relative prices of puts and calls. Remembering that cash dividends have a positive influence on the put's price, we will not be surprised to see that the upper boundary of a put's price is now increased by the amount of the dividends while the lower boundary remains identical to the one in Put-Call Relationship III for American options on nondividend-paying stocks. More formally, the price of an American put on a dividend-paying stock must never exceed the price of an identical call, plus the striking price, plus the present value of the dividends, and minus the stock's price:

$$P'(S, D, \tau, K) \leq C'(S, D, \tau, K) + K + D - S$$

The price of the put should always be greater than the call's price, plus the present value of the striking price, and minus the stock's price:

$$P' \geq C'(S, D, \tau, K) + KB(\tau) - S$$

Combining these two boundaries we can state the fourth put-call relationship for American options on dividend paying stocks as follows:

Put-Call Relationship IV:

$$C'(S, D, \tau, K) + K + D - S \geq P'(S, D, \tau, K)$$
$$\geq C'(S, D, \tau, K) + KB(\tau) - S \quad (2.30)$$

We will not prove the upper boundary since it involves exactly the same demonstration as for the upper boundary in the third relationship, except that here, when constructing the arbitrage portfolio, we would also have to buy the present value of the dividends to restitute those we owe on the stock held short.

To prove the lower boundary, we can again demonstrate its validity by contradiction. That is, if:

$$C'(S, D, \tau, K) + KB(\tau) - S > P'(S, D, \tau, K)$$

then construct an arbitrage portfolio by selling the call, buying the put, buying the stock (which now pays dividends), and borrowing the present value of the striking price. This net investment turns out to be an immediate profit (cash inflow) that is riskless. To see that this is true, consider what would happen at maturity if the call wasn't exercised prematurely. We would then close out the position by

	$S^* < K$	$S^* \geq K$
Selling the put	$K - S^*$	—
Buying the call	—	$-(S^* - K)$
Reimbursing the loan	$-K$	$-K$
Selling the stock	S^*	S^*
Retaining the dividends earned on the stock	D^*	D^*
Result	D^*	D^*

That is, no matter what happens at maturity, we end up making a profit D^* equal to the amount of the dividends paid on the stock and the interest earned on them.

If the call happened to be exercised prior to maturity, we would use the stock initially bought to deliver it, pay back the loan by using the $\$K$ received from the owner of the option, and we would realize a profit since we still hold the put as well as the dividends paid on the stock until the call is exercised. Therefore, regardless of when the call is exercised, we actually hold a "sure profit" investment strategy under the following condition:

$$C'(S, D, \tau, K) + KB(\tau) - S > P'(S, D, \tau, K)$$

Therefore by contradiction, this must be a precluded relationship. Hence the lower boundary of the put-call relationship IV must also hold.

We observe that the put-call relationships are much more powerful and precise for European options, where they price calls (or puts) exactly, than for American options, where they can only give a "fair" range of prices for the put (the call) given the price of the call (the put). This is unfortunate since most traded options are in fact American options. Moreover, since we have assumed known dividends, which are in fact unpredictable, and since we have ignored transaction costs, short selling restrictions, margin requirements, et cetera, it should be true that those boundaries are much broader, and therefore, less reliable when they are used in active trading strategies focusing on the call-put relative mispricing.

5   CONCLUSION

This chapter may seem to be a "compendium of laws" that is difficult to synthesize. However, all these rational boundaries for call and put option prices are fundamental and apply without any further assumptions about the stock's price behavior. By knowing that the option's payoff structure has a specific relationship to the stock's payoff structure, and by assuming no riskless arbitrage opportunities, we derived a set of boundaries that call and put prices must satisfy. These restrictions will help us test whether a specific option pricing model is relevant, since the theoretical pricing should be consistent with these general boundaries.

Moreover, while going through these price restrictions for calls and puts we encountered two key features—early exercise and dividend payments—that make it more difficult to value an American option than a European call option, and even more difficult to value an American put than an American call option. Also, while showing that in an arbitrage free setting, put and call relative pricing should conform to some specific relationship, we noticed that this restriction could be precisely identified for European options but that it only led to upper and lower boundaries for American options. Again, this is due to the fact that early exercise is always possible for American put options while it isn't necessarily the case for American call options. The latter fact is important since it implies that while we only need to value one security (for example, the European call) and use the put-call parity relationship to derive the price of an "identical" put, a similar argument doesn't apply to American options. Here we must value each option (put and call) separately, considering its specific features regarding the dividends and the early exercise possibilities.

We now have a better understanding of how both put and call option prices are related to the stock price, exercise price, expiration time, dividends, and interest rates. Further, we have a better understanding on the relative pricing of call options versus put options and of American options versus European options.

However, these qualitative generalizations (for example, "the lower the stock price, the lower the call's price") aren't very useful if one needs to know, for example, by how much the call's price will vary given a 10 percent increase in the stock price. The next step will therefore address option pricing models that allow us to jump from theoretical judgments to some functional relationships, thereby relating the option's price to its basic explanatory variables. During this incursion in the theory of option pricing, we shall see that the previously defined pricing restrictions are relevant in describing option prices, in building option pricing models, and in checking the validity of some existing models' conclusions.

CHAPTER 3

THE PRICING OF
A EUROPEAN
OPTION ON A
NONDIVIDEND-PAYING
STOCK

1 INTRODUCTION

Until now, we have stated some general restrictions that option prices should not violate in an efficient market. This allowed us to derive fair ranges for option prices, however no exact pricing relationship could be derived except at their expiration date. Following Restriction 2 of Chapter 2, we know that at maturity a call's price should equal

$$C(S^*, K, 0) = \max[0, S^* - K]$$

Similarly a put's price should equal

$$P(S^*, K, 0) = \max[0, K - S^*]$$

This is obviously insufficient information, since we need to be able to price an option at any point in time in order to assess if it is correctly valued by the market, and in turn, to determine what optimal investment strategies can be implemented. However, to derive an option pricing relationship for a European call option, we need to make some additional assumptions about the capital market's structure, interest rates, and the probability distribution of the underlying stock's return, which is the most important consideration. We begin our theoretical explanation of option pricing by assuming a very simple random behavior of stock prices, which will enable us to derive the binomial option pricing formula. The binomial approach has the advantage of being easy to understand for those unfamiliar with advanced mathematics, while emphasizing the main principles and methodology of the valuation process.

In this chapter we focus on the fundamental pricing techniques—the replicating strategy and the perfect hedge—that lead to the binomial option pricing formula. We will also review the basic assumptions of the binomial distribution and apply them to our option pricing problem. The use of the binomial pricing approach will be illustrated through an example. We will conclude by summarizing the most salient properties of this option pricing framework.

2   THE REPLICATING PORTFOLIO

A call option can be viewed as a leveraged position in the stock. This means that by simply adjusting the amount invested in the stock and the number of bonds sold, we can in fact replicate the payoff structure of the European call at maturity. Therefore to avoid riskless arbitrage, the current values of the call and replicating portfolio must be equal. We will now present a simple example of a replicating portfolio.

Suppose that Stock S.O.S. is currently trading at $32 and you can buy riskless zero-coupon bonds that have a face value of $100 and that mature in one period at a current price of $90.90. At the same time, the one-period call option on stock S.O.S. with an exercise price of $30 is trading for $4.73. Moreover, we know that the stock's price one period ahead is going to be worth either $33 or $30.

First, we will show that a portfolio containing one share of stock held long and 0.3 bonds sold (Portfolio B) exactly replicates the cash flow pattern of the S.O.S. call option (Portfolio A) on its expiration date. The following table illustrates their payoffs at the maturity date of the call option.

	$S^* = 33$	$S^* = 30$
A) Sell the call	$3	0
B) Sell the stock and buy back 0.3 bonds now trading at their face value of $100	$33 - (0.3 \times 100)$	$30 - (0.3 \times 100)$
Payoff of the replicating portfolio	$3	0

Clearly, if the replicating portfolio and the option have the same payoffs, the current option price must be equal to the current value of a portfolio containing 1 share of S.O.S. stock held long and 0.3 bonds sold. Is this the case?

$$\text{Current value of S.O.S. call} = \$4.73$$

$$\text{Current value of portfolio} = 32 - 0.3(90.90)$$

$$= \$4.73$$

In this case, the replicating portfolio and the option are identically priced, and therefore profitable riskless trading opportunities involving the call and the portfolio are effectively prevented. However, this example represents more than just another illustrated arbitrage restriction on call pricing. What it really shows is that by correctly choosing the amounts invested in the underlying stock and bond, we can replicate the payoff structure of a European call option. To do that, however, we need some "predictions" on the future stock price (S^*). We are now going to see that even by allowing the stock price to follow a specific random pattern over a period of time, we are able to value the option as if it were a leveraged position in the stock. Note that not any leveraged position in the stock will do; there is a unique combination of Δ shares of stock and Y bonds sold short that will replicate the call's value at each point in time. In this example, the values $\Delta = 1$ and $Y = 0.3$ were already given. We will now describe the methodology used to derive these parameters for the purpose of pricing a call option when the stock price follows a multiplicative binomial process through time.

3 ASSUMPTIONS UNDERLYING THE BINOMIAL APPROACH

To describe the valuation process leading to the binomial option pricing formula, we must make some additional assumptions.[1]

1. The markets are competitive, and each individual acts as a price taker. Moreover, there are no transaction costs or taxes, and short selling is allowed without restrictions. We also assume that investors act rationally and they prefer more wealth to less.

2. The riskless interest rate is constant through time. We will denote the interest rate per period by the letter i and the compounding factor for one period by the letter R:[2]

$$R = (1 + i)^1 = (1 + i)$$

3. The stock does not pay any dividends throughout the option's remaining time to maturity.

---

[1] The effect of relaxing some of these assumptions will be discussed in the following chapters.

[2] It then follows that the price $B(\tau)$ of a one-period discount bond equals

$$B(1) = \frac{1}{1 + i} = \frac{1}{R}$$

4. The stock price follows a multiplicative binomial process in discrete time. That is, over each period there is a probability q that the stock will rise by U percent and a probability $(1 - q)$ that the stock will decrease by D percent. Here U and D represent the rates of return on the stock[3] in the case of an upward and downward movement, respectively.

While the first three assumptions require no further comment, we offer further discussion about the last one. We said previously that to derive an exact option pricing formula, it was necessary to specify the probability distribution associated to the stock's return. In other words, we do not need to know or predict future stock prices to price the call, but we must be able to adequately describe how the stock price moves from one period to the other.

Let us introduce the binomial multiplicative process through a simple example. Individual A agrees to play the following game: he will toss a coin and everytime it falls on heads he earns 5 percent ($H = 1.05$) everytime it falls on tails he loses 10 percent ($T = .90$). Furthermore, he has a total of $100 to gamble. If he only tosses the coin once, he will end up owing either $100 \times H$ ($105) or $100 \times T$($90). If he tosses it twice, the possible outcomes are: HH, HT, TH, and TT, which is the same as $H^2, 2HT$, and T^2 with corresponding wealth of $110.25, $94.50, and $81. He could play like this n times, but for each toss there are always only two possible outcomes: head or tail. Of course, the total number of possible combinations will grow at a rate of 2^n as represented by the tree diagram in Fig. 3.1.

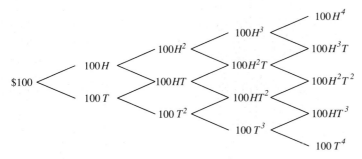

FIGURE 3.1
Tree diagram of possible coin-toss combinations.

---

[3] Note that to prevent arbitrage opportunities between the stock and riskless lending (or borrowing), U and D must satisfy

$$U > i > D$$

Obviously, individual A is interested in knowing his final financial situation. After n trials, the possible combinations of $j (j = 0, 1, 2, 3, \ldots, n)$ head tosses and hence $(n - j)$ tail tosses are given by[4]

$$\frac{n!}{j!(n - j)!}$$

So, for example, if he wanted to know how many combinations would result in three heads $(j = 3)$ after four tosses $(n = 4)$, he would compute

$$\frac{4!}{3!(4 - 3)!} = \frac{4 \times 3 \times 2 \times 1}{3 \times 2 \times 1 \times 1} = 4$$

Indeed this is true since he could have obtained: *HHHT* or *THHH* or *HTHH* or *HHTH*, as we can clearly see from the tree diagram of Fig. 3.1. After each number n of trials, the final wealth Z_n is unknown: it is a stochastic variable that varies through the state space (trials here) according to some probability rules. Here, however, we do have some knowledge about the probability rules governing Z_n.

- Since we are dealing with a binomial process, there are only two possible outcomes from each node on the tree. Hence, we can denote the probability of a head toss by q and the probability of a tail toss by $(1 - q)$.
- The probability of tossing a head or a tail is independent for each trial; that is, whether this is the first, second, or nth trial, the probability of tossing a head is always equal to q.
- The probability of tossing a head is independent of the path history of previous tosses, and is always equal to q. This means that whether the results follow the path *HHHT*, or *THHH, HTHH*, or *HHTH* up to $n = 4$, the probability of tossing a head in the fifth trial remains the same and is equal to q.

Therefore, we can say that the random variable Z_n denoting his final wealth after n trials follows a multiplicative binomial process with probability[5] that equals

$$\frac{n!}{(n - j)! \, j!} q^j (1 - q)^{n-j} \tag{3.1}$$

For example, if the gambler wanted to know the probability of ending up with three head tosses after four trials, which corresponds to $100(1.05)^3(0.9) = \$104.19$,

---

4
  $n! = n \cdot (n - 1)(n - 2)(n - 3) \cdots (3)(2)(1); 1! = 1$ and $0! = 1$.

5 Note that $\sum_{j=0}^{n} [n!/(n - j)! \, j!] q^j (1 - q)^{n-j} = 1$ confirms that the sum of the probabilities associated with each possible outcome $(j = 0, j = 1, \ldots, j = n)$ out of n trials must be equal to 1.

assuming that for a "fair" game the probability q of tossing a head must be equal to 1/2, he would obtain

$$\text{prob}[j = 3] = \frac{4!}{(4 - 3)!\, 3!}(1/2)^3(1/2)^1 = 0.25$$

$$= \text{prob}[Z_n = \$104.19]$$

More generally, we wish to know the probability of ending up with "at least" a specific result corresponding to $j = a$ successes out of n trials. Therefore we compute the complementary binomial distribution as follows:

$$B[n, a, q] = \sum_{j=a}^{n} \frac{n!}{(n - j)!\, j!}q^j(1 - q)^{n-j} \tag{3.2}$$

In our example, suppose the gambler wants to know the probability of ending up with at least \$104.19 after four trials. He has to fix his target level of successes (head tosses) at $a = 3$ and then compute the probability of the number of head tosses j being at least equal to or greater than 3 given $n = 4$. Using the binomial complementary distribution $B[4; 3; 1/2]$, he will obtain

$$B[4; 3; 1/2] = \sum_{j=3}^{4} \frac{4!}{(4 - j)!\, j!}(1/2)^j(1/2)^{4-j}$$

$$= \frac{4!}{1!\, 3!}(1/2)^3(1/2)^1 + \frac{4!}{0!\, 4!}(1/2)^4(1/2)^0$$

$$= 0.25 + 0.0625$$

$$= 0.3125$$

Thus, the gambler has a 31.25 percent chance of ending up with at least \$104.19 after four trials.

We now have a better understanding of the properties of the binomial multiplicative process in a state space dimension. Returning to our problem and focusing on the assumption specifying the stock price process, we must first make the following comment: The random variables $\tilde{S}_t$ (the stock price at time t) follows a stochastic process through time since, at each new time period, $\tilde{S}_t$ can take one of several possible values. A stochastic process is a family of random variables $[\tilde{S}_t, t = 1, 2, 3, \ldots, T]$ indexed by a parameter t to show that $\tilde{S}_t$ varies according to probability laws over time. At each point of time t, there is a distribution function that allows us to assess the probability associated with each possible outcome of S; in our case, we used the binomial distribution to describe the stock's price behavior.

This implies that all our previous conclusions regarding the binomial distribution can be directly applied to the stock price process. We can now view n (previously defining the number of trials) as the number of periods, and hence $\tilde{S}_n$

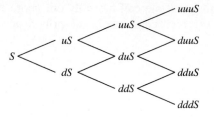

FIGURE 3.2
Price path of a stock under the multiplicative binomial process.

as the random value of the stock after n periods. Since $\tilde{S}_n$ follows a multiplicative binomial process, this implies that from each previous node S_{n-1}, the stock price can either go up by U percent or down by D percent with a probability of q and $(1 - q)$ respectively.[6] These probabilities have to be independent of previous outcomes as well as of the number of previous periods. This implies that they are always the same, and therefore, the stock's relative values $S_t/S_0, S_2/S_1, \ldots, S_n/S_{n-1}$ have a stationary and identical distribution that is independent of the stock price level.

Let us denote the one-period growth factors of the stock price for upward and downward movements by $u = (1 + U)$ and by $d = (1 + D)$ respectively. We can then illustrate the stock's price path under the multiplicative binomial process as shown in Fig. 3.2. Now that we can determine a stock's price path through the call option's expiration date, we can return to our primary objective of valuing a European call option.

4 THE BINOMIAL OPTION PRICING FORMULA

Let us value a European call option—relying on the assumptions described in Section 3—by constructing a replicating portfolio with Δ stocks and $\$Y$ of bonds that exactly matches the call's payoff structure at each point in time. Since we know the payoff structure of the call at maturity, the valuation process has to be recursive: starting to value the call at its expiration date T, we proceed backwards, valuing it at time $T - 1, T - 2$, and so on, until we reach the current date and hence the desired call price.

---

[6] We shall examine later in this chapter whether it is realistic, over any arbitrary period of time, to assume that constant rate of return—U and D respectively—are driving prices up and down. The fact that an increase in price can be followed—through independent probabilities—by either an increase or decrease in prices over the next period is, however, consistent with the random walk hypothesis.

Let us first state the methodology assuming that the call has only one more period until expiration. We know the stock price process can be described as follows:

$$S \begin{cases} uS \\ dS \end{cases}$$

Hence the corresponding call's price path is given by

$$C = ? \begin{cases} C_u = \max[0, uS - K] \\ C_d = \max[0, dS - K] \end{cases}$$

where

C_u denotes the call price one period ahead given that the stock price increased by $U\%$

C_d denotes the call price one period ahead given that the stock price decreased by $D\%$

Now, we want to construct a replicating portfolio with Δ shares of stock and $\$Y$ borrowed at the riskless interest rate so that the expiration date the portfolio has a value equal to C_u if the stock price goes up and a value equal to C_d if the stock price comes down:

$$\Delta S + Y \begin{cases} C_u \\ C_d \end{cases}$$

But we also know that the value of this portfolio should have grown to[7]

$$\Delta S + Y \begin{cases} \Delta uS + YR \\ \Delta dS + YR \end{cases}$$

Hence, since we require the same payoffs for the call and the portfolio at maturity, it must be that:

$$C_u = \Delta uS + YR \tag{3.3}$$

$$C_u = \Delta dS + YR \tag{3.4}$$

---

[7] Note that the rate of return on riskless bonds is constant and equal to i. Hence, at the end of the period the $\$Y$ borrowed will have grown to $Y(1 + i) = YR$.

Subtracting Eq. (3.4) from Eq. (3.3) we obtain

$$\Delta = \frac{C_u - C_d}{S(u - d)} \tag{3.5}$$

Plugging the value of Δ in either Eq. (3.3) or (3.4) we obtain

$$Y = \frac{uC_d - dC_u}{(u - d)R} \tag{3.6}$$

Since Δ and Y have been chosen so that they equate the final payoffs of the call and the portfolio, it should be true, to avoid arbitrage, that the current option price be equal to the current value of the replicating portfolio:

$$C = \Delta S + Y$$

Substituting for the values of Δ and Y, we obtain

$$C = \left[\frac{(R - d)}{(u - d)} C_u + \frac{(u - R)}{(u - d)} C_d \right] \Big/ R \tag{3.7}$$

Equation (3.7) values a call option as a function of the stock's price, the stock's price process parameters u and d, the striking price, and the interest rate. The first observation we can make by looking at the terms in brackets of Eq. (3.7) is that they express the expected value of the call at expiration. Can we really talk about "expected" value? Yes, because $(R - d)/(u - d)$ and $(u - R)/(u - d)$ can be interpreted as probabilities since they are strictly positive[8] and since their sum is one. We can then write Eq. (3.7) as follows

$$C = (pC_u + (1 - p)C_d)/R \tag{3.8}$$

where $p = (R - d)/(u - d)$ and $1 - p = (u - R)/(u - d)$

and we see that the call's price is equal to the discounted value of its expected payoff one period ahead.

Now since the stock's price process is stationary, we can use exactly the same replicating methodology with Eq. (3.8) to recursively value a call that has two periods until expiration. The stock's price now describes the following path:

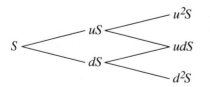

---

[8] Remember we made the assumption that U and D satisfy $U > i > D$, hence $u > R > d$ must also hold.

The corresponding call's price path looks like this:

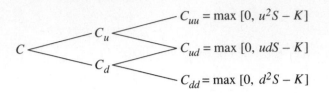

$$C_{uu} = \max [0, u^2 S - K]$$
$$C_{ud} = \max [0, udS - K]$$
$$C_{dd} = \max [0, d^2 S - K]$$

We can obtain C_u and C_d as equal to the value of two replicating portfolios respectively at the end of period one. So from Eq. (3.8) we can express C_u and C_d in a two-period context as follows:

$$C_u = [pC_{uu} + (1 - p)C_{ud}]/R \qquad (3.8a)$$
$$C_d = [pC_{du} + (1 - p)C_{dd}]/R \qquad (3.8b)$$

Hence the current price of the option is equal to

$$C = [pC_u + (1 - p)C_d]/R$$

Plugging the values C_u and C_d in Eqs. (3.8a) and (3.8b), we obtain the following expression for C:

$$C = [p^2 C_{uu} + 2p(1 - p)C_{du} + (1 - p)^2 C_{dd}]/R^2 \qquad (3.9)$$

Since we know the values of the call at expiration from the tree diagram, we can substitute them for C_{uu}, C_{du}, and C_{dd} in Eq. (3.9) to obtain

$$C = \{p^2 \max[0, u^2 S - K] + 2p(1 - p) \max[0, udS - K]$$
$$+ (1 - p)^2 \max[0, d^2 S - K]\}/R^2 \qquad (3.10)$$

Again, we can see that the option's current price is equal to the discounted value of its expected terminal payoff [9] that now occurs two periods ahead.

Since we don't need to worry about early exercise for a European call and we assumed that the stock isn't paying any dividends, we can exploit the one period step-by-step recursive valuation equation in a more rational fashion. We already saw that the price of the call is always equal to its expected value one period ahead discounted with the discount factor $1/R$. By extending this procedure over two, three, ... ,n periods, we can conclude that the call's current price is equal to the present value of its expected payoff at maturity.

This concept is very useful since it allows us to value European call options without considering all the intermediary one-period recursive steps. For example,

---

[9] The sum of the probabilities of Eq. (3.10) is equal to 1 ($p^2 + 2p(1 - p) + (1 - p)^2 = 1$), and we have seen previously that p and $1 - p$ are themselves positive probabilities that add up to 1.

a two-period European call can be priced directly from Eq. (3.10) without worrying about its possible prices (C_u and C_d) at period 1. The only additional factor we must account for in a multiperiod framework is the number of periods (n) that separate the call from its maturity date, and hence the increasing number of combinations the stock price and the option price may therefore follow over the total number of periods considered.

Now recalling our previous comments on the binomial distribution, we can look at the term in brackets of Eq. (3.10) as representing the total number of combinations the value of the call can take after two periods, that is for $n = 2$, given that the stock price makes j upward movements and hence $(n - j)$ downward movements, with probability p and $(1 - p)$ respectively. Hence we can write Eq. (3.10) as follows:

$$C = \left[\sum_{j=0}^{2} \frac{2!}{(2 - j)!\, j!} p^j (1 - p)^{2-j} \max[0,\, S u^j d^{2-j} - K] \right] \Big/ R^2 \qquad (3.11)$$

where $p = (R - d)/(u - d)$ and $1 - p = (u - R)/(u - d)$

In the general case where we would value an n-period call option, we would simply restate Eq. (3.11) as follows:

$$C = \left[\sum_{j=0}^{n} \frac{n!}{(n - j)!\, j!} p^j (1 - p)^{n-j} \max[0,\, S u^j d^{n-j} - K] \right] \Big/ R^n \qquad (3.12)$$

Note, however, that for some stock paths and hence for some values of j, the call will expire worthless. Therefore, it would be much more useful to use the complementary binomial distribution starting at $j = a$, where we know that for $j \geq a$ the call will expire in-the-money. We would then only need to sum up the $n - a$ strictly positive expected call values at expiration and discount them to the present in order to value the call.

a can be defined as the smallest integer satisfying

$$S u^a d^{n-a} > K$$

Taking the logarithms on both sides, we find

$$a > \frac{\ln(K/S d^n)}{\ln(u/d)} \qquad (3.13)$$

Combining this result with Eq. (3.12), we can then use the binomial complementary distribution $B[n, a, p]$ to price the call:

$$C = \left[\sum_{j=a}^{n} \frac{n!}{(n - j)!\, j!} p^j (1 - p)^{n-j} (S u^j d^{n-j} - K) \right] \Big/ R^n$$

Rearranging the formula, we obtain

$$C = \left[S \sum_{j=a}^{n} \frac{n!}{(n-j)!\,j!} p^j (1-p)^{n-j} u^j d^{n-j} \right] /R^n$$

$$- KR^{-n} \left[\sum_{j=a}^{n} \frac{n!}{(n-j)!\,j!} p^j (1-p)^{n-j} \right] \qquad (3.14)$$

Entering $1/R^n$ into the first term in brackets and observing that:

$$p^j (1-p)^{n-j} \frac{u^j d^{n-j}}{R^n} = \left(\frac{pu}{R}\right)^j \left(\frac{(1-p)d}{R}\right)^{n-j}$$

we can denote the new probabilities b and $1 - b$ such that:[10]

$$b = pu/R \text{ and } 1 - b = (1-p)d/R \qquad (3.15)$$

With these substitutions, we can finally set the general binomial option pricing formula by writing Eq. (3.14) as follows:

$$C = S \left[\sum_{j=a}^{n} \frac{n!}{n-j!\,j!} b^j (1-b)^{n-j} \right] - KR^{-n} \left[\sum_{j=a}^{n} \frac{n!}{n-j!\,j!} p^j (1-p)^{n-j} \right]$$

$$(3.16)$$

$$\Longleftrightarrow$$

$$C = SB[n, a, b] - KR^{-n}B[n, a, p] \qquad (3.17)$$

where

S denotes the current stock price

K denotes the striking price of the call option

n denotes the number of periods until the call's expiration date

$B(n, a, p)$ denotes the complementary binomial distribution with parameters n, a, and p, or in other words, the probability that the stock will make at least a upward movements over n periods knowing that the per period probability of an upward movement is equal to p.

$B(n, a, b)$ denotes the complementary binomial distribution with parameters n, a, and b, or in other words, the probability that the stock will make at least a upward movements and hence end up being greater than the exercise price (K) at the end of n periods given that the per period probability of that event occurring is equal to b $(b = pu/R)$.

At this stage we can look at Eq. (3.17) as implying that the call's price is equal to the discounted expected future value of the stock given that the stock

---

[10] We can again state that b and $(1 - b)$ are strictly positive and that they add up to 1.

will end up in-the-money: $SB[n, a, b]$ less the present value of the expected cost incurred by exercising the call: $-KR^{-n}B[n, a, p]$.

Before going much deeper into the interpretation of the binomial pricing approach, we shall now use an example to illustrate how the replicating portfolio strategy leading to the recursive valuation procedure and the binomial option pricing formula can both be easily implemented to price options.

5 APPLYING THE BINOMIAL APPROACH: AN EXAMPLE

Suppose we observe the following data on stock of company Axis and on the European call written on this stock: $S = 40$, $K = 38$, and $n = 2$. We also know that in each period the stock price will either increase by 15% or decrease by 5% with probabilities 0.6 and 0.4 respectively, hence, $u = 1.15$; $d = 0.95$; $q = 0.6$; and $1 - q = 0.4$. We also observe that the interest rate is constant and equal to 10% per period, hence:

$$R = (1 + 0.1) = 1.10$$

A The Recursive Approach

This approach enables us to determine the call's price at each node by using the recursive replication technique described in Section 3.4. First, we can diagram the stock's price path:

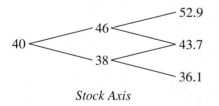

Stock Axis

Then we can diagram the call's path:

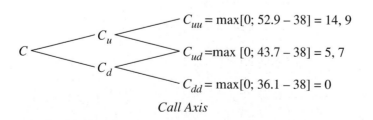

Call Axis

Since the procedure is recursive, we must first compute the call option prices at the end of the first period: C_u and C_d.

To determine the call option price C_u, we can create a replicating portfolio consisting of Δ_1 shares of Axis stock and $\$Y_1$ invested in riskless bonds, so that this portfolio exactly replicates the payoff structure of C_u at the end of the second period. To do that, we have to compute the parameters Δ_1 and Y_1, and from Eq. (3.5), we obtain[11]

$$\Delta_i = \frac{C_{uu} - C_{ud}}{S_u(u - d)} = \frac{14.9 - 5.7}{46(1.15 - 0.95)} = 1$$

$$Y_i = \frac{uC_{du} - dC_{uu}}{(u - d)R} = \frac{(1.15)(5.7) - (0.95)(14.9)}{1.1(1.15 - 0.95)} = -34.545$$

Hence, at the end of the first period, the portfolio containing one share of stock at $46 held long and $34.545 of riskless zero coupon bonds sold replicates the payoff structure of C_u. The portfolio's value at the end of period one must therefore be equal to C_u in order to avoid riskless arbitrage opportunities. So we must observe that

$$C_u = \Delta_1 S_u + Y_1$$

$$= 1 \times 46 - 34.545$$

$$= \$11.455$$

We can apply the same methodology to find another portfolio that exactly replicates the payoff structure of C_d at the end of the second period. This duplicating portfolio will consist of Δ_2 shares of stock and $\$Y_2$ of bonds, where Δ_2 and Y_2 respectively satisfy

$$\Delta_2 = \frac{C_{ud} - C_{dd}}{S_d(u - d)} = \frac{5.7 - 0}{(38)(0.2)} = 0.75$$

$$Y_2 = \frac{uC_{dd} - dC_{ud}}{R(u - d)} = \frac{(1.15)(0) - (0.95)(5.7)}{(1.1) \times (0.2)} = -24.613$$

and hence the call's price C_d must be equal to the value of this portfolio consisting of 0.75 shares of stock Axis at a price $S_u = \$38$ held long and of $24,613 of zero coupon riskless bonds sold:

$$C_d = \Delta_2 S_d + Y_2$$

$$= 0.75 \times 38 - 24.613$$

$$= \$3.887$$

---

[11] Note that since we are working with two periods, we compute the call's price C_u as a function of C_{uu} and C_{ud}, so that formula (3.5) must be adjusted considering the following transformations: S becomes S_u, C_u becomes C_{uu}, C_d becomes C_{du} and C becomes C_u; hence (3.5) can be written as follows:

$$\Delta_1 = (C_{uu} - C_{ud})/S_u(u - d).$$

The same transformations are valid when we compute Y_1.

Now, to compute the current call's price C, we shall replicate its payoff structure one period ahead using a third portfolio whose value at the end of the first period must be equal to C_u or C_d. This portfolio will contain Δ_3 shares of stock levered by an amount Y_3 of riskless debt, where Δ_3 and Y_3 respectively must satisfy

$$\Delta_3 = \frac{C_u - C_d}{S(u - d)} = \frac{11.455 - 3.887}{(40)(0.2)} = 0.946$$

$$Y_3 = \frac{uC_d - dC_u}{R(u - d)} = \frac{(1.15)(3.887) - (0.95)(11.455)}{(1.1)(0.2)}$$

$$= -\$29.147$$

The current value of this portfolio must be equal to the current call's price. Therefore, we can easily compute the call's price as satisfying

$$C = \Delta_3 S + Y_3 = (0.946)(40) - 29.147$$

$$= \$8.693$$

The recursive approach is very instructive since it shows us that, to value a call option we must readjust the replicating portfolio whenever the stock price changes. The following table illustrates this need for portfolio rebalancing.

Time 0			Time 1		
S	40	S_u	46	S_d	38
Δ_3	0.946	Δ_1	1	Δ_2	0.75
Y_3	-29.147	Y_1	-34.545	Y_2	-24.613
C	8.693	C_u	11.455	C_d	3.877

We can see that the higher the stock price, the more shares we need to buy to replicate the (more "in-the-money") call option. Although we shall present the properties of replicating and hedging portfolios in Chapter 4, it is important to observe that the replicating binomial approach already emphasizes the dynamic structure of option pricing. Whenever the stock price—the random variable—changes, the portfolio's risk exposure is altered and must be adjusted to maintain the replicating strategy throughout the option's remaining time to maturity.

However, the replicating strategy seems also very heavy and time consuming, especially if it has to be applied to long-term options. In fact, this approach would only be used in cases where one really needs to assess the option's value at each intermediate tree node. This is obviously the case with American call options on dividend-paying stocks or with American put options, since for these options early exercise must be explicitly considered during the valuation procedure. We shall see that the recursive approach is precisely a powerful instrument to value these options: the step-by-step pricing technique allows us to verify at each node whether early exercise is optimal or not. Even with those options, however, we wouldn't bother with the calculations of Δ and Y at each node, and hence a much quicker procedure would rely on the one-period recursive formula:

$$C = [pC_u + (1 - p)C_d]/R \qquad (3.8)$$

This is the direct result of the replicating portfolio strategy followed from one period to the other.

Since we don't need to bother with early exercise, we could have used Eq. (3.10) to price this two-period European call directly. In our example, we need to compute: $p = (R - d)/(u - d) = 0.75$ and hence $1 - p = 0.25$. The we just have to substitute the values of C_{uu}, C_{ud}, and C_{dd} in Eq. (3.10) to compute the current call's price:

$$C = \frac{[(0.75)^2(14.9) + 2(0.75)(0.25)(5.7) + (0.25)^2 \times 0]}{(1.1)^2}$$

$$C = \$8.693$$

Note that we obtain the same call price that was generated using the step-by-step recursive procedure. This had to be expected, since Eq. (3.10) is simply a straightforward extension of Eq. (3.8), which is the direct valuation formula obtained through a one-period replicating portfolio strategy.

When we use Eq. (3.10) for $n = 2$, or even extend it to an arbitrary number of periods, we are assuming implicitly that the replicating portfolio is periodically rebalanced so as to validate Eq. (3.8) throughout the option's time to maturity. Hence the call's price is equal to its discounted expected value at maturity and we can skip the intermediary steps when we deal with a European call option.

The most general result of the binomial valuation approach is of course the binomial pricing formula Eq. (3.17), and we can now use it in our example to price the two-period call option.

B   The Binomial Pricing Formula

To apply the binomial pricing equation (3.17), we need to compute the probabilities p and b and the integer a such that for $j > a$ the call will necessarily end up in-the-money at expiration. Since we previously computed $p = 0.75$ and $1 - p = 0.25$, we can calculate b as follows:

$$b = \frac{pu}{R} = \frac{0.75 \times 1.15}{1.1} = 0.784$$

and

$$1 - b = \frac{(1 - p)d}{R} = \frac{0.25 \times 0.95}{1.1} = 0.216$$

Then we can compute a using Eq. (3.13).

$$a > \frac{\ln(K/S\,d^n)}{\ln(u/d)}$$

$$\Longleftrightarrow$$

$$a > \frac{\ln(38/(40 \times (0.95)^2))}{\ln(1.15/0.95)}$$

$$\Longleftrightarrow$$

$$a > 0.267$$

However, since a is defined as the smallest integer greater than the right-hand side of Eq. (3.13), we must set a equal to one. We can then compute $B[n, a, b]$:

$$B[2, 1, 0.784] = \sum_{j=1}^{2} \frac{2!}{(2-j)!\,j!}(0.784)^j(0.216)^{2-j}$$

$$= [2 \times (0.784)^1(0.216)^1] + [1 \times (0.784)^2 \times 1]$$

$$= 0.9534$$

and $B[n, a, p]$:

$$B[2, 1, 0.75] = \sum_{j=1}^{2} \frac{2!}{(2-j)!\,j!}(0.75)^j(0.25)^{2-j}$$

$$= [2 \times 0.75 \times 0.25] + [1 \times (0.75)^2 \times 1]$$

$$= 0.9375$$

Finally, we may now apply the binomial pricing formula in Eq. (3.17) to compute the call's price.

$$C = SB[n, a, b] - KR^{-n}B[n, a, p]$$

$$= (40)(0.9534) - (38)(1.1)^{-2}(0.9375)$$

$$= \$8.692$$

It is of course the same price (omitting rounding differences) as the one previously computed with the recursive approach. This was expected since the binomial pricing formula simply summarizes the result of the recursive replicating portfolio valuation procedure into a general pricing equation. From this example, we see that applying the binomial option pricing formula is quite easy when we are dealing with a two-period option. If we want to price a longer-lived option, the preliminary computations of a, p, and b would be as simple. However, the calculation of the binomial complementary distributions $B[n, a, p]$ and $B[n, a, b]$ becomes very tedious as n increases. Therefore one would generally use powerful computer software that is designed to price European call options with the binomial formula given arbitrary large values of n.

6 A CLOSER LOOK AT THE BINOMIAL OPTION PRICING FORMULA

Although we now have all the relevant tools to price European call options with the binomial formula, it is important to analyze the basic assumptions, implications, and limits of this valuation approach. First, it is clear that although we were only focusing on European call options in this chapter, the binomial approach can be applied without restrictions to value a European put option on a nondividend-paying stock. To derive the put pricing formula, we could again use a replicating portfolio that recursively mimics the payoff structure of the put from its expiration date to the present. The only difference is that, given Restriction 2 in Chapter 2, we know that the put's value at expiration must be equal to

$$P(S^*, 0, K) = \max[0, K - S^*]$$

Therefore, our previous relationships and replicating portfolio would have to be constructed considering the specific payoff structure of the put. A much quicker way to derive the European put option pricing formula is to use the put-call parity relationship I from Chapter 2, which can be restated[12]

$$P = C - S + KR^{-n} \tag{3.18}$$

Since Eq.(3.17) gives the binomial pricing formula for the call, all we have to do is to plug it in Eq. (3.18) to derive the put's price, hence:

$$P = SB[n, a, b] - KR^{-n}B[n, a, p] - S + KR^{-n}$$

$$\Leftrightarrow P = S\left[\sum_{j=a}^{n} \frac{n!}{(n-j)!\, j!} b^j (1-b)^{n-j} - 1\right] +$$

$$KR^{-n}\left[1 - \sum_{j=a}^{n} \frac{n!}{(n-j)!\, j!} p^j (1-p)^{n-j}\right]$$

We obtain[13]

---

[12] Note that from Chapter 2 we had $P = C - S + KB(\tau)$. But since $B(\tau)$ is now the price of an n-period zero coupon bond $B(n) = 1/R^n = R^{-n}$

[13] Since $1 = \sum_{j=0}^{n} \frac{n!}{(n-j)!\, j!} b^j (1-b)^{n-j}$, we have that:

$$1 - \sum_{j=a}^{n} \frac{n!}{(n-j)!\, j!} b^j (1-b)^{n-j} = \sum_{j=0}^{a-1} \frac{n!}{(n-j)!\, j!} b^j (1-b)^{n-j}$$

The same argument applies for the complementary binomial distribution $B[n, a, p]$.

$$P = KR^{-n} \left[\sum_{j=0}^{a-1} \frac{n!}{(n-j)!\,j!} p^j (1-p)^{n-j} \right] - S \left[\sum_{j=0}^{a-1} \frac{n!}{(n-j)!\,j!} b^j (1-b)^{n-j} \right]$$

$$\Longleftrightarrow$$

$$P = KR^{-n}[1 - B[n, a, p]] - S[1 - B[n, a, b]] \qquad (3.19)$$

where a is the smallest integer greater than:

$$\frac{\ln(K/S\,d^n)}{\ln(u/d)}$$

Equation (3.19) enables us to price a European put on a nondividend-paying stock in the same way as we did previously for the call. Hence, the current value of a put is equal to the present value of the exercise price given that the put will expire in-the-money ($K > S^*$) less the discounted expected value of the stock at maturity given that the stock will end up with a value strictly smaller than the exercise price. Since the put is precisely in-the-money when a call is out-of-the money, this explains why the complementary binomial distribution is now taken for a symmetric number of upward movements (from 0 to $a - 1$) to the one requested for the call to end up in-the-money (from a to n). Intuitively this result is straightforward, since as a put owner, the less upward movements in the stock price, the greater your expected final return. However, once $a - 1$ upward movements for n periods have occurred the put will expire worthless given any additional upward jump, and hence the summation of the complementary binomial distribution over the interval (a, n) leads to zero option prices.

Now that we have derived a binomial pricing formula for put and call options respectively, we can look at Eq. (3.17) and (3.19) to determine which parameters directly affect the prices of these options. We can see that put and call option prices depend on

S the current level of the stock price

K the striking price

R the value of the capitalization factor reflecting indirectly the interest rate $i = R - 1$

n the number of periods until the option's expiration date

u, d the rates of growth in the stock price under the binomial multiplicative stochastic process

Obviously, there is one factor that doesn't affect the option's price: it is the probability q that was originally assigned to an upward movement in the stock price under the binomial multiplicative process. This is important since it implies that even if two persons do not assign the same subjective probabilities q and $(1 - q)$ to stock price changes, they will nevertheless price the call equally provided that they agree on the range of the stock's upward and downward movements. This also implies that call and put option prices are computed without considering individuals' attitudes or preferences towards risk.

The call (or put) price is computed relative to a unique state variable: the stock price. In the binomial pricing framework, it is implicitly assumed that this variable already reflects all the relevant information that will "indirectly" affect the call price. This is the feature of all relative pricing models where one prices an asset (here an option) with respect to the values of some other assets (here the stock) without explicitly taking into account other macroeconomic or behavioral parameters except to the extent that they are already embedded in the stock price.

There is a third important feature concerning the preference-free setting in which the call (or put) binomial valuation procedure is cast. We already stated that call and put prices are independent of the subjective probabilities one associates to upward and downward movements in the stock price. There is, however, one set of probabilities p and $(1 - p)$ that directly affects the option price since it defines the binomial formula's complementary distribution functions $B[n, a, p]$ and $B[n, a, b]$.[14] How can we interpret these probabilities? Why are they—and not the subjective probabilities q and $(1 - q)$—relevant in the binomial option pricing framework?

To understand the significance of the probabilities $p = (R - d)/(u - d)$ and $(1 - p) = (u - R)/(u - d)$, we shall rely on an alternative approach to derive the binomial pricing formula. We already saw that options can be priced through a replicating portfolio strategy. They can also be valued using a "perfect hedge" strategy involving the stock and the call (or put) option.

Suppose we observe a call that has still one period before its maturity date and we want to create a perfectly hedged position involving the underlying stock and the call, so that no matter how the stock price moves (up or down) over the next period, our final position will be the same. We shall form a portfolio that is perfectly "immunized" against stock price movements and that provides the same payoff in all possible states of nature one period ahead. We can construct such a portfolio by buying one share of the underlying stock and selling short m call options. The given stock's price path is

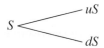

---

[14] Remember that $b = pu/R$ and $1 - b = (1 - p)d/R$ so that $B[n, a, b]$ is also a function of p and $1 - p$.

The resulting call's price path is

$$
C \begin{cases} \max[0,\ uS - K\,] = C_u \\ \max[0,\ dS - K\,] = C_d \end{cases}
$$

We end up with the following final position:

$$
S - mC \begin{cases} uS - mC_u \\ dS - mC_d \end{cases}
$$

The position is fully hedged. This implies that the final payoffs of the portfolio must be the same in both states of nature, or more formally stated

$$
uS - mC_u = dS - mC_d \tag{3.20}
$$

If Eq. (3.20) holds, our final wealth will be independent of the state of nature that prevails at expiration. Hence to create a perfect hedge, we shall have to sell m call options, where m can be found from Eq. (3.20)

$$
m = \frac{S(u - d)}{C_u - C_d} \tag{3.21}
$$

The position involving one share of stock held long and m options sold short is effectively riskless; therefore its rate of return must be equal to the risk-free rate of return, otherwise we could set up profitable riskless arbitrage strategies by selling the portfolio short and borrowing at the riskless rate.

Hence the return on this portfolio must satisfy

$$
\frac{uS - mC_u}{S - mC} = R \tag{3.22}
$$

From Eq. (3.22), we can isolate C:

$$
C = \frac{S(R - u) + mC_u}{mR} \tag{3.22}
$$

Substituting m in Eq. (3.22)$\prime$ by its value in Eq. (3.21) we obtain

$$C = \left[C_u \frac{(R - d)}{(u - d)} + C_d \frac{(u - R)}{u - d} \right] \Big/ R \tag{3.23}$$

$$\Longleftrightarrow$$

$$C = [pC_u + (1 - p)C_d]/R \tag{3.24}$$

where $p = (R - d)/(u - d)$ and $(1 - p) = (u - R)/(u - d)$. Equation (3.24) is exactly the same one-period pricing equation we obtained when we were valuing a one-period call with the "replicating strategy," Eq. (3.8).

Hence, providing the assumptions in Section 3 hold, we can use either the replicating portfolio strategy or the hedging strategy to price options in the binomial framework. This equivalence results from the relative pricing characteristic of the binomial valuation approach. In fact, we could use any two of the three parameters (stock price, call price, and riskless rate) involved in the relative pricing procedure to determine the value of the remaining parameter. For example, if the risk-free rate was unknown but the call and stock prices were known, we could use the perfect hedge strategy to find the value of the risk-free rate of return. Similarly, if we assumed that the stock price and the risk-free rate were known, we could either use a perfect hedge or a replicating portfolio strategy to price the call. Finally, if we assumed that the price of the stock was unknown, we could either replicate its structure with the call and the risk-free rate or again value the stock by creating a perfect hedge between the stock and the call option (this time S would be the unknown).

The basic assumption of any relative pricing methodology—whether applied through a replicating strategy or a hedging strategy—is essentially the no-arbitrage opportunities condition that is crucial in both valuation techniques to derive the (partial) equilibrium price of one asset with respect to the observed values of the others. The relationship between the two valuation strategies is even more pronounced, since we can view a perfect hedge strategy as a way of replicating the payoff structure of a risk-free asset with two risky assets, and hence we can define the "perfect hedge" as a specific replicating strategy where one mimics a risk-free rate of return with risky assets chosen in optimal proportions.

Now that we have defined the basic assumptions and characteristics of a perfect hedge relative pricing strategy, we can return to our main problem and show how this strategy may help us explain the nature of the probabilities p and $(1 - p)$ used in the binomial pricing formula. Since in a perfect hedge strategy, the call is valued by creating and rebalancing through time a fully riskless portfolio, it must be true that this portfolio has a rate of return equal to the risk-free rate of return in order to avoid arbitrage opportunities. We can see that this equilibrium condition doesn't require any specification about an individual's risk tolerance levels. This is true because individuals would always assign the same value and return (equal to the risk-free rate) to a perfectly hedged portfolio, no matter how risk-averse or risk-loving they are.

Thus, regardless of the particular economy, we would always obtain the same call pricing equation. To see that this is true, note that a riskless hedge must be valued equally by risk-neutral and risk-averse investors, so we can assume, for the sake of simplicity, that we are in a risk-neutral economy. Suppose further that the stock is valued identically in both the risk-averse and the risk-neutral economy. However, in the risk-neutral economy all assets have the same expected return equal to the risk-free interest rate because risk-neutral investors do not require any premium for bearing risk. Therefore the stock's expected one-period growth factor must also be equal to R:[15]

$$E(\Delta S/S) = q \frac{uS}{S} + (1 - q)\frac{dS}{S} = R \tag{3.25}$$

From this relationship we can compute q in a risk-neutral economy:

$$q = \frac{R - d}{u - d} = p \quad \text{and} \quad (1 - q) = \frac{u - R}{u - d} = 1 - p$$

Hence, we have just shown that the probabilities p and $(1 - p)$ used to value the call in the binomial formula Eq. (3.17) are equal to the subjective probabilities respectively associated with an upward and downward movement of the stock price in a risk-neutral economy. Therefore the probabilities p and $(1 - p)$ can be called the "risk-neutralized probabilities" and they can be used without restriction to price the call.

We have just shown that the call valuation procedure is preference-free; it is important to understand that this statement should not be interpreted to mean that the call must be valued in a risk-neutral environment. Rather we can value it in any economy, and since the risk-neutral economy has the simplest properties, let us price it as if we were in a risk-neutral economy. Of course, the resulting pricing equation, which is the binomial pricing equation (previously derived without any references to individuals' risk-tolerance level), is perfectly general. This last argument allowed us to pick a specific behavioral assumption—risk-neutrality—and to show that it generates the set of probabilities (p and $(1 - p)$) that are associated with the stock's upward and downward movements when we price European put and call options according to the binomial pricing Eq. (3.17) and (3.19).

7 CONCLUSION

In this chapter we have focused on a pricing relationship for European calls and puts on nondividend-paying stocks that only required some simple assumptions on the stock's price stochastic process; it follows a multiplicative binomial process on the interest rate (it is constant) and on the market (it is frictionless and efficient).

The binomial pricing approach imposes an equilibrium constraint on option prices since its derivation explicitly requires that they satisfy the no-arbitrage

---

[15] Remember that $R = 1 + i$ represents the one-period growth factor of $1 invested at the riskless interest rate i.

condition. This argument has been used when we discussed both the replicating strategy and the perfect hedge strategy. We are therefore sure that the option's theoretical price satisfies the nondominance criterion stated in Chapter 2.

The binomial pricing approach is also very instructive since it has shown that options can be valued without considering individuals' subjective probabilities associated with either upward or downward movements in the stock price. Hence, the option's price is independent of both the stock's expected return and any considerations about individuals' attitudes toward risk. Therefore it is a general preference-free pricing equation that can be derived in any economy. Since the framework of a risk-neutral economy is very simple, we can use it to show that the probabilities associated with upward and downward movements in the stock price used in the binomial pricing formula are in fact risk-neutralized probabilities.

Of course there are many other factors—the current stock price, the time to maturity, the striking price, the interest rate, the range of movements in the stock price—that affect option prices. How these factors individually affect option prices is discussed in the next chapter.

Through this presentation of the binomial approach, we can say that the key parameter to value an option is its underlying asset's price or more precisely—since it is a random variable—the underlying asset's price stochastic process. To emphasize this statement, we must remind ourselves that the binomial pricing formula is a relative pricing formula, one in which we implicitly assume that the stock price process embodies all the relevant information to price put and call options.

But, can we say that the binomial multiplicative process is a sufficiently close representation of a stock price "true" process across time? In other words, can we assume that the stock price varies only at discrete time intervals and that it can only go up or down? Isn't its path through time continuous? And finally is the stock price really restricted to only two possible outcomes given any length of the unitary period chosen to value the option? These are all questions we will answer in the next chapter by presenting a well-known Black and Scholes option pricing model. Despite this model's greater popularity, we will show that it is not very different from the binomial pricing approach since the former can in fact be derived as the limiting case of the binomial pricing model. Moreover, as we shall see later, for the pricing of American calls on dividend paying stocks and for the pricing of American put options in general, the binomial approach is very elegant in that it allows us to consider early exercise possibilities at each point in the option's price path.

We conclude this chapter by saying that the binomial approach has the great advantage of being a practical and a flexible tool that can be used to price a large variety of traded options. It is also a pedagogically suited framework that helps us understand the basic mechanisms underlying option pricing.

CHAPTER
4

THE BLACK
AND SCHOLES
OPTION
PRICING
MODEL

1 INTRODUCTION

In 1973, two professors of finance, F. Black and M. Scholes,[1] made an enormous
contribution to the theory of finance by deriving a formula to price European call
options on nondividend paying stocks. The significance of the Black and Scholes
option pricing model and its various extensions go beyond the theoretical framework since they have been widely used by practitioners to price stock options,
stock index options, currency options, et cetera.

Because it is the first academic contribution to have such an important and
widely diffused impact on the professional world, we think it is necessary for
people dealing with options to understand the methodology, assumptions, and
results obtained by applying the "magic" formula. Although it is quite easy

---

[1] F. Black and M. Scholes, "The Pricing of Options and Corporate Liabilities," *Journal of Political
Economy,* 81, May/June 1973.

to compute the pricing equation—especially with today's computer equipment technology—its underlying mathematical derivation is comparatively complex and tends to obscure the economic reasoning behind it. Therefore, the purpose of this chapter is to clarify the "black box" in which this pricing model is often cast to discuss all the assumptions one implicitly makes when using the Black and Scholes formula to price an option or to implement an option hedging strategy.

For that purpose we will first of all show how the Black and Scholes formula is related to the binomial pricing approach and hence how it can be derived with a much simpler mathematical setting than the one originally used. In other words we will prove that as the number of periods in which the option's time to maturity is expressed tends to infinity, the binomial pricing equation converges—under some specific assumptions—to the Black and Scholes formula.

Once we have derived the pricing equation, we will discuss its underlying assumptions, the nature of the results it provides, and their intuitive explanation. Finally, we will focus on the basic parameters of the Black and Scholes option pricing model and show how they individually affect the price of a call or a put.

2 THE BLACK AND SCHOLES FORMULA VIEWED AS THE LIMITING CASE OF THE BINOMIAL OPTION PRICING FORMULA

In the previous chapter, we valued options assuming that the stock price followed a discrete time binomial multiplicative process. Now, there are two criticisms of this hypothesis one may address when considering options in a broad sense.

1. If the length of the unitary period separating two consecutive stock prices is arbitrarily chosen, let us say a day, a week, or even a month, we cannot assume that the stock price is following a binomial process; that is, at the end of the specified period, the stock price can display more than two possible outcomes. This didn't matter in Chapter 2, since we were considering the binomial approach in its generality and we didn't have to define its unitary "period" length for that pedagogical purpose.

   However, in our economic environment, the fact that there are two possible outcomes—the stock can either go up or down—becomes a plausible stock's price path if and only if we are considering that this happens over a very short time period, or more precisely, if we are reducing the "unitary" time period to an "instant." This allows us to maintain the binomial multiplicative process and to ascertain that over a longer time period—whether it be an hour, a day, or a month—the stock price can then have many possible values.

2. Given the integration and the internationalization of current stock markets, we can trade (nearly) continuously in many major companies' stocks. For these reasons, the discrete stock price path postulated in the binomial pricing approach appears very disturbing unless we agree to use it in the limit; that is, by dividing the total period corresponding to an option's time to maturity

in very small time "units" to obtain a continuous time stochastic process for the stock price when we let the length of the unitary step go to zero (or the number of steps go to infinity).

To respond to these two critics, we must first divide the option's time to maturity τ into n intervals of (nearly) infinitesimal length l:

$$\tau = n \cdot l \tag{4.1}$$

So in the limit—as n goes to infinity—we are really dealing with continuous-time stock and hence option price paths. Since Black and Scholes assumed that the stock price was a continuous-time state variable, this is our very first step towards understanding their option pricing formula.

Our second step focuses on the parameters u, d, and q of the binomial multiplicative process as n goes to infinity. These parameters must be "scaled" or redefined since the magnitude of an upward or a downward movement in the stock price cannot be the same over a minute as it is for a day, a week, or even a year. For that purpose we need to define the continuously compounded rates of return of the stock—corresponding to an instantaneous upward or downward movement in the stock price—as well as their respective probabilities.

The continuously compounded rates of return are such that if A represents the one-period discrete growth factor,[2] then the continuously compounded rate of return a satisfies

$$A = \mathrm{Lim}\left(1 + \frac{a}{m}\right)^m \qquad \text{when } m \to \infty \tag{4.2}$$

where

$$m = \text{the number of "units" into which}$$
$$\text{we have divided the unitary period length}$$

This implies

$$A = e^a$$
$$\text{or} \quad a = \ln A \tag{4.3}$$

Hence, the continuously compounded rates of return on the stock are by analogy equal to $\ln u$ if the stock goes up, and $\ln d$ if the stock goes down. The continuously compounded risk-free interest rate is equal to r, where r satisfies

$$r = \ln(1 + i) = \ln R \tag{4.4}$$

Remember that in our discrete time setting the price of the stock S^* at the expiration date T of the option, hence n periods from now, is a function of its j upward movements and $n - j$ downward movements:

---

[2] The one-period growth factor A is simply equal to 1 plus the one-period interest rate.

$$S^* = Su^j d^{n-j}$$

with a probability of

$$\frac{n!}{(n-j)! \, j} q^j (1-q)^{n-j}$$

Now, in the continuous-time framework, we are concerned with the continuously compounded rate of return on the stock—equal to $\ln(S^*/S)$ from Eqs. (4.3) or (4.4)—and that can be defined as follows:

$$\ln(S^*/S) = \ln(u^j d^{n-j})$$

$$\Longleftrightarrow$$

$$\ln(S^*/S) = j \ln u + (n-j) \ln d \tag{4.5}$$

with a probability of

$$\frac{n!}{(n-j)! \, j!} q^j (1-q)^{n-j}$$

We are now going to show that in the limit, as n tends to infinity, the binomial multiplicative distribution converges to the lognormal distribution. Since Black and Scholes originally assumed that the stock price is lognormally distributed,[3] it is important to show under what conditions this convergence of the binomial multiplicative process obtains.

The first step is to show that the means and the variances of the two distributions converge as n approaches infinity. From Eq. (4.5) we can compute the expected value of $\ln (S^*/S)$:

$$E[\ln(S^*/S)] = \ln(u/d)E(j) = n \ln d \tag{4.6}$$

and its variance:[4]

$$\text{Var}[\ln(S^*/S)] = \text{Var}(j)[\ln(u/d)]^2 \tag{4.7}$$

---

[3] Under the lognormal distribution for stock prices, the random variable $\ln (S_T/S)$ has a normal distribution with mean $\mu\tau$ and variance $\sigma^2\tau$. This is equivalent to the assumption that continuously compounded rates of return of the stock follow a normal distribution since $\ln (S_T/S)$ is defined as the continuously compounded rate of return of the stock over the period $\tau \, (= T - t)$.

[4]
$$\text{Var}[\ln(S^*/S)] = E[\ln(S^*/S) - E[\ln(S^*/S)]]^2$$

Combining this expression of the variance with Eqs. (4.5) and (4.6) we obtain

$$\text{Var}[\ln(S^*/S)] = E[j \ln u + (n-j) \ln d - \ln(u/d)(E(j) - n \ln d)]^2$$
$$= E[j \ln(u/d) - E(j) \ln(u/d)]^2$$
$$= \text{Var}(j)[\ln(u/d)]^2$$

Note that j is a random variable representing the number of upward movements in the stock price given n periods. We know that each upward movement has a probability of q, it then follows that:

$$E(j) = \sum_{j=0}^{n} j\left(\frac{n!}{(n-j)!\,j!}q^j(1-q)^{n-j}\right) = nq \tag{4.8}$$

$$\text{Var}(j) = E(j^2) - E^2(j) = nq(1-q) \tag{4.9}$$

Plugging the values of $E(j)$ and of $\text{Var}(j)$ into Eqs. (4.6) and (4.7) respectively, we obtain

$$E[\ln(S^*/S)] = [\ln(u/d)q + [\ln d]on = wn \tag{4.10}$$

$$\text{Var}[\ln(S^*/S)] = q(1-q)[\ln(u/d)]^2]n = \Delta^2 n \tag{4.11}$$

Now, we want the mean and the variance of the binomial distribution to converge with the mean $\mu\tau$ and the variance $\sigma^2\tau$ of the "true" lognormal stock price process,[5] which we will call $\ln(S_T/S)$ to distinguish it from the binomial limiting case $\ln(S^*/S)$. Hence, we request that:

$$wn = [\ln(u/d)q + \ln d]n \quad \rightarrow \mu\tau$$
$$\text{as } n \rightarrow \infty \tag{4.12}$$
$$\Delta^2 n = [[\ln(u/d)]^2 q(1-q)]n \rightarrow \sigma^2\tau$$

At this stage, we can see that the choice of the initial parameters of the binomial multiplicative process u, d, and q cannot be arbitrary. In fact, the limit of the binomial multiplicative process is not unique, because depending on how we specify u, d, and q we can end up with a so called "jump process" that assumes the stock price will either stay constant over the next instant or will make a large jump with a very small probability of occurrence.[6]

When Black and Scholes derived their option pricing formula, they assumed that the stock price varies continuously and smoothly according to infinitesimal increments only. Hence, they explicitly identified the stock price path with a lognormal continuous time stochastic process. Therefore we must be sure that our choice of parameters in the binomial process allows us to converge to the lognormal distribution, otherwise we will not be able to prove that we obtain the Black and Scholes formula in the limiting case. To satisfy Eq. (4.12), first note that

---

[5] See footnote (1).

[6] We will discuss in Chapter 6 whether a pure jump or Poisson stochastic process more closely reflects the stock price's evolution across time. We will also see that the mixed or "jump-diffusion stochastic process" that allows prices to move smoothly with however small a probability of a jump affecting its path may be a good representation of large unexpected "swings" (like on October 19, 1987) that occasionally affect individual firms' values.

since the binomial pricing formula is independent of the subjective probabilities q and $(1 - q)$ associated to the stock price movements (and since as we will see this is true for the Black and Scholes formula), we can define the value of q arbitrarily.

Cox, Ross, and Rubinstein (1979), the first authors to formally prove the link between the Black and Scholes formula and the binomial pricing framework, chose the following value for q:[7]

$$q = \frac{1}{2} + \frac{1}{2}((\mu/\sigma) \sqrt{\tau/n}) \tag{4.13}$$

where

    μ is the instantaneous expected return of the stock under the "true" lognormal distribution

    σ is the instantaneous standard deviation of the stock return under the "true" lognormal distribution

    τ is the time until expiration of the option ($\tau = T - t$)

    n is the total number of periods used in the binomial pricing approach

Given the value of q in Eq. (4.13) and the two expressions in Eq. (4.12), Cox, Ross, and Rubinstein computed the desired values of u and d as equal to

$$u = e^{\sigma \sqrt{\tau/n}} \tag{4.14}$$

$$d = e^{-\sigma \sqrt{\tau/n}} \tag{4.15}$$

For the values $u = e^{\sigma \sqrt{\tau/n}}$, $d = e^{-\sigma \sqrt{\tau/n}}$, and $q = 1/2 + 1/2(u/\sigma) \sqrt{\tau/n}$, we can verify[8]

$$wn \equiv \mu\tau$$

as $n \rightarrow \infty$

$$\Delta^2 n \equiv \sigma^2 \tau$$

In other words, the mean and variance of the multiplicative binomial process converge to the mean and variance of the true lognormal diffusion process as n tends to infinity.

---

[7] Jarrow and Rudd (1983) set $q = 1/2$, and therefore obtained different values of the parameters u and d than those given by Cox, Ross, and Rubinstein (1979).

[8] Plugging the values of q, d, and u in Eq. (4.12) we obtain the desired results by taking the appropriate limits as n tends to infinity.

To complete the proof, we must show that given these values of u, d, and q, the binomial distribution functions $B[n, a, p]$ and $B[n, a, b]$ entering the binomial pricing formula

$$C = SB[n, a, b] - KR^{-n}B[n, a, p] \tag{3.17}$$

converge to the cumulative normal distribution functions we call $N(d_1)$ and $N(d_2)$, respectively.

This result is obtained by using the central limit theorem, which ensures that if, as n goes to infinity, the higher moments of the distribution (all moments higher than the variance) do not matter anymore, then we can assume that the state variable we defined—here $\ln(S^*/S)$—converges in probability to the normally distributed state variable—here $\ln(S_T/S)$)—or otherwise stated that:

$$\text{Prob}\left[\frac{\ln(S^*/S) - wn}{\Delta\sqrt{n}} \leq Z\right] \rightarrow$$

$$\text{Prob}\left[\frac{\ln(S_T/S) - \mu\tau}{\sigma\sqrt{\tau}} \leq Z\right] = N(Z) \quad \text{as } n \rightarrow \infty$$

where $N(Z)$ = the standard normal distribution function.

The proof of this convergence in probability is presented in Appendix 4-1, where we show that as $n \rightarrow \infty$:

$$B[n, a, p] \equiv N\left[\frac{\ln(S/KR^{-\tau})}{\sigma\sqrt{\tau}} - (1/2)\sigma\sqrt{\tau}\right]$$

$$\equiv N(d_2) \tag{4.16}$$

and that:

$$B[n, a, b] \equiv N\left[\frac{\ln(S/KR^{-\tau})}{\sigma\sqrt{\tau}} + (1/2)\sigma\sqrt{\tau}\right]$$

$$\equiv N(d_1) \tag{4.17}$$

Now, if we substitute these expressions of $B[n, a, p]$ and $B[n, a, b]$, we can write Eq. (3.17) as follows:

$$C = SN(d_1) - KR^{-n}N(d_2)$$

Moreover, since we are now dealing in a continuous-time framework and we have defined r as the continuously compounded rate of return (see Eq. 4.4), we can rewrite the previous equation as follows:

$$C = SN(d_1) - Ke^{-r\tau}N(d_2) \tag{4.18}$$

where

$$d_1 = \frac{\ln(S/Ke^{-r\tau})}{\sigma\sqrt{\tau}} + (1/2)\sigma\sqrt{\tau}$$

$$d_2 = d_1 - \sigma\sqrt{\tau} = \frac{\ln(S/Ke^{-r\tau})}{\sigma\sqrt{\tau}} - (1/2)\sigma\sqrt{\tau}$$

$N(\cdot) = $ the cumulative normal distribution function

$r = $ the continuously compounded interest rate satisfying $\ln R = r$

$K = $ the striking price of the call option

$S = $ the current stock price

$\tau = $ the time to maturity of the option

$\sigma = $ the instantaneous standard deviation of continuously compounded stock returns

Equation (4.18) is precisely the Black and Scholes European call valuation formula. Therefore, we have proven that as the number of periods of the binomial multiplicative stock price process tends to infinity, the binomial option pricing formula converges to the Black and Scholes formula if the parameters of the binomial distribution are chosen so that the logarithm of the stock price relatives becomes normally distributed in the limit.

To provide this convergence between the binomial distribution and the log-normal distribution, the parameters u, d, and hence p have to be chosen in the following way:[9]

$$u = e^{\sigma\sqrt{\tau/n}} \tag{4.14}$$

$$d = e^{-\sigma\sqrt{\tau/n}} \tag{4.15}$$

$$\lim_{n\to\infty} p = \frac{1}{2} + \frac{1}{2}\left(\frac{\ln R - (1/2)\sigma^2}{\sigma}\right)\sqrt{\frac{\tau}{n}} \tag{4.19}$$

Then, by applying the central limit theorem to $B[n, a, p]$ and $B[n, a, b]$, we have shown (see Appendix 4-1) that the Black and Scholes call valuation formula is the continuous-time valuation equation into which the binomial pricing formula Eq. (3.17) collapses.

---

[9] The definition of the risk neutralized probabilities p and $1 - p$ defining $B[n, a, p]$ and $B[n, a, b]$ is given in Appendix 4-1 for the limiting case ($n \to \infty$).

At this stage, it is useful to show through an example that the theoretical call option prices of the two formulas will coincide as n becomes very large if the parameters of the binomial pricing model are properly specified.

3 AN EXAMPLE

Suppose we observe the following data for the MAC stock call option:

$$S = \$38.00$$

$$r = 5\%$$

$$\sigma = 30\% \text{ on an annual basis}$$

$$\tau = 0.3333 \text{ years or 4 months}$$

$$K = \$35.00$$

Using the Black and Scholes option pricing formula, [10] we can compute the price of that call option as equal to

$$C = SN(d_1) - Ke^{-r\tau}N(d_2)$$

where

$$d_1 = \frac{\ln\left(38/(35)\left(e^{-0.05\times0.333}\right)\right)}{0.3\sqrt{0.333}} + (1/2)\left(0.3\sqrt{0.333}\right)$$

$$= 0.657654$$

$$d_2 = d_1 - \sigma\sqrt{\tau} = 0.484450$$

hence:

$$C = 38N(0.657654) - (35)(0.983473)N(0.484450)$$

Looking in the tables of the cumulative normal distribution[11] and interpolating to obtain the exact values of $N(d_1)$ and $N(d_2)$, we finally get

$$C = \$4.68$$

Now we will value this European call with the binomial option pricing formula Eq. (3.17) assuming in a first stage that $n = 5$. To apply the binomial formula we need to define u, q, R, and p from the continuous-time parameters given to compute the Black and Scholes formula, hence:

---

[10] We will discuss the applications and computation techniques of the Black and Scholes option pricing formula in more detail in the next chapter.

[11] The tables of the cumulative normal distribution are illustrated in Appendix 4-2.

$$u = e^{\sigma \sqrt{\tau/n}} \qquad = e^{0.3 \sqrt{0.333/5}} = 1.080538$$

$$d = e^{-\sigma \sqrt{\tau/n}} \qquad = e^{-0.3 \sqrt{0.333/5}} = 0.925465$$

$$R = e^{r\tau/n} \qquad = 1.00333$$

$$p = (R - d)/(u - d) = 0.502118$$

Then, apply Eq. (3.17) to obtain the binomial call option price:

$$C_{n=5} = SB[n, a, b] - KR^{-n}B[n, a, p]$$

$$= 38B[5, a, b] - 35R^{-5}B[5, a, p]$$

$$= \$4.59$$

Using five steps we already obtain a good approximation of the Black and Scholes call value. The difference of $0.09 is quite small given the fact that each step size corresponds to approximately 24 days—which is very far from the continuous-time assumption.

Let us increase the number of steps to 30. In this example, we then work with a step size of approximately 4 days and are therefore closer to the continuous-time assumption than in our previous trial with $n = 5$. The new values of the parameters required to compute the binomial call price must be equal to

$$n = 30$$

$$u = e^{\sigma \sqrt{\tau/n}} \qquad = e^{0.3 \sqrt{0.333/30}} = 1.032128$$

$$d = e^{-\sigma \sqrt{\tau/n}} \qquad = e^{-0.3 \sqrt{0.333/30}} = 0.968872$$

$$R = e^{\tau r/n} \qquad = e^{(0.05)(0.333)/30} = 1.00056$$

$$p = (R - d)/(u - d) = 0.500885$$

And the resulting binomial call price is now equal to

$$C_{n=30} = SB[30, a, b] = KR^{-30}B[30, a, p]$$

$$= \$4.70$$

With 30 steps, we have obtained a more accurate approximation of the Black and Scholes call's price since the difference between the two prices is now reduced to only $0.02.

We can go further in our search for convergence between the two formulas by letting n become very large in the binomial pricing equation Eq. (3.17). For that purpose we have chosen 150 steps, which corresponds to more than one step per day in our example. The value of the parameters requested to compute the binomial call price is now equal to

$$n = 150$$

$$u = e^{\sigma \sqrt{\tau/n}} \qquad = e^{0.3 \sqrt{0.333/150}} = 1.014242$$

$$d = e^{-\sigma \sqrt{\tau/n}} \qquad = e^{-0.3 \sqrt{0.333/150}} = 0.985957$$

$$R = e^{\tau r/n} \qquad = e^{(0.05)(0.333)/150} = 1.000111$$

$$p = (R - d)/(u - d) = 0.500407$$

This yields the following call price:

$$C_{n=150} = SB[150, a, b] - KR^{-150}[150, a, p]$$
$$= \$4.68$$

Since $C_{n=150}$ is equal to the Black and Scholes theoretical price—if we are considering both prices on a cent basis—we can say that this example has numerically illustrated how the price computed with the binomial pricing equation converges to the Black and Scholes theoretical call value when n becomes very large, provided that the parameters of the binomial multiplicative process are chosen so that the continuously compounded rates of return on the stock become normally distributed in the limit.

This example also shows that even with a fairly reasonable number of steps ($n = 30$), the binomial call price is very close to the Black and Scholes computed price, suggesting that for practical needs a good accuracy can be obtained without requiring an unmanageable number of steps. The trade-off between the number of steps required to obtain convergence and the additional (computer) costs incurred is a very important consideration for every user of the binomial pricing approach; the decision must be based on the user's specific needs and targeted accuracy.

4   SOME INSIGHTS INTO THE BLACK AND SCHOLES OPTION PRICING MODEL

Now that we have shown a possible but not unique derivation of the Black and Scholes formula, we will discuss the basic assumptions and methodology originally employed to derive this well-known option pricing model.

Black and Scholes assumed frictionless markets, a constant risk-free interest rate, and as in the binomial pricing approach, they treated the option's price as determined entirely by the stock's price path and the time to maturity of the option. In addition, they assumed that the stock price follows a continuous-time lognormal stochastic process, that is, the continuously compounded rates of return on the stock are normally distributed with a constant mean μ and a constant variance σ^2 per unit of time.

Given this set of hypotheses, Black and Scholes used the same perfect hedge methodology to price the call—the one we already described in the binomial pricing framework. The authors constructed a perfectly hedged position between the stock and the option; in other words, a position consisting of a nonarbitrary quantity Δ of shares held long for every call option written such that regardless of the direction the stock is moving over the next instant, the investment is fully protected. The gains (losses) on the Δ shares of stock are exactly offset by the losses (gains) on the written call option. Since this position is perfectly riskless over the next instant, it must earn the riskless rate of return to prevent riskless arbitrage opportunities. From this "no-arbitrage" condition and given the distributional properties of the stock price, the authors were able to derive a partial differential equation that the call's price must satisfy.

The solution of that equation is, of course, the Black and Scholes formula [see Eq. (4.18)], and its original derivation is very similar—through its underlying methodology—to that of the binomial. In both cases. it is assumed that a perfect hedge can be formed and readjusted (discretely or continuously for the Black and Scholes formula) throughout the option's remaining time to maturity, and it is also assumed that prices are competitively set in an arbitrage opportunity free market. The main differences between both approaches arise from their underlying time dimension—continuous for the Black and Scholes formula and discrete for the binomial pricing formula—and from the distributional properties—lognormal process for the Black and Scholes formula and binomial multiplicative process for the binomial formula—they assign to the stock price path.

Given that these two option pricing approaches have many common assumptions and that they are both derived in an arbitrage-free economic setting, it is not surprising that many properties and interpretations of the Black and Scholes formula have already been stated in our analysis of the binomial pricing equation.

We shall now discuss some fundamental characteristics of the Black and Scholes European call option pricing formula:

1. The theoretical call prices satisfying equation Eq. (4.18) are equilibrium prices only with respect to the stock price and the riskless interest rate. This is because the Black and Scholes formula stems from a relative pricing approach: the pricing equation is derived by forming a riskless hedge between the stock and the option, and the resulting equilibrium (no-arbitrage) condition involves only the stock, the option, and the riskless interest rate. Hence, there is no concern about other assets' (bonds, stocks, options, etc.) equilibrium prices. Further, there is even no concern about whether the underlying stock price is itself an equilibrium value with respect to the market. In other words, when using the Black and Scholes formula, we take the stock price as given and assume implicitly that it already reflects the relevant information to price the call.

2. The Black and Scholes formula does not depend on the expected rate of return on the stock or on any other parameter reflecting investors' tastes or preferences. It is therefore a preference-free pricing formula that can be derived in any type—risk-neutral, risk-averse, or so on—of economy.

   We can therefore choose a specific environment (for example, the risk-neutral environment) and value the call accordingly, keeping all our previous assumptions and knowing additionally that in a risk-neutral economy all assets have an expected return equal to the risk-free rate of return. We shall, of course, obtain the Black and Scholes valuation formula since it is valid for any type of individual preference structures.

However, in a risk-neutral economy, the Black and Scholes formula solves the following system:[12]

$$C_t = e^{-r\tau}E[C_T]$$

$$= e^{-r\tau}E[\max(0, S_T - K)] \qquad (4.20)$$

with

$$E[\Delta S_t/S_t] = r\Delta t$$
$$\text{the expected instantaneous rate of return on the stock}$$

where

$C_T =$ the price of the call option at maturity

$S_T =$ the price of the stock at the option's maturity date T, assuming it is lognormally distributed

$C_t =$ the current call price

Therefore, we can say that the Black and Scholes formula's theoretical call price is equal to the expected future value of the call at maturity discounted at the risk-free rate of return. When we interpret the option pricing formula in this way, we know—from our previous discussion about the binomial pricing model—that the standard cumulative normal distribution functions $N(d_1)$ and $N(d_2)$ used to compute the stock's and hence the option's future expected value can be interpreted as "risk-neutralized" distribution functions.

The preference-free characteristics of the Black and Scholes formula enables us to compute the theoretical option's price in any kind of economic environment. Deriving the Black and Scholes pricing equation in a risk-neutral framework is simply a corollary of that statement. However, it does not imply that we need "risk-neutrality" to obtain the formula since it is general with respect to people's risk-tolerance levels. The risk-neutral environment is often assumed for technical purposes since it enables us to solve rather complex option pricing equations that would otherwise require assumptions on investors' risk premiums. In the risk-neutral framework, the problem is simplified since the expected rate of return on all assets is equal to the risk-free interest rate.

3. A third important property of the formula is related to its underlying "continuous-time perfect hedge" assumption. Its main corollary is that one

---

[12] See Cox and Ross (1976) and Jarrow and Rudd (1983) for further explanations about the risk-neutral option pricing framework.

should be able to continuously rebalance the hedged position in the market until the option's expiration date.

If markets are not open continuously (or nearly so) and particularly if trading barriers (margin requirements, short selling restrictions, etc.) are too strong to allow frequent portfolio rebalancing, obviously market prices will tend to diverge from theoretical option prices. Hence, one may expect that the relevance of the Black and Scholes formula will be greater for liquid and active markets than for illiquid and thin option exchanges. This is an important observation since it is irrelevant to compare theoretical prices to market prices when the underlying assumptions of the model are in contradiction with the structure of the specific market. Whenever the latter is true, using the formula to detect profitable strategies arising from a temporary option's mispricing may be a completely absurd policy, since the mispricing results from structural differences between the "ideal" market assumed in the model and the exchanges we are dealing with. Hence, the mispricing can be all but temporary, and can even lead us to lose money on what first seemed to be a "sure profit" strategy. However, on most actively traded stock option exchanges (especially in the United States of America and in the United Kingdom), the Black and Scholes pricing formula may be properly used to detect over- and underpriced options[13] and to set up dynamic portfolio strategies accordingly. We will discuss the implementation of such strategies involving the Black and Scholes formula's parameters in Chapter 5.

4. At all stages of the Black and Scholes formula's derivation, it is explicitly assumed throughout this chapter that the underlying stock is not paying any dividends until the option's maturity date. Since we saw in Chapter 2 (Restriction 11) that the price of an American call option on a nondividend paying stock is equal to the price of an otherwise identical European call, it follows that the Black and Scholes formula can be used to price American call options on nondividend paying stocks.

We will see in the next chapter how—under some specific assumptions about the dividends—we can modify the Black and Scholes formula to price European call options on dividend paying stocks, and even price some American call options on dividend paying stocks providing that they satisfy the no-early exercise Restriction 13 of Chapter 2.

However, if early exercise must explicitly be considered—because Restriction 13 is violated—then we will usually rely on the more general framework of the binomial pricing equation to value American call options on div-

---

[13] We will discuss in Chapter 6 the main empirical evidence on the Black and Scholes formula's pricing performance. However, we can already note that even in liquid and actively traded markets the formula may lead to some pricing inconsistencies (for example, it tends to systematically overprice out-of-the-money call options).

idend paying stocks. We reasoned that the Black and Scholes option pricing model cannot explicitly handle the early exercise possibilities of American options and will therefore systematically underprice them every time it may be "optimal" to exercise American call options written on dividend paying stocks prior to their expiration date.

5. Finally, it is important to show that the Black and Scholes formula can also be used to price European put options on nondividend paying stocks. For that purpose, we simply have to rely on the put-call parity relationship I (see Chapter 2) that can be expressed under the continuous-time assumption as follows:[14]

$$P = C - S + Ke^{-r\tau} \tag{4.21}$$

Hence to value a European put, one simply has to rewrite Eq. (4.21) knowing Black and Scholes' expression for the call price. Therefore, combining Eqs. (4.21) and (4.18), we obtain

$$P = SN(d_1) - Ke^{-r\tau}N(d_2) - S + Ke^{-r\tau}$$

$$= -S(1 - N(d_1)) + Ke^{-r\tau}(1 - N(d_2))$$

$$\Longleftrightarrow$$

$$P = Ke^{-r\tau}N(-d_2) - SN(-d_1) \tag{4.22}$$

where

$$d_1 = \frac{\ln(S/Ke^{-r\tau})}{\sigma\sqrt{\tau}} + \frac{1}{2}\sigma\sqrt{\tau}$$

$$d_2 = d_1 - \sigma\sqrt{\tau}$$

$$N(\cdot) = \text{the cumulative standard normal distribution}$$

$$N(-d_1) = 1 - N(d_1) \text{ and similarly for } N(-d_2)$$

Applying one of the general restrictions to option pricing, the well-known put-call parity, we were able to show that when we know how to price a call (or put) we can substantially simplify the whole valuation procedure of the put (or call). In the case of European options on nondividend paying stocks, we simply have to combine the Black and Scholes call valuation formula with the put-call parity relationship I, we then immediately obtain the put price valuation equation.

Now that we have reviewed the basic theoretical assumptions underlying the Black and Scholes formula and discussed the relevant cases in which it may

---

[14] To simplify the notations, we write C for $C(S, K, \tau)$ and P for $P(S, K, \tau)$.

be applied to value an option, we might go even further, asserting that, in those relevant cases, the formula can also be used to identify the fundamental parameters affecting an option's price.

5   THE DETERMINANTS OF AN OPTION'S PRICE

It is obvious that the Black and Scholes formula's main goal is to provide (partial) equilibrium prices for European call and put options written on nondividend paying stocks. However, the formula can also be used to measure the option's price sensitivity with respect to its explanatory variables. Before turning to this point, we must identify the parameters that are relevant in explaining option prices.

If we look at Eqs. (4.18) and (4.22), we see that there are essentially five parameters that will affect an option's price, or otherwise stated that call and put option prices depend on (1) the current stock price level S, (2) the striking price K, (3) the continuously compounded riskless rate r, (4) the time to maturity τ, and (5) the instantaneous standard deviation of the stock's return σ.

First, we can see that almost all of these parameters also explained an option's price under the binomial approach. There is, however, one difference between the two pricing equations. In the binomial pricing formula, the distributional properties of the stock price basically entered the formula through the parameters u, d (which reflect the relative upward and downward growth rates of the stock price) and through the "risk-neutralized" probabilities p and $1 - p$. However, there was no explicit—only implicit through the dispersion measure $(u - d)$—measure of the stock price riskiness in the binomial option pricing formula.

Contrarily, in the Black and Scholes formula, there is a parameter that explicitly accounts for uncertainty in stock returns, and this parameter appears to be the standard deviation of the continuously compounded rates of return of the stock. Although the expected rate of return on the underlying stock doesn't affect option prices, its riskiness obviously does. The Black and Scholes formula allows us to discover and understand the direct relationship between the risk of the underlying asset and the option's price. As a corollary, it reminds us that proper estimation of stock return variability is a delicate but necessary condition for consistent option pricing. These are clearly some of the Black and Scholes option pricing model's main contributions over the binomial pricing approach, in which the impact of "riskiness" (important for both option pricing and portfolio management) could only be indirectly determined.

Now that we have enumerated the relevant parameters that determine stock option prices, we will discuss how slight changes in those parameters modify the prices of European put and call options on nondividend paying stocks. [15]

---

[15] Note that since an American call option on a nondividend paying stock is priced like a European call option, all our statements about European call options are valid for this specific subset of American call options.

A   The Striking Price

The higher the striking price, the less valuable a call option since the striking price represents a higher cost of exercising the call and thereby purchasing the stock. The Black and Scholes formula can help us assess this relationship more formally. By computing the derivative of the call's price with respect to the exercise price from Eq. (4.18) we obtain

$$\frac{\partial C}{\partial K} = -e^{-r\tau}N(d_2) < 0 \qquad (4.23)$$

Since the derivative is negative it means that a small increase in the exercise price will decrease the call's price by a proportionality factor equal to $-e^{-r\tau}N(d_2)$. This inverse relationship between the call's price and the exercise price is fully consistent with Restriction 4 in Chapter 2 and thereby supports the Black and Scholes theoretical option prices.

Similarly, we would expect the put's price to be higher, the higher its exercise price. Since by exercising the put we are in fact selling the stock for $\$K$ when it is worth $\$S$ in the market, all things being equal the gain will increase if the striking price is greater.

The Black and Scholes formula clearly shows this positive relationship between a put's price and its exercise price. When we use the put pricing Eq. (4.22) to compute the derivative of the put's price with respect to the striking price, we obtain

$$\frac{\partial P}{\partial K} = e^{-r\tau}N(-d_2) > 0 \qquad (4.24)$$

Since the derivative is positive, we can say that the Black and Scholes theoretical put price is rationally determined (see Restriction 4 in Chapter 2) with respect to its exercise price.

B   The Time to Maturity

The longer the time to maturity of a European call option, the higher its price since by increasing the time period, we simultaneously increase our chances of ending in-the-money at expiration (in which case we shall make a profit) or of ending out-of-the-money, which does not affect us because we are not obliged to exercise the option at expiration. Given the dissymmetric payoff structure of the option at its expiration, additional time is always a beneficial factor that contributes to increase the profit potential while keeping the loss potential limited to the purchase price of the call option.

The derivative of Eq. (4.18) with respect to τ shows that this is indeed true:

$$\frac{\partial C}{\partial \tau} = \frac{S\sigma}{2\sqrt{\tau}}N'(d_1) + Ke^{-r\tau}\tau N(d_2) > 0 \qquad (4.25)$$

where

$$N'(d_1) = \frac{1}{\sqrt{2\pi}} e^{-d_1^2/2}$$

$$= \text{standard normal density function}$$

The positive derivative confirms that the Black and Scholes formula values longer-lived European call options more than otherwise identical shorter-lived call options.

Note that a modified version of the first derivative of the call's price with respect to time to maturity is often called "Theta":[16]

$$\theta = -\frac{\partial C}{\partial \tau} \tag{4.26}$$

Theta is a very useful tool for monitoring strategies involving options, as we shall see in the next chapter.

In Chapter 2 we mentioned that while there is always a positive relationship between an American option's price (whether it be a call or a put) and its time to maturity, the same need not be true for European options. In the context of the Black and Scholes model, we do obtain a positive relationship between the price and the time to maturity of call options; however, the same argument does not apply to European put options.

Taking the derivative of the put's price with respect to its time to maturity, from Eq. (4.22) we obtain

$$\frac{\partial P}{\partial \tau} = \frac{S\sigma}{2\sqrt{\tau}} N'(d_1) + K e^{-r\tau} r (N(d_2) - 1) \overset{>}{\underset{<}{=}} 0 \tag{4.27}$$

where

$$N'(d_1) = \frac{1}{\sqrt{2\pi}} e^{-d_1^2/2}$$

The derivative of the put's price with respect to time to maturity can be of any sign,[17] thereby suggesting an ambiguous relationship between these two variables, which we will now explain intuitively.

As previously mentioned for call options, longer time to maturity also has a positive influence on a put's price since it increases the chance of favorable outcomes ($K > S^*$) at maturity. However, in the case of a put option, a longer

---

[16] More precisely θ measures the time bias of the option's price associated with the passage of time. Since $\partial C/\partial \tau > 0$ for the call option, the latter has a negative θ, which means that a decrease in time to maturity decreases its price, or in other words, that the call suffers from a negative time bias (its value depreciates, *ceteris paribus*, with the passage of time).

[17] The put's theta, $\theta = -\partial P/\partial \tau$ can be positive or negative according to Eq. (4.27). A positive θ would imply that the put's price increases when time passes and a negative θ—reflecting the negative time bias—implies that the put's price decreases as time elapses.

time to maturity also has a negative impact on its price since it lowers the present value of the striking price $(Ke^{-r\tau})$, which is the actual value of the maximal proceeds (when $S^* = 0$) a put can generate at expiration. Usually, for at-the-money put options, we would expect the former effect to be dominant and hence to observe that $\partial P/\partial\tau$ is typically positive: the longer the time to maturity, the higher the chances of positive outcomes for these put options. For out-of-the-money and in-the-money puts, the same relationship applies when their time to maturity is relatively long. However, when these options are very close to maturity (one month or less), the reverse becomes true, and a small decrease in their time to maturity increases their price over this maturity segment. [18]

Note that this ambiguous relationship between a put's price and its remaining time to maturity does not apply for American put options that can be exercised prior to maturity and thereby avoid the negative impact associated to a "lower striking price effect" dominating the "favorable final outcome effect" as maturity is lengthened. Therefore, American put options will, *ceteris paribus,* always show a positive relationship between their prices and their time to maturity.

C   The Interest Rate

The higher the interest rate, the higher the call's price. To see why this is true, we refer to Restriction 10 of Chapter 2, where we stated that a European call's price should always be at least equal to the current stock price less the present value of the striking price: [19]

$$C \geq S - Ke^{-r\tau}$$

Obviously a higher interest rate will lower the present value of the cost of exercising the call at maturity, increasing the call's current price. We can assess the positive relationship between a call's price and the interest rate level more formally by taking the first derivative of C—as defined in the Black and Scholes formula—with respect to r. We obtain

$$\frac{\partial C}{\partial r} = \tau Ke^{-r\tau}N(d_2) > 0 \qquad (4.28)$$

---

[18] For very short term in-the-money options, the latter phenomenon is explained by the absence of early exercise opportunities for European put options and by the fact that they are relatively less sensitive to increased return dispersion.

[19] We have simply written Eq. (2.17) assuming a continuously compounded interest rate, hence:

$$B(\tau) = e^{-r\tau}$$

$$= \text{the price at time } t \text{ of a riskless bond}$$
$$\text{paying \$1 at maturity date } T$$

We then obtain $C \geq S - Ke^{-r\tau}$.

For European put options, there is an inverse relationship, since a higher interest rate lowers their prices. This is because the payoff of the put $\max[0, K - S^*]$ is symmetric to the payoff of the call $\max[0, S^* - K]$ at expiration. Hence, a higher interest rate decreases the present value of K and decreases the current exercise value $(Ke^{-r\tau} - S)$ of the put option accordingly.

More formally, by deriving the put's price in Eq. (4.22) with respect to the riskless interest rate, we obtain

$$\frac{\partial P}{\partial r} = \tau K e^{-r\tau}(N(d_2) - 1) < 0 \qquad (4.29)$$

The negative sign of the derivative confirms that the put's price is negatively affected by an increase in the interest rate.

D   The Stock Price

Since this is the unique random variable that explains the option's price in the Black and Scholes option pricing model, we will carefully analyze how option prices respond to changes in the underlying stock's price.

For European call options, it is obvious that a higher stock price induces, *ceteris paribus*, a higher current exercise value $(S - Ke^{-r\tau})$ of the option, thus increases its price. A call option is always more valuable when the stock price increases, which can be seen from the first derivative of C with respect to S:

$$\frac{\partial C}{\partial S} = N(d_1) > 0 \qquad (4.30)$$

This derivative is often called the "delta" of the call option. Its value is always positive, and as we shall see later, "delta" (Δ_C) is a fundamental tool for valuing and hedging option positions. This derivative tells us that a $1 change in the stock's price will lead to a $N(d_1)$ .1 change in the option's price.

Since[20] $0 \leq N(d_1) = \Delta_C \leq 1$, the call price will generally change by less than $1 if the stock price increases or decreases by $1. Hence, the absolute change in the call's price is always less than or equal to the absolute change in the underlying stock's price.[21]

---

[20] Strictly speaking, when the stock price tends to zero, $\partial C/\partial S$ becomes null.

[21] We can define the call's price elasticity Ω with respect to the stock price as equal to

$$\Omega = \left(\frac{\partial C}{\partial S}\right)\left(\frac{S}{C}\right) = \Delta_C\left(\frac{S}{C}\right) \geq 1$$

Since the call's price elasticity with respect to changes in S is generally greater than 1, we can say that a 1 percent increase in the stock price will lead to more than a 1 percent increase in the call's price. This confirms the traditional proposition stating that, in relative terms, the call is riskier than the underlying stock. We will discuss the concepts of an option's elasticity and riskiness in more detail in Chapter 5.

But is the call's price change, for a given $1 change in the price of the stock, the same at low stock price levels as it is at high stock price levels? To answer that question, we must analyze Δ_C and see if this parameter varies with the stock price level. To assess the sensitivity of Δ_C to small changes in the stock's price, we will refer to the Black and Scholes formula and take the first derivative of Δ_C with respect to S, which is equivalent to taking the second derivative of the call's price with respect to S:

$$\frac{\partial \Delta_C}{\partial S} = \frac{\partial^2 C}{\partial S^2} = \frac{1}{S\sigma\sqrt{\tau}} N'(d_1) > 0 \qquad (4.31)$$

where

$$N'(d_1) = \frac{1}{2\sqrt{\pi}} e^{-d_1^2/2}$$

Since the derivative is always positive, this implies that Δ_C increases when the stock price increases, or in other words, that changes in the call's price for a given $1 change in the stock price will be greater the higher the level of the stock price.

Using the second derivative of the call's price with respect to the stock price—usually called "Gamma" (Γ)—in conjunction with the call's Δ_C, we will now be able to describe the "call price-stock price" relationship more precisely. Δ_C is the slope of the function relating C to S since $\Delta_C \geq 0$ implies that C is an increasing function of S. Moreover, Γ_C, the derivative of Δ_C with respect to S, represents the rate of change in the slope of the "call price-stock price function." Since it is positive we know that Δ_C is an increasing function of S. Hence, we can say that C increases with $S(\Delta_C > 0)$ and that it increases at an increasing rate with $S(\Gamma_C > 0)$. It then follows that the call price is an increasing convex function of the stock price.

This is an important statement that we can now use in conjunction with Restriction 8 of Chapter 2[22] (the call's price is equal to zero when the stock price is worthless) to illustrate the convexity of the "call price-stock price" relationship at any time prior to the option's expiration date (see Fig. 4.1). The curve $C = f(S)$ in Fig. 4.1 shows the actual call option's price as a function of the stock price. We can see that before expiration, the call always sells at a higher price than its current exercise value[23] (the line max$[0, S - Ke^{-r\tau}]$) and that it always lies above its exercise value at maturity (the line max$[0, S - K]$). The latter fact is of course due to the "time value" embedded in an option's price. The graph clearly demonstrates that the call's price increases at an increasing rate with the stock price.

Hence, by applying the Black and Scholes formula, we are able to go further than just setting upper and lower limits to the call's price since we can, at any

---

[22] We also need the following statement: $C \to \infty$ when $S \to \infty$. This can be seen by taking the limit of C in Eq. (4.18) when S tends to infinity and using the property that $N(\infty) = 1$.

[23] This is consistent with Restriction 10 in Chapter 2 requiring that $C \geq S - Ke^{-r\tau}$.

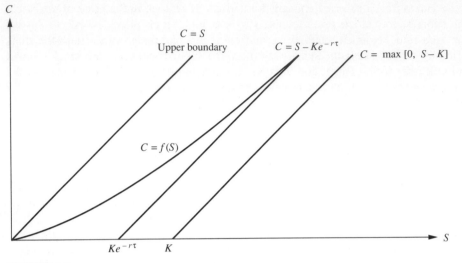

FIGURE 4.1
The European call price-stock price relationship.

time, compute the whole range of call prices corresponding to the set of possible stock prices ($S \in [0, \infty]$) and conclude graphically or mathematically, as we did previously, that the call price is an increasing convex function of the stock price.

We will observe that the price for a European put option is lower when the stock price is higher. Since a higher price of the underlying asset decreases the value of our right to sell this asset for a fixed price K, reducing the put's current exercise value ($Ke^{-r\tau} - S$), the put's price must decrease accordingly.

Using the Black and Scholes put option Eq. (4.22) derived with respect to the stock's price, we obtain

$$\frac{\partial P}{\partial S} = -N(-d_1) = \Delta_P < 0 \tag{4.32}$$

The put's price first derivative with respect to S, also called delta, is indeed negative, telling us that for each $1 increase in the stock price we will observe a decrease of $N(-d_1)$ ($1) in the put's price. Since the put's delta is negative[24] but never smaller than -1 ($-1 \leq \Delta_P \leq 0$), we can say that a given dollar change in the stock price will never lead to a greater—opposite direction—dollar change in the put's price. Hence, for a given change in the stock price, put and call option

---

[24] Strictly speaking, the put's Δ reaches zero when the stock price becomes very high and tends to infinity.

values move in opposite directions but the absolute changes in their prices never exceed those observed on the underlying stock.

We shall now proceed by analogy and ask ourselves how the put's delta changes when the stock price level changes. To answer that question we will compute the derivative of Δ_P with respect to S, which is equivalent to taking the second derivative of the put's price with respect to the stock's price:

$$\frac{\partial \Delta_P}{\partial S} = \frac{\partial^2 P}{\partial S^2} = \frac{1}{S\sigma \sqrt{\tau}} N'(d_1) = \Gamma_P > 0 \qquad (4.33)$$

We see that the Γ_p (gamma) of the put is positive and that its expression—compare Eqs. (4.31) and (4.33)—is exactly the same as that of an otherwise identical call's Γ. Hence the dollar change in the put's price—given a \$1 change in the stock price—is greater as the stock price increases. By the same argument and using our conclusions about the sign of the put's Γ and Δ, we can say that the put's price decreases ($\Delta_P < 0$) at an increasing rate ($\Gamma_P > 0$) with the stock price.

Hence, the put's price is a decreasing convex function of the stock price. Combining this statement with the fact that a European put can never be worth less than zero[25] (as S tends to infinity) and more than $Ke^{-r\tau}$ (when $S = 0$), we can illustrate the "put price-stock price" relationship as shown in Fig. 4.2. The curve

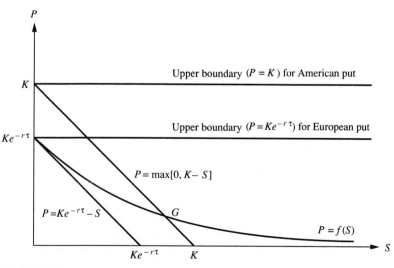

FIGURE 4.2
The European put price-stock price relationship.

---

[25] Since the put is a limited liability asset and since we are not obliged to exercise it under unfavorable conditions, our "right" to sell the stock for \$$K$ will simply be worthless as the stock price goes to infinity.

$P = f(S)$ represents the actual put price as a function of the stock price. We see that today's put value cannot exceed $Ke^{-r\tau}$ (should the stock be worthless) and the put's value approaches zero when the stock price becomes infinite. In between, the European put is a decreasing convex function of the stock price. However, since it is a European put, its actual value $P = f(S)$ will in fact lie—until point G on the graph—below its intrinsic value at maturity max$[0, K - S]$ because the lower boundary to the actual put price given that its remaining time to maturity is equal to τ is the line max$[0, Ke^{-r\tau} - S]$.

Note that since American puts must always satisfy Restriction 3 of Chapter 2 and sell at least for their exercised value, their lower boundary is always the line max$[0, K - S]$, which is higher than the lower boundary applying to European put options of identical maturity. Therefore, an American put option is always worth at least the same or more than an otherwise identical European put option since the former would definitely be exercised whenever its unexercised value happened to be lower than its exercise value. Clearly, the no-early exercise possibility affects the value of European put options and this is illustrated in Fig. 4.3 where we see that the European put's price function $P = f(S)$ lies always below the price function $P' = f'(S)$ of an otherwise identical American put.[26] We shall

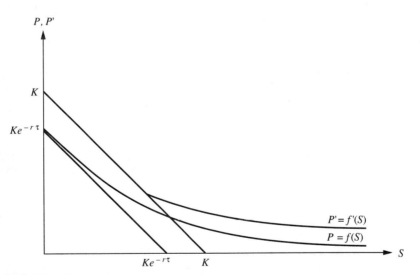

FIGURE 4.3
The American and European put prices as functions of the stock price.

---

[26] The curves $P\prime$ and P have a common horizontal asymptote since we know that the prices of both European and American put options are equal to zero when the stock price tends to infinity.

discuss the impact of the early exercise feature of American put options on their prices in greater detail when we discuss the methods used to value those rather complex options.

E   The Standard Deviation of Stock Returns

The standard deviation of the continuously compounded rates of return is a measure of the underlying asset's riskiness which, in the context of the Black and Scholes formula, is assumed constant over the option's remaining time to maturity. In other words, it is assumed that an unexpected change in the current instantaneous return is of the same magnitude as the unexpected change in the one month ahead instantaneous return on the stock. But how does stock riskiness affect option prices? Intuitively, we think of a stock with a higher standard deviation as having a greater dispersion of its possible—bad and good—outcomes (returns).

Now to show that both put and call options written on riskier stocks sell at higher prices, it is sufficient to focus on the dissymmetric pattern of those option payoffs at maturity. For a call option, the price at expiration satisfies

$$C = \max[0, S^* - K]$$

Similarly, for a put option the price is

$$P = \max[0, K - S^*]$$

In both cases, a higher standard deviation (greater unexpected variations in the stock returns) increases the option's set of favorable possible outcomes and hence its probability of ending in-the-money at maturity. A higher standard deviation also increases the set of unfavorable outcomes at maturity, but since call and put options bear no downside risk, they will expire worthless no matter how deeply out-of-the-money they are at maturity.

The dissymmetric payoff structure of options implies that they only capture the positive effect of a higher standard deviation in stock returns, and hence their prices will increase due to the fact that their set of expected in-the-money values at maturity is broader when the stock is more risky.

We can prove the positive relationship between option prices and the stock's return volatility by taking the derivative of the put and call prices with respect to σ. For the call price defined in Eq. (4.18), we obtain

$$\frac{\partial C}{\partial \sigma} = S \sqrt{\tau} N'(d_1) > 0 \tag{4.34}$$

For the put price defined in Eq. (4.22), we obtain

$$\frac{\partial P}{\partial \sigma} = S \sqrt{\tau} N'(d_1) > 0 \tag{4.35}$$

where

$$N'(d_1) = (1/\sqrt{2\pi})(e^{-d_1^2/2})$$

Since both derivatives are strictly positive this confirms our statement that put and call options will be more valuable the riskier their underlying stock. Note that the same conclusions remain valid for American options since a higher standard deviation of stock returns induces no downside (loss) risk while it increases the upside (profit) potential of American put and call options. However, since the Black and Scholes formula Eq. (4.18) applies[27] to American call options on nondividend paying stocks, this assertion has already been proven in Eq. (4.34) for this specific subset of American options.

By looking carefully at the five essential parameters affecting option prices in the Black and Scholes formula, we discover another useful feature of this pricing model. Since the market price of the stock, the current interest rate on a short-term discount bond or Treasury Bill, the striking price, and the time to maturity of the option can all be directly collected or computed from available market data, there is only one unobservable parameter in the formula.

However, the same isn't true for the instantaneous standard deviation of stock returns. It reflects the future variability of the stock but must be estimated from current and/or past price data—in the absence of "perfect forecast" ability. The estimation of the stock returns' future variability is certainly the most delicate task associated with the application of the Black and Scholes model since any biased estimation of the standard deviation directly leads to over- or underpriced theoretical call and put values and hence to misleading investment strategies. We will examine the techniques generally employed to estimate the stock return's variability in the next chapter when we present many applications associated with the Black and Scholes model.

6   ILLUSTRATING EUROPEAN OPTION PRICES BEHAVIOR

Before concluding this analysis of option price determinants, we will use a numerical example to summarize the various relationships presented. To preserve the homogeneity of the example, we will only focus on a put's option price sensitivity to a change in its five explanatory variables. Let us assume the data on ROY stock and a European put option written on that stock are as follows:

Current stock price $\qquad S_0 = \$42$

Standard deviation of stock returns (annualized) $\qquad \sigma_0 = 30\%$

Striking price $\qquad K_0 = \$40$

Time to maturity in years $\qquad \tau_0 = 0.5$

Continuously compounded riskless rate (annualized) $\qquad r_0 = 0.05$

---

[27] This result follows from Restriction 11 in Chapter 2.

If we apply the Black and Scholes put option pricing formula, this put's theoretical price equals[28]

$$P_0 = Ke^{-r\tau}N(-d_2) - SN(-d_1)$$
$$= 40 \times e^{-0.05 \times -0.5}N(-0.24179) - 42N(-0.45391)$$
$$= \$2.12$$

Now, we would like to assess how the put's price will react if—all other things being equal—we increase each of its explanatory parameters by a very small amount. The following table illustrates the individual impact of these parameter changes by computing the Black and Scholes theoretical value of the put for each new situation.

| | Initial data | New value of[*]: | | | | |
		S	σ	K	τ	r
S_0	42	43				
σ_0	30%		31%			
K_0	40			41		
τ_0	0.5				0.52**	
r_0	0.05					0.06
Put price	2.12	1.82	2.23	2.54	2.17	2.04
$P - P_0$		−0.30	+0.11	+0.42	+0.05	−0.08

[*] Assume that all other parameters remain the same as in the initial situation.
[**] Time to maturity of approximately six months and one week instead of six months in the initial situation.

As expected, the put price dropped (by \$0.30) given an increase of \$1 in the stock price. Conversely a \$1 increase in its striking price induced a \$0.42 increase in the put price. The put price also increased by \$0.11 following a one percent (in absolute terms) higher standard deviation of Roy stock returns. Thus, greater riskiness indeed positively affects put option prices.

The sensitivity of the put price to a change (of one week, in our example) in time to maturity clearly indicates that it has a negative "theta" since its price

---

[28] To compute the put's price, we are using the following property of the cumulative standard normal function: $N(-Z) = 1 - N(Z)$.

increases by \$0.05 with a one-week increase in time to maturity.[29] This is consistent with the fact that medium-term out-of-the-money European put options' prices generally drop when their time to maturity decreases.

Finally, as expected rising interest rates lower put prices and in this example this is reflected by a \$0.08 decrease in the put's value given a 1 percent (in absolute terms) increase in the continuously compounded riskless rate.

We could also illustrate these relationships by computing the numerical value of the derivative of the put price with respect to S, K, σ, r, and τ. Given a slight increase of each underlying parameter, our conclusions would have been exactly the same as to the direction of the put's price change.

This example also demonstrates how important it is to monitor the random variable S. Since in the Black and Scholes model, unpredictable changes in the stock price reflect the only source of uncertainty and since a given change in the stock price can substantially affect call and put prices, portfolio strategies should always be set considering the sensitivity parameters (the "delta" and the "gamma") of option prices to a given change in the stock price.

Computing the sensitivities of option prices to their underlying parameter changes may also be useful when one wishes to select a more aggressive or a more defensive option with respect to specific changes in some of these variables. For example, if we want to sell a put option but are not perfectly aware of the high degree of volatility in the underlying stock, we may be hurt twice if the stock moves down and if it simultaneously happened to be a highly volatile stock.

We will discuss the portfolio applications of the Black and Scholes formula's sensitivity parameters in the next chapter. At the current stage, we should see how useful these sensitivities are in explaining and measuring option price responses to changes in their fundamental explanatory factors.

7   CONCLUSION

In this chapter we introduced the well-known Black and Scholes option pricing model as a limiting case of the binomial pricing approach. Although the model was originally derived in a much more complex continuous-time setting, we have been able to show that if we let the number of periods in the binomial pricing formula tend to infinity and if we choose the parameters of the multiplicative binomial stock price process in such a way that the distribution of the continuously compounded rates of return of the stock does, in the limit, converge to the normal distribution, we obtain the Black and Scholes option pricing formula from a simpler mathematical setting than the one used by its authors.

---

[29] In other words, this put's price has a positive first derivative with respect to time to maturity: $\partial P / \partial \tau > 0$. The derivative $\partial P / \partial \tau$ tells us that the put price will increase by \$0.05 with an increase of one week in its time to maturity. While θ ($= -\partial P / \partial \tau$) tells us the same relationship but with respect to time and not time to maturity. Hence θ is negative in this example, since this put bears a negative time bias.

Moreover, since the basic assumptions used to derive the Black and Scholes formula are identical—except for the stock price stochastic process assumption—to those required in the binomial pricing framework, we were able to specify some properties of the Black and Scholes formula that were already familiar.

The pricing methodology of the Black and Scholes model is a relative one: we again—using a continuously rebalanced perfect hedge—price the call with respect to the risk-free interest rate and the stock price assuming that the no-arbitrage condition must hold in the markets. Hence, the theoretical option's price is again a partial equilibrium price since the option is valued without any general equilibrium consideration in the economy. We may therefore say that the call is fairly priced with respect to the underlying stock and the risk-free rate, but we do not know whether it is consistently priced with regard to all other assets. The latter would only be true if the riskless rate and the stock price were themselves "true" equilibrium values that reflected all the relevant information to price the option.

We stated that unlike the binomial pricing formula, the Black and Scholes formula does not depend on investors' preferences and that it can therefore be derived in any kind of economy. We then argued that we would have easily obtained the Black and Scholes formula by assuming a risk-neutral economy. Hence, as in the case of the binomial pricing formula, the probabilities used in the Black and Scholes formula's normal cumulative distribution functions $N(d_1)$ and $N(d_2)$ can be interpreted as "risk-neutralized" probabilities.

Although originally derived for a European call option on a nondividend paying stock, we have shown that the Black and Scholes pricing equation can also be used to price American call options on nondividend paying stocks as well as European put options (by applying the put-call parity relationship I of Chapter 2). In all those cases where the formula is relevant, we were then able to show how a change in each of the relevant parameters—interest rate, stock price, striking price, time to maturity, and standard deviation—affects both put and call option prices. These relationships can be stated directly from the Black and Scholes pricing equation, and they are all consistent with the rational boundaries to option pricing stated in Chapter 2.

However, there is more to understand about the Black and Scholes pricing model. First, it seems important to know how the formula must be used; that is, where to look for and how to compute the relevant parameters that enter Eq. (4.18). One should also be able to estimate the standard deviation of stock returns properly, and then introduce the dividends into the model if stock's theoretical option prices are to be considered as reliable investment tools.

These are some of the many extensions of the Black and Scholes pricing model addressed in the next chapter. We will also emphasize the importance of this pricing model for portfolio management strategies involving options. Thus far we have seen but one feature of the Black and Scholes model, namely its ability to price European call and put options in a simple and consistent manner. We still have much to learn about the practical applications and theoretical strengths and weaknesses of the Black and Scholes option pricing model.

APPENDIX 4-1

In this Appendix we follow the Cox, Ross, and Rubinstein (1979) proof of the convergence in probability of the binomial distribution functions $B[n, a, p]$ and $B[n, a, b]$ to the standard normal distribution functions $N(d_1)$ and $N(d_2)$. We will show that as $n \to \infty$:

$$B[n, a, p] \to N \left[\frac{\ln(S/KR^{-\tau})}{\sigma \sqrt{\tau}} - \frac{1}{2} \sigma \sqrt{\tau} \right] \qquad (4'.1)$$

First note that $p = (R - d)/(u - d)$, and given $u = e^{\sigma \sqrt{\tau/n}}$ and $d = e^{-\sigma \sqrt{\tau/n}}$, we obtain the limiting value of p satisfying

$$\lim_{n \to \infty} p = \frac{1}{2} + \frac{1}{2} \left(\frac{\ln R - (1/2\sigma^2)}{\sigma} \right) \sqrt{\frac{\tau}{n}} \qquad (4'.2)$$

Moreover, with the risk-neutralized probabilities p and $(1 - p)$, we can redefine the expected logarithmic return and its variance given in Eqs. (4.10) and (4.11) as follows:

$$E(\ln S^*/S) = [p \ln(u/d) + \ln d]n = wn \qquad (4'.3)$$

$$\text{Var}(\ln S^*/S) = [p(1 - p)[\ln(u/d)]^2]n = \Delta^2 n \qquad (4'.4)$$

Now $B[a, n, p]$ is the complementary binomial distribution that defines the probability that the number of up jumps (j) will be greater or equal to a, given a total number of n jumps in the stock price. The probability of each jump is equal to p if it is an upward movement and to $(1 - p)$ if it is a downward movement respectively.

We can therefore write

$$B[n, a, p] = \text{prob}[j \geq a]$$

$$\Longleftrightarrow$$

$$1 - B[n, a, p] = \text{prob}[j \leq a - 1] \qquad (4'.5)$$

Since we know that the random variable j is distributed[1] with a mean equal to np and a variance equal to $np(1 - p)$, we can write Eq. (4'.5) as follows:

$$1 - B[n, a, p] = \text{prob} \left[\frac{j - np}{\sqrt{np(1 - p)}} \leq \frac{a - 1 - np}{\sqrt{np(1 - p)}} \right] \qquad (4'.6)$$

---

[1] This can be seen from Eqs. (4.8) and (4.9). We only substitute p for q since the binomial pricing formula is a function of the risk-neutralized probabilities p and $(1 - p)$.

Using the definitions of $E(\ln(S^*/S))$ and $\mathrm{Var}(\ln(S^*/S))$ in Eqs. (4'.3) and (4'.4) and recalling that:

$$\ln(S^*/S) = j \ln(u/d) + n \ln d \tag{4'.7}$$

we obtain the following equality:

$$\frac{j - np}{\sqrt{np(1-p)}} = \frac{\ln(S^*/S) - wn}{\Delta \sqrt{n}} \tag{4'.8}$$

Hence, we can write Eq. (4'.6) as follows:

$$1 - B[n, a, p] = \mathrm{prob}\left[\frac{\ln(S^*/S) - wn}{\Delta \sqrt{n}} \le \frac{a - 1 - np}{\sqrt{np(1-p)}}\right] \tag{4'.9}$$

From Chapter 3, we know that a is the smallest integer greater than $\ln(K/Sd^n)/\ln(u/d)$; hence if

$$a > \ln(K/Sd^n)/\ln(u/d)$$

then

$$a - 1 = [\ln(K/Sd^n)/\ln(u/d)] - \epsilon \tag{4'.10}$$

where $0 < \epsilon < 1$

Given the definition of $(a - 1)$ in Eq. (4'.10) and using the definition of wn and $\Delta^2 n$ given in Eqs. (4'.3) and (4'.4), respectively, we can rearrange Eq. (4'.9) in the following way:

$$1 - B[n, a, p] = \mathrm{prob}\left[\frac{\ln(S^*/S) - wn}{\Delta \sqrt{n}} \le \frac{\ln(K/S) - wn - \epsilon \ln(u/d)}{\Delta \sqrt{n}}\right] \tag{4'.11}$$

Since the higher moments (of order greater than two) of the distribution do not matter in the limit,[2] we can now use the Central Limit Theorem to see what happens to Eq. (4'.11) when $n \to \infty$. From Eqs. (4'.3) and (4'.4):[3]

$$\lim_{n\to\infty} wn = (\ln R - (\tfrac{1}{2}\sigma^2))\tau \equiv \mu\tau \tag{4'.12}$$

$$\lim_{n\to\infty} \Delta \sqrt{n} \equiv \sigma \sqrt{\tau} \tag{4'.13}$$

Note that:

---

[2] This is proven in Cox, Ross, and Rubinstein's (1979) paper.

[3] Substituting u, d, and p by their respective values in (4'.3) and (4'.4) and taking the appropriate limits of wn and $\Delta \sqrt{n}$ gives the desired results.

$$\lim_{n \to \infty} \ln(u/d) - \lim_{n \to \infty} 2\sigma \sqrt{\tau/n} = 0$$

Hence, by applying the Central Limit Theorem, Eq. (4'.11) reduces to

$$1 - B[n, a, p] = \text{prob} \left[\frac{\ln(S^*/S) - wn}{\Delta \sqrt{n}} \le \frac{\ln(K/S) - (\ln R - ((1/2)\sigma^2))\tau}{\sigma \sqrt{\tau}} \right]$$

(4'.14)

Since $[\ln(K/S) - (\ln R - (1/2)\sigma^2)\tau]/\sigma \sqrt{\tau}$ is a standard normal variate, we can say that:

$$1 - B[n, a, p] \to N(Z) = N \left[\frac{\ln(K/S) - (\ln R - ((1/2)\sigma^2))\tau}{\sigma \sqrt{\tau}} \right]$$

Hence:

$$B[n, a, p] \to N(-Z) = N \left[\frac{\ln(S/K) + (\ln R - ((1/2)\sigma^2))\tau}{\sigma \sqrt{\tau}} \right]$$

$$\Longleftrightarrow$$

$$B[n, a, p] \to N(-Z) = N \left[\frac{\ln(S/KR^{-r})}{\sigma \sqrt{\tau}} - \frac{1}{2}\sigma \sqrt{\tau} \right] \qquad (4'.15)$$

Given that $\ln R = r$ where r is the continuously compounded interest rate, we can arrange Eq. (4'.15) to obtain

$$B[n, a, p] \to N(-Z) = N \left[\frac{\ln(S/Ke^{-r\tau})}{\sigma \sqrt{\tau}} - \frac{1}{2}\sigma \sqrt{\tau} \right]$$

$$= N(d_2) \qquad (4'.16)$$

where

$$d_2 = \frac{\ln(S/Ke^{-r\tau})}{\sigma \sqrt{\tau}} - \frac{1}{2}\sigma \sqrt{\tau}$$

In deriving Eq. (4'.16), we have just shown that the complementary binomial distribution $B[n, a, p]$ will in the limit tend to the standard normal cumulative distribution $N(d_2)$ entering the Black and Scholes formula Eq. (4'.18). By the same reasoning (i.e., by applying the Central Limit Theorem) we can show that:

$$B[n, a, b] \to N(d_1) \qquad \text{as } n \to \infty$$

This completes the proof, since we can now say that we obtain the Black and Scholes formula as the limiting case of the binomial pricing model when the parameters r, u, d, and hence p are appropriately chosen.

APPENDIX 4.2   AREA UNDER THE NORMAL CURVE

Areas under the standard normal distribution function $\int_0^s f(z)\,dz$									
z	.00	.01	.02	.03	.04	.05	.06	.07	.08	.09
0.0	.0000	.0040	.0080	.0120	.0160	.0199	.0239	.0279	.0319	.0359
0.1	.0398	.0438	.0478	.0517	.0557	.0596	.0636	.0675	.0714	.0753
0.2	.0793	.0832	.0871	.0910	.0948	.0987	.1026	.1064	.1103	.1141
0.3	.1179	.1217	.1255	.1293	.1331	.1368	.1406	.1443	.1480	.1517
0.4	.1554	.1591	.1628	.1664	.1700	.1736	.1772	.1808	.1844	.1879
0.5	.1915	.1950	.1985	.2019	.2054	.2088	.2123	.2157	.2190	.2224
0.6	.2257	.2291	.2324	.2357	.2389	.2422	.2454	.2486	.2517	.2549
0.7	.2580	.2611	.2642	.2673	.2704	.2734	.2764	.2794	.2823	.2852
0.8	.2881	.2910	.2939	.2967	.2995	.3023	.3051	.3078	.3106	.3133
0.9	.3159	.3186	.3212	.3238	.3264	.3289	.3315	.3340	.3365	.3389
1.0	.3413	.3438	.3461	.3485	.3508	.3531	.3554	.3577	.3599	.3621
1.1	.3643	.3665	.3686	.3708	.3729	.3749	.3770	.3790	.3810	.3830
1.2	.3849	.3869	.3888	.3907	.3925	.3944	.3962	.3980	.3997	.4015
1.3	.4032	.4049	.4066	.4082	.4099	.4115	.4131	.4147	.4162	.4177
1.4	.4192	.4207	.4222	.4236	.4251	.4265	.4279	.4292	.4306	.4319
1.5	.4332	.4345	.4357	.4370	.4382	.4394	.4406	.4418	.4429	.4441
1.6	.4452	.4463	.4474	.4484	.4495	.4505	.4515	.4525	.4535	.4545
1.7	.4554	.4564	.4573	.4582	.4591	.4599	.4608	.4616	.4625	.4633
1.8	.4641	.4649	.4656	.4664	.4671	.4678	.4686	.4693	.4699	.4706
1.9	.4713	.4719	.4726	.4732	.4738	.4744	.4750	.4756	.4761	.4767
2.0	.4772	.4778	.4783	.4788	.4793	.4798	.4803	.4808	.4812	.4817
2.1	.4821	.4826	.4830	.4834	.4838	.4842	.4846	.4850	.4854	.4857
2.2	.4861	.4864	.4868	.4871	.4875	.4878	.4881	.4884	.4887	.4890
2.3	.4893	.4896	.4898	.4901	.4904	.4906	.4909	.4911	.4913	.4916
2.4	.4918	.4920	.4922	.4925	.4927	.4929	.4931	.4932	.4934	.4936
2.5	.4938	.4940	.4941	.4943	.4945	.4946	.4948	.4949	.4951	.4952
2.6	.4953	.4955	.4956	.4957	.4959	.4960	.4961	.4962	.4963	.4964
2.7	.4965	.4966	.4967	.4968	.4969	.4970	.4971	.4972	.4973	.4974
2.8	.4974	.4975	.4976	.4977	.4977	.4978	.4979	.4979	.4980	.4981
2.9	.4981	.4982	.4982	.4982	.4984	.4984	.4985	.4985	.4986	.4986
3.0	.4987	.4987	.4987	.4988	.4988	.4989	.4989	.4989	.4990	.4990

Source: Thomas E. Copeland and J. Fred Weston, *Financial Theory and Corporate Policy,* Third Edition, Addison-Wesley Publishing Company, MA., 1988, from Chapter 8, p. 290. Reprinted with permission.

CHAPTER
5

THE BLACK AND SCHOLES FORMULA AS AN INVESTMENT DECISION MAKING TOOL

1 INTRODUCTION

Now that we have presented the Black and Scholes formula, we will analyze more carefully the various features and applications that contributed to its popularity among the academic and the financial community. It is the first theoretical valuation model to be widely accepted and used by practitioners to value options, to speculate, or simply to hedge underlying equity positions.

The first problem in applying the Black and Scholes formula is a purely technical one that addresses the identification and estimation of relevant parameters from the available market data. In this context, we will essentially analyze the difficulties related to the variance estimation, and discuss their impact on the computed theoretical option prices.

We will then present some simplifying assumptions and techniques that enable the Black and Scholes formula's extension to both American and European options on dividend paying stocks. While the formula can be adjusted consistently for certain types of dividend payments and hence price European dividend paying stocks, the same is not true for American call options written on dividend paying stocks since the problem of early exercise is not satisfactorily solved in the "ad hoc" modifications of the Black and Scholes formula. This suggests that the early exercise feature of both American call and put options requires a specific redefinition of the option valuation procedure to explicitly handle these options' additional rights.

This discussion of the main technical and theoretical problems is very useful since it will allow us to distinguish the option types and the market conditions for which the Black and Scholes formula is relevant from those for which it is not. In light of the frequent inappropriate applications of the Black and Scholes formula to options for which it is not suited, awareness of its validity domain is very important since it can limit misleading—costly—investment decisions that affect the performance of option portfolios.

In the next part of the chapter we will move temporarily from option pricing to the concepts of risk and return associated with an option's position. How can we define and measure the return and the risk of an option? How can we relate the risk and the return of an option to the same characteristics of the underlying stock?

The Black and Scholes option pricing framework provides useful measures of an option's price sensitivity to various parameter changes. These sensitivity measures (for example, delta, gamma, and theta) prove to be very useful and effective tools for monitoring an option's position risk exposure. We will illustrate through an example how these risk parameters can be used to create or to control a position with a targeted risk level to satisfy the objectives and the constraints of an investment plan.

By the end of the chapter we will have broadened our understanding of the main applications of the Black and Scholes option pricing model. We will also have a detailed description of the main strengths and weaknesses found in its pricing and risk monitoring abilities for a large variety of options.

2 HOW TO COMPUTE THE BLACK AND SCHOLES FORMULA: SOME TECHNICAL CONSIDERATIONS

We already mentioned in the previous chapter that the Black and Scholes formula Eq. (4.18) can be easily computed since—except for the estimation of the variance—it essentially relies on observable market data (for example, the stock price) and on contractual data (for example, the exercise price).

However, in applying the formula, the choice of the relevant data doesn't seem obvious since it involves self-judgment as well as the consideration of many structural features of the market that can affect the option price. We will now examine more thoroughly the problems related to the choice and the computation of each of the five parameters entering the Black and Scholes formula:

$$C = SN(d_1) - Ke^{-\tau r}N(d_2) \tag{4.18}$$

where

$N(\cdot)$ represents the cumulative standard normal distribution

$$d_1 = \frac{\ln(S/Ke^{-\tau r})}{\sigma \sqrt{\tau}} + \frac{1}{2}\sigma \sqrt{\tau}$$

$$d_2 = d_1 - \sigma \sqrt{\tau}$$

A The Stock Price: S

The main problem in choosing the relevant stock price is to obtain simultaneity between the option price and the stock price. If this condition does not hold, any price differential between the market value of the option and its theoretical price (computed with the Black and Scholes formula) may be mistakenly considered as an arbitrage opportunity while it results from asynchronous stock price data plugged in the formula. Of course, this problem cannot be solved by the user unless he has access to on-line information on every transaction or quote that occurs in the market.

More generally, the user will only obtain opening, closing, and settlement prices for the stocks and hence cannot avoid the simultaneity problem since option and stock markets hardly ever open, close, or clear at the same time. Moreover, given a set of stock prices for a particular trading day, it is not obvious to fit its nature to that of the traded option prices. For example, in the case of illiquid options, we may face a situation in which the closing price of the stock stems from a transaction while the option price is just a bid or an ask quote.[1] Hence, every time the market data does not allow the matching of the observed stock prices with the nature of the observed option prices, caution must be used in comparing the computed option price to its market value.

B The Exercise Price: K

The exercise price is the simplest parameter that enters the Black and Scholes formula since it is clearly specified in each standardized option contract. The only problem may arise from the adjustment technique that the exchange applies in cases of right issues, stock splits, or stock dividends. If the adjustment of the exercise price does not correspond to the effective dilution of the stock price, the option holder is penalized,[2] and this phenomenon is even more pronounced

---

[1] We cannot generally infer if the closing price for the option was on the bid or on the ask side.

[2] Note that it has been proposed in Switzerland [see Cordero and Zimmerman (1987)] to compensate the option holders against right issues and stock dividends only at the exercise or maturity date of the option. At each of these two dates, the option owner is entitled to buy an additional amount of shares corresponding to the proportion of shares issued relative to the previously outstanding shares (at the issue price for right issues and at a zero price for stock dividends). Hence, he effectively holds a "deferred" right that he can exercise or convert into cash. The only problem with this adjustment technique is that it doesn't compensate the option owner for the true dilution that occurred in the stock price at the time of the new stock issue. This problem may be neglected for short-term options and hence does only become serious for longer-term (six months) traded options in Switzerland.

for European options since early exercise possibilities do not exist. However, the latter problem does only affect the pricing performance of the Black and Scholes formula to the extent that market participants are aware of the phenomenon and have hence bidded option prices down according to the remaining dilution. Generally, this situation can be easily avoided by implementing adjustment technique in cases of stock splits, right issues, and stock dividends.

For example, suppose Company Beta decides to split each of its existing shares into five new ones. Call option contracts written on Beta stock previously entitled you to buy 100 Beta shares at an exercise price of $150 per share. On the split date, the stock's value will drop by a fifth (the split ratio) and this suggests that the terms of the option contract must be adjusted accordingly. This can be done by entitling the option owner to a "modified" call option either by

a) increasing the number of shares he can buy with a single option contract and reducing the exercise price according to the split ratio. In our example, the call option owner now has a contract entitling him to buy 500 shares of Beta stock at an exercise price of $30 per share.

b) increasing the number of option contracts and reducing the exercise price according to the split ratio. In our example, each call option holder now owns five call options entitling him to buy 100 shares of Beta stock at an exercise price of $30 per share.

Note that when the split ratio is not an integer number, the first solution will usually be adopted since dealing with a fractionary number of option contracts becomes confusing.

In the case of right issues, the procedure may become more complex as illustrated by the following example. Company A decides to issue 20,000 new shares. Each shareholder owning four old shares is entitled to buy one new share at the price of $150. The last traded price of stock A prior to the right issue was equal to $420.

First we need to define the dilution factor resulting from this issue; that is, the theoretical value of the preemptive right (d) belonging to the old shareholders is equal to

$$d = \frac{\dfrac{\text{Last traded}}{\text{stock price}} - \text{Issue price}}{\dfrac{\text{Old shares}}{\text{New shares}} + 1} = \frac{420 - 150}{5 + 1} = \$45$$

Hence, the theoretical price of the diluted "stock" is equal to

$$S^* = S - d = 420 - 45 = \$375$$

and the dilution factor (f) obtains

$$f = S^*/S = 375/420 = 0.8928$$

Now suppose that prior to the issue, a three-month call option on stock A entitled its owner to buy 5 shares of stock at an exercise price of $400. After the issue, the terms of the call option contract must be adjusted to reflect the stock price dilution. Again, this can be done either by

a) increasing the number of contracts and reducing the exercise price according to the dilution factor f. In this example, the option owner then holds $(1/0.8928) = 1.12$ contracts entitling him to buy 5 shares of stock A at an exercise price of $400 \times 0.8928 = \$357.12$.

b) increasing the number of shares and reducing the exercise price of the option contract according to the dilution factor f. In this example, the option owner will then hold one call option entitling him to buy $5 \times (1/0.8928) = 5.6$ shares of stock A at an exercise price of $357.12.

Of course, both methods face the problem of either a fractionary number of contracts or shares resulting from the stock issue. This problem is generally solved at the expiration or at the exercise date of the option by allowing cash compensation for the remaining fractionary amounts of shares or option contracts. We suggest that the second method be used so the quoted prices for the option always apply on a unitary contractual basis.

C   The Time to Maturity: τ

Standardized option contracts are generally issued with one to twelve months until expiration and their last trading day is generally specified as a standard norm by each exchange. For example, on the Swiss Option Exchange, the expiration date will always be the third Friday of the relevant month.

When we need to value an option at a particular time, the most common and intuitive approach is to count the effective number of calendar days from the observation date until the expiration date. Then, since the Black and Scholes formula expresses time to maturity as a fraction of a year, we simply divide the number of effective days by 365 (or 366) to obtain the desired parameter τ.

As Jarrow and Rudd (1983) pointed out, however, there are some cautions in choosing the number of calendar days as a reference. Indeed, in the Black and Scholes formula [Eq. (4.18)] time to maturity is used to discount the exercise price $(Ke^{-\tau r})$ as well as to project the instantaneous variance of stock returns $(\sigma^2 \tau)$ until the option's expiration date. For the first "discounting function," the number of calendar days is relevant since interest is earned over the weekends and during the holidays. However, the variance of stock returns can only be—historically—estimated over effective trading days. Moreover, several empirical studies found stock return patterns (the overnight pattern, the weekend effect, etc.) that suggested different volatility for trading and nontrading periods. Therefore, an alternative in computing τ is to count the effective number of trading days and divide it by the total number of business days in the year.

Unfortunately, there is no available empirical evidence about the difference those two methods may induce on computed option prices. We therefore suggest—according to the parsimony principle—using the calendar year as a reference[3] as long as further performance comparisons are not available.

D The Riskless Interest Rate: r

This is the first parameter that cannot be totally derived from some simplifying assumptions. First, note that the Black and Scholes model assumes that the riskless rate is unique and constant. In the continuous-time framework—in which the authors derived their formula—the riskless rate is defined as the rate of return on an instantaneously maturing default-free discount bond. Therefore, if $B(\tau)$ is the price at time t of a default-free bond paying $1 at time T, the riskless interest rate r is defined as

$$\lim_{r \to 0} \frac{dB(\tau)}{B(\tau)} = r \ dt \qquad (5.1)$$

Moreover, since the authors assume a constant riskless rate over the life of the option, they are implicitly allowing for a flat term structure of interest rates (because the instantaneous riskless rate can only stay constant through time if all bonds with longer maturities also have an instantaneous rate of return that is and will remain equal to r). Under this hypothesis, the current price $B(\tau)$ of any default-free discount bond can be written as follows

$$B(\tau) - e^{-r(T-t)} = e^{-r\tau} \qquad (5.2)$$

The choice of the maturity of the relevant bond from which r must be computed becomes irrelevant precisely because the term structure is—and will remain—flat.

In practice, however, this hypothesis is very strong since the term structure of interest rates can have any shape, and hence default-free bonds of different maturities will bear different yields (or spot rates). Moreover, when future interest rates are uncertain, the risk-free asset's maturity is not irrelevant. For example, if we wish to lock in a certain interest rate over 120 days, our best strategy is to buy and to hold a Treasury Bill that matures in 120 days. However, we would certainly not buy the same asset if our objective is to lock in a sure return over a two-year holding period. Indeed, what would we do with the amount invested in the Treasury bill at the end of 120 days? We would not be able to avoid the risk related to the unknown interest rate at which we would have to reinvest the

---

[3] The number of business days may vary from one country to the other, which may prevent us from comparing the computed prices to the market prices of similar options—this is particularly relevant for currency options—traded in different countries.

proceeds from the maturing T-Bill over the remaining 20 months. It follows that a riskless strategy consists in this case of buying a two-year default-free zero-coupon bond and holding it until it matures. This strategy would guarantee the realization of the ex ante yield to maturity (or spot rate) of this default-free bond over our two-year holding period.

The relevant default-free asset from which the riskless rate must be computed cannot be chosen arbitrarily, it has to be a default-free discount bond or note (or T-Bill) with a time to maturity as close as possible to the remaining time to maturity of the option. Since standardized option contracts rarely last longer than one year, one would use the annualized[4] yield to maturity of the T-Bill with a maturity date as close as possible to that of the option to approximate r.

The problem of finding the relevant interest rate proxy can become tedious in some markets (like Switzerland) which do not have a well-developed secondary money market. Moreover, when one values longer-term options, or warrants, it is often impossible to find a zero-coupon default-free bond that matches the time to maturity of the warrant since government debt issues in most countries bear a coupon rate. Hence, one would then have to approximate the riskless spot rate with the yield-to-maturity of a default-free coupon bearing bond. The existence of the coupon as well as the differential tax treatment of income versus capital gains that prevails in several countries can lead to substantial biases when using this latter proxy of the riskless interest rate.

Finally, in addition to these technical considerations related to the choice of the relevant riskless rate proxy, the obvious one related to the Black and Scholes formula is that it assumes a constant riskless rate over the life of the option. We will see in the next chapter how this restrictive assumption can be relaxed to price options in a world with interest rate uncertainty.

E   The Variance of Stock Returns: σ^2

This unobservable parameter entering the Black and Scholes pricing equation is certainly the most important and controversial one for both practical and theoretical reasons. Remember that the Black and Scholes formula is based on the assumption that stock prices are lognormally distributed,[5] or in other words, the continuously compounded rates of return of the stock follow a normal distribution characterized by a constant mean (μ) and a constant variance (σ^2) per unit of time. The variance must be precisely estimated to determine the variance of stock returns over the option's remaining time to maturity ($\sigma^2 \tau$).

---

[4] U.S. Treasury Bill yields are quoted on a 360 day basis and since option prices are generally computed assuming a 365 day calendar year, the quoted yields of the T-Bills should be adjusted accordingly. For a detailed explanation of the adjustment method see Cox and Rubinstein (1985).

[5] We have examined the behavior of the stock prices under the lognormal distribution in Chapter 4, Section 4.

The lognormal stock price distribution implies that the variance over any given time period is proportional to its length. Therefore, one method of computing the (constant) future instantaneous variance (σ^2) is to simply rely on past stock return data; that is, to assume that this past variability of the stock's returns is indeed invariant across time.

THE HISTORICAL VARIANCE OF STOCK RETURNS. To compute the historical variance of stock returns, we first need a time series of price data on the stock to compute its continuously compounded rates of return (equal to the logarithms of the stock price relatives). Suppose that we have 16 weekly price observations on stock ABC.

Week #	Price	$\ln(S_t/S_{t-1})$	Week #	Price	$\ln(S_t/S_{t-1})$
1	51.0		9	51.1	0.0157
2	50.5	-0.0098	10	49.3	-0.0358
3	52.0	0.0290	11	49.8	0.0100
4	51.7	-0.0050	12	51.5	0.0034
5	51.2	-0.0097	13	52.1	0.0116
6	50.6	-0.0117	14	52.5	0.0076
7	50.1	-0.0099	15	51.9	-0.0115
8	50.3	0.0040	16	50.3	-0.0310

We can then estimate the mean of the series of continuously compounded rates of return:

$$\hat{\mu} = \frac{1}{n} \sum_{j=1}^{n} R_j \tag{5.3}$$

where

$\hat{\mu}$ = mean of the continuously compounded rates of return in the sample

$R_j = \ln(S_t/S_{t-1})$ = the continuously compounded rate of return over week j, $j = 1, \ldots, n$

n = total number of available continuously compounded rates of return

Hence, in our example, the mean weekly rate of return equals

$$\hat{\mu} = \frac{1}{15} \sum_{j=1}^{15} R_j = -0.00287$$

We can then calculate the variance of the historical weekly returns around their mean given that the unbiased estimator of the variance is equal to[6]

$$\hat{\sigma}^2 = \frac{1}{n-1} \sum_{j=1}^{n} [R_j - \hat{\mu}]^2 \tag{5.4}$$

The unbiased estimator of the variance of the weekly returns in our example is then equal to

$$\hat{\sigma}^2 = \frac{1}{14} \sum_{1}^{15} [R_j - (-0.00287)]^2 = 0.0002934$$

Now, to infer the proper variance parameter σ^2 that enters the Black and Scholes formula, we must remember to annualize the estimated weekly historical variance $\hat{\sigma}^2$, hence

$$\sigma^2 = 52.\hat{\sigma}^2 = 0.01526$$

Finally, the annualized standard deviation σ is equal to

$$\sigma = \sqrt{\sigma^2} = \sqrt{0.01526} = 12.35\%$$

Assuming that the standard deviation (or the variance) of stock ABC's returns will indeed remain constant over time and equal to 12.35% (or 0.01526) per year, we can then use it in conjunction with the Black and Scholes pricing formula to compute the theoretical prices of European options—of any maturity and/or exercise price—written on stock ABC.

---

[6] Note that the variance of a sample: $\sigma_S^2 = (1/n) \sum_{j=1}^{n} [R_j - \hat{\mu}]^2$ is biased. This means that its expected value will differ from the true value of the population's variance (σ_0^2):

$$E[\sigma_S^2] = \left[\frac{1}{n} \sum_{j=1}^{n} E[R_j - \hat{\mu}]^2 \right] = \frac{1}{n} \sum_{j=1}^{n} E\left[(R_j - \mu)^2 - (\hat{\mu} - \mu)^2 \right]$$

$$= \frac{1}{n} (n\sigma_0^2 - \sigma_0^2)$$

$$= \sigma_0^2 \left(1 - \frac{1}{n} \right)$$

where $\hat{\mu}$ = sample mean, μ = population's true mean and var[$\hat{\mu}$] = σ_0^2/n.

Hence, an unbiased estimator of the variance ($\hat{\sigma}^2$) is obtained by multiplying σ_S^2 with the correction factor $n/(n-1)$, so that we obtain

$$\hat{\sigma}^2 = \frac{n}{n-1} \sigma_S^2 = \frac{n}{n-1} \times \frac{1}{n} \sum_{j=1}^{n} [R_j - \hat{\mu}]^2 = \frac{1}{n-1} \sum_{j=1}^{n} [R_j - \hat{\mu}]^2$$

Of course, the number of stock prices (and continuously compounded rates of return) should in practice be greater[7] than 16 (15) to get a reliable estimate of the variance. Generally, one would rely on one year of weekly data (or 52 price observations) to compute the historical variance. However, going so far into the past may be very misleading for some cyclical or growth stocks since their current characteristics (profit level, leverage, management policy, etc.) can vary substantially from what they were twelve months ago. Even for very stable stocks, this procedure can be criticized since a long time span increases the probability of general shifts in the economy and hence of systematically induced changes in the stock's return variability. If we use more closely spaced data—for example, daily stock prices—we can certainly minimize the problem caused by too distant price observations while keeping a sufficient number of observations to estimate the variance accurately.

Using 52 daily price observations would only lead us one month and 22 days into the past and we may expect that such a recently computed historical volatility will be more appropriate to price options. However, we still must assume that the economy changes slowly over time, assuming that this recent but nevertheless historical estimate of stock returns' volatility can adequately approximate the unknown future volatility over the option's remaining time to maturity.

Parkinson's (1980) "extreme values" variance measurement procedure is a second method used to obtain variance estimates based on recent past market data. Assuming that stock prices are lognormally distributed, he suggested estimating the variance with high and low daily prices rather than with closing prices. He defined the following formula to compute the variance from daily high- and low-price relatives[8]

---

[7] In this example, we essentially emphasize the technique that should be used to compute the variance of the continuously compounded rates of return. In practice, the choice of the relevant sample size (n) is very delicate since we need a lot of observations (large n) to compute a consistent estimator of the variance while, paradoxically, going too far in the past decreases the extrapolative power of the estimated historical variance. For many highly liquid stocks, this problem can be partially solved by relying on more frequently spaced data and typically on daily stock prices. Note that for currency options, some studies have even relied on intra-daily data to estimate the variance of the exchange rate relative changes [see Wasserfallen and Zimmerman (1986)].

[8] If $p(l, t)$ is defined as the probability that $(X_{max} - X_{min}) \leq l$ during a time interval t where X is a variable following a continuous-time random walk, then Parkinson has shown

$$E[l^2] = 4\ln2\sigma^2 t$$

Hence over a unit time interval, we have

$$\sigma^2 = 0.361E[l^2]$$

Over n unit time intervals we obtain

$$\sigma^2 = \frac{0.361}{n} \sum_{j=1}^{n} l_j^2$$

This corresponds exactly to Eq. (5.5) with

$$l = \ln(S_{Hj}/S_{Lj})$$

$$\sigma_{HL}^2 = \left[\frac{0.361}{n} \sum_{j=1}^{n} \ln(S_{Hj}/S_{Lj})^2 \right] \tag{5.5}$$

where

$$\sigma_{HL}^2 = \text{Estimated variance from daily high and low prices}$$

$$n = \text{Total number of days in the sample}$$

$$S_{Hj} = \text{Highest quoted price of the stock on day } j$$

$$S_{Lj} = \text{Lowest quoted price of the stock on day } j$$

This method requires even less data than the daily closing prices based variance since each continuously compounded rate of return now relies on data occurring within the same day and not within two consecutive days. Hence, Parkinson proves that this method is more efficient, providing the same accuracy as the variance estimated from daily closing prices while requiring only a fifth of the data. Instead of using, for example, 60 daily closing prices, we can compute a historical estimate of the variance with the 12 most recent daily high and low prices with the same level of accuracy.

As pointed out by Cox and Rubinstein (1985), this method is very sensitive to errors in data reporting, which can lead us to compute the variance from erroneous high and low daily prices. Since the method does not necessarily rely on a large number of price observations, such reporting errors can severely bias the estimated historical variance. Also, the Parkinson's extreme values method for option pricing cannot be broadly recommended due to the absence of empirical evidence establishing its accuracy of variance estimates and due to the limited number of stock exchanges that report the highest and the lowest daily stock prices.

THE IMPLIED STANDARD DEVIATION METHOD. An even more ambitious attempt toward "refreshing" the variance estimation is provided by the implied standard deviation (ISD) method that estimates the stock returns' variability from the most recent available market data, namely current market prices. The concept is original and appealing since it tries to estimate the variance of stock returns implicitly reflected in current option prices.

Take a careful look at the Black and Scholes European call pricing formula:

$$C = SN(d_1) - Ke^{-r\tau}N(d_2) \tag{4.18}$$

where

$$d_1 = \frac{\ln(S/Ke^{-r\tau})}{\sigma\sqrt{\tau}} + \frac{1}{2}\sigma\sqrt{\tau}$$

$$d_2 = d_1 - \sigma\sqrt{\tau}$$

We can see that although this call option is slightly out-of-the-money ($51.7 < $52), it still has some time value due to its remaining time to maturity of 46 days and to the underlying stock's volatility of 12.35 percent per annum. As an investment decision, one can compare the market price of that ABC call option to its theoretical value and then decide to buy the call option if it is underpriced or to sell it short if it is overpriced.

Of course other investment considerations focusing on fundamental or technical analysis based estimations of stock ABC future volatility over the next 46 days will lead to different theoretical prices and hence to heterogeneous conclusions about the opportunity to buy this call option.

3 EXTENDING THE BLACK AND SCHOLES FORMULA TO THE PRICING OF DIVIDEND PAYING STOCK OPTIONS

The practical usefulness of the Black and Scholes pricing model has two severe limitations. First, the model was originally built to value options written on nondividend[16] paying stocks, and second, the model was developed to price only European options. Since most stocks pay dividends and nearly all standardized stock option contracts are of the American type,[17] we will now determine the extent to which the Black and Scholes model can be modified to account for the dividend payments and for the early exercise feature of American options.

A Introducing Dividends into the Black and Scholes Pricing Model

In this section we will only be concerned with the pricing of European call and put options when the underlying stock pays dividends.[18] Under some specific assumptions about the nature of the dividend flows, we will see that the Black and Scholes formula requires only some slight modifications to remain valid.

---

[16] We have already mentioned in Chapter 2 that this limitation does not affect the pricing validity of the Black and Scholes formula equally among different countries. For Switzerland, where most companies pay a dividend only once a year, this restriction is much weaker than for the United States where companies are generally paying quarterly dividends.

[17] In Chapter 2, we derived the conditions under which it can be optimal to exercise an American call or put option prior to its expiration date.

[18] We are effectively excluding from our discussion payout-protected options—i.e., options whose contractual features are always adjusted when a dividend flow occurs—which can be treated like options on a nondividend paying stock. Most traded options are not payout-protected and to our knowledge only over-the-counter traded stock options are protected against cash dividends. As pointed out by Merton (1973), payout-protection is achieved if, at each payout date, the contract is adjusted so that each option to buy a share at the exercise price K is "exchanged" for another option which allows to buy a total of λ [$\lambda = 1 + (d/s)$] shares at a total price of $\$K$. Note: d is the dollar amount of the payout and s is the ex-dividend price of the stock.

The crucial assumption is that the dividends payable over the remaining time to maturity of the option are at most a known function of time and/or of the stock price. Indeed, if we would let the dividends vary randomly over time, their shifts would represent an additional source of uncertainty—to that stemming from stock price movements—affecting the option's price. But the Black and Scholes formula[19] is derived on the basis of a hedging argument that asserts that by combining an option with a given quantity of the underlying stock, one can effectively form a riskless position that should earn a rate of return equal to the risk-free rate. This is true because this position is perfectly hedged against any unexpected change in the stock price, that is, any gain (loss) on the value of the stocks held long is exactly offset by an equivalent dollar loss (gain) on the call option sold short.

However, if dividends also vary stochastically over time, the latter position is not risk-free anymore since it remains unhedged against unexpected dividend fluctuations. Hence, the underlying assumptions of the Black and Scholes model are violated if we assume that the dividend is an additional random variable that is independent of the stock price since the latter model only allows for uncertainty arising from stock price fluctuations over time. We will now distinguish between cases where dividends are either known—in terms of their amount and date of occurrence—or unknown (but still at most deterministically related to the stock price).

KNOWN DIVIDEND PAYMENTS. Under this hypothesis, there is no uncertainty related either to the payment dates or to the amount of dividends payable until the option's expiration date. This assumption is not unrealistic given the short-term life of traded options (generally less than one year) and given the stable dividend policy most companies tend to follow over a short horizon. Moreover, dividends are generally paid on the same calendar dates from one year (or quarter) to another, hence the dividend payment dates can be fairly accurately predicted.[20]

To apply the Black and Scholes formula under this ideal scenario, we simply need to subtract the present value of the dividends payable over the option's remaining time to maturity from the stock price (S). The latter modification is consistent with the fact that the owner of a call is not entitled to the dividends payable over its time to maturity. Therefore this call should be worth less than an otherwise identical call written on a nondividend paying stock.[21] To illustrate how

---

[19] The hedging argument, which has been explained in detail in Chapters 3 and 4, is also valid for the derivation of the binomial pricing formula.

[20] Of course there may be problems related to weekends or holidays affecting the yearly or quarterly calendar rule, but this uncertainty around the predicted dividend dates should be negligible for most options. The main difficulty arises for options that expire very close to an ex-dividend date. It is important to assess as precisely as possible if those options will mature before or after the dividend payment occurred since any forecast error in the predicted ex-dividend date may severely bias their computed theoretical prices.

[21] This point has already been discussed in Chapter 2, Section 3.

the formula should be modified, suppose that over the call's time to maturity, one dividend of amount D_1 will be paid at time t_1 ($t < t_1 < T$). Hence the current price of this call must satisfy

$$C = (S - D_1 e^{-r\tau_1})N(d_1) - Ke^{-r\tau}N(d_2) \qquad (5.8)$$

where

$$S = \text{current stock price}$$

$$T = \text{expiration date of the call option}$$

$$t_1 = \text{dividend payment date}$$

$$\tau_1 = t_1 - t = \text{remaining time until the dividend payment}$$

$$D_1 = \text{amount of the dividend payable at date } t_1$$

$$K = \text{exercise price of the call}$$

$$N(\cdot) = \text{standard normal cumulative distribution}$$

$$d_1 = \frac{\ln(S - D_1 e^{-r\tau_1}/Ke^{-r\tau})}{\sigma\sqrt{\tau}} + \frac{1}{2}\sigma\sqrt{\tau}$$

$$d_2 = d_1 - \sigma\sqrt{\tau}$$

To illustrate how we can price European call options on dividend paying stocks, let us return to our previous example on stock ABC[22] and assume that this stock pays its quarterly dividend of $1.50 on March 15, 1988. The required parameters to price the call are now defined as follows:

$$S = 51.7$$

$$\tau = 0.125683$$

$$r = 5.61\%$$

$$K = \$52$$

$$D_1 = \$1.50$$

$$\tau_1 = 36/366 = 0.09836$$

Hence, we can compute ABC's stock call option price under the hypothesis of a known dividend payment by using Eq. (5.8):

$$C = (51.7 - 1.5e^{-(0.0561)(0.09836)})N(d_1) - 52e^{-(0.0561)(0.125683)}N(d_2)$$

---

[22] See point F in Section 2 of this chapter.

where[23]

$$N(-0.6178061) = 1 - N(0.6178061) = 0.2709051$$

$$N(-0.6616204) = 1 - N(0.6616204) = 0.2546217$$

We finally obtain

$$C = \$0.37$$

The impact of the dividend for an out-of-the money short-term call option is dramatic since the price of this call option is now only worth $0.37 against $1.035 under the no-dividend scenario.

We can also apply this discussion to the pricing of European put options. We simply need to apply the put-call parity relationship II of Chapter 2 to obtain the theoretical put price from the relevant Black and Scholes call pricing Eq. (5.8). Hence, the price of a European put on a (known) dividend paying stock satisfies the following equation:

$$P = Ke^{-r\tau}N(-d_2) - (S - D_1e^{-r\tau_1})N(-d_1) \tag{5.9}$$

where

$$d_1 = \left\{ \left[\ln\left(\frac{S - D_1e^{-r\tau_1}}{Ke^{-r\tau}} \right) \middle/ \sigma\sqrt{\tau} \right] + \left(\frac{1}{2} \right)\sigma\sqrt{\tau} \right\}$$

and

$$d_2 = d_1 - \sigma\sqrt{\tau}$$

If there are two or more known dividends payable over the put or the call's remaining time to maturity, we would simply subtract from the current stock price the present value of all those cash payments, and hence replace $S - D_1e^{-r\tau_1}$ by

$$S - \sum_{i=1}^{I} D_i e^{-r\tau_i}$$

where

D_i = dividend payment at date t_i

I = total number of dividends payable until
    the option expires

$\tau_i = t_i - t$ = time until payment of the ith dividend

in Eqs. (5.8) and (5.9), respectively.

---

[23] The values of $N(d_1)$ and $N(d_2)$ are found by interpolating between the two nearest values of the standard normal cumulative distribution found in the tables.

UNKNOWN DIVIDEND PAYMENTS. Whenever the payment dates and the amount of the dividends cannot be precisely determined, a common practice[24] has been to assume that the dividend yield $\delta(S, t)$ is a known function of the stock price level. More generally, option pricing models have relied on a constant dividend yield

$$\delta(S, t) = \delta$$

and hence allowed for a dividend payment per unit of time which represents always the same fraction (δ) of the stock's price.

Of course, one may object to the fact that firms maintain a constant dividend yield over time since this hypothesis contradicts the constant dollar dividend payment policy. Nevertheless, in the absence of additional information on the dividend policy of the firm, this simplifying assumption is well justified for the pricing of medium- and long-term options.[25]

Finally, it should be noted that several companies do state their remuneration objectives exclusively in terms of yields and not dollar amounts. This is often done by moderate growth firms to provide comparability between the income rates of their shareholders and their debtholders. For such firms, the constant yield assumption over the long run is even more appropriate.

Since the Black and Scholes formula is derived in continuous time, the main preliminary task is to estimate the continuously compounded constant dividend yield, which is consistent with the expected dividend policy of the firm over the option's remaining time to maturity. Usually, this constant yield is inferred from historical price and dividend data, and it may be updated if some changes in the dividend policy of the firm have already been announced.

To price European call options under this assumption, we simply need to reduce the stock price by the total value of the dividend flow accrued over the option's remaining time to maturity. This adjustment is necessary since option holders are only entitled to the capital gains but not to the dividend income provided by the underlying stock.

Hence, when the stock earns a continuously compounded constant dividend yield δ, the European call option satisfies the following modified Black and Scholes pricing equation:

$$C = S e^{-\delta\tau} N(d_1) - K e^{-r\tau} N(d_2) \tag{5.10}$$

where

---

[24] See Merton (1973), Roll (1977), and Jarrow and Rudd (1983) for a thorough discussion of the continuous dividend yield assumption.

[25] As pointed out by Cox and Rubinstein (1985), firms tend to maintain a constant dollar dividend policy over the short run and a constant dividend yield policy over the long run. Hence, the latter assumption is more appropriate for the pricing of long-term options.

$$d_1 = \frac{\ln(S/K) + (r - \delta)\tau}{\sigma \sqrt{\tau}} + \frac{1}{2}\sigma \sqrt{\tau}$$

$$d_2 = d_1 - \sigma \sqrt{\tau}$$

δ = continuously compounded dividend yield per unit of time

The same methodology is of course applicable to European put options whose price will now satisfy the following equation:

$$P = Ke^{-r\tau}N(-d_2) - Se^{-\delta\tau}N(-d_1) \tag{5.11}$$

with d_1 and d_2 as defined under Eq. (5.10).

Indeed, the constant yield assumption may even be relaxed and replaced by a more complex yield function as long as the dividend yield still remains deterministically related to the stock price and still allows for stock price shift–induced dividend changes.

To conclude, European traded options can be consistently priced under the Black and Scholes model when the underlying stock is paying dividends over the option's time to maturity. A problem will arise, however, for the pricing of very long-term traded options or warrants since it is unclear how the future dividends should be meaningfully related to the stock price over a three-, five- or even a ten-year horizon.

B   The Black and Scholes Formula and the Pricing of American Options

Since most traded options are actually American options, it is very important to distinguish the cases in which the Black and Scholes formula can be used to price American options from those where it would lead to inconsistent results. To analyze the consequences of the early exercise feature, we will analyze its impact on the pricing of call and put options individually.

For American call options, we will distinguish among three possible situations.

1. The underlying security does not pay dividends until the expiration date of the call option.
2. The underlying security pays dividends but the dividends satisfy the no-early exercise condition.[26]
3. The underlying security pays dividends and we cannot exclude the possibility of early exercise.

---

[26] Restriction 13 of Chapter 2 is giving the necessary condition for no-early exercise when the underlying stock pays dividends.

Under the first situation, it has been shown in Chapter 2 (Restriction 11) that an American call will never be exercised before its expiration date, therefore its price is equal to the price of an otherwise identical European call option. Hence the standard Black and Scholes formula Eq. (4.18) developed in Chapter 4 can be used to price American call options on nondividend paying stocks without any further restriction.

This observation has important practical implications for countries where the dividends are paid only once or twice a year since it suggests that the Black and Scholes formula can be consistently applied to most short- and medium-term American call options.

Under the second situation, it is assumed that the present value of the interest earned on the striking price over the option's remaining time to maturity is always greater than the present value of the dividends, and therefore, it will not "pay" for the call owner to exercise his right before the expiration date. This scenario implies that we know the dividend payments and their occurrence dates, or alternatively, that we know the continuously compounded dividend yield applicable over the option's remaining time to maturity. If the no-early exercise condition is satisfied, we can price American call options on dividend paying stocks in the same way we priced European calls on dividend paying stocks in Section A.

It should be pointed out that in the case of known dividend payments satisfying the no-early exercise condition, this approach and hence Eq. (5.8) provide the "exact" theoretical price of an American call option. However, when the dividends are unknown and approximated by a constant yield δ over the option's time to maturity, we cannot be sure that the no-early exercise condition will hold over the option's remaining time to maturity.

As Jarrow (1983) mentioned, when the stock price becomes very large, Eq. (5.10) collapses into[27]

$$C \simeq Se^{-\delta\tau} - Ke^{-r\tau} \tag{5.10}'$$

For a positive value of δ and for a large stock price the unexercised value of the American call given by Eq. (5.10)$'$ can become smaller than its exercise value $[S - K]$ so that we cannot avoid the possibility of early exercise.

Hence, when the dividends are not known and when we instead assume a constant continuously compounded dividend yield to price the American call option according to Eq. (5.10), we will not obtain an "exact" theoretical price for the American call because the early exercise possibility cannot be definitively ruled out. Therefore, Eq. (5.10) will only provide a lower bound for the price of the American call since, in the case of early exercise, this option should always be worth more than an otherwise identical European call option.[28]

---

[27] When $S \to \infty$, $N(d_1) \simeq 1$ and $N(d_2) \simeq 1$, hence Eq. (5.10)$'$ follows.
[28] See Chapter 2, Restriction 6.

In practice, we see that only under very restrictive conditions can an American call option on a dividend paying stock be valued like an otherwise identical European call option. We need to know ex ante the occurrence dates as well as the amount of the dividends, which must also fulfill the no-early exercise condition to obtain an "exact" price of the American call option using the modified Black and Scholes formula Eq. (5.8).

More often we will confront the third situation; that is, it might be optimal to exercise an American option prior to maturity. This will be true whenever future dividends cannot be meaningfully predicted[29] or whenever their known (predicted) amount violates the no-early exercise restriction.

Since the Black and Scholes formula cannot explicitly handle the early exercise possibilities, it has been a common practice to use an "ad hoc" American call valuation procedure based on both the Black and Scholes formula and on the fact that the optimal early exercise dates for these call options arise just before the ex-dividend dates.[30] This approach, originally proposed by Black (1975), accounts for each early exercise possibility by computing the Black and Scholes price of the American call at different maturities, each of which corresponds to an ex-dividend date and to the final expiration date of this American call. Among the several European options' prices then obtained, we pick the option with the highest price and identify the latter with the theoretical value of the American call option.

This so-called "pseudo-American" call valuation procedure defines the American call's price as the maximum of the values of European calls that differ only through their time to maturity, the latter being chosen to match the possible early exercise dates and the final maturity date of the American option. The American call has the "highest" possible European call's value which reflects that it only bears additional rights but has no obligation to exercise prior to maturity.

We can illustrate the "pseudo-American" call valuation procedure by assuming that the stock bears a continuous dividend yield (δ) —which is substituted for its unknown dividend payments—and that the ex-dividend dates over the option's remaining time to maturity can be reasonably well predicted. In the case of two ex-dividend dates over the American call's remaining time to maturity, its price will then satisfy

$$C^* = \max[C_1, C_2, C_3] \qquad (5.12)$$

where

$C^* =$ price of the American call written on a stock whose current price is S, with an exercise price of K and a time to maturity equal to $\tau \ (= T - t)$

---

[29] Since we already saw that using the constant dividend yield assumption in those cases will not exclude early exercise whenever the stock price becomes very large.

[30] The reasons accounting for the fact that it can only be optimal to exercise an American call option just before the ex-dividend dates have been discussed in Chapter 2, Section 3.

C_1 = price of an otherwise identical European call option that expires an instant before the first ex-dividend date t_1 and whose time to maturity is equal to τ_1 $(= t_1 - t)$

C_2 = price of an otherwise identical European call option that expires an instant before the second ex-dividend date t_2 and whose time to maturity is equal to τ_2 $(= t_2 - t)$

C_3 = price of an otherwise identical European call that has the same time to maturity (τ) as the American call option

The prices of the three European call options satisfy the following equations:

$$C_1 = SN(d_1) - Ke^{-r\tau_1}N(d_2) \qquad (4.18)$$

where

$$d_1 = \frac{\ln(S/Ke^{-r\tau_1})}{\sigma\sqrt{\tau_1}} + \frac{1}{2}\sigma\sqrt{\tau_1}$$

$$d_2 = d_1 - \sigma\sqrt{\tau_1}$$

$$C_2 = Se^{-\delta\tau_1}N(d_1) - Ke^{-r\tau_2}N(d_2) \qquad (5.13)$$

where

$$d_1 = \frac{\ln(Se^{-\delta\tau_1}/Ke^{-r\tau_2})}{\sigma\sqrt{\tau_2}} + \frac{1}{2}\sigma\sqrt{\tau_2}$$

$$d_2 = d_1 - \sigma\sqrt{\tau_2}$$

$$C_3 = Se^{-\delta\tau_2}N(d_2) - Ke^{-r\tau}N(d_2) \qquad (5.14)$$

where

$$d_1 = \frac{\ln(Se^{-\delta\tau_2}/Ke^{-r\tau})}{\sigma\sqrt{\tau}} + \frac{1}{2}\sigma\sqrt{\tau}$$

$$d_2 = d_1 - \sigma\sqrt{\tau}$$

We see that the price C_1 of the shortest maturity European option is computed under the standard Black and Scholes formula Eq. (4.18) since the option matures an instant before the first dividend payment occurs. The price of the medium-term European option C_2 is computed using the adjusted Black and Scholes formula Eq. (5.14), but since this option matures just before the second dividend occurs, we only need to adjust the stock price for the first dividend payment (by deflating it according to the dividend flow due until date t_1). Finally, the price of the third call option C_3 must also be computed using the adjusted Black and Scholes formula Eq. (5.15) but this time since the option expires after both dividend dates we must deflate the stock price by the total dividend flow accruing until date t_2.

Note that here, since the payment dates of the dividends are known, we only adjust the stock price over the period for which the dividend stream is due. In our original presentation of Eq. (5.10), we assumed that the dividend payment dates were unknown, and we therefore adjusted the stock price over the entire remaining time to maturity of the option. In the first case, this adjustment is motivated by the assumption that we can replace an unknown dividend by a constant dividend stream until the dividend actually occurs. In the second case, it is motivated by the assumption that we can fit a constant dividend yield over the remaining lifetime of the option to substitute for its unknown dividend payments occurring at random points in time.

To illustrate how the "pseudo-American" call valuation method works, let us focus on the following example of an American call written on stock ZZ:

$$S = 50$$

$$K = 45$$

$$\tau = 73 \text{ days} = 0.2 \text{ years}$$

$$\sigma = 0.30$$

$$r = 0.05$$

Suppose stock ZZ pays a dividend 30 days before the call expires. But since the amount of this dividend is unknown, we substitute it by an estimated continuously compounded dividend yield of 10% per year ($\delta = 0.10$). The time until the next dividend payment is equal to

$$\tau_1 = 43 \text{ days} = 0.1178 \text{ years}$$

We will first compute[31] the price C_1 of the European call maturing an instant before t_1 (the ex-dividend date) and which hence satisfies the standard Black and Scholes formula Eq. (4.18):

$$C_1 = 50N(d_1) - 45e^{-(0.05)(0.1178)}N(d_2)$$

where

$$d_1 = \frac{\ln(50/45e^{-(0.05)(0.1178)})}{0.3\sqrt{0.1178}} + \frac{1}{2}(0.3\sqrt{0.1178})$$

$$= 1.1319416 \text{ so that } N(d_1) = 0.870766$$

$$d_2 = 1.0289756 \text{ so that } N(d_2) = 0.846157$$

We obtain

$$C_1 = \$5.685$$

---

[31] For simplicity, we shall assume a flat term structure of interest rates and use the same riskless rate to compute the prices C_1 and C_2 of both European call options.

The price C_2 of the second European option maturing at the same date as the American option is obtained with the following equation:

$$C_2 = Se^{-\delta\tau_1}N(d_1) - Ke^{-r\tau}N(d_2)$$

$$\Longleftrightarrow C_2 = 50e^{-(0.1)(0.01178)}N(d_1) - Ke^{-(0.05)(0.2)}N(d_2)$$

with

$$d_1 = \frac{\ln(50e^{-(0.10)(0.1178)}/45e^{-(0.05)(0.2)})}{0.3\sqrt{0.2}} + \frac{1}{2}(0.3\sqrt{0.2})$$

$$\Rightarrow d_1 = 0.8391256 \text{ so that N}(d_1) = 0.7967563 \text{ and}$$
$$d_2 = 0.7049615 \text{ so that N}(d_2) = 0.7580517$$

The price of the second European call option is then equal to

$$C_2 = \$5.598$$

Applying the "pseudo-American" call pricing rule Eq. (5.12), we find that the American call on stock ZZ should be worth

$$C^* = \max[5.685; 5.598] = \$5.685$$

Hence, under the "pseudo-American" call valuation procedure, this American call should be priced as if it were going to be exercised an instant before the ex-dividend date t_1. This isn't surprising given that we have assumed a very high dividend yield ($\delta = 10\%$) and a fairly low interest rate ($r = 5\%$). So the interest forgone on the exercise price—when the option owner exercises an instant before t_1—is more than compensated by the fact that he will earn a high dividend payment.

Unfortunately, the "pseudo-American" call valuation procedure does not give an "exact" theoretical price for American call options. Indeed, it does not take into account the flexibility left to the owner of such options. In other words, it neglects the fact that the owner can change his mind if adverse shifts in the stock price occur because he can de facto exercise or postpone his decision at any time.

Hence, by definitively restricting the occurrence dates as well as the number of exercise possibilities belonging to the owner of the option to a finite set of opportunities, the "pseudo-American" valuation procedure provides only a lower bound to the true value C' of this call:

$$C' \geq C^*$$

This lower bound is certainly a better approximation than the one we would obtain by simply ignoring the early exercise feature, but it nevertheless suggests that the Black and Scholes option pricing model is not suited to price American options whenever the dynamics of their exercise policy must be explicitly modeled.

Since the "pseudo" call price is only a lower bound, it is not appropriate for any investment strategy that tries to detect arbitrage opportunities by comparing theoretical and market values of traded options. If we were to use the "pseudo-American" call price as a benchmark, we would find many apparent "arbitrage opportunities." They would induce us to sell the call although its market price is not overpriced but simply reflecting the additional value stemming from the early exercise feature's flexibility that the "pseudo-American" call valuation method cannot capture. For that reason and given that there are other theoretical models that can explicitly handle the early exercise possibilities of American call options,[32] we would not recommend using the Black and Scholes framework for that purpose. Exceptions are either when one only needs to rely on some approximate values or lower bounds for those options' prices or when one can be fairly confident that the conditions for no-early exercise over those options' remaining time to maturity will be met.

As far as American put options are concerned, we would be even more categoric since they can always be exercised prior to maturity. Of course, the existence of dividends[33] lowers the probability of an early exercise, and it also reduces the number of optimal exercise possibilities to only those instants that immediately follow an ex-dividend date. However, once the last dividend date over the option's remaining time to maturity has elapsed, we are again left with complete uncertainty as to the timing of the exercise possibilities; that is, they no longer obey any specific occurrence rule. An equivalent to the "pseudo-American" call valuation method is therefore ruled out in the case of American put options since their early exercise possibilities are a priori unlimited. Hence, in the next chapter we will examine how one can value those options relying on more complex valuation models or simply by returning to a binomial pricing framework.

As a conclusion to this survey of the different ways in which the Black and Scholes model can be modified to allow for the pricing of a larger category of stock options, we say that it remains a robust model for the valuation of European options on dividend paying stocks, but that it still provides a crude and incomplete means of valuing American (especially put) options whenever early exercise may be optimal.

4 MEASURING THE RISK EXPOSURE OF OPTION POSITIONS

A Defining and Using Option Price Sensitivity Measures

So far, we have only focused on the Black and Scholes formula as a pricing tool that can be used to detect under- and overpriced European options and hence to build investment strategies accordingly. We will now show that the Black and Scholes model can also be employed to monitor option positions since it provides fundamental tools to evaluate an option's risk exposure. The major source of

---

[32] We will discuss in particular the model originally proposed by Roll (1977) and the binomial approach to the pricing of American call options in the next chapter.

[33] A description of the conditions leading to the put option's early exercise are given in Chapter 2, Section 3.

risk that affects an option's expected return arises from unexpected shifts in the underlying stock's price.

We saw in Chapter 4 that we can define from the Black and Scholes valuation equation a sensitivity measure of the option's price response to an infinitesimal change in the stock's price. This sensitivity measure—also called the delta of an option—is defined as follows for a call option:

$$\Delta_C = \frac{\partial C}{\partial S} = N(d_1) \geq 0 \tag{5.15}$$

where

$$d_1 = \frac{\ln(S/Ke^{-r\tau})}{\sigma\sqrt{\tau}} + \frac{1}{2}\sigma\sqrt{\tau}$$

$N(\cdot)$ = the standard normal cumulative distribution

An option's delta plays a key role in determining the Black and Scholes formula. We know[34] that this formula is based on the assumption that we can construct and maintain over time a perfectly hedged position in the stock and in the option. This position is immunized against any change in the stock price since we gain (lose) on the long position in the stock exactly what we lose (gain) on the written call.

To obtain a perfectly hedged position, how many stocks must we buy for every written call option? Precisely, we must buy $N(d_1) = \Delta_C$ shares of stocks to hedge any option sold short and to create a riskless position. Hence, the delta of a call or of a put option[35] is often called the "hedge ratio" since it tells us how many shares of stock are necessary to build a riskless position with the involved option. Since the delta of a call has a value between 0 and 1, we will generally need less than one share of stock for every written option.

We see that this absolute (in dollar terms) measure of an option's riskiness tells us that both puts and calls will experience smaller (in dollar terms) fluctuations in their prices than the underlying stock.

A closer look at Δ_C shows that this sensitivity measure depends on the stock price and on the time to maturity of the option and that it cannot therefore stay constant through time: as time passes and/or as the stock price moves, so will the option's delta.

---

[34] We discussed the procedure originally used by Black and Scholes to develop their pricing formula in Chapter 4. Note that like the binomial formula, the Black and Scholes model is based on the feasibility of a perfect hedge.

[35] For the put option:

$$\Delta_P = \frac{\partial P}{\partial S} = -N(-d_1) \leq 0$$

The delta of a put has a value which is never smaller than -1.

Hence, to maintain a hedged position over time we will need to continuously recalculate the Δ of the option and to rebalance the initial position—by buying or selling more stocks—over the option's time to maturity. We now understand why we needed the continuous-trading assumption to derive the Black and Scholes formula since it is based on a dynamic continuous hedging argument. In practice, due to transaction costs, such a frequent portfolio reallocation is unfeasible and one will generally rebalance the portfolio when the position's delta has moved noticeably from its target level.

Since we saw that an option's delta varies with the stock price level, we should not only focus on an option's delta but also on the way in which the latter measure responds to movements in the stock price. The option's gamma, defined in Section 5 of Chapter 4, will help us assess precisely how frequently one should rebalance the initial portfolio to maintain a targeted position[36] despite any stock price changes. For a call option, Γ is defined as:[37]

$$\Gamma_C = \frac{\partial^2 C}{\partial S^2} = \frac{\partial \Delta_C}{\partial S} = \frac{1}{S\sigma\sqrt{\tau}}N'(d_1) > 0 \qquad (5.16)$$

where:

$$N'(d_1) = (1/\sqrt{2\pi})e^{-d_1^2/2}$$

The higher the Γ, the higher the sensitivity of the hedge ratio (Δ) to any stock price movement, hence inducing more frequent portfolio rebalancing to maintain a target position over time. Since at-the-money options have the highest Γ, these options will require more attention than in- or out-of-the money options. This monitoring becomes even more desirable over time since the Γ of at-the-money options—contrary to other options—rises as they get very close to their expiration date.

We emphasize that Δ and Γ are very useful price sensitivities measures not only for the monitoring of riskless positions but also for the purpose of controlling the risk exposure of any strategy involving stock[38] and options or options

---

[36] We assume that the target position has been defined in terms of Δ. A hedged position should have a target Δ equal to zero to be completely insensitive to stock price movements. As we shall see later in this chapter, this condition is, however, not sufficient to guarantee a perfect hedge. For that purpose, the position's Γ should also be equal to zero over the holding period.

[37] For a put option:

$$\Gamma_P = \frac{\partial^2 P}{\partial S^2} = \frac{\partial \Delta_P}{\partial S} = \frac{1}{S\sigma\sqrt{\tau}}N'(d_1) > 0$$

The gammas of identical European call and put options are equivalent.

[38] Note that for a stock:

$$\Delta_S = \frac{\partial S}{\partial S} = 1$$

$$\Gamma_S = \frac{\partial^2 S}{\partial S^2} = 0$$

alone. For example, if one has bullish expectations about the stock price's future movements, one might want to select an option with a high Δ (i.e., with large positive option price shifts occurring in response to increases in the underlying stock price) and with a positive Γ to profit from any large movements in the stock price. Typically, this can be accomplished by buying an at-the-money call option on the underlying stock. However, if one is not sure that such large price fluctuations can only occur on the positive side (i.e., by increases in the underlying stock price) one may want to choose a less risky bullish position (or in other words) an in-the-money call option with a smaller Γ.

B A Numerical Example

We can now use an example to illustrate how the Δ and the Γ of options can be used to create more complex strategies involving two or more financial assets. Suppose we want to create a riskless hedge with the stock of company BIP and the underlying call written on that stock given the following information on those assets:

$$S_o = \$41$$
$$K = \$40$$
$$\tau = 0.5$$
$$r = 0.05$$
$$\sigma = 0.30$$

Using the Black and Scholes formula Eq. (4.18), we find that the current price C_0 of this call is equal to

$$C_0 = 41 \times N(0.3401) - 40e^{-(0.05)(0.5)}N(0.1278)$$
$$= \$4.465$$

If we want to create a perfect hedge with this call option and the underlying stock, we must set up our portfolio in such a way that it is "delta-neutral" (the Δ^* of the portfolio equals zero), hence:

$$n_1\Delta_S + n_2\Delta_C = \Delta^* = 0$$

where

$$\Delta^* = \text{the delta of the portfolio}$$
$$n_1 = \text{number of shares of stock in the portfolio}$$
$$n_2 = \text{number of call options in the portfolio}$$

Since we know that Δ_S is equal to one, this requires that:

$$n_1 = -n_2\Delta_C$$

In other words, every option sold short ($n_2 = -1$) will be hedged by a number of shares held long (n_1) equal to the call's delta.

Note that from the Black and Scholes computation of Eq. (4.18), we obtained the hedge ratio's value as equal to

$$N(d_1) = N(0.3401) = \Delta_C = 0.633$$

So if we start by selling 1000 options short, we simultaneously need to buy 633 shares of stock to create the "delta-neutral" or perfectly hedged position.

Accordingly, the initial value of our portfolio will be equal to

$$(-1000 \times 4.465) + (633 \times 41) = \$21488$$

Now suppose that at the end of the day stock BIP closed at \$40.5. How will this decrease in the stock price affect our position? First, we need to compute the new price of the option C_1 using Eq. (4.18), and we obtain

$$C_1 = \$4.154$$

So at the end of the day our portfolio will be worth:

$$(-1000 \times 4.154) + (633 \times 40.5) = \$21482.5$$

The loss of \$5.5, corresponding to less than 0.03% of the initial value of the portfolio, is due to the fact that a delta-neutral position is not completely immunized against stock price movements. Indeed, for infinitesimal shifts in the stock price the portfolio is hedged; however, for larger stock price movements, the portfolio's value can only decrease. Although the Δ^* of the position was set equal to zero, this is true because we didn't care about the value of its gamma (Γ^*).

From the definition of Γ_C and from the Black and Scholes formula, we know that its value satisfies Eq. (5.16):

$$\Gamma_C = \frac{1}{S\sigma\sqrt{\tau}}N'(d_1) = 0.0433$$

Since the Γ_S of a stock is always equal to zero, the gamma (Γ^*) of the initial position is indeed equal to

$$\Gamma^* = -1000(0.0433) + (663) \times 0 = -43.3$$

The highly negative value of our position's gamma is due to the fact that we sold short 1000 options that are at-the-money, and thereby induced a high exposure of our position's delta to any given change in stock BIP's price. Moreover, the negative gamma of the position implies that we can only lose from a given stock price movement and that the portfolio's large gamma value—in absolute terms—requires a very frequent rebalancing of the portfolio if we wish to maintain its delta-neutral or perfect hedge feature over time.

To see that this is indeed true, notice that at the end of the day when the stock price drops to \$40.5, the call's delta becomes equal to

$$\Delta_{C_1} = 0.6112$$

Hence, we are not hedged anymore since now, for any option sold short, we only need 0.6112—and not 0.633—stocks held long in our portfolio.

Given that we have initially sold short 1000 options, we must therefore sell[39] 22 (633-611) shares of stock to remain "delta-neutral" at the end of the day. This confirms the fact that the delta of a position will be very sensitive to stock price changes—and hence requires frequent adjustments—the higher (in absolute terms) the value of its gamma. It also suggests that unless "very frequent" trading can indeed be accomplished, a "delta-neutral" position or otherwise called perfect hedge is not perfect at all as long as the position is not simultaneously tracking a zero Γ target over time.[40]

Of course, one might be willing to elaborate similar strategies that focus not only on the price response of an option to changes in the underlying stock price but also to changes in the stock price volatility, in the time to maturity of the option, et cetera, by relying on other price sensitivities measures ($\partial C / \partial \sigma, \partial C / \partial \tau$) derived from the Black and Scholes formula.

Of particular interest is a measure of the option's price sensitivity to the passage of time, often referred to as the option's theta (θ). The option's theta measures how the price of an option is affected by the passage of time, and it can therefore be computed by deriving the call's price with respect to time (t). However since the passage of time and the time to maturity of an option are exactly negatively related, the θ of a call (or put) can also be computed as the negative of the derivative of the option's price with respect to its time to maturity, hence:

$$\theta_C = -\frac{\partial C}{\partial \tau} < 0$$

$$\theta_P = -\frac{\partial P}{\partial \tau} \gtrless 0$$

Generally, the θ of both put and call options will be negative,[41] suggesting that—ceteris paribus—any long position in either a call or a put will lose its "time value" with the passage of time. This negative "time bias" inherent to options can only be avoided by setting up a θ neutral position consisting of short and long holdings in options that have the same θ or reversed by shorting either a put or a

---

[39] We consider the fact that fractions of stock cannot be traded hence we only sell 611 instead of 611.2 shares of stock.

[40] Since the Γ of a stock is equal to zero, we will generally require at least two options to create a zero-delta and a zero-gamma position. The positive value of both put and calls options' Γ requires that one be able to exactly offset the Γ of the long option's position with that of the short option's position. This confirms that we need at least three assets since we also require that the total position be delta-neutral.

[41] The only exception has to be found for European short term in- and out-of-the money put options whose θ actually increases with the passage of time.

call option. However, in this latter case the expected gain on the written option resulting from the passage of time must be weighted against the potential losses that may happen with adverse stock price movements whenever the short option position is naked.

Hence, one should always try to simultaneously monitor a portfolio or an option's exposure to the various parameters that may affect the option's price and therefore its expected return over the holding period. In the context of the Black and Scholes model, there is only one source of uncertainty, namely that stemming from unexpected stock price movements. If one agrees with this statement, then option positions should essentially be monitored with respect to their Δ and their Γ. Contrarily, if one believes that volatility is not constant and that interest rates change stochastically over time, then the sensitivity of the option's price with respect to those factors must also be assessed and monitored. Although the Black and Scholes model does not explicitly account for those sources of uncertainty, it still provides—through the theoretical values of $\partial C / \partial \sigma$ and $\partial C / \partial r$—useful tools to quantify the potential for gains or losses arising from a shift in the stock returns' volatility or from a change in the interest rate level.

C   The Concept of an Option's Price Elasticity

So far we have essentially focused on dollar measures of an option's price response to a given absolute change in the stock price, time to maturity, etcetera. However, for the purpose of measuring an option's risk we must be able to assess how uncertainty affects an option's return—or in other words, its percentage price change—since risk is essentially defined as the degree of dispersion of the returns around their expected value.

Therefore we will assume—in the spirit of Black and Scholes single factor option pricing model—that the "only" source of risk affecting options' prices (and hence returns) has to be found in unexpected stock price movements. Hence, if we know how to measure a stock's riskiness (through its standard deviation, or its beta, for example) we can easily determine the resulting option's riskiness using the concept of "elasticity."

The price elasticity Ω measures the relative option's price response to a given percentage change in the stock price. Hence, the elasticity of a call option is equal to

$$\Omega_C = \frac{\partial C}{\partial S} \cdot \frac{S}{C} = N(d_1) \cdot \frac{S}{C} = \Delta_C \cdot \frac{S}{C} \tag{5.17}$$

Typically, if the option price is a convex function of the stock price,[42] a call option's elasticity will always be equal to or greater than one, suggesting that a

---

[42] We have shown in Chapter 4 that under the lognormal stock price distribution this is indeed the case since $\partial C / \partial S \geq 0$ and $\partial^2 C / \partial S^2 \geq 0$. Merton (1973) stated that a sufficient condition for the option price to be a convex function of the stock price is that the stock return distribution be independent of the stock price level.

1% increase in the stock price will be followed by an increase of $(\Omega_C \cdot 1\%)$ more than 1% in the call price.

The elasticity of a put option can similarly be defined as

$$\Omega_P = \frac{\partial P}{\partial S} \cdot \frac{P}{S} = -N(-d_1) \cdot \frac{S}{P} = \Delta_P \cdot \frac{S}{P} \qquad (5.18)$$

It will always be less than zero, suggesting that a put may, if $\Omega_P < -1$, or may not, if $-1 \leq \Omega_P \leq 0$, have larger—in absolute terms—percentage price changes than the underlying stock. It follows that although options are generally viewed as riskier financial assets than their underlying stocks, this statement is not necessarily valid for all put options.

Furthermore, we should also emphasize the fact that the elasticity of both put and call options will be greater[43] the more "out-of-the money" they are and the closer they get to their maturity date.

Now that we have defined an option's elasticity we can easily compute its riskiness measures simply by multiplying the underlying stock's dispersion measures by the relevant elasticity factor. Given that the most common measure of a stock's variability is given by the standard deviation of its returns, we can compute the standard deviation of a call or a put's returns[44] as follows:

$$\sigma_C = \Omega_C \cdot \sigma_S \qquad (5.19)$$

$$\sigma_P = -\Omega_P \cdot \sigma_S \qquad (5.20)$$

where

σ_S denotes the annualized standard deviation of the stock returns

σ_C and σ_P denote the annualized standard deviations of the call and the put returns.

Another frequently computed risk measure for stocks is the beta coefficient.[45] The beta measures the nondiversifiable or systematic portion of a stock's riskiness. More precisely, it tells us how a given stock responds to unexpected fluctuations in the market. An aggressive stock will amplify market movements (its beta will

---

[43] We are referring to the absolute values of Ω_P for different put options in this comparison.

[44] $\sigma_P = -\Omega_P \sigma_S$; we add the sign minus to the definition of σ_P, since Ω_P is negative and a standard deviation is by definition positive.

[45] The coefficient beta of a stock is defined as

$$\beta_i = \frac{\text{Cov}(\tilde{R}_i, \tilde{R}_m)}{\text{Var}(\tilde{R}_m)}$$

where

$\tilde{R}_i, \tilde{R}_m$ denote the returns of stock i and of the market respectively.
$\text{Var}(\tilde{R}_m)$ denotes the variance of the returns on the market portfolio.
$\text{Cov}(\tilde{R}_i, \tilde{R}_m)$ denotes the covariance between the returns of stock i and those of the market portfolio

be greater than one) while a defensive stock will attenuate them (its beta will be smaller than one). Once the beta of the underlying stock (β_S) has been estimated, we only need to use the elasticity coefficients Ω_C and Ω_P to compute the beta of call or put options, hence:

$$\beta_C = \Omega_C \cdot \beta_S \qquad\qquad (5.21)$$

$$\beta_P = \Omega_P \cdot \beta_S \qquad\qquad (5.22)$$

where

β_S is defined as the beta of the underlying stock

β_C and β_P are defined as the beta coefficients of the call and the put option respectively

Focusing on both the standard deviations and the beta coefficients of individual call and put options we can conclude that a call option is a more risky and more volatile instrument than the underlying stock (since $\Omega_C \geq 1$) while the same statement is only true for put options that have an elasticity (Ω_P) smaller than -1.

We now have a complete description of an option's risk and return[46] characteristics as they relate to the same characteristics of the underlying stock. It will be useful to illustrate how these parameters should be computed and analyzed in practice. To do this, let us come back to the data on stock BIP used in our previous example (see Section 4B). We observed the following data initially:

$$S_0 = \$41$$

$$C_0 = \$4.465$$

$$\sigma = 30\%$$

$$N(d_1) = \Delta_C = 0.633$$

At the end of the day, the stock price dropped to $S_1 = \$40.5$, hence the rate of return R_S on the stock during that day was equal to

---

[46] Focusing on relationships in Eqs. (5.18) and (5.17) we can define an option's rate of return over a small time interval $((\Delta t) \to 0)$ in terms of the rate of return (relative price change) of the stock since:

$$\frac{\Delta C}{C} \cong \Omega_C \cdot \frac{\Delta S}{S}$$

$$\frac{\Delta P}{P} \cong \Omega_P \cdot \frac{\Delta S}{S}$$

where

$\Delta C/C$ and $\Delta P/P$ represent the (almost) instantaneous rates of return on the call and on the put option respectively, $\Delta S/S$ represents the (almost) instantaneous rate of return on the stock.

$$R_S = \frac{S_1 - S_0}{S_0} = -1.22\%$$

We can compute the call's elasticity Ω_C from Eq. (5.17):

$$\Omega_C = \Delta_C \frac{S_0}{C_0} = 0.633 \times \frac{41}{4.465} = 5.8125$$

From there we can estimate the rate of return on the option—or its relative price change—induced by the 1.22% price drop in stock BIP's price:

$$R_C^* \cong \Omega_C \cdot R_S = 5.8125 \times (-1.22\%) = -7.09\%$$

Indeed, if we calculate the "true" rate of return of the call knowing that the new theoretical call price (C_1) was equal to \$4.154 at the end of the day, we would obtain:

$$R_C = \frac{C_1 - C_0}{C_0} = \frac{4.154 - 4.465}{4.465} = -6.96\%$$

This confirms the well-known statement that for small relative price changes, the elasticity can be reliably used to predict the relative price change of the derived asset. Since the call's elasticity is fairly high, we see that the call's value drops nearly six times more—in relative terms—than did stock BIP.

Knowing that the volatility of the stock is equal to 30%, we can compute the standard deviation of the call option using Eq. (5.19):

$$\sigma_C = (30\%) \times (5.8125) = 174.375\%$$

This needs no further comments that an at-the-money call option is a much riskier security than its underlying stock since its annualized standard deviation[47] is worth nearly 175%. Hence, although the expected return on a call option is much greater than the expected return on the underlying stock this is essentially "a reward" for the higher volatility associated to this derivative instrument.

Finally, we must remember that, like all elasticity measures, Ω_C and Ω_P are only valid for infinitesimal percentage changes in the stock price. Under the lognormal distribution these are the only type of stock price changes one would expect to occur over a short-time interval, and this suggests that the price elasticities Ω_C and Ω_P can under this stock price path behavior validly measure the instantaneous riskiness of both put and call options relative to that of the underlying stock. However, if stock price movements are essentially characterized by large infrequent jumps, then we can no longer use those price elasticities to measure an option's resulting return dispersion.

---

[47] Note that since we are dealing with daily figures:

The stock's daily standard deviation of returns is equal to $(1/\sqrt{365})(0.3) = 1.5\%$.

The call option's daily standard deviation is equal to $(1/\sqrt{365})(1.74375) = 9.1\%$.

Moreover, a closer look at Eqs. (5.18) and (5.17) suggests that Ω_P and Ω_C are functions of the option's remaining time to maturity (τ) and of the stock's price level (S). Hence, these elasticity measures will change over time and/or with any change in the stock price level, thereby suggesting that the standard deviation and the beta of an option are not constant over time.

The elasticity and the riskiness measures—the standard deviation and the beta—of an option are only valid over very short time intervals, and in practical portfolio management decisions they should be recalculated as often as possible. This variability in an option's risk exposure also clearly points out how inappropriate it is to estimate the current standard deviation or the beta of an option from the historically estimated standard deviation or beta of the underlying stock. A more precise static risk measure can be obtained by computing the stock's implied standard deviation and then—according to Eqs. (5.19) or (5.20)—the resulting option's standard deviation.

Hence, we can conclude by saying that if options are only subject to one source of uncertainty resulting from continuous unexpected infinitesimal movements in the stock price, the Black and Scholes model will provide useful and reliable tools to measure and monitor their nonstationary risk exposure over time. This still leaves us, however, in the next chapter, with the task of assessing whether the stock price movements are "really" smooth over time and whether they represent the only relevant risk factor to be considered when we price or manage an option's position. The answers to these questions are essential for understanding the limits of the Black and Scholes model and for seeking solutions and models that give a better representation of an option's price dynamics.

5 CONCLUSION

We are now able to understand and use the Black and Scholes model to price and analyze a variety of option positions. We are also aware of the limits—in terms of market conditions and option characteristics—to this model's applicability, which essentially refer to its inability to price American call and put options on dividend paying stocks. Despite that fact, the Black and Scholes model represents a fundamental contribution to the option pricing theory that leads to a simple pricing formula—unlike many other financial models—which relies almost exclusively on observable parameters, and that provides several risk exposure measures to monitor numerous types of dynamically managed option strategies.

One question remains, namely how accurate are the model's theoretical prices? Or in other words, can we be confident when we identify its results to "true" or "fair" option values? To answer this question, we must examine the empirical evidence regarding the model's pricing performance and ask ourselves whether its theoretical assumptions can still be maintained in light of these empirical findings. We shall therefore discuss in the next chapter the main weaknesses attributed to the Black and Scholes model's underlying theoretical framework and analyze the most important academic research since 1973 that has contributed to the improvement and extension of this "pioneering" contingent claims valuation model.

CHAPTER 6

IMPROVING AND
EXTENDING
THE SINGLE
FACTOR
OPTION
PRICING
MODEL

1   INTRODUCTION

Since the development of the Black and Scholes option pricing model in 1973, there have been several empirical studies[1] that have focused on its ability to price put and call stock options consistently. Allowing for the problems related to the nonsimultaneity of options' and stocks' closing prices, to the bid and ask spread, and to the neglected transaction costs, those tests have shown that the theoretical model does nevertheless induce some price biases. According to Black (1976a) and Macbeth and Merville (1979, 1980), the model tends to overprice in-the-money call options while it underprices out-of-the-money call options. Moreover,

---

[1] Some of the well-known studies were conducted by Black and Scholes (1972), Galai (1977), Chiras and Manaster (1978), Macbeth and Merville (1980), Sterk (1983), and Whaley (1982).

Whaley (1982) found that even a model adjusted for the dividend payments—
by a constant dividend yield assumption—will not price American call options
adequately on average because it fails to properly account for the early exercise
feature of those options.

Hence, despite the great popularity of the Black and Scholes model, there are
still some "caveats" and anomalies limiting the ability of its theoretical prices to
detect under- or overpriced options. This assertion is particularly true for strategies
that rely on the Black and Scholes theoretical values to detect mispricing among
in- or out-of-the-money call options and among American options that may be
optimally exercised prior to their expiration date.

In this chapter we will therefore focus on the main assumptions of the Black
and Scholes model that need to be revised to account for the "real" economic
environment in which options are traded. Since it is obvious that all underlying hypotheses cannot be simultaneously relaxed, we will discuss the effects of
removing each restrictive assumption individually.

First we will focus on the constant risk-free interest rate assumption and
show how this unrealistic description of the interest rate behavior can be removed
to capture the effect of interest rate risk on the pricing of options. Second, we will
return to the problem created by the early-exercise feature of American options
and present some theoretical models that have tried to account explicitly for them.

The third critical assumption of the Black and Scholes model—which certainly deserves the most attention—claims that the underlying stock's price is
lognormally distributed. Since the stock price represents the only state variable
with which we price the option, it is essential that its stochastic path over time be
correctly described. In particular, we will examine whether it is realistic to assume
that the stock returns have a stationary distribution (constant mean and variance
per unit of time) and also whether stock prices will only change smoothly. Recent
evidence from the worldwide stock market "crash" on October 19, 1987 clearly
emphasizes that infrequent large jumps in stock prices should not be excluded.
Finally, we will analyze the effects of some institutional features of both stock and
option markets (for example, restrictions on short sales, bid and ask spreads, liquidity, etc.) on the pricing performance of any contingent claim valuation model
developed under the "perfect market" paradigm.

At the end of this survey on the main improvements and extensions that
have enriched the option pricing theory since 1973, we will be able to distinguish
the problems that have been successfully solved from those that require further
research to improve the performance of existing stock option pricing models.

2   RELAXING THE CONSTANT RISK-FREE
INTEREST RATE ASSUMPTION

The Black and Scholes model assumes a flat and constant term structure of
interest rates, and hence prices options of all maturities with the same riskless interest rate r. We have already shown in Chapter 5 that the formula can

be modified to account for the fact that default-free discount bonds with different maturities bear different yields. Hence, to explicitly allow for the possibility of a nonflat term structure of interest rates, one should price each option with the riskless rate computed from the price of a default-free discount bond whose maturity is as close as possible to that of the option.

Unfortunately, this modification is only valid if we assume that interest rates change predictably over time.[2]

This is obviously a restrictive assumption since unexpected interest rate shifts are unquestionably the major source of uncertainty in the bond market. Given that interest rates vary stochastically over time, we need to modify the Black and Scholes option pricing formula to introduce a second variable that will reflect the effects of interest rate risk on option prices. Merton (1973) was the first to explicitly derive a European call valuation model that relied on a stochastic interest rate. He assumed that the price $B(\tau)$ of a discount bond maturing in $\tau(= T - t)$ periods is a random variable distributed according to a nonstationary[3] process. Hence, its instantaneous return $(dB(\tau)/B(\tau))$ can no more be assumed constant—or changing predictably over time—since it is subject to unexpected shifts that definitively affect option prices.

In such a framework, the prices of the stock and the default-free ordinary bond whose maturity matches that of the option are the two relevant random variables that determine the price of a European call option. Then, following a similar procedure to the one originally suggested by Black and Scholes, Merton constructed an arbitrage portfolio[4] with the call option, the default-free discount bond, and the stock. This zero net investment portfolio bears no risk and it should therefore, in equilibrium, earn a zero expected (and realized) return to avoid arbitrage opportunities among these three assets.

From this equilibrium condition, Merton derived a partial differential equation whose solution is the price of a European call that is subject to both stock

---

[2] If we denote by $R(t,T)$, the spot rate derived from the price of a default-free discount bond maturing in $\tau(= T - t)$ years:

$$R(t, T) = -\frac{1}{T - t} \ln B(t, T) = \frac{1}{T - t} \int_{t}^{T} r(s)ds$$

where $r(s)$ represents the instantaneous continuously compounded interest rate that is changing predictably over time. Hence, we see that in this case the spot rate $R(t, T)$ is simply the average of the instantaneous interest rates—derived from immediately maturing discount bonds—prevailing over the period $T - t$.

[3] In Merton's model, the instantaneous return on the bond $(dB(\tau)/B(\tau))$ has an expected mean $\mu(B, \tau)$ that can depend on the bond's price level, on its time to maturity, et cetera. However, the instantaneous variance $\gamma^2(\tau)$ of its returns is restricted to be at most a deterministic function of the bond's time to maturity (τ).

[4] An arbitrage portfolio is riskless and requires zero net investment. For example, if we sell the call and buy "delta" shares of stock we will take an additional position (by issuing or short selling) in the discount bond to form an arbitrage portfolio.

price and interest rate uncertainty. In Merton's model the European call will satisfy the following valuation equation:

$$C(S, B, \tau) = SN(X_1) - KB(\tau)N(X_2) \qquad (6.1)$$

where

$C(S, B, \tau) =$ the price of a European call option maturing in τ years as a function of the stock price (S) and the discount default-free bond price $B(\tau)$

$B(\tau) =$ the price at time t of a default-free discount bond maturing in τ periods

$$X_1 = \frac{\ln(S/K) - \ln B(\tau) + (\hat{\sigma}^2/2)\tau}{\hat{\sigma}\sqrt{\tau}}$$

$$X_2 = \frac{\ln(S/K) - \ln B(\tau) - (\hat{\sigma}^2/2)\tau}{\hat{\sigma}\sqrt{\tau}}$$

$N(\cdot) =$ the standard normal cumulative distribution function $\hat{\sigma}^2 = \sigma^2 + \gamma^2 - 2\rho\gamma\sigma$, with σ^2 defining the variance of stock returns, γ^2 defining the variance of bond returns, and ρ defining the correlation coefficient between unexpected changes in the stock returns and in the discount bond returns.

Equation (6.1) is an extended version of the Black and Scholes European call option pricing formula Eq. (4.18) and it differs from the latter in replacing the constant[5] discount factor $(e^{-r\tau})$ by the now stochastic discount factor $B(\tau)$—which is simply the price of the discount bond—and in depending on the variance of the returns of the stock (σ^2) and of the bond (γ^2) as well as on the interdependence between bond and stock returns' unexpected co-movements through the covariance term $-2\rho\gamma\sigma$. We can hence interpret $\hat{\sigma}^2$ as the total variance—stemming from bond and stock individual and correlated unexpected shifts—that will affect the call's price.

Notice that although the formula is very similar to the single factor Black and Scholes pricing equation, it depends on three unobservable parameters: the variance of the stock returns (σ^2), the variance of the discount bond returns (γ^2), and the correlation coefficient (ρ) between unexpected stock and bond returns. It is therefore subject to additional estimation problems that may alter its pricing reliability.

---

[5] Remember that when interest rates are assumed to be constant and the term structure is flat, the price of a discount bond of any maturity will satisfy:

$$B(\tau) = e^{-r(T-t)} = e^{-r\tau}$$

where r is the instantaneous continuously compounded riskless interest rate.

Moreover, the application of this formula is severely compromised in many financial markets where default-free borrowing instruments without coupons are simply never or only occasionally issued. Hence, it might be very difficult or even impossible to find a traded riskless bond for every call option we wish to value according to Eq. (6.1).

In the cases where default-free discount bonds are not traded, we can still use a given interest rate, for example the short-term interest rate, instead of the bond price itself, as the relevant state variable inducing stochastic shifts in the entire term structure of interest rates. Given that the short-term interest rate is not a traded asset, we will not be able to price the call option in a preference-free setting because the market premium for short-term interest rate risk is unobservable. [6]

Hence, the resulting valuation model will be much more complex since it requires estimations of the market price of short-term interest rate risk and the expected change in the short-term rate in addition to the variance of stock returns, the variance of the short-term rate changes, and the coefficient of correlation between the short-term interest rate changes and stock returns. This additional complexity[7]—which arises every time one introduces a state variable that is not defined as the price of a traded asset—can only be justified if interest rate risk is really an important factor for the pricing of stock options.

Unfortunately, there have been no empirical tests that enable us to conclude Merton's two factor option pricing model prices European call options more precisely than the Black and Scholes formula. Given the lack of empirical evidence as to whether interest rate risk is really an important factor for the pricing of stock options and given that the sensitivity of an option's price with respect to a change in the interest rate is typically small,[8] we may say that in the absence of default-free discount bonds, one should simply rely on the deterministic interest rate assumption presented in Chapter 5 and apply the Black and Scholes formula Eq. (4.18). Of course, for stock options that have a longer maturity (this will typically be the case for warrants issued by corporations) and for options written on some other financial instruments (such as Treasury bills or bonds), interest rate risk will become an important—and for bond options, essential—issue that cannot be ignored even if it requires the computation of rather complex valuation models.

---

[6] Unlike the market premium for stock price risk that can be observed and is defined as the excess return—over the risk-free rate—from expected stock price relative changes plus the dividend payments.

[7] The introduction of a nontraded state variable breaks the preference-free framework in which standard option pricing models are cast. We then always observe that the pricing equation does depend on the expected rate of change in the state variable and on the market price of this state variable's risk while these two parameters did not appear in either the Black and Scholes or the binomial stock options pricing models.

[8] This can be seen from our example in Chapter 4, Section 5, where we computed the price of a six months put option for two different interest rates (5% and 6% respectively) and noticed that a 100 basis points increase in the interest rate only decreased the put's price by 8 cents.

3 THE EARLY EXERCISE FEATURE OF AMERICAN OPTIONS REVISITED

One of the most disturbing assumptions underlying the Black and Scholes model states that it applies only to those options that can be exercised at their expiration date. As we have shown in Chapter 5, only under very special conditions can we then use the Black and Scholes model to price American call options, and generally whenever early exercise may be optimal the formula will only give lower bounds for the prices of both American put and call options. Since standardized stock option contracts traded on most exchanges are of the American type, we have both a theoretical gap as well as a practical need to fulfill that extend beyond the Black and Scholes pricing framework.

We will therefore present some theoretical models that address the early exercise feature of American options explicitly and thereby attempt to provide theoretical values for these options under very general conditions with regard to the existence of dividend flows and the frequency of early exercise.

A   The Binomial Approach

Since the binomial approach values options in a recursive step-by-step procedure, it provides us with the required sequential ability to check for the possibility of early exercise. Indeed, we can make the step sizes as small as required and allow for a nearly "continuous" early exercise checking procedure that is particularly suited for put options since their early exercise feature does not obey any particular timing rule.

To illustrate how the binomial framework should be used to price American options, we will go through the formal steps, assuming that we have to value a call option written on a stock that pays a constant dividend yield δ.[9] The notation will be the same as the one used in Chapter 3 when we developed the binomial pricing formula for European options.

The stock price path must be described in such a way as to allow on each ex-dividend date for the fact that the stock price has dropped by the amount of the dividend flow (δS). Combining the following restriction with the multiplicative binomial stock price path, we can illustrate its evolution as shown in Fig. 6.1,[10]

---

[9] Remember that the early exercise feature of American call options can only become "valuable" if the underlying stock pays dividends. To simplify the formal derivation of the American call valuation model we have assumed a constant dividend yield δ. The analysis would be essentially the same had we instead assumed a constant dollar dividend payment. The latter dividend pattern would only require more computations since the stock price and option price trees expand more rapidly when we consider such a dividend policy. Any dividend policy for which the dividends are at most a deterministic function of the stock price and time will allow us to use the binomial approach. The reasons for this restriction were explained in Chapter 5, Section 3.

[10] Here we have assumed that at the end of each step, the stock is paying a dividend.

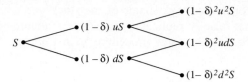

FIGURE 6.1
The binomial stock price path.

where

δ = the constant dividend yield

S = the initial stock price

$u = (1 + U)$ the growth factor of the stock price given that it increases by $U\%$ over the interval

$d = (1 + D)$ the growth factor of the stock price given that it decreases by $D\%$ over the interval

q = the probability that the stock price will increase by $U\%$ over the interval

Before we can value the call, we must first separate the nodes that correspond to ex-dividend dates from those where no dividend is actually paid. Hence for a total of n steps in the stock price, we will use m_n to denote the total number of dividend payments that actually occurred. Therefore, the final stock price satisfies

$$S^* = u^j d^{n-j}(1 - \delta)^{m_n} S \tag{6.2}$$

where

j = total number of upward movements in the stock price ($j = 0, 1, 2, \ldots, n$)

m_n = total number of dividend payments dates over the entire period ($m_n \leq n$)

S^* = price of the stock after n periods and given that the stock price experienced j upward movements

Similarly, we can use m_{n-i} to denote the number of ex-dividend dates that already occurred after any arbitrary number $(n - i)$ of steps. For example, if $n - i = 2$ and the stock already paid one dividend ($m_{n-i} = 1$), we can determine the stock price after two $(n - i)$ steps as follows:

$$S_2 = u^j d^{n-i-j}(1 - \delta)^{m_{n-i}} = u^j d^{2-j}(1 - \delta)^1$$

We can now value the American call with the same recursive procedure we used earlier to value European options assuming in a first stage that the call has only one period until expiration ($n = 1$) and that the stock pays a dividend at the end of that period. The American call's price (C') path is illustrated in Fig 6.2.

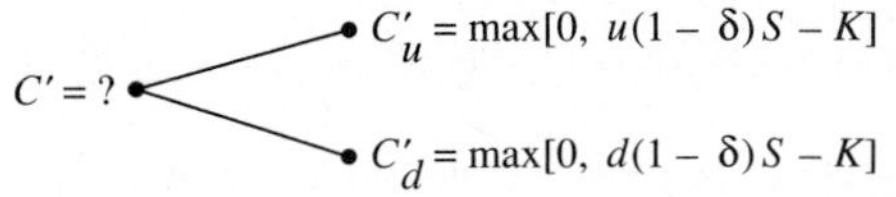

$C' = ?$

$C'_u = \max[0, u(1 - \delta)S - K]$

$C'_d = \max[0, d(1 - \delta)S - K]$

FIGURE 6.2
Price path of an American call on a dividend paying stock.

Hence, we can select a portfolio consisting of Δ shares of the stock and a dollar amount Y of default-free bonds that exactly replicates the payoff structure of this call at the end of the period. Following the same procedure as in Chapter 3, we find

$$C = [pC'_u + (1 - p)C'_d]/R \tag{3.8}$$

where

$$p = \frac{R - d}{u - d} \text{ and } (1 - p) = \frac{u - R}{u - d}$$

However, Eq. (3.8) only gives the price of this American call if his unexercised value is greater than its exercise value $(S - K)$, otherwise the holder of the call will exercise his call before the expiration date (which is also an ex-dividend date). Hence, the value of a one-period American call will satisfy the following relation:

$$C' = \{\max[S - K; [pC'u + (1 - p)C'd]/R]\} \tag{6.3}$$

We can follow the same recursive procedure to value a two- or three- or n-period American call option. At each step, we compute the value of the call as being equal to the value of an equivalent portfolio consisting of Δ shares of stock and a Y-dollar investment in riskless bonds.[11] The latter value of the call will then be compared to its current exercise value to identify the "true" American call's price at that given node as the highest of these two values.

We can already see that the early exercise feature necessitates that one checks at each node preceding a dividend payment date whether the computed binomial price is greater than, equal to, or smaller than the exercise value of the call at that node. Hence, an American call option will always have to be priced with a sequential procedure because we cannot find an analytical solution for its price analogous to the binomial European call option pricing Eq. (3.17).

We can now state the general recursive valuation formula for an American call that still has i periods until expiration as follows:[12]

---

[11] Note that at each ex-dividend date, the owner of the replicating portfolio that is long in the stock will invest the amount of the dividends in riskless bonds. If we had instead a short position in the stock we would have to borrow the amount of the dividends so that we can restitute them at the end of the period.

[12] In fact, whenever the subsequent node does not correspond to an ex-dividend date, Eq. (6.4) simplifies to

$$C'(n, i)^* = [pC'_u(n, i - 1) + (1 - p)C'_d(n, i - 1)]/R \tag{6.4'}$$

where

$C'(n, i)^*$ is the price of an American call at the $n - i^{th}$ node given that the stock does not pay a dividend an node $n - i - 1$.

$$C'(n, i) = \max\{u^j d^{n-i-j}(1 - \delta)^{m_{n-i}} S - K;$$

$$[pC'_u(n, i - 1) + (1 - p)C'_d(n, i - 1)]/R\} \quad (6.4)$$

where

$C'(n, i)$ = the value of an American call that still has i periods to live

m_{n-i} = the total number of ex-dividend dates at the $(n - i)^{th}$ node

$C'_u(n, i - 1)$ = the price of the American call one period ahead (at node $n - i - 1$) given that the stock made an upward movement

$C'_d(n, i - 1)$ = the price of the American call one period ahead (at node $n - i - 1$) given that the stock price experienced a downward movement

$p = (R - d)/(u - d)$ and $(1 - p) = (u - R)/(u - d)$

A Numerical Example. We can now illustrate with an example how an American call option should be valued according to the binomial step-by-step procedure. Suppose we observe that stock M.I.A. is currently trading at $80 and that we want to value a two-period ($n = 2$) call option written on that stock with an exercise price of $45.

Moreover, we know that the stock price process is driven by the two growth rate factors $u = 1.5$ and $d = 0.5$. The interest rate per period is equal to 10%, hence $R = 1.1$ and $p = (R - d)/(u - d) = 0.6$.

Stock M.I.A. has a constant dividend yield of 20%, and there is only one ex-dividend date (when $n - i = 1$) over the call's remaining time to maturity.

We can now illustrate the stock's price path over those two periods as shown in Fig. 6.3(a). When we plug in the values of S, u, d and δ, we find that stock M.I.A. evolves as shown in Fig. 6.3(b).

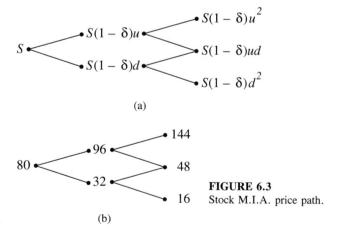

(a)

(b)

FIGURE 6.3
Stock M.I.A. price path.

We will now proceed backwards and value the call one period before its expiration date (when $n - i = 1$). Graphically, we observe the M.I.A. call price path as shown in Fig 6.4.

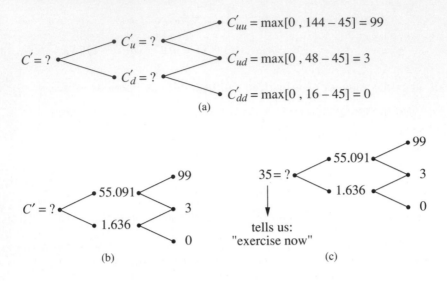

(a)

(b)

(c)

35 = ?

tells us:
"exercise now"

FIGURE 6.4
Call M.I.A. price path.

Using Eq. (6.4) we can compute the two unexercised values C'_u and C'_d of call M.I.A. one period before its expiration:

$$C'_u = [pC'_{uu} + (1 - p)C'_{ud}]/R$$
$$= [(0.6) \times 99 + (0.4) \times 3]/1.1$$
$$= 55.091$$

and

$$C'_d = [pC'_{ud} + (1 - p)C'_{uu}]/R$$
$$= [(0.6) \times 3 + (0.4) \times 0]/1.1$$
$$= 1.636$$

Since there was no dividend payment at the call's expiration date (when $n - i = 0$), we don't need to check whether the call's prices one period before—C'_u and C'_d—are greater than their exercise values[13] since this condition only applies when a dividend is paid subsequently. Hence, the call's price path can now be completed as shown in Fig. 6.4(b).

---

[13] Indeed, the reader may easily verify that

$$C'_u = 55.091 > 96 - 45$$

and that

$$C'_d = 1.636 > 32 - 45$$

This confirms that there will never be an incentive to exercise the call if the following node does not coincide with an ex-dividend date. However, when the opposite is true will we need to compare the binomial option prices to the exercise values of the American call.

To determine the current call's price C' (when $n - i = 2$) we again use the same recurrent relationship Eq. (6.4) to compute the binomial option price:

$$C = [p \cdot C'_u + (1 - p)C'_d]/R$$
$$= (0.6 \times 55.091 + 0.4 \times 1.636)/1.1$$
$$= 30.645$$

However, since we are now determining the call's price (at $n = 2$) just before an ex-dividend date, we will also apply the maximization condition of Eq. (6.4) to determine whether the computed call's price (30.645) is greater than the call's exercise value.

The American call's exercise value two periods before expiration is equal to

$$S - K = 80 - 45 = 35$$

Applying Eq. (6.4) we find

$$C' = \max[30.646; 35] = \$35$$

Therefore, the call should be immediately exercised—since $35 > 30.646$—and its current price is equal to its exercise value of $35. We can therefore illustrate the entire call's path obtained with the recursive binomial approach as shown in Fig. 6.4(c).

This example shows that the binomial framework is well-designed to price American call options on dividend paying stocks. In practice, one would select very small time intervals and hence work with a large number of steps to be sure to really capture the "instants" before the ex-dividend dates when early exercise may indeed be optimal.

This refinement and the resulting increase in the number of steps is well-suited for the valuation of American put options, which can be valued with exactly the same recursive procedure already presented for call options except that we will have to account for their symmetric exercise value $(K - S)$ with respect that of the call. Hence, the price of an American put written on a dividend paying stock that still has i periods until expiration will satisfy the following recursive valuation equation:

$$P'(n, i) = \max \{K - S(1 - \delta)^{m_{n-i}} u^j d^{n-i-j};$$
$$[pP'_u(n, i - 1) + (1 - p)P'_d(n, i - 1)\}i \tag{6.5}$$

where

$P'(n, i) = $ the price of an American put with i remaining periods until expiration

$\delta = $ constant dividend yield

$m_{n-i} = $ total number of ex-dividend dates until the $(n - i)^{\text{th}}$ node

$P'_u(n, i - 1) = $ price of the put option one period ahead given that the stock price experienced an upward movement

$P'_d(n, i - 1) = $ price of the put option one period ahead given that the stock price experienced a downward movement

$n = $ total number of periods initially considered to value the put

$p = (R - d)/(u - d)$ and $(1 - p) = (u - R)/(u - d)$

Even if the underlying stock does not pay any dividends we would still have to apply the recursive valuation Eq. (6.5) with $\delta = m_{n-i} = 0$ since we know that for sufficiently low values of the stock price, American put options can be exercised prior to maturity without obeying any specific timing rule. In fact, in the absence of dividends, the probability that an American put option will be exercised prior to maturity is—*ceteris paribus*—even greater since the put owner is not sacrificing any future stock price declines due to dividend payments if he exercises earlier.

This explains why in practice we must rely on powerful computers that enable us to price American call and put options using between 150 to 300 steps in the stock price over the option's time to maturity. The accuracy provided by the binomial approach[14] has proved to be very satisfactory despite the fact that it generally approximates a cash dividend—usually paid on a quarterly basis—by a fixed dividend yield.

Of course, the binomial method is also much more "costly" for put options than for call options, which we must check at each step whether the computed put price is greater than its exercise value, while the latter check will only be done one to three times—just before ex-dividend dates—for call options. Since the binomial procedure can be "carried" over and hence substantially reduced from one ex-dividend date to the other, we will of course consume much less computer time when valuing American call options than we do with otherwise equivalent put options.

We can conclude by saying that with its pedagogical structure and its implementation facilities, the binomial valuation approach is certainly the most appealing procedure for valuing American call and put options in the absence of an analytical formula that would directly price these options. This doesn't mean, however, that we should ignore other models or other approximation techniques that serve the same purpose.

B Other Solutions to the Pricing of American Options

There are no simple dynamic portfolio strategies—such as the one consisting of buying the underlying stock and borrowing at the risk-free rate used for a European call option—that will enable us to replicate the exact payoff structure of American options simply because of the uncertainty around the dates when those payoffs may actually occur. This statement, which is directly related to the dynamic property of the early exercise feature, severely compromises the derivation of an analytical solution for the pricing of those options.

One might think that because American call options on dividend paying stocks can only be exercised at some specific known[15] dates, the problem may

---

[14] For a detailed analysis of the efficiency of the binomial pricing approach in terms of its accuracy and its cost (computer time), see Geske and Shastri (1985).

[15] We assume that the number and the timing of each dividend flow are known or can at least be accurately predicted.

be more easily solved than for American put options. Indeed, this is true and has been confirmed through Roll's (1977) American call valuation model,[16] which applies when the underlying stock pays one known dividend D (in dollars) over the remaining time to maturity of the option.

The crucial point is that the payoff structure of such an American call option an instant before the (known) ex-dividend date t_1 is as follows:

$$C' = \begin{cases} S_{t_1} + D - K & \text{if } S_{t_1} \geq \underline{S} \\ C(S_{t_1}, K, T - t_1) & \text{if } S_{t_1} < \underline{S} \end{cases} \tag{6.6}$$

where

$S_{t_1} + D - K$ = the exercise value of the American call an instant before the ex-dividend date t_1 with S_{t_1} denoting the ex-dividend stock price

$C(S_{t_1}, K, T - t_1)$ = the unexercised value of the call an instant before the ex-dividend date t_1

$\underline{S}$ = the critical stock price above and for which the call will be exercised

Of course, Eq. (6.6) is similar to the condition we used in the binomial pricing procedure since they both express—with different notations—that the call should be exercised if its exercise value is greater than its unexercised value an instant before the ex-dividend date.

Moreover, as every call option, the American call should also satisfy the well-known boundary condition at expiration, namely that:

$$C' = \max[S^* - K, 0] \tag{6.7}$$

where

S^* = the stock price at the expiration date ($\tau = 0$) of the American call

Roll (1977) has shown that the payoff structure of such an American call can be replicated by the one of a portfolio consisting of the following:

1. A long position in a European call option written on the same stock and that has the same maturity date as the American call option. We will denote the price of this European call by $C_1(S - De^{-r\tau_1}, K, \tau)$.
2. A long position in a European call option that expires an instant before the ex-dividend date t_1 and whose exercise price is equal to $\underline{S}$ (the critical stock price for which the American call option will be exercised at t_1). We will denote the value of this European call option by $C_2(S - De^{-r\tau_1}, \underline{S}, \tau_1)$.

---

[16] In fact, the model was developed and extended in three papers written by Roll (1977), Geske (1979), and Whaley (1979).

3. Finally, the portfolio also involves a short position in a European "compound" call option.[17] A European compound call option is an option that at expiration allows you to buy another call option written on the stock. In this case, the compound option is written on the first European call option $C_1(S - De^{-r\tau_1}, K, \tau)$ defined under 1, and it allows its owner to buy this call an instant before the ex-dividend date t_1 at an exercise price of $\underline{S} + D - K$. We will denote the price of the compound option by $C^*(C_1, \underline{S} + D - K, \tau_1)$.

We can illustrate the payoff structure of this portfolio at the ex-dividend date t_1

	$S_t \geq S$		$S_{t_1} < S$	
	Action	Value	Action	Value
European call C_1	Abandoned for the exercise of C^*	$S_{t_1} - K + D$	Alive	$C_1(S_{t_1}, K, T - t_1)$
European call C_2	Exercised	$S_{t_1} - \underline{S}$	Expires worthless	0
Compound call C^*	Exercised by abandoning call C_1 to the owner of the compound call	$[S_{t_1} - K + D$ $-\underline{S} - D + K]$	Expires worthless	0
Result $(a + b - c)$		$S_{t_1} - K + D$		$C_1(S_{t_1}, K, T - t_1)$

---

[17] See Geske (1979) for a detailed analysis of the concept of a compound option. In general, $C^*(C, K^*, \tau_1)$ is the price of a European compound option that expires at date T_1 and that allows you at that date to buy at an exercise price of K^* another call option written on the stock that expires at date $T(T > T_1)$ and whose current price is equal to $C(S, \tau, K)$. At maturity, the compound option is worth

$$C^*(C, K^*, 0) = \max[0, C_{T_1} - K^*]$$

When the underlying stock follows a lognormal stochastic process, Geske (1979) has shown that a compound call option on a non-dividend paying stock satisfies the following pricing equation:

$$C^* = SM(q + \sigma\sqrt{\tau_1}, h + \sigma\sqrt{\tau_1}, \tau_1/\tau)$$
$$- Ke^{-r\tau}M(q, h, \sqrt{\tau_1/\tau}) - K^*e^{-r\tau_1}N(q) \tag{6.A}$$

where

$q = (\ln(S/S') + (r - (1/2)\sigma^2)\tau_1)/\sigma\sqrt{\tau_1}$

$h = (\ln(S/K) + (r - (1/2)\sigma^2)\tau)/\sigma\sqrt{\tau}$

$M(\cdot) = $ bivariate normal cumulative function

$N(\cdot) = $ standard normal cumulative function

S' satisfies $C(S', K, \tau_1) - K^* = 0$

We see that this portfolio perfectly replicates the payoff structure of the American call an instant before the ex-dividend date by comparing Eq. (6.6) to the resulting payoff table of the portfolio. Moreover, it is clear that if the price of the stock at date t_1 is less than the critical value $\underline{S}$, only C_1 remains alive[18] and it will clearly satisfy Eq. (6.7) at its expiration date ($\tau = 0$).

It then follows that the current value of the replicating portfolio must be equal to the price of the American call option to avoid riskless arbitrage opportunities. We can therefore compute the theoretical price of the American call as equal to the price C_1 (of the first European call) plus C_2 (the price of the second European call) minus C^* (the compound call option's price). Those three assets can be valued analytically using the Black and Scholes formula—modified for the dividends as in Eq. (5.8)—to price C_1 and C_2 and using Geske's compound call option valuation formula[19] presented in the footnote 17 to price C^*.

Once the theoretical values of C_1, C_2 and C^* have been computed, the American call's price C' is easily derived from the following relation:

$$C' = C_1 + C_2 - C^* \tag{6.8}$$

Roll's valuation approach is very elegant since it determines—through Eq. (6.8)—an exact theoretical price for the American call option. As pointed out by Geske (1979), the model can also be extended to allow for more than one dividend payment over the option's remaining time to maturity, however, this involves additional computational difficulties since we begin to consider "options on options on options..." whose values are determined by multivariate normal distribution functions.

A recent empirical study by Whaley (1982) has shown that Roll's American call valuation model does indeed provide accurate price estimates (the pricing error is \$.01 or less) for American call options written on dividend paying stocks. However, the same study also shows that the simpler "pseudo-American" call valuation model performs almost as well (the pricing error is \$.02). This conclusion suggests that the complexity underlying Roll's model is only partially compensated by a superior pricing performance relative to that of simpler and less costly option pricing models. This modest gain in pricing accuracy might lead many users to make a parsimonious choice and hence to use alternative valuation models especially when stocks are expected to pay more than one dividend over the option's remaining time to maturity or when ex-dividend dates cannot be accurately predicted.

---

[18] Note that after date t_1, the American call and an otherwise identical European call have the same value since there are no more dividend payments. Hence:

$$C'(S, \tau, K) = C(S, \tau, K) \text{ for } t > t_1$$

[19] Geske's compound call option pricing formula Eq. (6.A) presented in footnote 17 will have to be modified since the underlying call—here C_1—is written on a stock that pays a dividend D. Hence, the price C^* of the compound call will have to be computed by replacing S by $S - De^{-r\tau_1}$ and by replacing the exercise price K^* by its value of $\underline{S} + D - K$ in Eq. (6.A) given in that footnote.

There have been several other attempts to price American call and put options and we can classify them into two main categories. The first has essentially focused on approximating numerically the solution of the rather complex partial differential equation that American put and call option prices must satisfy.[20] These numerical approaches used by Schwartz (1977), Brennan and Schwartz (1977, 1978), and Geske and Shastri (1985) are essentially computing the numerical solutions of the partial differential equation by replacing the partial derivatives with finite differences and then solving the finite difference equation backwards (starting at $\tau = 0$).[21] As shown by Geske and Shastri (1985), the numerical approximation techniques lead to reliable American call and put price estimates and they should be preferred to the binomial valuation technique everytime one needs to value a large sample of American options.

The second category of research addresses the problem of analytically approximating the (unknown) closed-form solution of the partial differential valuation equations governing American call or put option prices. This is done by approximating the option's price with a functional expression that matches it as closely as possible while being computationally tractable. For example, Johnson (1983) approximated the American put's price with a linear combination of two European put options prices. Geske and Johnson (1984) derived an analytical solution by defining an American put's price as an infinite truncated series of compound European put option[22] prices.

Basically, the choice of an approximating technique, whether it be numerical or analytical depends on the objectives, type, and number of options that have to be valued as well as on the technical skills and resources of the user. Indisputably,

---

[20] Assuming that the stock price is lognormally distributed, the interest rate r is constant, and the underlying stock pays a constant dividend yield, the American put's price P' will satisfy the following partial differential equation:

$$1/2 \frac{\partial^2 P'}{\partial S^2} \sigma^2 S^2 + \frac{\partial P'}{\partial t} + (r - \delta)S \frac{\partial P'}{\partial S} - rP' = 0$$

subject to the early exercise condition, i.e.:

$$P' = \max[P'(S, \tau, K); K - S]; \text{ for } \forall \tau > 0$$

and to the expiration date condition:

$$P'(S^*, 0, K) = \max [0, K - S^*] \text{for } \tau = 0$$

It can be shown that an American call will satisfy the same partial differential equation except that its early exercise conditions will have to be applied only before each ex-dividend date—if the latter are known—and remembering that its exercise value is symmetric $(S - K)$ to that of the put.

[21] The expression "finite difference" numerical approach is used to denote that the partial derivatives in the valuation equation are actually approximated by finite differences.

[22] A more recent analytical approximation technique proposed by Macmillan (1986) and by Barone-Adesi and Whaley (1987) approximates the "early exercise premium"—that is, the difference between the American option price and the otherwise "identical" European option price—by a quadratic function. The value of the American option is then computed as the sum of the identical European option's theoretical price and the approximated value of the "early exercise premium."

all these recently developed models and approximating techniques demonstrate that researchers have been able to provide a variety of methods to value American call and put options with much greater accuracy than was originally possible using the standard Black and Scholes option pricing model.

4   A CLOSER LOOK AT THE DISTRIBUTIONAL PROPERTIES OF THE STOCK PRICE

So far, nearly all option pricing models we have analyzed rely on the assumption that there is a single state variable—namely the stock price—that embodies all the relevant information to price put and call options. These relative pricing models are, of course, very sensitive to the specification of the state variable's random path through time (stochastic process) and will lead to more accurate theoretical prices if one has been able to correctly assess and estimate the behavior of the stock price.

Hence, if we agree[23] that there is only one state variable that can affect option prices, we are faced with a fundamental issue common to all single factor pricing models, namely that of correctly identifying and specifying the chosen state variable's path so that it matches as close as possible its observed random evolution.

The Black and Scholes model and many of its extensions explicitly assume that the stock price is a continuous-time state variable that will only move according to infinitesimal increments over any infinitesimal time interval. Hence, the resulting sample path of the stock price is continuous and smooth; it can be drawn without ever having to lift the pencil from the sheet of paper.

Moreover, these models assume that the continuously compounded rates of return of the stock are normally distributed[24] with a constant mean μ and variance σ^2 per unit of time. This implies that the stochastic process governing instantaneous stock returns is a stationary diffusion[25] process that can be represented as follows:

$$\frac{dS}{S} = \mu dt + \sigma dz \qquad (6.9)$$

---

[23] We will analyze later on in this chapter whether it is realistic to assume that the stock price is the only random factor that will determine option prices. We have already seen in the second section of this chapter how the Black and Scholes model can be extended to allow for a stochastic interest rate (see Merton, 1973).

[24] This follows from the fact that the stock price is itself assumed to be lognormally distributed over time.

[25] A random variable $\tilde{S}_t$ is said to follow a diffusion process if it is defined in continuous time and if its probability density function at each instant is also continuous. The latter fact and the lognormal distribution assumption jointly imply that at each instant t, the stock price S_t can take any of the continuum of values defined over the interval $[0, \infty]$ and not just a set of discrete values like, for example, $\tilde{S}_t \in [0; 0.5; 1; 1.5; 2; 2.5; \ldots]$.

where

μ = the instantaneous expected return or "drift" of the stock; μ is a constant

σ = the standard deviation of the stock's expected returns per unit of time. Hence, σ^2 is the instantaneous variance of stock returns; it is also a constant

dz = a standard normal variate that is also called a standard Wiener process. dz is normally distributed with a mean $E(dz) = 0$ and a variance Var $(dz) = dt$

According to the relationship in Eq. (6.9), the instantaneous return of the stock (dS/S) is driven by two components:

1. An expected relative price change of μ over any instant of time. Note that since μ is a constant, we expect the same instantaneous return today as in one year.
2. An "unexpected" departure from its expected return that is driven by a stochastic process (the standard Wiener process dz). The latter makes the stock return fluctuate randomly around its mean with a constant variance of σ^2 per unit of time.[26]

Although it is generally agreed that the return of a financial asset is consistently depicted as "fluctuating randomly around its mean," there are several objections as to how this behavior is restricted in Eq. (6.9). First, one may criticize the lognormal stock price distribution assumption by arguing that it is unlikely that the mean rate of return and the variance are inter-temporal constants. Since we saw that an option price is only a function of the variance of stock returns, we will discuss the limitations resulting from the constant variance assumption and analyze alternative stock return specifications that have tried to justify and allow for nonstationary unexpected shifts in the stock instantaneous returns.

The second criticism one may address to the stochastic process described in Eq. (6.9) is also relevant for any other stock price behavior's specification that will restrict it to evolve smoothly and continuously over time. Can we really allow for a complete description of stock price movements without considering that it may occasionally be driven by large jumps? As we saw on October 19, 1987, large unexpected jumps can play a significant role in explaining stock returns and hence imply that a pure diffusion process—which only accounts for continuous but infinitesimal relative price movements—may be an inappropriate representation of the observed stock returns dynamics. We will therefore present in the second part of this section some theoretical research that has focused on the integration of jumps in the specification of the stochastic process driving stock returns.

---

[26] Since dz is normally distributed with mean $E(dz) = 0$ and variance Var$(dz) = dt$, it only induces the unexpected random shifts in dS/S or, in other words, the variance—$\sigma^2 dt$—component driving dS/S.

A Nonstationarity of the Stock Returns' Variance

The constant variance assumption underlying the Black and Scholes model is very convenient since it suggests that variance estimates computed from historical data can be accurately used for extrapolative purposes and hence to price options.[27] Unfortunately, it turns out that even when we use the different variance estimation procedures that apply to the Black and Scholes model—essentially the historical variance and the implied standard deviation techniques—they generally will not lead to a constant and unique variance estimate for each stock. Indeed, the historical variance of the stock computed over the past five years is unlikely to be equal to its historical variance computed over the last six months, which, in turn, is unlikely to be equal to the current implied variance of the stock returns.

Obviously, the variance of stock returns is not constant through time, thereby suggesting that the lognormal distribution assumption underlying Black and Scholes model is not relevant. Indeed, there is considerable empirical evidence in the literature (see Fama [1965], Black [1976], Blattberg and Gonedes [1974], Kon [1984], etc.) supporting the nonstationarity of the stock returns' distribution. In particular, several authors including Black (1976), Schmalensee and Trippi (1978), Beckers (1980), and Christie (1982) have observed that the volatility of stock returns varies inversely with the level of the stock price. According to these authors, the negative relationship between the level of the stock price and the volatility is attributable to the financial leverage of the firm. For example, when the stock price of a firm falls, its debt-to-equity ratio[28] will increase, thereby increasing the riskiness of its stock and vice versa.

Parallel to this empirically identified relationship between the variance of stock returns and the level of stock prices, Cox (1975) derived a call option pricing model that explicitly assumes a nonstationary variance of stock returns and simultaneously provides another test of the previously documented negative relationship. The so-called Cox "constant elasticity of variance" option pricing model explicitly models the variance of stock returns as a known deterministic function of the stock price level.

More specifically, Cox assumed that the instantaneous rate of return on the stock obeys the following diffusion process:

---

[27] In the Black and Scholes formula Eq. (4.18), we need to know the variance of the stock returns over the option's remaining time to maturity ($\sigma^2(T - t)$). If the instantaneous variance per unit of time is assumed to be inter-temporally constant, then σ^2 can be computed from past stock returns data.

[28] Beckers (1980) assumed that the market price of the common stock will fall more rapidly than the market price of the firm's debt so that the debt-to-equity ratio will fall if the stock price increases. In other words, the elasticity of the stock's volatility with respect to the stock value $(\partial \sigma / \sigma)/(\partial S / S)$ should be negative (but greater than minus one). As pointed out by Christie (1982), this negative relation stems from the fact that stock returns volatility is an increasing concave function of leverage. When a firm has no debt a similar effect can be attributed to operating leverage. Higher fixed costs will lower the value of the firm (or its equity value) while simultaneously increasing its operating risk.

$$dS/S = \mu dt + \delta S^{(\theta/2)-1} dz \tag{6.10}$$

where

$$\mu = \text{the instantaneous expected rate of return on the stock}$$

$$\delta S^{(\theta/2)-1} = \text{the instantaneous standard deviation of stock returns. It is as-sumed that } \delta \text{ is a constant and that } \theta \text{ is an elasticity parameter whose value is strictly smaller than 2}$$

$$dz = \text{a standard Wiener process that is normally distributed with a mean } E[dz] = 0 \text{ and a variance Var } (dz) = dt$$

Although Eq. (6.10) looks more complex than Eq. (6.9), their main difference is that in Cox's model we can explicitly account for the fact that the stock price affects the variance of stock returns $(\delta^2 S^{\theta-2})$. This will be true as long as the elasticity coefficient θ is different[29] from 2. Moreover, since it has been proven that the relationship between the stock returns' variance and the stock price level is negative, we would expect to find a value of θ strictly smaller than 2.

If we denote by $\sigma^2 = \delta^2 S^{\theta-2}$ the variance of the stock returns, we can compute its elasticity η_S with respect to the stock price as follows:

$$\eta_S = \frac{\partial \sigma^2}{\partial S} \cdot \frac{S}{\sigma^2} = \frac{\partial(\delta^2 S^{\theta-2})}{\partial S} \cdot \frac{S}{\delta^2 S^{\theta-2}} = \theta - 2 \tag{6.11}$$

Hence, the elasticity η_S will be negative for $\theta < 2$. Moreover, it is a constant and this is why we call Cox's model a "constant elasticity of variance option pricing model."

Assuming a constant interest rate r, a nondividend paying stock whose instantaneous return follows the stochastic process described in Eq. (6.10), Cox derived the theoretical European call option pricing formula using the risk-neutral or preference-free valuation framework.[30] The price of the call is then simply the expected value of its terminal payoff discounted at the risk-free interest rate r.

---

[29] When $\theta = 2$, we obtain the result that the stock price does not affect the variance of stock returns and Eq. (6.10) collapses to the following well-known stationary process:

$$dS/S = \mu dt + \delta dz$$

This is the same as Eq. (6.9) since both assume a stationary stock return distribution. Hence, the Black and Scholes model can be obtained as a specific case of Cox's constant elasticity of variance option pricing model for which $\theta = 2$.

[30] Although the variance is not stationary anymore it is defined as a deterministic (constant) function of the stock price as can be seen from Eq. (6.10). We therefore still have a single-factor pricing model where the only state variable is the stock price. We have already seen that in this case we can form a "perfect hedge" portfolio with the stock and the call option that under the no-arbitrage condition leads to the call option valuation equation. Since the equation can be obtained using only arbitrage restrictions it is perfectly general and will hold for any type of assumptions about investors' preferences. Therefore, Cox has chosen to derive the constant elasticity of variance option pricing model using a risk-neutral environment since in this case the valuation procedure is much simpler. This is true because as we already mentioned in Chapter 3, in a risk-neutral economy all assets have the same expected rate of return equal to the risk-free interest rate due to the fact that individuals do not require any additional premium for bearing risk.

$$C_V = e^{-r\tau}\hat{E}_t[\max(0, S^* - K)] \tag{6.12}$$

where

C_V = the price of a European call with an exercise price of K and maturing in $\tau(T - t)$ years given by the Cox constant elasticity of variance pricing model

$\hat{E}_t$ = expectation operator applying to the risk-adjusted process

S^* = the price of the underlying stock at the expiration date T of the call

The pricing equation is easily computed once the distribution of the terminal stock price S^*—under the assumption that it follows a constant elasticity of variance diffusion process as described in Eq. (6.10)—has been determined.

The latter fact is more easily said than done since the probability density of S^* is now a less tractable expression than it was in the case of the binomial or the lognormal stock price distributions. Therefore, the resulting constant elasticity of variance call pricing equation derived[31] by Cox can seem much more complicated than the Black and Scholes pricing equation. It still remains true in both cases that the price of the call is equal to the present value of the expected value of the stock price at expiration conditional upon the fact that it will expire in-the-money less the present value of the exercise price multiplied by the probability that it will expire in-the-money. The main difference is that the expectations and the probabilities are defined under the lognormal stock price distribution in the case of the Black and Scholes model while they are defined under the constant elasticity of variance stock price distribution in Cox's call option pricing model.

There have been several empirical studies (for example, Macbeth and Merville [1980] and Emanuel and Macbeth [1982]) suggesting that Cox's constant elasticity of variance option pricing model precisely removes one disturbing bias of the Black and Scholes model, which (as has been shown previously by

---

[31] Cox's constant elasticity of variance call option pricing formula is defined as follows:

$$C_V = S \sum_{n=0}^{\infty} g(\lambda S^{-\phi}, n + 1)G\left(\lambda(Ke^{-r\tau})^{-\phi}, n + 1 - \frac{1}{\phi}\right)$$

$$-Ke^{-r\tau} \sum_{n=0}^{\infty} g\left(\lambda S^{-\phi}, n + 1 - \frac{1}{\phi}\right)G(\lambda(Ke^{-r\tau})^{-\phi}, n + 1)$$

where

C_V = the price of a European call option that expires in $\tau(T - t)$ years and that has a striking price equal to K

$\phi = 2\theta - 2$

$\lambda = 2r/\delta^2\phi e^{(r\phi\tau - 1)}$

$\Gamma(n) = \int_0^{\infty} e^{-v}v^{n-1}dv$ = the gamma function

$g(x, n) = e^{-x}x^{n-1}/\Gamma(n)$ = the gamma density function

$G(a, n) = \int_a^{\infty} g(x, n)dx$ = the complementary gamma distribution function

Black [1972] and by Macbeth and Merville [1980]) tends to overprice in-the-money call options while it tends to underprice out-of-the-money call options. However, if we look at the formulation of the constant elasticity of variance stock price distribution in Eq. (6.10), we see that very high stock prices (and hence in-the-money call options) will simultaneously tend to have lower volatilities (for $\theta < 2$) while low stock prices (and hence out-of-the-money call options) will simultaneously be associated to higher volatilities. Hence, the negative effect of the stock price level on the variance creates offsetting effects on the resulting call's price of in- and out-of-the money call options. This explains why Cox's constant elasticity of variance option pricing model is able to substantially remove this "moneyness" pricing bias attributed to the Black and Scholes model.

However, this also suggests that whenever the Black and Scholes model underprices some in-the-money call options while overpricing some out-of-the-money call options, using Cox's model will only result in increasing the observed bias. Moreover, Cox's model requires that one estimates two variance related parameters, namely δ and θ. Both are supposed to be inter-temporal constants and hopefully the elasticity parameter θ should be the same for all stocks. Unfortunately, studies by Beckers (1980) and by Emanuel and Macbeth (1982) have shown that this parameter—although usually smaller than 2—can vary substantially among stocks and across time and that we cannot exclude over some time periods to find stocks for which the value of θ will be greater than two. This is very disturbing since there is no rational explanation for why the relationship between the stock price level and its variability should be positive over some time periods and negative over others.

Indisputably, Cox's constant elasticity of variance call option pricing model has the advantage of capturing changes in volatility induced by price changes. Hence, since the stock's return variability can be updated continuously according to the most recent price changes, the model should have greater predictive power than the Black and Scholes (constant variance) model. This is indeed the case when θ is smaller than 2. However, as Emanuel and Macbeth (1982) have pointed out, the prices predicted by Cox's model (using parameter θ and δ computed at time t with the stock price at time $t + k$ to predict the option price at time $t + k$) when θ is greater than two are even worse than predictions based on Black and Scholes model (using the implied standard deviation σ computed at time t and the stock price at time $t + k$ to compute the option price at time $t + k$). Finally, we must admit that even in those cases where θ is less than 2 and although this relationship between the stock's variance and the stock's price has been empirically validated, the latter deterministic nonstationary variance specification cannot fully account for the observed changes in a stock's variability over time. At the end of their study, Macbeth and Emanuel recognize that Cox's specification of a nonstationary variance will at most explain 20% of its observed shifts over time. Given the additional parameter estimates required by the implementation of Cox's European call option pricing model as well as its greater mathematical complexity, this conclusion is disappointing and discouraging for both the practitioners and the academics who expected a noticeable pricing accuracy improvement relative to the Black and Scholes model.

The fact that stock prices can only partially explain movements in the stock returns' variance has led several researchers including Wiggins (1986), Hull and White (1987), and Scott (1987) to the conclusion that the variability of stock returns may itself be a random variable that evolves according to a specific inter-temporal pattern. Since in the latter case, shifts in the variance are not any more determined by the stock price level and are moreover stochastic, we have to introduce a second state variable in the option pricing framework. Hence, these authors explicitly assume that the stock price and the standard deviation of stock returns are the two relevant state variables that jointly determine option prices. In this framework, unexpected changes in the call's price are induced by stochastic movements in the stock price and/or in the volatility.

Since we now have two state variables in the model—the stock price S and the volatility σ—we cannot use the perfect hedge assumption underlying the Black and Scholes model anymore. Indeed, this hedge is only effective with respect to unexpected shifts in the stock price but it does not provide any protection against unexpected shifts in the volatility. Moreover, the valuation procedure based solely on an arbitrage argument (i.e., the fact that riskless profitable arbitrage strategies cannot exist) is not sufficient to determine the price of an option when the latter depends on state variables that are not traded or that cannot be hedged by an existing traded security or portfolio (as it is the case for the stock's return variability). To develop the option pricing model, these authors are therefore relying on a more sophisticated framework, namely an equilibrium asset pricing model under which they are able to define the option's price as a function of the two state variables and of investors' preferences. The latter parameter will enter the valuation equation in the form of a compensation for bearing uncertainty attached to the stock's variance or, in other words, as a market premium for stochastic variance risk.

Indeed, since the volatility cannot be "hedged" away with traded assets, the option pricing equation will not be preference-free anymore, and it will re-quire that one estimates the market price for volatility risk bearing unless some simplifying assumptions are made about this parameter's value. The two-factor option pricing formula that allows for a stochastic volatility will generally not lead to a closed form solution and, therefore, will require approximating tech-niques to compute the options' theoretical prices. Moreover, the implementation of the model presupposes that one first estimates the random process governing the volatility over time, the market price of volatility risk, and the volatility itself (as in classical single-factor option pricing models). This is a rather delicate task, since we have limited empirical evidence on the volatility's stochastic process[32]

---

[32] Wiggins (1986), Hull and White (1987), and Scott (1987) assumed that changes in the volatility follow a mean reverting diffusion process. This implies that the volatility is expected to revert to its long-term mean value and that it fluctuates randomly around its mean reverting expected path, driven by a constant variance. The constant variance of the volatility's stochastic process implies that its unexpected shifts are stationary over time.

over time and even less knowledge about investors' required risk premiums for unexpected shifts in the volatility.

Despite these technical difficulties, recent empirical studies and simulations do indicate that stochastic volatility option pricing models are a promising direction for further research since they lead to a greater pricing accuracy than the Black and Scholes model (see Scott, 1987) and since they can eliminate some pricing biases of the latter model. However, the empirical evidence currently available is too limited to derive any stronger conclusions except perhaps that these models will only become a feasible alternative once the stochastic process of the variance has been properly identified.

Finally, we can say that it is definitively recognized today that the volatility of stock returns is not constant and that it is even unlikely to be a deterministic function of the stock price. Given that volatility is more likely to behave stochastically over time, there is an indisputable need for further empirical studies that will enable us to specify its stochastic process more accurately. However, it seems that the more we progress and the more we have to rely on estimated parameters and on behavioral variables (risk premiums) that can only be computed under restrictive assumptions. Therefore, the additional computational costs associated with stochastic volatility option pricing models may not necessarily be offset by their gains in pricing accuracy. As long as specification or measurement errors dominate, one will certainly find it more efficient and parsimonious to simply rely on the Black and Scholes model with updated—daily or even hourly—estimates of the implied standard deviation of stock returns. This is the current state of the art, which strongly encourages further theoretical and empirical studies to improve our knowledge of the stochastic properties of the variance and to determine the extent its randomness really affects option prices.

B   Discontinuities in the Stock Price Sample Path

Indisputably, the lognormal distribution is not an adequate representation of the stock price's path since it fails to capture the nonstationarity inherent in the stock returns' variance. However, even if we allow for a stochastic volatility, this will not eliminate a second criticism of the Black and Scholes model and all its extensions presented so far. These option pricing models do not allow for jumps in the stock price path since they explicitly assume that the latter is described by a continuous-time diffusion process.

The only exception is the binomial option pricing model described in Chapter 3. It can be shown that in the limit—as the number of stock price steps tends to infinity—we can let the binomial multiplicative stock price process converge to a log-Poisson continuous-time stock price process that will explicitly allow for jumps in the stock price. This pure jump process can be obtained with an appropriate choice of the parameters u, d, and q describing the binomial stock price process. Cox, Ross, and Rubinstein (1979) have shown that if those parameters are chosen so that:

$$u = u$$

$$d = e^{\varepsilon(\tau/n)} \text{ where } \varepsilon \text{ is an infinitesimal increment, } \varepsilon \to 0$$

$$q = \lambda(\tau/n)$$

$$\lambda = \text{ the intensity of the jump process (i.e., the number of jumps per unit of time)}$$

We are in fact describing a pure jump process in which each successive stock price is with very high probability $(1 - \lambda(\tau/n))$ close to its previous value $(S \to dS)$ and has a small probability $\lambda(\tau/n)$ of making a jump from S to uS. As $n \to \infty$, the probability that S moves to dS becomes increasingly greater while the probability of a jump from S to uS tends to zero. In the limit, with this choice of parameters, the binomial multiplicative stock price distribution will converge to a log-Poisson distribution. Under the log-Poisson continuous-time stock price distribution, Cox, Ross, and Rubinstein (1979) have shown that call options written on nondividend paying stocks satisfy the following "jump process option pricing formula":

$$C = S\psi(x, y) - Ke^{-r\tau}(x; y/u)$$

where

$$y = (r - \varepsilon)u\tau/(u - 1)$$

$$x = \text{ smallest nonnegative integer greater than } (\ln(K/S) - \varepsilon\tau)/\ln u$$

$$\psi(x; y) = \sum_{i=x}^{\infty} (e^{-y}y^i)/i! \text{ denotes the complementary Poisson distribution}$$

Note that a similar formula results if we chose the parameters so that:

$$u = e^{\varepsilon(\tau/n)}$$

$$d = d$$

$$1 - q = \lambda(\tau/n)$$

In this case there is a small probability $\lambda(\tau/n)$ that the stock price jumps from S to dS while there is a large $((1 - \lambda(\tau/n))$ probability that it remains close to its previous value $(S \to uS)$. In these two examples, the jump is deterministic in magnitude and either upward or downward oriented, respectively.

Cox and Ross (1976) were the first authors to analyze the possibility of valuing options under the assumption that the underlying asset follows a continuous-time jump process. In the case of a simple jump process, we can describe the stochastic behavior of the instantaneous stock return (dS/S) as follows:

$$\frac{dS}{S} = \mu dt + \begin{cases} \dfrac{\lambda dt}{1 - \lambda dt} & \begin{matrix} K - 1 \\ 0 \end{matrix} \end{cases}$$

$$\Longleftrightarrow \tag{6.13}$$

$$\frac{dS}{S} = \mu dt + (K - 1)d\pi$$

where

μ = the expected rate of return on the stock per unit of time

π = a continuous-time Poisson process

λ = the intensity of the jump (i.e., the number of jumps per unit of time)

$K - 1$ = the magnitude of the jump, which is assumed to be constant in a simple jump process

The instantaneous stock return's stochastic process defined in Eq. (6.13) has two components. As in the case of a lognormal distribution, it has a deterministic constant component μ that defines the expected rate of return on the stock over each small time interval. However, the second component, namely the unexpected stock return—expressed by the term $(K - 1)d\pi$—is not continuous anymore since it allows for jumps in the stock price. Indeed, with a small probability λdt the stock return will experience a jump of magnitude $K - 1$ over the next instant, and with a probability $1 - \lambda dt$ it will experience no unexpected discontinuous shift over the next instant. Hence, when we consider a pure jump continuous-time stochastic process, we explicitly allow the random component in the stock price distribution to be discontinuous. As a result, the stock price will occasionally shift to a new level according to a stepwise pattern.

To get a better understanding of the stock price behavior implied by the pure jump process, we can illustrate its path implied by Eq. (6.13) as shown in Fig. 6.5. The stock price follows a positive trend and will at some fixed-time intervals—whose length depends on the intensity λ of the Poisson process—experience a sudden jump of magnitude K that breaks its continuous path. Although a pure

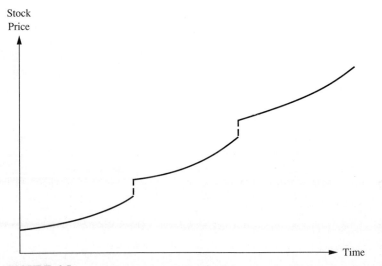

FIGURE 6.5
The stock price path under a pure jump process.

jump process may seem appealing precisely because it captures discontinuities in the stock price path, we cannot identify Fig. 6.5 with a realistic description of a stock price random behavior over time.

Indeed, according to a pure jump process, the stock price process is purely deterministic—the stock grows at a rate μ per unit of time—between the occurrence of two jumps while this is unlikely to be the case in reality. Moreover, the magnitude and the sign of each jump $(K - 1)$ in the stock returns as well as their frequency are unlikely to stay constant over time. If the latter was true, jumps wouldn't create the surprise or even "panic" effects that we experienced worldwide on October 19, 1987. Hence, it is more realistic to assume that jumps have different sizes, different signs—sometimes upward while other times downward—and that they are unevenly spread across time.

From these considerations it follows that a better representation of the stock price path could be provided by a mixed "jump-diffusion process" or, in other words, by a process that allows for continuous infinitesimal random changes in the stock price (induced by the diffusion process) as well as for occasional unexpected large swings or jumps (induced by the Poisson process) that would vary in both magnitude and frequency. Such a mixed "jump-diffusion process" would give a more realistic representation of the stock's price erratic behavior over time since it is not only due to occasional discontinuities but also to continuous infinitesimal random changes "in between" two successive jumps. Hence, a jump-diffusion stochastic process leads to the following more reliable evolution of the stock price shown in Fig. 6.6.

Merton (1976) was the first to "extend" the assumptions of the Black and Scholes model to allow both for smooth and continuous as well as for sharp

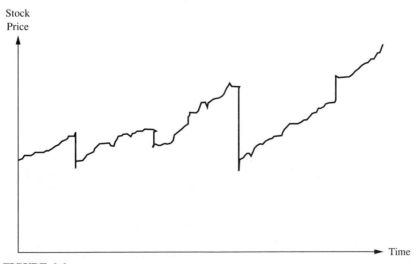

FIGURE 6.6
The stock price path under the jump diffusion stochastic process.

and discontinuous variations in the stock price. He therefore assumed that the instantaneous stock's return is driven by the following jump-diffusion stochastic process:

$$\frac{dS}{S} = \mu dt + \sigma dz + (J - 1)d\pi \qquad (6.14)$$

where

μ = the expected rate of return of the stock over the next instant; μ is a constant

σ = the instantaneous standard deviation of the stock's return conditional upon the fact that no jump occurred over that instant; σ is a constant

π = a continuous-time Poisson process such that with probability λdt a jump can occur over the next time interval and with probability $1 - \lambda dt$ no jump should occur over the next time interval. λ is defined as a positive constant measuring the intensity of the Poisson process (i.e., the number of jumps per unit time)

$J - 1$ = the size of the jump in the stock's instantaneous rate of return. $\ln J$ is a normally distributed random variable with mean $E[\ln J] = \alpha$ and variance $\mathrm{Var}(\ln J) = \gamma^2$

This jump-diffusion stock price process has two components: (1) a pure diffusion process[33] describing the stock price continuous sample path and (2) a Poisson jump process allowing for occasional discontinuities in the stock price's evolution. We can also notice that Merton doesn't restrict the magnitude of the jump to a constant value, or sign; rather, at each time a jump occurs, its random magnitude J is derived from a lognormal distribution. The frequency of the jumps, however, is restricted to be constant over time since the probability λdt that a jump occurs over each small time interval is assumed to be constant.

Given this very general stock price behavior while keeping all other hypotheses identical to those initially stated by Black and Scholes, Merton (1976) derived a jump-diffusion option pricing formula to value European call options on nondividend paying stocks. The derivation of an option pricing model when the underlying stock experiences infrequent jumps is a rather delicate task because we cannot use the perfect hedge argument directly.

Indeed, if we form and maintain—by continuous rebalancing over time— a perfectly hedged position involving the stock and the option, we are in fact only protected against unexpected infinitesimal stock price changes arising from the diffusion component of the stock price's path. But here, contrary to the Black

---

[33] The pure diffusion component of the stock's instantaneous rate of return is defined by the first two terms in Eq. (6.14), namely: $\mu dt + \sigma dz$. The jump component is defined by the last term in Eq. (6.14), namely $(J - 1)d\pi$.

and Scholes option pricing framework, we have a second source of uncertainty, namely that arising from occasional unexpected jumps in the stock price. A perfect hedge involving only the stock and the call option cannot eliminate this second source of uncertainty, and we must, therefore, make some assumptions as to how the market "prices" the remaining risk component affecting option prices.

To deal with the latter problem, Merton (1976) assumed that the risk stemming from unexpected jumps in the stock price is diversifiable. Hence, by holding a portfolio consisting of a large number of stocks from different firms, every investor should be able to eliminate this "jump" risk component. Since it is an avoidable source of uncertainty, it will not be rewarded by the market.

Arguing that "jump risk" is socially irrelevant and hence not priced allowed Merton to go back to the perfect hedge argument and to value the call option accordingly. Indeed, although a long position in Δ_C shares[34] of stocks and a call option sold short is not hedged against "jump risk," the latter fact will not matter since the position is still "riskless" as far as "market" priced sources of uncertainty are concerned.[35] The rate of return on this hedged position must therefore be equal to the risk-free rate of interest—since the remaining "jump risk" component is not rewarded by the market—to avoid profitable arbitrage opportunities. This equilibrium condition then enables Merton to derive the valuation equation that applies to European call options on nondividend paying stocks when their price follows a jump-diffusion stochastic process:

$$C_j = \sum_{n=0}^{\infty} \frac{e^{-\eta\tau}(\eta\tau)^n}{n!} C(S;K;\tau;\sigma^2 + n\gamma^2/\tau; r + n(\alpha + \frac{1}{2}\gamma^2)/\tau - \lambda(e^{\alpha+\frac{1}{2}\gamma^2} - 1))$$

(6.15)

where

C_j = the price of a European call option when the underlying stock price follows the mixed jump-diffusion process defined in Eq. (6.14)

$\eta = \lambda e^{\alpha+\frac{1}{2}\gamma^2}$

$C(S;K;\tau;\sigma^2 + n\gamma^2/\tau; r + n(\alpha + \frac{1}{2}\gamma^2)/\tau - \lambda(e^{\alpha+\frac{1}{2}\gamma^2} - 1))$ is the Black and Scholes pricing Eq. (4.18) computed for a call whose time to maturity is equal to τ, whose exercise price is equal to K when the underlying stock price is equal to S, when the instantaneous variance of stock returns is equal to $\sigma^2 + n\gamma^2/\tau$, and when the risk-free rate of interest r is replaced by the following expression: $r + n(\alpha + \frac{1}{2}\gamma^2)/\tau - \lambda(e^{\alpha+1/2\gamma^2} - 1)$.

---

[34] $\Delta_C = \partial C/\partial S$ is the hedge ratio under the Black and Scholes option pricing model that tells us how many shares of stock must be held long to perfectly "mimic" and hence neutralize the price changes affecting the written call option.

[35] In this case it is the uncertainty arising from continuous infinitesimal stock price unexpected changes that is considered relevant (or in other words, nondiversifiable).

Although the jump-diffusion option pricing formula looks rather complex it can be viewed as an infinite weighted sum of Black and Scholes call option values that have been computed using a "modified" variance of stock returns and a "modified" expression for the risk-free interest rate.

In practice however, the jump-diffusion option pricing formula will be much more cumbersome to implement than the Black and Scholes option pricing model since it requires the estimation of three additional parameters defining the size and frequency of the jumps. Indeed, in the Black and Scholes model, we only needed to estimate the instantaneous variance of stock returns σ^2. Now, we must also estimate the mean (α) and the variance (γ^2) of the lognormally distributed jump magnitude J as well as the intensity parameter λ defining the frequency of the jumps.

Given these additional implementation constraints, one is immediately tempted to ask whether the jump-diffusion model is really more powerful and more reliable than the standard Black and Scholes option pricing model. The answer to that question depends on the extent to which a jump-diffusion stochastic process is an adequate description of the observed stock price behavior over time. An empirical study by Ball and Torous (1985) has shown that there was evidence of statistically significant jumps in the daily returns of 30 common stocks listed on the New York Stock Exchange over the period January 1, 1981 to December 31, 1982. Moreover, Ball and Torous (1985) confirmed Merton's conjecture that "jump risk" is diversifiable since they found no evidence of statistically significant jumps in the daily returns of the CRSP value-weighted Index. This suggests that a well-diversified portfolio of common stocks will not be subject to "jump risk" and therefore the latter can justifiably be considered as an avoidable and hence not rewarded uncertainty factor.

However, when comparing the theoretical prices obtained with the Black and Scholes formula to those obtained with Merton's jump-diffusion option pricing model, Ball and Torous observed that there are only minor price discrepancies between results derived from the two models. Therefore, Merton's model neither fully explains nor eliminates the well-known pricing biases attributed to the standard Black and Scholes model. The small differences between the two models' theoretical prices are due to the fact that the jump component observed on these stock prices is neither too large nor too scarce. Ball and Torous proved that large infrequent jumps are cumulatively required to obtain a noticeable pricing improvement of Merton's jump-diffusion option pricing formula over the Black and Scholes option pricing model.

Obviously we need more empirical data to draw any definitive conclusion regarding the jump-diffusion option pricing model's performance. However, it seems that for the call options on the 30 American stocks analyzed by Ball and Torous, discontinuities in the stock price path were not a relevant parameter since they did not affect option prices noticeably. This doesn't mean that we should reject the idea of modeling stock prices' paths according to a jump-diffusion stochastic process; but contrarily, we need additional empirical studies to ascertain how those jumps really occur (for example, can we assume that their frequency is constant?) and to identify a plausible cause for their size variations over time.

After the worldwide market crash on October 29, 1987, large infrequent jumps in stock prices definitively cannot be rejected as potential patterns in a stock's random behavior over time. This phenomenon will certainly shed new light on the necessity to determine whether jumps really affect option prices and hence require the implementation of more sophisticated jump-diffusion option pricing models.

It has already been shown by Jorion (1987) that for regulated markets, for example, the foreign exchange market during the fixed regime period, jumps had a significant impact on the determination of the exchange rate's stochastic behavior. In this perspective, it will be interesting to analyze whether some recently proposed—after the October 19, 1987 stock market crash—stock and stock futures markets regulations such as daily price limits or increased margin requirements will contribute to reinforce the jump-component inherent in stock prices' dynamic behavior and hence develop a stronger incentive to value stock and futures options with jump-diffusion pricing models.

In summary, we have seen how important it is to define the stochastic process of the stock price consistently to improve the accuracy and performance of existing option pricing models. However, we must recognize that no definitive agreement has yet been reached among researchers in this field. Obviously, every one is willing to admit that stock prices do not follow a lognormal distribution characterized by a constant mean and variance of stock returns. We can also confidently claim that the variance of stock returns is not stationary.

Moreover, there is strong empirical evidence suggesting that the variance itself fluctuates randomly over time and, therefore, a two-factor—the stock price and the variance of stock returns—option pricing model should be even more appropriate. However, the models focusing on a nonstationary variance have ignored the impact of stock price jumps on option prices. Similarly, option pricing models that have allowed for a discontinuous stock price path did not cope with the problems raised by the nonstationarity of the stock's return total variance.[36] Hence, there is still a gap between the research that focused on the nonstationarity of the stock's return variance and research that extended the stock's price path description to a mixed jump-diffusion process.

Before we can claim that a reunification of those two streams of research is desirable, additional empirical studies are required to establish whether stock price jumps and/or stock's returns' total variance really bear a significant causal influence on option prices. This is a fundamental issue since there is no point in building sophisticated and technical option pricing models that cannot outperform the standard Black and Scholes model simply because their specification of the state variables' path is at odds with the stock price and the stock returns' variability "true" behaviors.

---

[36] In a mixed jump-diffusion process, the total variance is defined as the sum of the diffusion induced uncertainty component and the jump-Poisson process induced uncertainty component. The total instantaneous variance of stock returns is equal to $\sigma^2 + \lambda \gamma^2$. There are no covariance terms since it is explicitly assumed that the Poisson process ($d\pi$) and the Wiener process (dz) in Eq. (6.14) are independent.

5   CONCLUSION

We have reviewed the tremendous research effort of the past ten years that has substantially contributed to overcoming the main weaknesses of the Black and Scholes
option pricing model. These efforts initially focused on the constant interest
rate assumption, criticized it, and then relaxed it by allowing interest rate risk—
through the introduction of an additional state variable defined as the price of a
default-free discount bond—to be integrated into the option pricing model. Other
research has successfully extended the Black and Scholes model for pricing options on dividend paying stocks as well as on American options that may be
optimally exercised before their expiration date. Finally, we have seen that there
have been several contributions providing a more realistic—than the lognormal
distribution—description of the stock price behavior over time. This research has
extended Black and Scholes model in two different ways: (1) by assuming a nonstationary variance of stock returns or (2) by explicitly accounting for occasional
jumps in the stock price path.

Hence, we are now confronted with a variety of option pricing models,
each of which solves one or two of the original caveats of the Black and Scholes
pricing formula. Although this variety reflects the considerable research effort that
has strengthened the option pricing theory, it simultaneously creates confusion
whenever one has to decide which model to use for specific practical or academic
purposes. For example, should one be better off valuing European calls with a
two-factor—stochastic volatility—option pricing model or with Merton's jump-
diffusion option pricing model?

Moreover, whatever the choice, it will only offer a partial solution if the
sample also contains American options. We could mention many other similar
ambiguities and they would all lead to the same conclusion: there is definitively a
need for additional empirical studies to reach an agreement on the relative pricing
performance of currently existing option pricing models and to help us weigh
the accuracy of alternative valuation models against their computational costs and
limits.

Whatever the issue, it remains true that option pricing models, like any
other financial or economic model, will only provide a simplifying representation
of the economic environment in which options are actually traded. Hence, there
will always remain some minor differences between market and model prices
and we can essentially explain these pricing discrepancies by the following two
observations:

1. The main characteristic of the presented option pricing formulas is that they are
   derived from partial equilibrium models. Indeed, we have never considered the
   problem of valuing puts and calls given that the financial market, the market for
   consumer goods, the labor market, et cetera, should be in equilibrium. Instead,
   we were focusing on a very thin—or in other words, "partial"—relationship
   that relates the price of the option to the price of the stock and to the risk-
   free interest rate through the nonarbitrage condition. Hence, the price of the
   call will be an equilibrium price with respect to the risk-free interest rate and

to the stock price, but it will only be an equilibrium price from a broader macroeconomic perspective if the stock price and the riskless interest rate are themselves "fairly" valued.

In these relative pricing models it is explicitly assumed that one or two state variables contain all the relevant information to determine option prices. Hence, it is obvious that if we haven't identified all the relevant state variables or if the latter are themselves not reliably observable in the market, we will not be able to price the options consistently.

Moreover, in all single-factor option pricing models, we are only considering a one-way relationship in which the stock price contains information that is both necessary and sufficient to price the option. However, it is not a priori excluded to think that the development of option markets has itself changed some structural properties of the underlying stock markets and that, therefore, such a unilateral causal relationship between the stock price and the option price may actually become spurious.

2. Another feature that should explain differences between theoretical and actual option prices lies in the assumption that a perfect hedge can be established and maintained over the option's remaining time to maturity. This is the fundamental hypothesis that underlies all the previously mentioned option pricing models, and it leads to the well-known "no arbitrage" condition[37] from which the formulas are then derived.

Obviously, the hedge cannot be continuously rebalanced for several institutional reasons:

- transaction costs
- restrictions on short sales in some markets or countries
- lack of liquidity in certain stocks and options
- impossibility of continuous trading in most stocks and options that are not quoted simultaneously in different countries, et cetera.

Depending on the relative importance of these trading barriers, one may be able to rebalance a hedged position frequently in a very active and efficient market while only seldomly in some narrow, thin volume exchanges. In the first case, the option pricing models are expected to give meaningful theoretical option prices that can be exploited for practical as well as for academic purposes. In the second case, the discrepancies between the model's "ideal" hypotheses and the real "imperfect" trading environment strongly preclude the theoretical prices from having a meaningful informational content that could be exploited by portfolio managers.

---

[37] The instantaneous rate of return on the riskless hedge should be equal to the risk-free interest rate to avoid profitable riskless arbitrage opportunities.

The idea that a perfect hedge can be continuously rebalanced over time is essential not only to guarantee the consistency of option models' theoretical prices but also to assure that strategies based on these models may actually be implemented. We will now show that this is indeed the case for a very appealing portfolio strategy that stems directly from the option pricing theory, namely the "dynamic asset allocation" or "portfolio insurance" strategy.

In some cases one may want to buy or sell an option—on a stock or more typically on an existing portfolio—that is not traded in the market. However, it has been shown that we can use the stock and the risk-free asset to replicate the payoffs of a given option in the same way that a long position in the stock and a short position in the call replicates the risk-free asset. A call option is equivalent to a long-levered position in the stock while a put option can be replicated by selling the stock short and lending.

Given this statement one can "insure" or hedge an existing portfolio by replicating the payoff of a written call or of a long put[38] whenever the latter does not exist in the market. This is precisely the dynamic asset allocation strategy proposed by Leland (1980) which consists of protecting the value of an existing portfolio by creating and holding over a predetermined time period a "synthetic" put on this portfolio. The insurance—or long put position—is implemented by selling some of the existing shares of the portfolio and by investing a specific amount of cash in default-free bonds.[39] Then, whenever the stock prices vary the portfolio must be rebalanced to remain insured. This is done by selling more stocks and investing more heavily in risk-free bonds whenever stock prices go down (since the hedge ratio then decreases) and by selling risk-free bonds to increase the equity portion of the portfolio whenever the stock prices go up (since the hedge ratio is then also increasing). If the rebalancing can be done very frequently—theoretically, it should be done continuously—the terminal value of the portfolio after a prespecified time period will be insured at the initially chosen exercise price of the put—or target level—and at a cost equal to the value of the initially created "synthetic" put.

For this dynamic portfolio insurance strategy to be effective, we essentially require the same market conditions as those that guarantee the relevance of the option pricing formulas described in this study, namely, a high degree of market liquidity, low transaction costs and small bid/ask spreads. Whenever

---

[38] A long position in a portfolio as well as in a put on this portfolio provides "insurance" in the sense that the value of the portfolio has a lower boundary equal to the striking price of the put. The cost of this insurance or "covered" position is, of course, equal to the price initially paid for the put. A similar strategy can also be accomplished by synthetically replicating short call options on this portfolio. In the following discussion we will only talk about the long put hedge although it has to be understood that in practice both hedging alternatives may be considered.

[39] The exact fraction of shares to be sold and the amount of cash that has to be invested in default-free bonds are respectively given by the hedge ratio ($\Delta_P = -N(-d_1)$) and by the term $Ke^{-r\tau}N(-d_2)$ in the Black and Scholes put pricing Eq. (4.22) of Chapter 4.

markets do not fulfill these efficient trading conditions, the relevance of the currently existing option pricing models and of the synthetic portfolio strategies based on these models becomes questionable. This is precisely illustrated by the failure of most dynamic asset allocation strategies to maintain the value of their underlying portfolios protected when the market dropped on October 19, 1987. Indeed, the overwhelming trading trend turned to the selling side putting downward pressure on the prices and drying of the market's liquidity. Hence, portfolio insurers were not able—due to the lack of liquidity and the abnormally large bid/ask spreads—to sell the huge blocks of stocks required by their strategy to keep the "hedge ratio" in line with the substantially lower level of the stock market.

This example is particularly revealing of the main strengths and limits faced by the current state of the art of option theory. Its strengths can essentially be related to the variety of alternative option pricing models and option portfolio management strategies that have emerged through recent researches and have been able to solve numerous problems faced by portfolio managers as well as by academics. Its weaknesses are to a large extent the same as those faced by any financial valuation model, namely that it cannot exactly reproduce the environment in which options and stocks are actually traded. Hence, as users, we should remember that we cannot apply these models when their underlying assumptions are too far apart from our given trading environment. Recognizing this limitation would help us avoid many irrelevant portfolio management decisions based on "artificial" price discrepancies. Indeed, such decisions and their consequences are too often shown as proofs of these models' irrelevance while they are actually attributable to the user's bad appraisal of the conditions under which these models can be trusted.

As a corollary, there is one more reason for price discrepancies between market and theoretical option prices, which is strongly related to our previous discussion about the "perfect hedge" assumption underlying all previously examined option pricing models. We cannot ignore the institutional characteristics of the stock, option markets, and trading restrictions that investors in those markets are actually facing. They are often in sharp contrast with the "perfect market" paradigm of most option pricing models. With their simplified representation of the world, these models ignore the transaction costs and the bid/ask spread investors actually incur. In addition, margin requirements as well as short selling restrictions can also explain deviations in actual option prices from their theoretical values. Finally, sensible differences between the borrowing and the lending rate as well as tax considerations will also refrain investors from trading as frequently as predicted by these models. All these structural barriers will definitively have an impact on the liquidity of the stock, option, and default-free bond markets. We should therefore keep in mind that the more they slow down or restrict the volume and the speed of trading, the more we should suspect that existing models are giving inaccurate "fair" option values. By "inaccurate" we do not mean that these models are theoretically inconsistent; rather they are "too clean" to capture some noisy parameters that will necessarily affect option prices in illiquid and highly regulated markets.

However, despite these institutional problems that may affect the pricing performance of existing stock option pricing models, their contribution is invaluable from a theoretical and conceptual standpoint. Not only do they enable us to value options on traded stocks but, as we will see in the next chapters, these partial equilibrium models can also be extended to the pricing of options written on a variety of underlying financial assets such as stock indexes, stock index futures, gold, foreign currencies, Treasury bills, et cetera.

The theory of option pricing has really led to a powerful asset valuation methodology, and through our analysis of stock options so far, we have mainly presented its originality and its tractability. This is only part of the contribution since the variety of its extensions to all kinds of contingent claims will now prove how robust and flexible the option pricing theory actually is.

CHAPTER
7

GENERALIZING THE ARBITRAGE-FREE PRICING APPROACH TO STOCK INDEX AND STOCK INDEX FUTURES WRITTEN OPTIONS

1 INTRODUCTION

In April 1973, the Chicago Board of Options Exchange started trading standardized option contracts on stocks. This innovation was only the beginning of a continuously growing and expanding segment of the financial markets. Today, stock option markets have exploded both geographically and numerically. The daily volume of options traded on the New York Stock Exchange exceeds that of physical stocks negotiated on this exchange. Moreover, in every major market, such as Tokyo, New York, London, Paris, Singapore, and Geneva, one can currently buy or sell call and put options written on the main stocks traded in those financial centers.

However, the most distinguishing feature of the development of option markets is related to their so-called "underlying asset" diversification. Today, stock options represent only a segment of the variety of options investors may use to manage their investment risk exposure. Indeed, since 1983 when the Chicago Board of Options Exchange introduced option contracts on the Standard & Poor's 100 Index, the market risk exposure of any portfolio can be monitored by buying or selling index option contracts. The same can also be accomplished by trading options written on stock index futures contracts, which are now available on the Standard & Poor's 500 Index futures contracts, the New York Stock Exchange Composite Index, futures contracts, et cetera.

In addition, the introduction of options on Treasury bills, Treasury notes, and Treasury bonds by the American Stock Exchange and by the Chicago Board of Options Exchange has enabled investors to manage their interest rate risk exposure by buying or selling options on short-, medium-, and long-term default-free bonds. They hence represent useful hedging tools in light of the increasing volatility of interest rates over the past decade. A similar interest rate risk-monitoring service is also provided by options written on Treasury bills and Treasury bond futures contracts, traded on the International Monetary Market and on the Chicago Board of Trade respectively, which have proved to be even more liquid and successful than their counterparts written on spot fixed-income securities.

Finally, we should point out that an investor whose portfolio is internationally diversified can today also hedge his foreign currency exposure by buying or selling foreign currency options written on the spot exchange rate or on a foreign currency futures contract. Indeed, in 1982 the Philadelphia Stock Exchange began trading options on the spot foreign exchange rate of major currencies including the German mark, British pound, French franc, Swiss franc, Japanese yen, et cetera, and in 1984, the International Monetary Market in Chicago started trading options on futures contracts written on these major foreign currencies. An interesting feature of foreign currency options is that they represent valuable hedging instruments not only for investors but also for a much broader category of economic agents—such as producers or consumers—who at one point or another share an exporter's long position or an importer's short position in a foreign currency.

As we can see, the variety of traded standardized options written on securities or other financial assets has expanded dramatically over the last decade. We also note that there has been a parallel development of commodity and commodity futures options contracts—on gold, gold futures, silver futures, oil futures, heating oil futures, et cetera—that has enabled industrialists, manufacturers, traders, and consumers to hedge the variable cost (or revenue) associated with these commodities.

Since this book is essentially concerned with the analysis of options viewed as an investment vehicle, we will limit our presentation to those options that represent either directly or indirectly—by hedging certain types of portfolio investment risks—meaningful long or short positions that can be part of an investor's securities portfolio. This means that we will analyze stock index and stock index futures options as well as foreign currency options since those three main categories of traded contingent claims provide the investor with a variety of strategies and responses to market risk and foreign currency risk exposure that prove to be very important in light of the diversification characterizing today's portfolio management.

Since the two first categories of options, stock index and stock index futures options, have very similar characteristics and are designed to hedge the same type of "systematic" or market risk, they will be treated in the current chapter. However, since foreign currency options are written on a distinct underlying instrument (i.e., the spot exchange rate) and are used to monitor "currency risk exposure," they will be discussed separately in Chapter 8.

Given that a stock index can be viewed as a large basket or "portfolio" of common stocks, we expect stock index options to bear many features similar to those of individual common stocks written options. Hence, they represent the natural starting point in the following analysis of "other" types of traded options. In this chapter we will therefore focus exclusively on the characteristics, economic functions, and pricing of stock index options and of stock index futures options. This requires that we first define what a stock index actually is, explain how it is computed, and compare how its main difference—namely, that it is a *nontraded* asset—with an individual common stock affects the valuation of stock index written options.

We will then be able to describe stock index options, explain their main financial role—namely, the monitoring of market risk—and finally, ask whether a methodology similar to the one originally proposed by Black and Scholes can be applied to price those options. We will see that there are a lot of additional problems related to the non-negotiability of the stock index—and to the fact that these options must therefore be settled in cash if exercised—that preclude us from valuing those options accurately using a "no arbitrage" valuation framework.

Since options written on a futures contract on the stock index have developed in parallel, it is important that we understand how these instruments actually compare and compete with each other. For that purpose and since those instruments are actually written on a "futures contract," it is essential that we first explain what a futures contract actually is, what purposes it serves, how it differs from a forward contract, and finally how it should be priced relative to the spot value of the underlying asset or good.

After relating all these topics to the stock index futures contract, we will be able to value the rather complex financial instrument called "stock index futures contract written option." This will enable us, at the end of this chapter, to summarize the main similarities and differences between options written on the spot and options written on the futures price of a stock index, to compare their respective efficiency for hedging and monitoring the market risk exposure of a given equity portfolio, and finally to discuss the theoretical problems related to the valuation of these particular categories of options whose true underlying instrument is, *de facto*, the market price of a "basket" of stocks.

2 GENERAL CHARACTERISTICS OF STOCK INDEXES: AN OVERVIEW

A stock index measures the evolution and hence the performance of the stock market or of one of its segments over time. While broad-based stock indexes like the Standard & Poor's 500, the New York Stock Exchange Composite Index, or the Value Line Index are designed to track the evolution of the stock market as a "whole," it is clear that no index does, in fact, encompass the "entire" stock market either internationally or domestically. For example, the Standard & Poor's 500 and the New York Stock Exchange Composite Index provide an adequate measure of the evolution of the 500 largest stocks trading in the United States and of all the stocks listed on the New York Stock Exchange respectively. However, neither of them focuses on the stocks of small firms, and as far as the New York Stock Exchange Composite Index is concerned, over-the-counter traded American stocks do not enter into its composition.

Hence, even though broad-based indexes are supposed to accurately measure the performance of a stock market over time, they will always neglect—through their sampling—a more or less important fraction of the stocks actually traded in a domestic and a fortiori in the international market.

Narrow-based indexes typically rely on a smaller number of stocks and they essentially have one of the following objectives:

1. A stock index such as the Dow Jones Composite Average, based on a few (65) actively traded common stocks still measures how a "diversified" portfolio of major American stocks would have evolved through time. Hence, its objective is also to reflect the performance of the market as a "whole" although it does it with a much smaller selection of stocks.

2. In contrast, narrow-based indexes can be constructed to track the performance of a segment of the stock market by focusing in one of several ways: small versus large capitalization-based stocks, listed versus over-the-counter traded stocks, and more commonly, a firm's activity based partition of the stock market. For example, the New York Stock Exchange reports the following subindexes: the NYSE Industrial Subindex, the NYSE Transportation Subindex, the NYSE Utilities Subindex, and the NYSE Financial Subindex.

Although the composition of an index is essential in determining whether it represents the relevant benchmark against which the performance of a specific (private versus institutional, active versus passive, broadly diversified versus concentrated, national versus international, etc.) portfolio or management style should be evaluated, there is a second important factor to consider when dealing with indexes, namely, their computation method. In other words, one should always bear in mind how a specific index's value aggregates the prices of its component stocks. We will therefore quickly describe the most commonly used index computation techniques as well as their impact on the financial interpretation of the nature of the resulting indexes.[1]

A   Equally Weighted Stock Indexes

Intuitively, this is the most simple aggregation method that requires an equal dollar amount be invested in each stock. Let us illustrate through an example how an equally weighted arithmetic average index is constructed. If we decide that the

---

[1] Although this discussion doesn't seem to bear a direct link with the analysis and pricing of stock index options, we will see, however, that it becomes relevant when one has to assess whether an investor can actually replicate the portfolio composition of the underlying index and hence execute the perfect hedge from which the arbitrage based stock index option pricing formula is derived. This problem will be discussed in more detail in Section 3 of this chapter.

index should initially be based on an investment of $1000 to be allocated between two stocks A and B, currently trading at $500 and $250 respectively, then at time 0 the index will contain one share of stock A and two shares of stock B. One period later, stock A is trading at $550 and stock B is trading at $235. Given that the reference value of the index I_0 was arbitrarily set equal to 100, the value of the equally weighted arithmetic average stock index at time 1, I_1, is given by

$$I_1 = I_0 \times \frac{\text{Market value of index at time 1}}{\text{Market value of index at time 0}} \qquad (7.1)$$

$$I_1 = 100 \times \frac{(550 \times 1) + (235 \times 2)}{1000} = 102$$

Hence, we see that over the first period the index has increased from its initial value of 100 to 102 because the decline in the price of stock B was weaker $(2 \times (-15) = -\$30)$ than the observed increase in the amount invested in stock A $(1 \times 50 = +\$50)$.

An equally weighted arithmetic average price index would be appropriate for someone who aims to maintain over time equal dollar amounts invested in each stock building up his initial portfolio, and from this standpoint, it is clearly not a suited benchmark for portfolios based on a "buy and hold" policy. Finally, it should be pointed out that such an index is also an inadequate benchmark for the performance measurement of actively managed portfolios whose strategy is to switch from underperforming to outperforming stock positions. [2,3]

B   Price-Weighted Stock Indexes

A price-weighted arithmetic average index tracks the evolution of the simple average of the market prices of its constituent stocks over time. In other words, one share of stock belonging to each company has the same weight regardless of the latter's market capitalization; that is, only the price level will matter since it determines the degree to which each company's stock contributes to the index's total value. Formally, if I_0 represents the reference value of the index at time 0, the value of the index can be subsequently computed according to the following formula:

$$I'_t = \frac{\frac{1}{n} \sum_{j=1}^{n} P_{j,t}}{\frac{1}{n} \sum_{j=1}^{n} P_{j,0}} \cdot I_0 \qquad (7.2)$$

---

[2] Indeed, to "track" the equally weighted arithmetic average price index you would always have to sell the winning stocks and to buy the losing ones in order to maintain equal dollar amounts invested in each component stock.

[3] It should be pointed out that the CRSP (Center for Research in Security Prices) Index is an equally weighted stock index that is essentially used in academic studies on capital markets.

where

I'_t = value of the price-weighted arithmetic average index at time t

$P_{j,t}$ = price of the jth stock at time t

n = total number of stocks included in the index[4]

I_0 = reference value at time 0 of the index

A simple example illustrates how this index can actually be computed.

Stock	$P_{j,1}$	$P_{j,0}$	I_0
1	128	125	
2	80	81	100
3	27	27	

Applying Eq. (7.2), we can compute the value of the index at time 1 as follows:

$$I'_1 = \frac{(128 + 80 + 27)/3}{(125 + 81 + 27)/3} \times 100 = 100.85$$

We see that the index has slightly increased by 0.85% over the first period although only Stock 1 experienced a price increase (from $125 to $128). This result had to be expected since price-weighted indexes give more weight to highly priced stocks and, in our example, it is precisely Stock 1, the "highest weighted" stock, which accounts for 54.82% of the initial value of the index, that performed well over the period.

In using such an index, one doesn't discriminate between small and large capitalization firms; the only relevant factor is the price level of a specific share since the higher it is, the more it affects the index's performance over time, specifically if the total number of stocks included in the index is small. The Dow Jones Industrial Average, which reflects the evolution of 30 actively traded blue chip American stocks, is the most representative arithmetic average price-weighted index. It is the oldest and most well-known "stock market" indicator although it only tracks the "average" price evolution of a small number of industrial stocks.

It should be noted that in practice the divisor (n) used to compute the average value of the price-weighted indexes will have to be adjusted for stock splits and dividends as well as for newly entering or defecting stocks. Finally, it should be mentioned that price-weighted stock indexes are not recommended for countries (such as Switzerland) where the size of a unit share may vary consistently across firms.

---

[4] If the number of stocks included in the index may vary from one period to the other, then n should be indexed with the subscript t and read as n_t in Eq. 7.2.

C   Market-Weighted Stock Indexes

Most indexes, whether they be broadly or narrowly based, are computed as arithmetic averages of the market value of their underlying constituents. In other words, these market indicators weight each stock according to the size of its market capitalization relative to that of all other stocks in the sample. Hence, such indexes would essentially reflect the performance of large capitalization firms and would only be slightly affected by the performance of small firms.

We can now illustrate by example how the market-weighted arithmetic average index is computed using the same three stocks as in Section B.

Stocks	$P_{j,0}$	$P_{j,1}$	I_0
1	125	128	80
2	81	80	300
3	27	27	100

The value of the index at time t satisfies the following formula:

$$I_t^M = I_0 \frac{\sum_{j=1}^{n} N_{j,t} P_{j,t}}{\sum_{j=1}^{n} N_{j,0} P_{j,0}} \tag{7.3}$$

where

I_t^M = value of the market-weighted arithmetic average index at time t

I_0 = reference value of the index at time 0

$N_{j,t}$ = number of shares of stock j outstanding at time t

$P_{j,t}$ = price of a share of stock j at time t

n = total number of stocks in the index

In this example, if we assume that the reference value of the index I_0 was set equal to 100 and the number of outstanding shares of each stock didn't change, the value of the index at time 1 is equal to

$$I_1^M = 100 \times \frac{(128 \times 80) + (80 \times 300) + (27 \times 100)}{(125 \times 80) + (81 \times 300) + (27 \times 100)}$$

$$= 100 \times \frac{36940}{37000} = 99.84$$

When we compare the value of the market-weighted index I_1^M to that of the price-weighted index I_1', we see that the former actually decreased by 0.16% over the first period while the latter increased by 0.85%. This is because the "weight" of the well-performing Stock 1 in the market-weighted index is smaller since the capitalization of Firm 1 is less than that of the poorly performing Firm 2. Hence, we see that in a market-weighted index, a given trend of the index will essentially be driven by the performance of the large capitalization firms.

A market-weighted broad-based index will essentially measure the performance one could achieve by holding a large portfolio in which the proportion invested in each stock reflects its market share of the entire—or nearly so—stock market. Hence, it is an adequate performance measurement benchmark for most institutional well-diversified portfolios that attempt to track the stock market by investing in each stock according to the relative size of its capitalization value. Since market-weighted indexes are based on a buy and hold policy, they represent "feasible" investment strategies[5] for a portfolio manager or an investor. Therefore, they are commonly used to manage index funds or to measure managers' ability to "beat" the market.

The Standard & Poor's 500, the Standard & Poor's 100, and the New York Stock Exchange Composite Index are typical examples of broad-based market value-weighted stock indexes that track the performance of the American stock market while the Financial Times Stock Exchange Index, the SBS Swiss Index, and the Indice CAC fulfill the same mission for the British, Swiss, and French stock markets respectively.

Of course there are still a lot of technical problems to solve before an index actually becomes reliable. For example, the nature—bid, ask, or transaction prices—of the market prices of the stocks must be assessed, and liquidity criteria for the sample of stocks may therefore have to be imposed if one wants to rely only on transaction prices. Moreover, the problems related to events like stock dividends, stock splits, new issues, mergers, and the introduction or retrieval of some stocks must also be addressed. Generally, these technical issues are solved differently for every reported index. We will not discuss them in this study since they are beyond the scope of presenting the main criteria and objectives a stock index should globally fulfill, which is essentially through its specific composition—stock sample selection—and computation technique.

3   ANALYZING OPTIONS WRITTEN ON STOCK INDEXES

A   Description of a Stock Index Option Contract

We are now able to describe and analyze standardized call and put option contracts written on stock indexes. A European call (put) option written on a stock index gives its owner the right to buy (sell) at a specific date T, a specific "fraction" of the index at a predetermined exercise price (K).

---

[5] They require, however, an adjustment in the composition of the "replicating" portfolio when new shares are issued and when dividends are paid. The latter should be reinvested in the portfolio.

American call (put) options bear the same right over their entire lifetime, and are thereby distinguished from European options, which can only be exercised at a fixed time, namely their expiration date T.

The main difference between an option written on a stock and an option written on an index lies in their exercise policy. For example, if a call option of IBM stock is exercised at maturity, the owner will pay the exercise price and actually take "delivery" of the number of IBM shares specified in the standardized contract. However, if a call option on the Standard & Poor's 100 Index expires in-the-money, the owner can exercise it only through a so-called "cash settlement," which means that he will receive in *cash* the difference between the value of the index and its exercise price multiplied by the size (or multiplier) of the standardized contract. Indeed, since a stock index is not a traded asset, the delivery of the underlying asset that is associated with the exercise of the option is not relevant anymore and will be replaced by an equivalent "cash settlement" of the in-the-money position.

We will now illustrate with an example based on options traded on the American Stock Exchange Institutional Investor Index (XII)[6] how these contracts are actually specified, what purpose they serve, and how they should be priced. Call and put options written on this index are—contrary to most stock index options—of the European type and can only be exercised on their expiration date. The underlying trading "unit" of the contract is 100 times the dollar value of the index. The exercise price is quoted in the same units as the index itself and must therefore be multiplied by 100 to obtain the true cost of exercising one call or put option.

The "delivery" method, in case a call (or a put) should be exercised, is based on the "cash settlement" of the difference between the index value (the exercise price) and the exercise price (the index value) multiplied by 100. Usually, call and put options with five distinct expiration dates (the three nearest months and two more distant successive months) trade simultaneously.

Let us suppose that the XII Index actually closed at 251.86 on the expiration date of the 260 (exercise price) March put option contract written on that index. The owner of the put hence decides to exercise his in-the-money European put option and will be entitled to the following cash settlement:

$$\text{Exercise value of the put} = [\text{Striking price} - \text{XII closing price}] \times 100$$
$$= (260 - 251.86) \times 100$$
$$= \$814$$

---

[6] The XII is a market value-weighted index tracking the performance of the 75 American stocks that are held in highest dollar amounts in institutional portfolios that have a market value of at least 100 million dollars in investment funds. It is therefore a broad, well-diversified stock market index that can be used to measure the performance of institutional equity portfolios.

Similarly, we can show that a 260 March call option would have expired worthless on the same date since a stock index option provides—like stock options—limited liability to its owner.

B Stock Index Options and Portfolio Management Strategies

Now that we have shown the main difference between stock options and stock index options, we will discuss the purpose index options fulfill. Obviously, the buyers and the sellers of these options do not receive or sell the constituents of the XII Index when they exercise their options, and they are only "indirectly" interested by the price level of the index's component stocks. Rather, by buying or selling call and put options on a stock index, investors are essentially willing to take or to alter—if they already have a stock portfolio—their global "market risk" exposure.

To illustrate the first case, suppose an investor doesn't have any specific views on the trend followed by individual stocks but thinks that the market as a whole will follow a positive trend over the next two months. He may then buy a short-term call option on a broad-based index and hence profit from any potential increase in the market while limiting the potential loss of its forecasting error—if the value of the index actually declines—to the initial cost of the call.

A similar strategy for someone who is bearish about the stock market would lead to the purchase of a put option on a broad-based index. Again, if the index actually declines, the put owner may sell or exercise his option and realize a gain while if the market has actually evolved in the undesirable (upward) direction, the option owner has limited his loss to the initial cost of purchasing the put.

Hence, individuals placing "bets" on the future direction of the stock market are not required to purchase and hold a well-diversified stock portfolio anymore. By buying call (or put) options they can profit from any appreciation (depreciation) of a stock index without being required to liquidate a large stock portfolio at the end of their planning period. Indeed, by investing in naked options on stock indexes, investors and portfolio managers can profit from broad market movements without having to bear the large transaction costs associated with the construction and liquidation of a well-diversified stock portfolio; moreover, they can limit the cost of their market trend forecasting error. However, many market participants already own or manage existing equity portfolios and this category of agents will essentially use stock index options to increase the riskiness or to protect the value of an existing position.

We will illustrate through an example how the latter more conservative hedging objective can be fulfilled with stock index options. Suppose the manager of an institutional portfolio valued at $100,000 believes that the market will drop over the next month and decides to protect his entire position against a downward potential market trend. By purchasing a certain number of European at-the-money one-month put options written on XII Index,[7] he can insure his portfolio against any decline in the value of the index and hence indirectly any decline in the stock market. For simplicity, we will assume that his portfolio has a composition similar to that of the XII Index so that any $1 increase or decrease in the index is also accompanied by a $1 increase or decrease in the portfolio's value.[8]

Suppose that XII is currently trading at 250 and that a one-month at-the-money put option on the index is quoted at $4\frac{5}{8}$, which, given that by convention each point of quotation corresponds to $100, sets the put's price equal to $462.50. To cover the entire value of his portfolio, the investor can purchase four puts, since each put is only hedging a dollar value of $250 \times 100 = \$25,000$. Hence, the initial cost of insuring his $100,000 equity portfolio is equal to

$$4 \times 462.5 = \$1850$$

This represents 1.85% of the initial value of his portfolio.

Now, as he expected, suppose that one month later (which corresponds to the expiration date of the put) both the XII Index and his portfolio have experienced a 5% decline, so that we observe the following:

Market value of the portfolio: $95,000
Market value of the XII Index: 237.5.

By exercising his four puts that are clearly in-the-money, the investor obtains a cash amount equal to

$$4 \times [(250 - 237.5)100] = \$5000$$

In this "perfect hedge" example, the result exactly offsets the $5000 loss experienced on the portfolio's value. Hence, for a cost of $1850 the investor has insured himself against any decline in the value of his portfolio. This proved to be a "wise" strategy in this example since for an insurance premium of 1.85% of the value of his portfolio, the manager has been able to avoid the 5% decline that affected the stock market.

---

[7] Alternatively, such a hedging strategy can also be implemented by selling (writing) call options written on the XII Index. For this example, we will only illustrate the strategy involving put options written on that stock index.

[8] Of course, in practice the correlation between an index and a particular portfolio is never equal to one so that a perfect hedge will require that one focuses on the portfolio's beta coefficient with respect to the index to determine the number of puts that have to be bought. Also note that a perfect hedge is practically an illusory concept since a portfolio of assets will—due to transaction costs, dividends, etc.—never increase or decrease in value with the same magnitude and speed as a stock index. The latter is only "paper value" while a portfolio consists of real physical holdings that require reallocation—to be bought and sold—to "track" the index's composition over time.

It should be noted that a perfect hedge generally will not be attainable. Indeed, by purchasing put options on a broad-market index, one hedges the so-called "systematic" or market risk component of a portfolio. Whenever there are too few stocks in this portfolio, the latter will be essentially exposed to "residual" or diversifiable risk and will only to a minor extent respond to general market swings. Hence, a portfolio's value can be hedged by the purchase of put options—or the sale of call options—written on a broad-based stock index only if the portfolio is itself largely diversified (i.e., mainly exposed to market risk) and if, in addition, its composition is sufficiently close to that of the index itself over the required hedging "horizon."

Moreover, since most standardized stock index options have relatively short-term maturities, this implies that they will only be effective hedging instruments against short-term market movements but that they will be replaced by portfolio insurance[9] strategies—which are dynamic asset allocation strategies—whenever an investor seeks long-term portfolio protection against unexpected downward market movements.

Stock index options are gaining and will certainly continue to gain increasing popularity among portfolio managers and investors since they provide them with a way of monitoring the degree of market risk one wants to maintain in an equity portfolio. To assess the cost of these "market risk-monitoring" tools, one must understand how a stock index should be valued and hence becomes able to detect under- and over-priced stock index call and put options.

C   Valuing European Stock Index Options

Although they are very similar to stock options, we will now see that stock index options generate additional conceptual problems and technical constraints if they are to be priced consistently under the partial equilibrium valuation approach developed so far. For simplicity, we start by examining how a European call or put stock index option should be priced and then extend our analysis to the more complex nature of American stock index options.

Generally, one would start by identifying the value of a given index with the price of a share of stock or more precisely a "supershare" reflecting the arithmetical average market value[10] of its constituents. One may then assume,[11] as for an individual stock, that the price of the index follows a continuous-time lognormal

---

[9] We have already discussed in Chapter 6 the concept of "portfolio insurance." Basically, it is a dynamic asset allocation strategy that replicates the structure of a long put option by moving funds from bonds to equity—when the market goes up—and from equity to bonds—when it goes down—to keep an existing equity portfolio hedged over time. The same strategy can also be achieved by synthetically replicating the payoff structure of a written call option using stocks and riskless bonds.

[10] Stock index options are essentially written on market value-weighted indexes like the Standard & Poor's 500, the Standard & Poor's 100, the American Stock Exchange Institutional Index, et cetera.

[11] This also requires that the stock index be continuously updated.

distribution[12] or, in other words, that the continuously compounded rates of return of the index have a constant mean and variance per unit of time. Then, maintaining the assumptions underlying the Black and Scholes option pricing model, namely that markets are frictionless and open continuously, and that the riskless interest rate is constant over time, one could apply the Black and Scholes call option pricing formula Eq. (4.18) to price European call options written on the index.[13]

There is, however, a major problem related to this straightforward extension of the Black and Scholes model to European stock index options; that is, dividend payments can no more be ignored—even for short-term options—in the case of a stock index.

For broad-based stock market indicators, it is often assumed that the dividend flow for the index is evenly spread over time and that it is continuous. With this simplifying conjecture, one can then simply rely on the constant dividend yield adjusted Black and Scholes formulas Eqs. (5.10) and (5.11) developed in Chapter 5 to value European call and put options written on these indexes. For some market indexes, the dividend yields are already quoted separately from the index and one only needs to assume that the reported quoted value of the dividend yield will remain constant over the life of the option to use this valuation approach.

However, the latter procedure can be very misleading since individual companies tend to concentrate their quarterly, semiannual, or annual dividend payments during specific months. For example, in the case of the New York Stock Exchange Composite Index, a study by Brenner, Courtadon, and Subrahmanyam (1987) has shown that the minimum dividend monthly cycle lasts from the middle of June to the middle of July, while the maximum dividend month lasts from the middle of July to the middle of August. Hence, to maintain consistency and accurately value options written not only on broad-based but also on narrow-based stock indexes—such as the XII Index—it is more appropriate to apply the Black and Scholes formula adjusted for the "actual" dividend payments of all the representative stocks in the index over the option's remaining lifetime.

This means that we will use the same adjustment procedure as discussed in Chapter 5, namely, we will subtract the present value of each dividend payment occurring over the stock index option's remaining time to maturity from the current stock index value to price the call (or the put).

It should be noted that the amounts of dividend paid by each firm as well as their payment dates can be estimated from their previous year's value and timing. Moreover, they need to be weighted by each firm's relative market value before they can actually be subtracted from the stock index's value.[14] With these

---

[12] Notice that this statement creates a conceptual problem since a lognormally distributed stock index is generally inconsistent with lognormally distributed stock prices for its components.

[13] For a detailed analysis of the Black and Scholes option pricing model, see Chapters 4 and 5.

[14] In the case of an equally weighted stock index we would simply attribute to the amount of the dividend paid by each firm the same weights $1/N$, where N represents the total number of stocks included in the index.

adjustments, we can compute the value of a European call option written on a market-value weighted stock index using the Black and Scholes formula adjusted for the actual dividend payments of each stock in the index, namely:

$$C = (S - \sum_{j=1}^{J} \sum_{i=1}^{I} D_{j,i} e^{-r\tau_{j,i}}) N(d_1) - K e^{-r\tau} N(d_2) \qquad (7.4)$$

where

C = price of a European call option written on the stock index

S = value of the market-weighted stock index

K = exercise price of the call option

τ = time to maturity of the call option

r = constant riskless interest rate

σ = standard deviation of the index's continuously compounded rates of return per unit of time

$D_{j,i}$ = market value-weighted amount of the jth firm dividend paid at date t_i

$\tau_{j,i}$ = remaining time until the payment of the dividend due at time t_i by firm j

$$d_1 = \left[\log \left(\frac{S - \sum_{j}^{J} \sum_{i}^{I} D_{j,i} e^{-r\tau_{j,i}}}{K e^{-r\tau}} \right) \right] \Big/ \left[\sigma \sqrt{\tau} + \left(\frac{1}{2}\right) \sigma \sqrt{\tau} \right]$$

$$d_2 = d_1 - \sigma \sqrt{\tau}$$

$N(\cdot)$ = standard normal cumulative distribution function

We can now illustrate with a simplified example how a European call option [15] written on a market value-weighted index should be valued according to Eq. (7.4), given that we observe the following data on the index, the option, and the

---

[15] To value a European put option written on a stock index, one would also adjust the Black and Scholes put option pricing formula by subtracting from the index's value the present value of the market-weighted dividend payments paid by each firm over the put's remaining time to maturity. Hence, the price P of a European put written on a market-weighted stock index satisfies the following equation:

$$P = K e^{-r\tau} N(-d_2) - (S - \sum_{j=1}^{J} \sum_{i=1}^{I} D_{j,i} e^{-r\tau_{j,i}}) N(-d_1) \qquad (7.4)'$$

where the other parameters are defined as in Eq. (7.4)

dividend payments of the index's component stocks over the option's remaining time to maturity:

$$S = 230$$

$$\tau = 0.30$$

$$r = 6\%$$

$$K = 225$$

$$\sigma = 20\%$$

Firm	Dividend	% Market value of firm j in the index	$D_{j,i}$	$\tau_{j,i}$
1	$20	1	0.2	0.2
2	0	0	0	0
:	:	:	:	:
5	0	0	0	0
:	:	:	:	:
J	$10	3.5	0.35	0.1

Hence, during the remaining time (109 days) to maturity of this call only two firms pay dividends. Firm 1 pays a dividend of $20, which, given this firm's share of the index (1%), represents a dividend amount of $.20, which will be due in 73 days. The other firm J pays a dividend in 36 days, and given its contribution to the index, the market value-weighted dividend of firm J equals $0.35.

We can now apply Eq. (7.4) to value this call option as follows:

$$C = [230 - 0.2^{(-0.06)(0.2)} - 0.35e^{(-0.06)(0.1)}]N(d_1)$$
$$- [225e^{(-0.06)(0.3)}]N(d_2)$$

When evaluating $N(d_1)$ and $N(d_2)$ gives

$$C = \$14,681$$

Since most stock index option contracts are based on a multiple of the index equal to 100, this means that one call option on "100 units" of this index has a current theoretical value of $1468.10.

Of course, in our simple example where only two firms are assumed to pay dividends, the latter's influence on a European call or put's price is small. In practice, especially for short-term options that expire in months when a large number of firms pay their quarterly dividends, the latter may even more substantially decrease (increase) the value of a European call (put) especially when they are distributed by large capitalization firms.

D   The Valuation of American Stock Index Options

At this stage it is worth mentioning that with the exception of options written on the Standard & Poor's 500 Index and on the American Stock Exchange Institutional Index, most standardized option contracts are of the American type.

We will now see that for the valuation of this most common category of stock index options, we must devote even more care and judgment to the appropriate handling of the interim dividend payments on the index. For that purpose, it is often assumed in practice that the dividend flow is constant and continuous and that it therefore can be approximated by a constant dividend yield over the option's remaining lifetime. This "smoothing" of the dividend function is convenient since it results in the "no-early exercise" Restriction 13 of Chapter 2 being satisfied for most American stock index calls allowing one to use the constant dividend yield adjusted Black and Scholes formula, Eq. (5.10)—presented in Chapter 5—to price these claims.

However, this approach can be criticized in two respects:

1. As in the case of European stock index options, it is very unlikely that the dividend stream of stock indexes can be assumed continuous over time. It is true that there will be more ex-dividend dates than in the case of options written on individual stocks, but they will still obey a discrete time pattern over the option's remaining time to maturity.

2. In the case of American stock index call options, early exercise may be optimal before some ex-dividend dates if one considers the "actual" dividend payments of each firm in the index. This will tend to be true for options whose remaining time to maturity extends over a period when many firms tend to pay their dividends. It will be even more relevant—if the stock index is market value-weighted—when some large capitalization firms pay dividends during the period.

It is, therefore, essential to consider the actual dividend stream and its timing over the American call's time to maturity. As before, information about the amount and timing of the dividends paid by each firm in the index can be inferred from past data and should essentially be exploited in the following way: Over the time to maturity of each call to be valued, a preliminary checking is made as to whether the no-early exercise condition (i.e., the fact that the present value of the interest rate earned on the striking price is greater than the present value of the dividends over the remaining time to maturity of the options) holds at each ex-dividend date during the option's remaining maturity. If it holds, then the American call on a dividend paying stock index should be valued like its European counterpart, namely, relying on Eq. (7.4) presented in this section.

If the no-early exercise condition is violated or, in other words, if the possibility of early exercise cannot be ruled out, then we are in a similar situation to when we were valuing American call options on dividend paying stocks. There is again no analytical solution to the valuation equation[16] that an American call on a dividend paying stock index must satisfy, and this equation has to be solved numerically checking at each ex-dividend date if the exercise value of the option is greater—which means early exercise will occur—than its unexercised value.

For American put options written on stock indexes, early exercise may—as in the case of American put options on stocks—be optimal at any time regardless of whether there are dividends paid over the option's remaining lifetime. Since there is also no analytical solution to the partial differential equation that the American stock index put must satisfy, we will again use numerical approximation techniques to derive its theoretical value.[17] We should, therefore, always keep in mind that the theoretical prices of both put and call options written on a stock index will be more accurate and reliable if the actual dividend payments of each constituent firm of the index are considered. Otherwise, if one fits a continuous dividend yield to the dividend pattern of the index, the prices of American options will be biased because the dividends' positive (negative) impact on the early exercise frequency of American calls (puts) will be incorrectly assessed. This is particularly true for options written on narrow-based stock indexes for which the interim cash flow stream is obviously discretely and unevenly spread over time.

---

[16] The partial differential equation is the same as in the case of stock options, namely, the price C' of an American call option written on a stock index satisfies

$$\frac{1}{2}\frac{\partial^2 C'}{\partial S^2}\sigma^2 S^2 + \left(rS - \sum_{i=1}^{I}D_i^*\delta(t_i - t)\right)\frac{\partial C'}{\partial S} + \frac{\partial C'}{\partial t} - rC' = 0$$

where

D_i^* = the total value of all dividends paid at date t_i (by one or many firms) and assumed to be known or accurately estimated ex ante.

$\delta(t_i - t)$ = the so-called Dirac delta function defined as $\delta(x) = 0$ for all $x \neq 0$ and $\int_{-\infty}^{\infty}\delta(x) = 1$

The partial differential equation is subject to the following boundaries: (a) the condition at final maturity of the American call is

$$C'(S^*, T, T) = \max[S^* - K, 0]$$

(b) the early exercise condition occurring an instant prior to each ex-dividend date $t_i, i = 1, 2, 3, \ldots, I$ is

$$C'(S, t_i, T) \geq \max[S - K, 0]$$

[17] The partial differential equation for the American put written on a dividend paying stock index is the same as for the American call. Hence, the put's price P' will satisfy the partial differential equation in footnote 15 with the symbol P' replacing C' and with the following boundary conditions:

$$P'(S^*, T, T) = \max[K - S^*, 0]$$
$$P'(S, t, T) \geq \max[K - S, 0] \text{ for all } t < T$$

It should be noted that in the case of the American put, the early exercise condition should be checked at any point of time ($t < T$) while for an American call this condition needed only to be verified at each instant prior to an ex-dividend date t_i.

However important, dividends are neither the only nor most delicate problem to solve when valuing traded stock index options. The former is essentially related to one characteristic of those options' underlying instrument, namely to the fact that an index is *not a traded asset*.

E General Problems Related to the Pricing of Stock Index Options

So far we have valued both European and American stock index options with the same methodology initially devised by Black and Scholes for stock options. Hence, the analytical formula Eq. (7.4) that applies to European Stock Index options as well as the numerically solved valuation equations that apply to American Stock Index options rely—like all the relative pricing models previously discussed in this study—on the well-known "no arbitrage" restriction. Remember that in this framework it is explicitly assumed that an investor can form a perfectly hedged position with the option and the underlying instrument. This means that to value a stock index call option, for example, one should be able to sell the call option short and hedge it by buying all the securities comprising the index in proportions such that this market value-weighted portfolio has the appropriate "hedge ratio" [18] computed from the index's current value. [19] Further, it is assumed that over time, the investor will be able to remain "hedged" by selling or buying the securities comprising the index so that his long position in the latter's aggregate value is always tracking the evolution of the "hedge ratio" (Δ_C). If these conditions are continuously fulfilled, "the short call/long replicated index" position will be effectively riskless and should therefore, from the no arbitrage condition, earn the riskless rate of interest over any infinitesimal time period. This no arbitrage condition then allows us to derive the partial differential equation whose solution defines the call's theoretical price.

By a similar argument, it can be shown that the put's theoretical value obtained by assuming that a long put position and a long position in all the securities comprising the index can be continuously hedged over the put's remaining time to maturity. In the case of an option written on an individual stock, the perfect hedge—ignoring transaction costs—is a feasible strategy whose main practical deficiency is that the stock/option position cannot be continuously but only very frequently rebalanced.

---

[18] Remember that the hedge ratio for a call option is given by $\partial C / \partial S = N(d_1) = \Delta_C$. As time passes and as the value of the underlying instrument varies, the hedge ratio will also change accordingly. For a detailed discussion of the concept of a "hedge ratio," see Chapters 4 and 5.

[19] We suppose for this explanation that the underlying "instrument" is a market-value weighted stock index. Of course, the same reasoning applies to an option written on an equally weighted stock index except that in this case the long (short) replicating portfolio would have to attribute equal dollar amounts to each stock entering its composition. For a description of the equally weighted indexes' computation see section 2A of this chapter.

In the case of stock index options, however, it is definitely much more controversial and unrealistic to assume that a perfect hedge represents a feasible strategy an investor will be able to successfully implement in practice. If we suppose that he has a short position in a call option written on a broad-based index, like the Standard & Poor 500 or the NYSE Composite Index, this would require that he simultaneously initiates a long position in the 500 or 1500 stocks comprising those indexes and that he should further be able—by buying and selling these stocks—to adjust his long position everytime the index's value and hence the hedge ratio change.

Even if we examine options written on narrow-based indexes, like the Standard & Poor 100 or the XII Institutional Index, trading and monitoring around 100 different stocks in such a way as to always hold the same proportions of the latter as the index does and moreover maintaining the appropriate hedge ratio level over time will prove to be a very utopic goal.

In very simple terms, the main reasons that prevent an investor from implementing a perfect hedge are found in the legal and institutional barriers that preclude him from maintaining a replicating fraction—equal to the hedge ratio—of the index over the option's remaining lifetime. The most important of these trading restrictions are identified as follows:

1. The first restriction is the magnitude of the transaction costs associated with the continuous—or very frequent—rebalancing of such large stock portfolios. These costs are far more important than those required by the hedging of an individual stock option. This is particularly true if some of the stocks comprising the index are not very liquid and hence bear non-negligible bid and ask spreads.

2. The index does not necessarily reflect the current value of all its constituents. Indeed, at each time the index's value is reported, some of its component stocks have actually not been traded for the last minutes, hours, or even longer. The computed index's value as well as the hedge ratio, therefore, rely on "past" information that might induce the investor to be incorrectly hedged against the "true" (unknown) current value of the index. This phenomenon becomes particularly relevant for indexes reflecting the value of thin markets or whenever there are too many illiquid stocks entering its composition. Even for very liquid markets, whenever a rapid downfall (also called "panic" decline) in stock markets occurs, most of the stocks will not trade actively, some will even not trade at all, thereby implying that the index's value can be completely disconnected from the "true" value of its component stocks. In such situations, like on October 19, 1987, the "jumps" that affect the stock market as a whole may even result in a temporary trading suspension for some stocks and, therefore, severely compromise the required rebalancing of the "pseudo" hedged position.

3. Finally, the trading rules prevailing in each stock option exchange can—even under normal market conditions—severely limit the high volume or the nature of the transactions required by a perfect hedge. For example, the investor will

generally not be able to execute orders in many stocks as rapidly as necessitated by his changing hedge ratio. This is particularly true when we consider that short selling rules may preclude an investor from selling short stocks that have already dropped in value over the previous days.

To avoid some of these institutional barriers, the investor can, of course, choose a sample or a subset of the most liquid stocks included in the index and take appropriate positions. This will guarantee that his portfolio is highly correlated with the index and that it enables him to simultaneously track the index's hedge ratio over time. While this may be a solution for largely diversified stock indexes to avoid transaction and liquidity costs,[20] it still does not solve the main problem created by a perfect hedge involving a stock index option.

Indeed, we have mentioned that a specific feature of stock index options lies in their exercise rule; that is, when an option is exercised there is no asset delivery involved. Instead, stock index options are exercised on the basis of a cash settlement. This procedure is practical and convenient—since the option owner generally has no intention of receiving a fraction of the index's constituents—but it simultaneously compromises the existence of a perfect hedge. Even if one happened to be long in a portfolio that exactly replicates the stock index and if one continuously updated this long portfolio to hedge his short stock index call option, this strategy would provide an uncertain outcome should this option be exercised at (or before) its expiration date.

Obviously, when the writer of a call receives an exercise notice, he will subsequently have to liquidate his entire portfolio to obtain the cash he has to "deliver" to meet his obligation. Hence, even if the value of the index doesn't change, the prices of some stocks on which it is based may actually be "too old" to reflect the current values at which the option writer will actually be able to sell these stocks. In addition, he will not be able to avoid losses—due to the large bid and ask spreads—everytime the liquidation of his portfolio involves buying or selling illiquid stocks.

Indisputably, even though the position has been "hedged" against unexpected variations in the stock index's value, this is not sufficient to guarantee that it will earn a risk-free rate of return should the option be exercised. This is because holding an offsetting long position in a portfolio of stocks will not allow the option writer to *directly* settle his obligation in cash.

He faces an additional source of uncertainty, namely an "exercise risk" associated with the fact that he generally will be unable to liquidate his entire "offsetting" position in the portfolio of stocks at an aggregate price equal to the value of the index at the time when he received the exercise notice. Hence, the cash equivalent of the exercise value of his option will usually fail to be exactly

---

[20] These costs can be associated with the large bid and ask spreads some thinly traded stocks prices may reflect.

matched by the proceeds of the liquidation of his long (or short) position in the constituents of the index, involving a new type of risk exposure so far unknown for all options that are exercised through physical delivery of the underlying instruments. In the latter case, the hedged option writer needn't be concerned by any decline or rise in the value of the underlying instrument between the exercise notice date and the delivery "date" since he already had the offsetting physical short or long position. From that perspective, it is true that for all options based on traded underlying assets that involve physical delivery if exercised, the hedge really is perfect as far as its exercise obligation settlement is concerned.

It follows that the general arbitrage restrictions developed in Chapter 2 will not necessarily hold for stock index options. Indeed, these restrictions fail to recognize the difference between exercising an option by taking or receiving delivery of the underlying security and exercising it by paying the cash equivalent amount of its exercise value. In the latter case, the fact that an American option trades for less than its "exercise value" ($S - K$, in the case of a call option) will not necessarily lead to a riskless arbitrage profit. Indeed, if the price of the call is less than its exercise value, buying the call and exercising it (in cash) will not necessarily lead to a riskless arbitrage profit since the cash equivalent actually may not be risklessly reinvested in all the stocks comprising the index.

More serious is the problem related to the justification of using the no arbitrage approach to value stock index options. In other words, can we accurately assess the theoretical value of these options on the basis of the same pricing framework that has already been used in the case of common stocks, and "ignore" the impact of "exercise risk" on the perfect hedge strategy's outcome?

This question clearly depends on the degree of uncertainty that the "cash settlement" procedure will generate for each particular type of traded stock index option contract. If the options and the stocks underlying a specific index trade in a fairly active and liquid market and if we moreover observe an efficient price and transaction data processing on this specific exchange, we can be confident about the no-arbitrage-based pricing results.

Hence, in markets where the value of the index is continuously updated, the delay between exercise notice and cash settlement is small, and transactions can be rapidly executed with minimal institutional barriers, the "exercise rule" associated with stock index options will only have a negligible influence—and can therefore be ignored—on their prices. Contrarily, if one is interested in pricing a stock index option that trades on a highly regulated or less informatively efficient exchange where in addition the stock index components are not necessarily actively traded, the cash settlement exercise rule may play a key role in explaining why our traditional option pricing models fail to value these stock index options accurately.

Given the growing expansion of portfolio management strategies involving the use of stock index options, a major weakness of traditional arbitrage-based-option-pricing models is clearly pointed out. We obviously need further research that focuses on the specificities of options written on non-traded underlying assets and attempts to value these options without forcing them to fit in the general approach developed for common stocks. Indeed, we could safely apply the perfect hedge-based valuation approach for common stock written options since there was not such controversy about either the feasibility or the final settlement of such a strategy. In the case of stock index options, these are the two essential factors that will obviously require an explicit integration in any meaningful and accurate arbitrage pricing approach to be developed. Their importance is not only theoretical but should also prove useful for the analysis of "market oriented" portfolio management strategies, which need a precise estimate of the cost associated with the hedging and for the monitoring of market risk using stock index options.

As an alternative, wouldn't it be more advisable to choose options contracts written on stock index futures—since the latter represent traded financial assets—to fulfill the same objectives? This is precisely one of the interesting questions we will analyze in the following presentation of stock index futures options.

4   GENERAL CHARACTERISTICS OF FORWARD CONTRACTS, FUTURES CONTRACTS, AND STOCK INDEX FUTURES

Stock index futures options are contingent claims written on the value of a futures contract whose underlying instrument is the spot value of the stock index. Hence, these options prices are primarily related to the value of the futures contract and will only indirectly depend on the underlying index's spot price.

Since a futures contract—the "underlying" financial asset on which the stock index futures option is written—differs from an underlying physical or spot instrument with regard to its price settlement procedure, trading rules, and economic functions, we will first describe and analyze the main features of a futures contract, and more precisely, focus on the stock index futures contract.

Historically, economic agents such as farmers, traders, producers, or bankers have used "forward contracts" to buy or sell a commodity (agricultural product, asset, currency, etc.) on a specific future date for a price due at delivery that is determined on the day the contract is settled between both parties. We will therefore start by defining the concept of a "forward contract" since most of its characteristics have been precisely adapted, some even improved, with the development of standardized futures contracts.

A   Forward Contracts: Basic Properties

We can define a forward contract as an arrangement between two parties whereby the seller agrees to deliver to the buyer on a specified date and at a fixed price—to be paid at delivery—a specific quantity of a given good or asset. In such contracts, the quality, quantity, future delivery date, and the so-called forward price of the good to be paid on that date are settled through a common agreement between both parties. Hence, forward contracts are "tailored" to the specific needs of a given buyer and seller as opposed to option contracts that have *standardized* features (exercise price, expiration date, quantity, exercise settlement, etc.).

A second major difference between forward contracts and options contracts lies in the legal relationship they respectively establish between the two parties. In a forward contract, both parties have an *obligation*, namely the buyer must buy at the forward price the specified quantity of the good or asset no matter what its current market price is at the time of delivery. Similarly, the seller is *obliged* to deliver at this future date the fixed quantity of the good he has agreed to provide in exchange for a cash retribution equal to the forward price of the good. Hence, if at the expiration date of the contract the spot price of the good is greater than its forward price, the buyer will effectively realize a gain—and the seller a loss—equal to the difference between these two prices. We can therefore say that the payoffs of a forward contract are *symmetric* for both parties. Conversely, standardized option contracts have a dissymetric payoff structure in which the owner of the option has the *right* to decide whether or not to exercise his option and hence buy (sell) the good at the exercise price at (or before) the expiration date of the contract. Only the seller or so-called option writer faces the obligation to buy or sell the specified quantity of the good at the exercise price whenever the option owner decides to exercise his right.

Finally, a third difference between forward contracts and standardized option contracts lies in their initial price settlement procedure. The forward price is settled so that "no cash transfer" between the buyer and the seller occurs on the day of their agreement. Only at the expiration date—or delivery date—will the buyer transfer the cash equivalent of the forward price to the seller in exchange for the good. During the forward contract's "life" there will be no cash movements between the two parties. Conversely, standardized option contracts have arbitrarily defined exercise prices that require the buyer of the option to pay the premium or option price as soon as he acquires the option. This is because he has in fact bought a "right" and must hence compensate the other party for being the only one to face an "obligation" in this contract.

We will now closely examine how the price of a forward contract is actually settled. If the fixed price, $_0H_T^-$, to be paid at delivery (T) but defined at the time (0) the contract is initiated was too low, the buyer would have to pay a positive amount to compensate the seller at time (0) when the contract is negotiated. Similarly, if the fixed price was initially set too high, the seller would have to pay the "buyer" to induce him to accept the contract. There always exists an intermediate price, which we will call the forward price $_0H_T$ for which the initial value of the contract is equal to zero. This is the price that is commonly used in all forward agreements to guarantee their no initial cash-flow transfer characteristic.

Of course, this price is related to the spot value of the good S on the day the contract is initiated. As the spot price of the commodity or good changes, the forward price originally set becomes either too high or too low and hence the value of the contract will subsequently differ from zero.

If we use $_0H_T$ to define the forward price of a contract settled at time 0 for delivery at time T, we know that the following relationship must hold

$$V_0(_0H_T) = 0 \tag{7.5}$$

where

$$V_0(_0H_T) = \text{the value of the forward contract at time } t = 0$$

We also know that at the maturity date T of the contract, the buyer will pay an amount $_0H_T$ to receive a good whose current spot price will be equal to S_T, hence it must be true that the value of a forward contract at expiration is equal to

$$V_T(_0H_T) = S_T -_0 H_T \tag{7.6}$$

where

$$V_T(_0H_T) = \text{the value of the forward contract at its expiration date } T$$

$$S_T = \text{the spot value of the good or of the commodity at time } T$$

$$_0H_T = \text{the initially settled forward price of this contract}$$

But how does the value of a forward contract evolve between those two extreme dates? We can show by a simple arbitrage strategy involving two forward contracts initiated at time 0 and at time 1 respectively and expiring at the same date T, how the value of a forward contract will vary through time.

Suppose that at date 1, an investor sells a new contract with forward price $_1H_T$ to offset his long forward position initiated at time 0. Hence the value of his total position at time 1 is equal to

$$V_{1,P} = V_1(_0H_T) - V_1(_1H_T) \tag{7.7}$$

$$= V_1(_0H_T)$$

where

$$V_{1,P} = \text{the value of the portfolio at time 1}$$

Equation (7.7) follows from the fact that the value of the short position in the forward contract initiated at time 1 is such that its initial value $V_1(_1H_T)$ is equal to zero by virtue of Eq. (7.5).

At the maturity date of both contracts, we find that the value of the investor's portfolio $V_{T,P}$ satisfies

$$V_{T,P} = V_T(_0H_T) - V_T(_1H_T)$$

Using Eq. (7.6) to define the terminal value of both contracts, we can define $V_{T,P}$ as follows:

$$V_{T,P} = (S_T -_0 H_T) - (S_T -_1 H_T) \tag{7.8}$$

$$=_1 H_T -_0 H_T$$

This amount is certain since it is equal to the difference between the forward prices of the two contracts. Since the final outcome of this strategy is perfectly predictable and hence riskless, its rate of return should be equal to the riskless interest rate to avoid arbitrage opportunities in the market. Therefore, we have the following equation:[21]

$$\frac{V_{T,P}}{V_{1,P}} - 1 = \frac{1}{B(1,T)} \tag{7.9}$$

where

$B(1,T)$ = the price at time 1 of a riskless default free discount bond maturing at date T and paying \$1 for sure at that date. $B(1,T)$ can also be defined as the discount factor to be applied to a certain cash flow occurring in $(T-1)$ periods.

Plugging the expressions of $V_{T,P}$ and $V_{1,P}$ in Eq. (7.9) we obtain

$$\frac{_1H_T - _0H_T}{V_1(_0H_T)} = \frac{1}{B(1,T)} \tag{7.10}$$

From Eq. (7.10), we can now easily obtain the value of the long contract at date 1, hence:

$$V_1(_0H_T) = (_1H_T - _0H_T) \cdot B(1,T) \tag{7.11}$$

By a similar argument, we can show that at any subsequent date t, the value of a forward contract is simply equal to the present value of the difference between the forward price of an "identical" contract issued at time t and its own forward price $_0H_T$, formally written

$$V_t(_0H_T) = (_tH_T - _0H_T)B(t,T) \tag{7.12}$$

where

$V_t(_0H_T)$ = the value at time t of a forward contract initiated at time 0 for delivery at time T at a forward price equal to $_0H_T$

$_tH_T$ = forward price of a contract initiated at time t for delivery at date T

$B(t,T)$ = present value at time t of one riskless dollar to be paid at time T, or in other words, price at time t of a discount riskless bond maturing at date T

We can illustrate with a simple example how the value of a forward contract should be computed through time. Suppose a contract for delivery in one year is

---

[21] We are dealing with a discrete time setting but still assume that the interest rate is continuously compounded over time. Hence we have

$$B(t,T) = \exp(-r(T-t)) = \exp(-r\tau)$$

where

r = riskless interest rate assumed to be constant

τ = time to maturity of the riskless discount bond

initiated at date 0 for a forward price of $110. What is its value six months later given that at that time a six-month forward contract has been initiated at the price of $115? Furthermore, we know that the price of a six-month discount bond at that time is equal to $0.94. We can apply Eq. (7.12) to compute the value of this contract, let us call it $V_6(_0H_{12})$, at the end of six months:[22]

$$V_6(_0H_{12}) = (115 - 110) \times 0.94$$

$$= \$4.70$$

However, although we can now value a given forward contract whether it be written on an underlying currency, commodity, agricultural good, or financial asset, simply by knowing the forward prices of subsequently issued contracts for the same delivery date, we still don't know how the forward price of a given agreement is settled and how it should relate to the value of the underlying good. We definitely need those clarifications to understand which factors determine the forward price's evolution as well as the contract's value path over time.

The cost-of-carry model states that the forward price should reflect the current spot value of the good plus the net costs (benefits) of carrying it until the delivery date T:

$$_0H_T = S_0 + c_{0,T} \tag{7.13}$$

where

S_0 = the spot value of the good or commodity at date 0

$c_{0,T}$ = the net cost (benefit) at time 0 of carrying the good until date T

$_0H_T$ = the forward price of the contract at time 0

Obviously, the "net cost-of-carrying" will be given a different interpretation for each type of underlying instrument.

Historically, the cost-of-carry model was defined for commodity forward contracts. The "net carrying cost" consists of all the expenses associated with the holding of a given commodity or good—insurance costs, storage expenses, inventory financing interest rate charges, et cetera—less the benefits or so-called convenience yield—no transportation costs, no shortage problems, . . . , or typically the dividend payments of a financial asset—one may obtain by holding the commodity or the asset instead of having it delivered at a future date T. Hence, the net carrying costs account for both the reduction and increase in costs the ownership of a particular good may involve relative to a forward contract agreement.

The difference between the forward price and the spot price of a given good is generally referred to as the "basis." At the time of delivery T, the basis should be equal to zero since the forward price for immediate delivery cannot differ from

---

[22] We have used monthly notation in this example, hence $V_6(_0H_{12})$ is the value after six months of a 12-month forward contract initiated at date 0.

the then prevailing spot price without creating riskless arbitrage opportunities. Hence, at time T:

$$B_T =_T H_T - S_T = 0 \qquad (7.14)$$

where

$$B_T = \text{the basis at time } T$$

$$S_T = \text{the spot price of the commodity at time } T$$

$$_T H_T = \text{the forward price for "immediate delivery" at time } T$$

During the period from date 0 to T, the basis will vary, tending to shrink towards zero as the maturity date T approaches. However, at any arbitrary point in time t, the basis (i.e., the difference between the then prevailing forward price and the spot price) should be equal to the net cost-of-carrying the good if arbitrage opportunities are to be avoided in the market.

$$B_t = {}_t H_T - S_t = c_{t,T} \qquad (7.15)$$

For, suppose the converse were true and we would observe at time t that the basis is greater than the net cost-of-carrying the good (i.e., $B_t > c_{t,T}$). Further, assume that for this specific commodity the cost-of-carrying is simply equal to the interest rate costs of financing the commodity over the period. We can then construct a riskless self-financing portfolio by buying the commodity (or good), financing its purchase through riskless borrowing, and selling the forward contract short. This initial position involves no cash inflow or outflow at date t. Suppose we then hold this portfolio until the expiration date of the forward contract. At that time we liquidate the portfolio by (1) delivering the security and hence closing the forward position at the "locked in" forward price ${}_t H_T$:

$$S_T + ({}_t H_T - S_T)$$

and (2) paying back the loan S_t and the interest costs on the loan:[23]

$$-(S_t + c_{t,T})$$

Adding these two expression results in the outcome:

$$_t H_T - S_t - c_{t,T}$$

Since the strategy required no initial investment and it is perfectly riskless — its final outcome doesn't bear any uncertainty — it should provide a zero return to avoid riskless arbitrage opportunities. However, it is obvious that the final outcome will be different from zero since the basis (${}_t H_T - S_t$) was initially greater than the net cost-of-carrying ($c_{t,T}$). Hence, this situation is not viable, since it would imply, by contradiction, that arbitrage opportunities exist.

---

[23] To simplify we have assumed that the interest rate on the loan is equal to the net cost-of-carrying the commodity. The same arbitrage argument can also be obtained without making this simplifying assumption.

By a similar argument we can show that riskless arbitrage profits can be locked in by buying the forward contract, selling the security short, and lending the proceeds of the short sale until we liquidate the entire position at the expiration date T of the forward contract whenever the basis happens to be lower than the net cost-of-carrying the commodity of the asset until date T. Therefore the only viable relationship consistent with arbitrage-free markets is

$$B_t = c_{t,T} \qquad \forall t \tag{7.16}$$

If we now plug the definition of $_tH_T$ as given by Eq. (7.15) into the definition of the value of a contract given by Eq. (7.12), we obtain

$$V_t(_0H_T) = (_tH_T - _0H_T)$$

$$= S_t + c_{t,T} - S_0 - c_{0,T}$$

$$= (S_t - S_0) + (c_{t,T} - c_{0,T})$$

By virtue of the identity Eq. (7.16), we obtain

$$V_t(_0H_T) = (S_t - S_0) + (B_t - B_0) \tag{7.17}$$

Hence, we can see that the value of a forward contract will change if the value of the underlying good or asset changes and/or if the basis changes over time. This is an important result that emphasizes how the contract's value can be related to either changes in the forward price or in more fundamental parameters such as changes in the basis and the underlying good's spot price. It should also be noted that even if the price of the underlying good remains constant over time, the value of the contract will vary since we know that the basis—and the net cost-of-carrying the good—tend to zero as we approach the maturity date of the contract.

For precious metals, the basis will usually be positive since it essentially represents costs—like storage, financing, or insurance—the owner must pay if he holds the commodity from time t to time T while it is generally observed that there are only small or negligible benefits from storing such commodities. Hence, the forward price of a contract written on silver, gold, or platinum will generally be higher than the currently observed spot price of such commodities.

However, this is not a general rule. Commercial commodities like copper or plywood, for example, appear to have a net convenience yield that varies with the level of their respective inventories.[24] Hence, in case of shortage we may well observe a negative basis (i.e., the forward price is less than the prevailing spot price) suggesting that there is a direct benefit from holding and storing such commodities. Moreover, political events, cyclical consumption or production patterns, relative weight of hedgers versus speculators, and increasing marginal production costs are also some of the relevant factors one should try to integrate into the analysis of the basis level and evolution over time for each specific forward contract.

---

[24] For a detailed discussion and empirical investigation of the relationship between the convenience yield of a given commodity and the level of inventories, see Brennan (1986).

For storable commodities it is often assumed that the net cost-of-carrying is a function of the commodity's spot price. If such an assumption is made and if we use c' to denote the continuously compounded net cost-of-carrying yield—or net convenience yield—we can express the forward price $_tH_T$ as follows:

$$_tH_T = S_t e^{c'(T-t)} \qquad (7.18)$$

The basis is then equal to

$$B_t =_t H_T - S_t = [e^{c'(T-t)} - 1]S_t \qquad (7.19)$$

We can see in Eq. (7.19) that depending on whether the net instantaneous convenience yield is positive or negative (i.e., whether $c' > 0$ or $c' < 0$) we will observe a positive or negative basis.

It is, of course, an empirical issue beyond the scope of this study to state the type of commodities for which the forward contract pricing Eq. (7.18) really is relevant. This discussion was, however, necessary to help us understand the basic mechanisms governing the price of a forward contract based on a storable good or commodity since it now becomes straightforward to extend our discussion to financial forward contracts. Typically, such contracts consist of an agreement between two parties to buy or sell a specific quantity of a financial asset at a future date T, for a forward price initially settled. The "assets" we will refer to can be stocks, T-bills, bonds, or financial assets like foreign currencies, et cetera.

The main difference between forward contracts written on commodities and those written on financial assets is that the net cost-of-carrying for a financial instrument is considerably different from the net cost-of-carrying for a commodity, agricultural product, or precious metal. In the latter case, this net cost essentially involved storage related expenses while such expenses are typically irrelevant in the case of marketable securities or other financial assets. If the underlying asset does not pay any dividends, like, for example, a Treasury bill or a discount bond, then the net cost-of-carrying is simply equal to the—assumed constant—riskless interest rate.

Indeed, by holding the T-bill from time t until the expiration date T of the contract, the investor essentially bears an "opportunity" cost related to the fact that if he had bought the forward contract on the T-bill instead, he would have been able to invest the current value of the T-bill at the risk-free interest rate over that period $(T - t)$. Hence, the forward price of a contract whose security to be delivered at time T pays no interim payments (coupons or dividends) is simply equal to

$$_tH_T = S_t e^{r(T-t)} \qquad (7.20)$$

$$= S_t e^{r\tau}$$

where

$_tH_T$ = the price at time t of a forward contract written on a security that doesn't make any interim cash disbursements

$r =$ continuously compounded riskless interest rate, which is assumed to be constant

$\tau = T - t =$ the time until the expiration or delivery date of the forward contract

$S_t =$ the spot value of the security at time t

We can easily show that if the relationship in Eq. (7.20) doesn't hold, an investor can earn a riskless arbitrage profit. Suppose, for example, that the basis at time t was smaller than the net cost-of-carrying the T-bill, which is equal to [25] $S_t(e^{r\tau} - 1)$, and that hence we observe the following: ${}_tH_T < Se^{r\tau}$.

An investor could then implement a self-financing strategy by buying the forward contract, selling the security, and investing the proceeds of the short sale over the period $T - t$. Hence, initially no cash enters in or out of the position. At the expiration date T of the forward contract, the investor would liquidate his position by

1. Liquidating the forward contract $\qquad\qquad S_T - {}_tH_T$
2. Delivering the security he has sold short $\qquad -S_T$
3. Collecting the proceeds of his loan $\qquad\qquad S_t e^{r(T-t)}$

$$\text{Final outcome:} \qquad S_t e^{r(T-t)} - {}_tH_T$$

Since ${}_tH_T < S_t e^{r(T-t)}$, this represents a riskless arbitrage profit and hence Eq. (7.20) must therefore hold by contradiction.

When the underlying security is a stock or a coupon paying bond, the valuation Eq. (7.20) doesn't hold anymore since it ignores the fact that the owner of such an asset is entitled to the dividend or coupon stream over the lifetime of the forward contract. In these cases, owning the security has a direct cost related to the foregone interest rate one may have earned by buying the forward contract instead, but it is partially or even totally offset by the direct benefit of earning the dividends or the coupons paid during that period.

If we assume, like in the case of the stock option valuation procedure presented in Chapter 5, that the dividend stream over the forward contract's remaining lifetime can be validly approximated by a constant dividend yield δ, then the forward price equation can be written

$$\begin{aligned} {}_tH_T' &= S_t' e^{(r-\delta)(T-t)} \\ &= S_t' e^{(r-\delta)\tau} \end{aligned} \tag{7.21}$$

---

[25] By assumption, the net cost-of-carrying in Eq. (7.20) is taken to be simply equal to the interest rate earned by investing S_t over the period $T - t$. From our previous definition—see Eq. (7.13)—of the net cost-of-carrying, the latter therefore satisfies

$$c_{t,T} = S_t(e^{r\tau} - 1)$$

where

$_tH'_T$ = the forward price at time t of a forward contract on a dividend-paying security to be delivered at time T

S'_t = the spot price at time t of the dividend-paying security

δ = the continuously compounded constant dividend yield or coupon paid by the security.

An example will help illustrate how the price of a forward contract on a dividend paying stock should be computed. Stock BAC is currently trading at $98, its estimated dividend yield is equal to 3%, and we want to assess the current price of a forward contract for delivery in 6 months of one share of stock BAC. The riskless rate of interest is equal to 7% on an annual basis. Applying Eq. (7.21) we find[26] that the current price at time t of that forward contract on stock BAC is equal to

$$_tH'_T = 98 \exp[(0.07 - 0.03) \times 0.5]$$

$$_tH'_T = \$99.98$$

The existence of the dividends lowers the net cost-of-carrying a security with respect to the forward contract. We will observe that when the dividend yield is less than the riskless rate of interest $(\delta < r)$, the basis is positive; when the dividend yield is equal to the riskless interest rate $(\delta = r)$, the forward price is equal to the spot price; and finally, when the dividend yield is greater than the risk-free rate of interest $(\delta < r)$, the basis is negative.

At this stage, there are several theoretical and practical problems related to pricing forward contracts that still remain to be solved—for example, how do we estimate the dividend yield? What if the dividend stream is stochastic over time? What is a relevant proxy for the riskless rate? Are these relationships still valid in the case of cash settlement? We will not discuss them, however, since they are beyond our objective of emphasizing the main features of forward contracts to facilitate our analysis of financial futures contracts, and more specifically, of stock index futures contracts.

B   Financial Futures Contracts: Basic Properties

A futures contract can be defined as an agreement by which the seller commits to deliver a specified amount of a specified good—or commodity or asset—to the buyer at a specified date in the future and for the "futures price" prevailing at the time the contract is initiated. Hence, like forward contracts, futures contracts

---

[26] Note that all numbers are expressed on an annual basis (i.e., over a fraction of the year equal to 0.5 since the contract expires in six months).

create an obligation for both the buyer and the seller. They also do not[27] require a cash inflow or outflow on the day the contract is initiated, and they can only be exercised (i.e., settled for delivery) at a specified date in the future.[28]

However, futures contracts differ from the previously analyzed forward contracts in several respects.

1. Unlike forward contracts, they are not tailored to the specific needs of a particular buyer and seller. Conversely, futures contracts are *standardized* with regard to the quality and the quantity of the asset, time to maturity, price quotation, and delivery procedure. Hence, a potential buyer or seller using such contracts might, therefore, commit himself for a period or quantity that does not exactly match his original needs.

2. Futures contracts are traded on exchanges while forward contracts typically take place in the over-the-counter or interbank markets. Hence, unlike forward contracts, the former are negotiable and provide the seller (buyer) with the flexibility to close the futures position by buying (selling) an offsetting contract at any time prior to the expiration date. Obviously, to provide the negotiability as well as a high degree of liquidity to futures markets, the standardization of these contracts now appears to be a necessary prerequisite.

3. Finally, the most important difference between a futures and a forward contract lies in their respective price settlement procedures. We have already seen that there is no cash inflow or outflow in a forward position until its delivery date T. However, futures contracts have a *daily settlement procedure* that requires the buyer and seller adjust their position daily according to the gains or losses they might actually incur everytime the futures price changes. In other words, the daily settlement often referred to as the "marking-to-market" procedure guarantees that the market value of a futures contract will—unlike the market value of a forward contract—always be equal to zero.

Formally, if we use $_tF_T$ to denote the "futures price" at time t of a futures contract that expires at time T, we know that this price—like the forward price—is initially settled so that no "cash" transfer takes place at the date the contract is initiated. Hence, when it is initiated, the value of a futures contract $V_0(_0F_T)$ is simply equal to zero:

$$V_0(_0F_T) = 0 \qquad (7.22)$$

Now, suppose that one day later, the newly issued futures contract on the same underlying asset and for the same expiration date T has a price equal to

---

[27] We ignore for the moment the initial margin both parties to a futures contract may have to deposit when they enter the contract.

[28] Note that some futures contracts may actually have a delivery period. For example, the delivery period for crude oil futures contracts lasts between the fifth and the last business day of the delivery month.

$_1F_T$. Depending on whether $_1F_T$ is greater than, equal to, or less than $_0F_T$, the value of the futures contract initiated at time 0 will be greater than, equal to, or less than zero. Hence, to maintain the market value of the contract equal to zero, the futures contract will be "marking-to-market," which means that the buyer will receive (pay) the positive (negative) difference between $_1F_T$ and $_0F_T$ and that the seller will pay (receive) this difference to eliminate any change in the market value of the contract.

Obviously, the differences in the futures prices $(_tF_T - _{t-1}F_T)$ prevailing at the end of each day will always have to be settled in cash to guarantee at each date t the following relationship:

$$V_t(_tF_T) = 0 \qquad \forall t, 0 \le t \le T \tag{7.23}$$

Through this procedure, we are implicitly reopening at the end of each day t a new futures contract for delivery at date T at the current prevailing futures price $_tF_T$.

Hence, the difference between the initially contracted price $_0F_T$—at which the buyer entered the contract—and the final spot price of the good will have been compensated daily during the futures contract remaining lifetime. Therefore, at expiration, the futures price is simply equal to the prevailing spot price of the commodity (or goods) at time T:

$$_TF_T = S_T \tag{7.24}$$

This is perfectly consistent with a futures contract having a market value of zero at maturity—given that the relationship in Eq. (7.23) must always hold. This contrasts with the no day to day adjustment in the forward price of a forward contract that implied the latter's value was equal to the difference between the spot price at time T and the initial forward price $_0H_T$ at the expiration date. [29]

We will now illustrate with an example how the "marked-to-market" of futures contracts procedure is actually implemented at the end of each day by the exchange. Suppose that a futures contract has been bought at date 0 for a futures price equal to $10 and that it has been held until its expiration date, three days later. We can, ex post, examine how the changes in the futures price induced cash inflow or outflow in the buyer's account.

We see through this simple example that the buyer is credited (debited) at the end of each day of the positive (negative) change that occurred in the futures

Day	0	1	2	3
Spot price	9.0	10.5	10	9.5
Futures price	10	11	9	9.5
Cash flow to the buyer's account	0	+$1	-$2	+$0.51
Market value of futures contract	0	0	0	0

---

[29] See Eq. (7.6) in Section 4A.

price. Notice that at the expiration date, marking to-the-market can be done with respect to the spot or the futures price because their value must be the same, and equals $9.5 in this example. The marking-to-market would have been perfectly symmetric for a seller, of course. In practice, however, each exchange can impose additional regulations that should guarantee that both buyers and sellers always meet their obligations and that transactions can be efficiently processed. Typically, this will require an initial margin deposit as well as margin calls each time a buyer or seller's account is below a certain limit.

Daily marking-to-market may in this perspective be viewed as one of the regulating measures established by futures exchanges to protect investors against default risk. This kind of protection wasn't required in the case of forward markets since the identity of each party to the contract is known. Indeed, a forward agreement generally remains—due to its non-transferability—in the hands of its initial contracting parties until the expiration date.

Until recently, it was believed[30] that only market "imperfections" could explain the differences often observed between the prices of otherwise "identical" futures and forward contracts. Indisputably, such statements were made with the implicit assumption that the "marking-to-market" pricing settlement is irrelevant for the pricing of futures contracts. However, Cox, Ingersoll, and Ross (1981) made a pioneering contribution to the analysis of futures markets by showing that the price discrepancy between a futures contract and an "identical" forward contract can be explained by the marking-to-market procedure when interest rates are stochastic. Since, in the latter case, the futures position must be settled daily, and hence involves the investment (financing) of the daily inflows (outflows) in the buyer or seller's account at an unknown varying daily interest rate, a hedge involving the forward contract and an otherwise identical futures contract will not be perfect.

Cox, Ingersoll, and Ross (1981) have shown in their model that a forward contract can be replicated by a combination involving a long position in an otherwise identical futures contract and daily borrowing or lending. They then showed with an arbitrage argument that when interest rates are uncertain, the difference between the futures price and the forward price will depend on the covariance between the spot value of the underlying good and the product of the daily interest rates accumulated over the futures contract remaining time to expiration.

For example, when this covariance is positive, as the price of the good or commodity increases, interest rates also tend to be at higher levels. But, when the price of the commodity rises, the buyer's account is typically credited with a positive amount at the end of each day, enabling him to reinvest those positive cash flows at even higher interest rates. In the opposite case, when the good's price declines, interest rates will also tend to be lower so the buyer will be able to finance his debited daily account more "cheaply." Hence, the buyer is willing to pay more for such a contract written on a commodity that is positively correlated with the level of interest rates.

---

[30] See Capozza and Cornell (1979), and Rendelman and Carabini (1979).

For commodities or assets whose price is negatively correlated with interest rates—for example, a bond—the buyer will be willing to pay less for a futures contract than for a forward contract since the former implies that when the price of the underlying commodity or good decreases, not only will he see his account debited but he will also have to finance it at higher interest rates. Unfortunately, there is not enough empirical evidence to definitively assess the sign of this covariance term for each commodity or asset underlying a futures contract. We would, however, agree that it is negative for a futures contract written on fixed-income securities and also—but less strongly—negative for contracts written on stocks since it has been observed[31] that stock prices tend to be higher when interest rates are low. For other commodities or goods, the degree of correlation will of course vary according to their specific nature, storage facility, and individual capacity to provide a hedge against—or in other words, to be positively correlated with—inflation.[32] Empirically[33] however, the effect of this covariance term has proven to be negligible, so that most futures contracts pricing models have actually ignored it. They have been derived as if they were actually concerned with forward contracts, or in other words, as if futures prices were equal to forward prices thereby suggesting that interest rate uncertainty is irrelevant. We will return to this pricing issue later and analyze it in light of the specific futures contract we are interested in, namely a stock index futures contract.

C Stock Index Futures Contracts: Basic Properties

A stock index futures contract is a commitment by which the buyer (seller) agrees to purchase (sell) at a predetermined date a specific "fraction" of the index at a predetermined "futures price" to be paid at the expiration date of the contract. Since the underlying instrument, the spot index, is not a traded asset, at expiration we are facing the same situation previously examined with stock index options, namely that there can't be "physical" delivery of the underlying instrument.

The contract will be settled in cash at the maturity date, requiring from both parties to pay (receive) the difference between the then prevailing index's spot price and the previous day's futures price times the "multiplier" (i.e., the size of the index futures' contract). The "cash delivery" of a financial futures contract implies that at the expiration date, the contract will be closed by the same marked-to-market procedure as the one prevailing over the futures contract's entire lifetime involving no additional commitment either for the buyer or seller except that their

---

[31] See in particular the study by Fama and Schwert (1977) that reports a significant negative correlation between stock market and Treasury bill returns over 3-month and 6-month holding periods.

[32] For example, for a futures contract based on the consumer price index, we would expect the correlation between the underlying instrument—the consumer price index (CPI)—and interest rates to be positive.

[33] The studies by Cornell and Reinganum (1981) and by Elton, Gruber, and Rentzler (1984) do not find much difference caused by interest rate uncertainty in the cases of foreign exchange and Treasury bills futures contracts, respectively.

positions should be adjusted to reflect that the futures price is equal to the spot index's value at that date.

Hence, the difference between the spot index's value at expiration and the futures price at which the futures contract was originally bought (or sold) has been gained (or lost) daily over the future's contract remaining time to maturity, rather than at a single point in time as for forward contracts. This "cash settlement," which is based on the closing price of the spot index at the expiration date, is very easy to implement, of course. It does, however, rely heavily on the fact that the price of the underlying spot index is neither manipulated nor "too" old—in the sense that it is based on past transaction prices for some stocks—in order to be "fair" for both parties.

Currently, there are futures contracts trading on broad-market indexes—like the Standard & Poor's 500 futures contract, the Value Line Average futures contract, and the New York Stock Exchange Composite Index futures contract—as well as on narrow-based market indexes—such as the Major Market Index futures contract. The size of these contracts is expressed as a multiple of the underlying index. Usually, one futures contract allows you to buy or sell 500 times the value of the spot index. Furthermore, these contracts typically trade on a quarterly maturity cycle, which means for instance, that there will be four contracts for delivery in March, June, September, and December that are available on a turnover basis depending on the current calendar date.

The introduction of stock index futures contracts was an important innovation in the context of portfolio management since it provided investors and managers with the first financial instrument enabling them to easily monitor and hedge the nondiversifiable or systematic risk component of their portfolios, namely "market risk."[34] Indeed, equity index futures can be used to monitor—increase/decrease— the exposure of a given portfolio to unexpected market shifts, or in other words,

---

[34] It is assumed that the total risk of a share or portfolio of stocks can be decomposed into a diversifiable or residual component and into a systematic or nondiversifiable component. Typically, an individual stock's total variance of returns σ_i^2 can be decomposed as follows:

$$\sigma_i^2 = \beta_i^2 \sigma_m^2 + \sigma_{c_i}^2$$

where

$\beta_i = \text{Cov} (\tilde{R}_i, \tilde{R}_m)/\sigma_m^2$, defines the sensitivity or β of the stock's return $(\tilde{R}_i)$ to unexpected shifts in the market's return $(\tilde{R}_m)$

σ_m^2 = the variance of the returns on the market portfolio

$\sigma_{c_i}^2$ = the residual variance or nondiversifiable risk component of stock i

For a portfolio of stocks that is well-diversified, the systematic risk component will dominate and it is in this sense that diversification actually "pays" since it helps to reduce the total risk of a given portfolio. The total variance σ_P^2 of a portfolio can also be decomposed into its nondiversifiable and diversifiable components:

$$\sigma_P^2 = \beta_P \sigma_m^2 + \sigma_{c_P}^2$$

where

$\beta_P = \sum_{i=1}^{n} X_i \beta_i$ represents the beta of the portfolio

X_i = weight of security i in portfolio P

$\sigma_{e_P}^2$ = residual variance of portfolio P.

they enable a manager to increase or decrease the β of his portfolio without having to add or exclude some stocks from his portfolio and hence having to incur a potential "selection bias." They can also be used to manage index funds since a mixture of stock index futures and cash is an almost perfect substitute for a well-diversified market portfolio that has the advantage of avoiding the turnover costs as well as the dividend reinvestment problem.

Stock index futures have also been used in dynamic portfolio insurance strategies—instead of the previously applied technique of buying and selling stocks and simultaneously borrowing or lending in the default-free bond market—since a put option on an existing equity portfolio can be replicated much more easily using index futures and riskless bonds. Hence, we can say that stock index futures have two essential functions: (1) "clearing" relative price discrepancies with the underlying equity market—since any such mispricing would induce arbitrageurs to take appropriate spot and futures positions—and (2) allowing agents to alter their equity portfolio's market risk exposure.

We will illustrate with an example how stock index futures can actually be used to protect the market value of an existing equity portfolio. Suppose an investor actually owns a $100,000 equity portfolio and believes that over the next three months the market is likely to decline. He would, therefore, like to protect his position but without having to modify the current asset mix of his portfolio. As an alternative, he can take an offsetting short position in the Standard & Poor's 500 futures contract at a current futures price of 260 for "delivery" in three months.

The main problem associated with the hedge is to compute the number of contracts one must buy to be "perfectly" immunized against market movements. Obviously, no matter how well a portfolio is diversified, it will never behave exactly like the underlying stock index. We therefore need to compute the beta[35] or sensitivity of the portfolio's returns with respect to the index's returns to compute the hedge ratio. Indeed, if a given portfolio has a beta that is greater than one, we must buy more futures contracts since any $1 change in the index involves more than a $1 change in the portfolio, and obviously the converse will be true for a defensive portfolio[36] whose beta is smaller than one.

---

[35] The beta of a portfolio is the weighted average of the betas of its constituent stocks. The beta of an individual stock and portfolio have been defined in footnote 33. The beta of an individual stock is empirically estimated by regressing the past returns R_{it} of a security over the past returns R_{mt} of the index that is used as a proxy of the market portfolio. The beta coefficient β_i of each stock is simply the estimated slope of the regression line:

$$\hat{\beta}_i = \text{Cov}(R_{it}, R_{mt})/\sigma^2(R_{mt})$$

where

$\hat{\beta}_i$ = estimated beta coefficient for stock i

[36] In fact, since we are hedging with stock index futures and not with the underlying spot index and since the correlation between the futures and the spot index is not perfect, Figlewski (1986) has suggested that the β^* of the portfolio be computed with respect to the index futures' value rather than with respect to the spot index's value. Indeed, due to nonsynchronous trading, marking-to-market, et cetera, the two values of the index generally will not be perfectly correlated and typically we would expect the futures index to be more volatile than the underlying spot index. However, the latter distinction is only important for very short-term hedges for which basis risk plays an essential role.

Having computed the beta of the portfolio as being equal to 1.3, the investor can now use the following formula to determine the number of contracts of Standard & Poor's 500 futures contracts he should sell to be fully hedged:

$$n = \frac{\text{beta of portfolio} \times \text{market value of portfolio}}{\text{futures price} \times \text{(index multiplier)}} \tag{7.25}$$

where

n = number of futures contracts to be bought or sold in a perfect hedge.

Given that each futures contract on the Standard & Poor's 500 has a multiplier of 500, which represents a commitment to sell (or buy) 500 times the index, he should sell

$$n = \frac{1.3 \times 100,000}{260 \times 500} = 1 \text{ contract}$$

Now suppose that three months later, he observes the following:

$$\text{Spot index's value} = 247$$
$$\text{Portfolio's value}^{37} = \$93,500$$

We can now examine the outcome of the hedge:

$t = 0$	Initial value of portfolio	100,000
$t = 1$	Final value of portfolio	93,500
	Loss on equity portfolio	6,500
$t = 0$	1 contract sold at 260	
$t = 1$	1 contract settled in cash at current spot value of 247	
	net profit on the futures	
	position: $(1 \times 500 \times (260 - 247))$	6,500
	Global result	0

Of course, in practice the hedge will not be perfect due to (1) the marked-to-market procedure at random interest rates, (2) an investor's inability to buy or sell the required number of contracts—when it is not an integer number, (3) transaction costs, and (4) lack of absolute correlation between the spot and the futures value

---

[37] We have assumed that the portfolio's value decline of 6.5% was exactly equal to the decline in the S&P 500 spot value times the portfolio's beta (i.e, $0.05 \times 1.3 = 6.5\%$). Of course, in reality this relationship will not hold since any portfolio bears some non-market related or residual risk component.

of the index. Moreover, there still remains the fundamental question about the choice of the index given that it should be the closest possible proxy of the true—unobservable—market portfolio and should therefore reproduce unexpected market movements accurately. In addition, factors such as the liquidity of the stock index futures contract, margin deposits, price limits, and temporary disconnection between the quoted futures price and the reported spot index's value can certainly create problems whenever hedging or dynamic portfolio insurance policies need to be implemented or rebalanced.[38]

D   Valuing Stock Index Futures Contracts

We are now ready to discuss the delicate issue in this analysis of financial futures contracts, namely the problems related to the valuation of such contracts. Since stock index futures large volumes in trade and compete as hedging tools with other instruments such as stock index options, it is essential for investors, portfolio managers, and stock market analysts be able to determine what the "fair" price of a stock index contract should actually be.

We have previously argued that the price of any futures contract—regardless of the nature of its underlying instrument or asset—will be equal to the price of an otherwise identical forward contract if and only if we assume that there is no interest rate uncertainty. In fact, since it has been shown that the covariance term between the underlying asset's price and the level of interest rates is typically negligible for most futures contracts, we will omit interest rate uncertainty in the following argument and assume that the price of a stock index futures contract can be derived as if it were a forward contract written on the same multiple of the index and expiring at the same date. This will not affect our principal conclusions, and it will enable us to concentrate on the most important problems associated with the pricing of stock index futures.

Under this assumption, the price at time t of a futures contract for delivery at time T, will—with the same arbitrage argument as the one previously employed for the pricing of forward contracts—satisfy the following equilibrium relationship:

$$_tF_T = S_t + c_{t,T} \tag{7.26}$$

where

S_t = the spot value of the index at time t

$c_{t,T}$ = the net cost-of-carrying the index over the period $T - t$

Obviously, to determine the equilibrium or "parity" price of a stock index futures contract, one must be able to clearly define and quantify the net cost-of-carrying the index $c_{t,T}$.

We have already shown, in the case of financial forward contracts, that the equilibrium price of such a contract can be obtained by an arbitrage argument. In-

---

[38] Indeed, for simplicity we assumed that we can find a futures contract that matures at the end of the hedging horizon. In practice, this is seldom the case, thus leaving room for basis risk and "residual" uncertainty as to the outcome of the hedge.

deed, we proved that forming a self-financing portfolio by buying the underlying spot instrument, borrowing the amount required to pay the purchase price, selling a forward contract, and holding the entire position until the expiration date of the forward contract is a perfectly riskless strategy. Hence, the final value of this position should be equal to zero, which implies that the forward price of a contract written on an underlying asset paying no dividends must satisfy the following arbitrage-free relationship:

$$_tH_T = S_t e^{r(T-t)} = {_t}F_T \tag{7.20}$$

In the absence of interest rate uncertainty, the price of a futures contract written on a nondividend paying security should therefore satisfy the same pricing relationship, thereby explaining the second identity of Eq. (7.20).

However, when the underlying instrument is a stock index, we will obviously receive dividends during the period over which the riskless strategy is implemented, like previously, owning a long position in the stock index is now "less" costly since the payment of dividends reduces the net cost-of-carrying the index to its holder. But, for the reasons already explained in the section on stock index options, it would be inappropriate to assume that the dividend stream over the futures contract remaining time to expiration is continuous, which would ignore the clustering of the dividends paid by most firms during specific months—for example, July, August, September, and March—while in other months their frequency and hence amount will be very low—for example, December and January.

Hence, to compute the net cost-of-carrying an index, the *actual* dividend stream over the period $(T - t)$ should be deducted from the "interest rate" cost of financing the long position in the stock index since it is now "cheaper" for the holder of a physical position to carry this position over the futures contract remaining time to maturity. Therefore, by using the same arbitrage argument as before and replacing the constant dividend yield by the more realistic actual dividend stream assumption,[39] we can define the "parity futures price" of a stock index futures contract as

$$_tF_t = S_t e^{r(T-t)} - \sum_{j=1}^{N} D_j e^{r(T-t_j)} \tag{7.27}$$

where

$_tF_T$ = the price at time t of a futures contract on the stock index for "delivery" at time T

S_t = the market value of the stock index at time t

D_j = the value of the dividends paid by all firms in the index at time t_j

r = the riskless rate of interest assumed to be constant over $T - t$

---

[39] Moreover, we need to assume that the amount and the payment dates of all dividends are known or can be accurately predicted.

Hence, we see that the net cost-of-carrying the index is now equal to

$$c_{t,T} = {_t}F_T - S_t$$

$$= S_t e^{r(T-t)} - \sum_{j=1}^{N} D_j e^{r(T-t_j)} - S_t$$

$$= S_t(e^{r(T-t)} - 1) - \sum_{j=1}^{N} D_j e^{r(T-t_j)} \qquad (7.28)$$

The interest rate cost-of-carrying the spot index

$$S_t(e^{r(T-t)} - 1)$$

is now reduced by the future value of all dividends actually paid by the firms in the index over the futures contract remaining time to maturity

$$\sum_{j=1}^{N} D_j e^{r(T-t_j)}$$

An example will help illustrate how the parity futures price of a stock index futures contract should actually be computed with Eq. (7.27). Suppose that the Standard & Poor's 500 spot index's current value is equal to 265 and that we want to determine the equilibrium price of the stock index futures contract written on that index that expires in 130 days, having further estimated that over this period, firms will pay dividends for a total—market value weighted amount[40]—of $2 in five days and $1.20 in one hundred days. The continuously compounded interest rate is supposed to be constant and equal to 6%. Using Eq. (7.27), we find that the theoretical price of this futures contract should be equal to

$${_t}F_T = 265 \exp(0.06 \times (130/365)) - 2 \exp(0.06 \times (125/365))$$

$$- 1.2 \exp(0.06 \times (30/365))$$

$$= 267.47$$

Multiplying the resulting price by the multiplier of each Standard & Poor's 500 futures contract, we find that the parity price of one futures contract should be equal to

$${_t}F_T \times 500 = 267.47 \times 500 = \$133,735$$

The important issue for both practitioners and academics is to determine whether this equilibrium pricing relationship actually holds in the market. Several empirical studies conducted by Modest and Sundaresan (1983), Figlewski (1986), and Cornell and French (1983) conclude that the equilibrium or parity futures pricing relationship can be severely violated. For example, in their study dealing

---

[40] Note that since the Standard & Poor's 500 is a market value-weighted index, the dividends paid by each firm on date t_j should be multiplied according to this firm's specific weight in the index. We have already described this procedure in Section 3 of this chapter.

with the Standard & Poor's 500 futures contract, Cornell and French reported evidence that the observed Standard & Poor's 500 futures price traded 10% below its theoretical value. In other words, the equilibrium condition imposing that the basis be equal to the net cost-of-carrying the index appears to be violated as far as stock index futures contracts are concerned. This may partially be explained by the technical problems related to the assessment of the net cost-of-carrying a stock index. These technical problems relate to the estimation of the future dividend flows from past data and to the fact that we have ignored interest rate uncertainty and priced the stock index futures contract as if it were a forward contract. Although important, the practical difficulties related to both forecasting of the index's component firm dividend payments and the marking-to-market procedure do not represent the main explanation of this "apparent" arbitrage opportunity.

We say apparent, since at first sight it would seem that a futures price below—or above—its equilibrium value could lead arbitrageurs to make profits by taking relevant offsetting positions in the spot and futures market. We will see that it is precisely this arbitrage argument—on which the parity futures pricing formula is actually based—whose conceptual validity and practical implementation must be severely questioned in the context of stock index futures.

Indeed, the equilibrium pricing relationship Eq. (7.27) is precisely based on the fact that it is riskless to hold a long (short) position in the futures contract and an offsetting short (long) position in the spot index combined with some lending (or borrowing). Yet, a zero profit should be earned on this self-financing riskless strategy to preclude arbitrage opportunities in the market. But is such a strategy really riskless? There are several reasons that explain why it isn't actually a pure "arbitrage" strategy and why we therefore incur "basis risk" by setting up such a position.

1. Since the index is not a traded asset, several problems will appear when we take an offsetting long- or short-spot position to hedge the futures position. As previously mentioned, it will be impossible for an investor to hold a position in all the constituent stocks of an index that will perfectly replicate the index's composition over time. This is due to the large transaction costs, dividend reinvestment problems, and computation methods of some indexes that precludes them from being replicated by any "managed" portfolio.

   This is indeed the case for the Value Line Composite Stock Index that is an equally weighted geometric index. It calculates each stock's daily return and then geometrically averages the computed returns for the 1700 firms represented in the index.[41] Due to its particular computation technique—geometric

---

[41] The value of the geometric equally weighted index at date t, I_t is obtained as follows:

$$I_t = \sqrt[N]{(P_{t,1}/P_{t-1,1})(P_{t,2}/P_{t-1,2})\ldots(P_{t,N}/P_{t-1,N})} \, I_{t-1}$$

where

$$N = \text{total number of stocks in the index}$$
$$P_{t,1} = \text{price of security 1 at date } t$$
$$P_{t-1,1} = \text{price of security 1 date } t-1$$

averaging of a stock's returns—this index is not reproducible by any portfolio strategy and it further underestimates the "feasible" arithmetic average return an investor can actually earn on a portfolio.[42] Hence, we will never be able to perfectly hedge a long (or short) position in a Value Line Composite Index futures contract.

2. For those stock indexes that represent "attainable"—in the way they aggregate security returns—portfolios we still need to monitor and rebalance a replicating portfolio over time to track the index's composition. The problem can be simplified by building the replicating portfolio with a subset or small sample of stocks entering the composition of a given stock index. However, since the replicating portfolio should be tracking, and therefore be perfectly correlated with the index over time, this implies that we will very frequently need to revise and rebalance it, and hence not really be able to reduce transaction costs while bearing the additional risk that such a small portfolio will never be a perfect surrogate for a largely diversified or broad-based index.

3. Whenever the arbitrage position has to be implemented with a long futures position and an offsetting short position in a replicating portfolio containing all or part of the index's stocks, it will generally be an infeasible strategy. This will be the case when short sales of individual stocks are prohibited or severely regulated in the market. Hence, the fact that the parity futures price—computed with Eq. (7.27)—is below its actual value does not necessarily imply an arbitrage opportunity at all if the offsetting short position in the individual stocks is prohibited or involves high margin deposits.

4. Moreover, the problem of asynchronous trading plays an essential role in explaining why the parity futures price may actually diverge from its market price. This problem exists at two levels. First, the spot index and the futures contract may actually trade on different exchanges or on the same floor but with different opening and closing hours, and even if trading hours were identical, the prices will seldom reflect synchronous "true" arbitrage opportunities since trading never takes place continuously.

    Second, since the spot index is not itself a traded asset, the problem of asynchronous trading also exists at another level. Namely, the reported index's value at a given time will never exactly reflect the current market value of all its component stocks. Basically, we will observe a situation in which the spot index's value leads the value of the thinly traded stocks while it lags behind the value of the most actively traded stocks. Hence, due to the fact that trading is not continuous and that new prices are not instantaneously reflected in the spot index's value, most "arbitrage" opportunities are in fact more "apparent" than real since they rely on the comparison of nonsynchronous price data.

5. Finally, since stock index futures contracts are settled in cash and not through physical delivery, we are facing the same situation as previously examined

---

[42] It is well-known that the geometric mean is always less than the arithmetic mean return computed from the same aggregate data.

in the case of stock index options, namely that an arbitrageur is not hedged against what we might call "delivery risk." Indeed, he will never be able to sell (buy) all the stocks in the index's replicating portfolio at the determining prices as the closing spot index's value for settling the futures contract. Due to the time delay, unexpected downward (upward) movements in the prices of some stocks, and transaction costs, the closing of a perfectly hedged position may reflect additional gains or losses and is therefore not riskless.

Hence, the determination of the equilibrium price of a stock index futures contract suffers from the same weaknesses we previously encountered when defining the equilibrium price of a stock index option, namely that both pricing models assume the feasibility of a perfect hedge between two "assets," the index futures contract and the spot index and the option and the spot index, respectively. In reality, the main obstacle to both arbitrage based pricing models is that the underlying instrument (the spot index) is not a traded asset and it can't be perfectly replicated by trading in its component stocks due to trading barriers, illiquidity, transaction costs, inefficient information processing, et cetera. This suggests that practitioners be careful when they rely on such arbitrage opportunities based on the parity futures pricing formula since they are not necessarily riskless and profitable. It also suggests the need for more academic research on the market imperfections of pricing futures contracts written on nontraded assets such as stock indexes.

5   ANALYZING OPTIONS WRITTEN ON STOCK INDEX FUTURES

Now that we have analyzed stock index futures contracts and understood their main pricing characteristics and economic functions, we are ready to present the last and perhaps most complex category of options whose market value is indirectly related to the value of the market portfolio, namely stock index futures written options. Since the underlying instrument of these options is a futures contract, our previous discussion will be helpful. Since stock index options and stock index futures already offer most symmetric and asymmetric payoff structures a hedger or a speculator may choose to combine with his existing equity portfolio, we will examine whether stock index futures options provide some new benefits or functions in the monitoring of market risk that could justify their existence. Finally, we will be able to draw some conclusions about the efficiency of the risk monitoring functions provided by these three financial instruments—options on the spot index, futures contracts on the spot index, and index futures options.

An option on a futures contract provides its holder with the right to buy or sell the underlying "futures contract" at the exercise price of the option, at a specified date (or during a specified time period) in the future. Unlike options whose underlying instrument is a traded or physical asset, no cash exchange equal to the amount of the exercise price of the option occurs when an option on a futures contract is exercised. Rather, upon exercise, the option holder will receive a long or short position in a futures contract at a futures price equal to the exercise price of the option. At the end of the day when the futures contract is marked-to-market, the holder of the exercised option can withdraw the cash equivalent of the difference between the futures price and the exercise price of the call or between the exercise price of the put and its futures price.

In fact, when a futures contract written option is exercised, the "exercise value" of the option is settled in cash at the end of the day. Additionally, the option owner receives a long (if it is a call) or a short (if it is a put) position in the underlying futures contract. Hence, the physical potential delivery of the spot instrument is deferred until the time the futures contract itself expires.

Currently, there are options trading on a variety of stock index futures contracts that are themselves based on the most important broad-based stock market indexes. In particular, we mention options trading on the Standard & Poor's 500 futures contract, the Value Line Index futures contract, and the New York Stock Exchange Composite Index futures contract.

Typically, the "unit" size of an option contract involves the same index multiplier as the futures index contract, so that for example, a call option on the Standard & Poor's 500 futures contract allows you the right to buy 500 times the futures index or equivalently one futures contract on the Standard & Poor's 500 Index. Like their underlying futures contracts, options on stock index futures trade on a March–June–September–December annual cycle, and they generally expire on the last trading day of the futures index contract.

These options contracts are generally of the American type and can hence be exercised at any time prior to their expiration date. Note that if the option is actually exercised at the expiration date, which is also the "delivery date" of the underlying futures contract, the call holder will receive the cash value of the difference between the closing price of the Standard & Poor's 500 spot index and the exercise price since the futures price must be equal to the spot value of the index at that date. Hence, exercising a call or a put at maturity will involve a cash settlement of the exercise value of the option, as was previously the case with the settlement of stock index options and of futures contracts on the index. Conversely, if a stock index futures option is exercised before its expiration date, the owner will receive a long or a short position in the index futures contract in addition to the cash amount of the exercised value of his call or put option.

To gain some insight into the specification of stock index futures written options, an abstract of the daily quotation for the New York Stock Exchange futures index written options as it appeared in the Wall Street Journal on April 18, 1988, is provided below. This shows that we could actually buy one call option on the NYSE futures contract expiring in June with an exercise price of 144 for $7.55 \times 500 = \$3775$.[43] Since on the same day the futures price of the June NYFE futures contract was equal to 146.15, this call is clearly in-the-money.

---

[43] The price of one option contract is obtained by multiplying the quoted price by the size of the contract, which means by 500, the same multiplier used to determine the price of one futures contract on the stock index.

NYSE Composite Index (NYFE) $500 Times Premium

Strike Price	Calls			Puts	
	June	September	...	June	September
142	8.90	12.45	...	4.75	7.50
144	7.55	11.15	...	5.40	8.20
146	6.40	10.05		6.15	9.00
⋮	...	...		...	...

On the other hand, exercising the same call option—we are not discussing for the moment whether such a strategy is optimal or not—would provide its owner a long position in one NYSE futures contract expiring in June and the cash equivalent of the exercised value of his call, namely the futures price less the exercise price times the multiplier (i.e., $1075 in our example) credited to his account.

As we will see, whether or not it is optimal to exercise an American option on a futures contract before its expiration date is a slightly more complex issue than the problem related to the early exercise of an American option written on the spot value of an asset or financial instrument. Before we address that question and relate it to the more general topic of valuing American options written on an index futures contract, we will analyze the more simple case of valuing a European option written on a futures contract.

A The Pricing of European Options Written on Stock Index Futures Contracts

Using a methodology similar to the one originally proposed by Black and Scholes to value European options on common stocks, Black (1976b) was the first to derive a model to value European options on futures contracts. His model is based on some preliminary assumptions about market characteristics and asset prices' dynamics with which we are already familiar.

1. Markets are frictionless, there are no transaction costs or taxes, and trading takes place continuously.
2. The continuously compounded interest rate r is assumed to be constant over time.
3. The futures price[44] F is assumed to follow a continuous time lognormal diffusion process, or in other words, it is assumed that the continuously compounded relative changes in the futures price (dF/F) are normally distributed

---

[44] To simplify the notation we will now use the letter F to denote the price at time t of a futures contract for delivery at time T, previously denoted $_tF_T$.

with a constant mean μ and variance σ^2 per unit of time. More formally, we can write the stochastic differential equation characterizing the futures price relative changes as follows:

$$\frac{dF}{F} = \mu dt + \sigma dz \qquad (7.29)$$

where

μ = the expected relative price change of the futures contract per unit of time

σ = the standard deviation of the relative price changes of the futures contract per unit of time

dz = a standard Gauss Wiener stochastic process that is normally distributed with a mean $E[dz] = 0$ and a variance $\text{Var}[dz] = dt$

The assumptions of Black's model are essentially the same as those Black and Scholes invoked when they derived their European common stock call option pricing formula. The main difference is that here the futures price of the asset is assumed to follow a lognormal distribution. Moreover, Black's model is perfectly general in that it doesn't require any specification about the relationship between the futures price and the underlying asset or commodity's spot price. However, since the model assumes interest rate certainty, it can be shown[45] that the stochastic behavior of the futures price defined in Eq. (7.29) is perfectly consistent with the parity pricing relationship for a futures contract previously defined, namely:

$$F = S e^{(r-\delta)(T-t)} \qquad (7.30)$$

where δ = the continuously compounded dividend or convenience yield on an asset or commodity if we assume that the spot price of the underlying asset S does itself follow a lognormal diffusion process. Hence, even though we do not care about the relationship between the spot and the futures prices in Black's option pricing model, it is comforting to know that it doesn't violate the net cost-of-carrying pricing relationship under interest rate certainty.

Using these assumptions, Black constructed a perfectly hedged portfolio consisting of a long position in the futures contract and a short position in the European call option written on that futures contract. Note that since a long futures position doesn't require any initial fund commitments it allows—unlike hedges with underlying spot assets—its holder to earn interest on the free cash amount.

---

[45] See Whaley (1986).

If the hedge is continuously rebalanced to perfectly offset any gain (loss) in the short option by equal dollar amount losses (gains) in the long-futures position, it is a riskless strategy that should therefore yield no more than the riskless interest rate over the option's remaining time to maturity. Applying this no arbitrage condition, and relying on the fact that at its expiration date[46] T^*, the value of the call should be equal to the maximum between its exercise value and 0, Black obtained the valuation equation a European call written on a futures contract should satisfy, namely:

$$C(F^*, K, T^*) = \max(F^* - K, 0) \tag{7.31}$$

where

F^* = futures price at the expiration date T^* of the European call option

K = exercise price of the call option

Black was able to solve the valuation equation and hence obtain an analytical formula for the theoretical price of the futures contract written European call option, which is more formally written

$$C(F, K, T^*) = e^{-r(T^* - t)}[FN(d_1^*) - KN(d_2^*)] \tag{7.32}$$

where

$C(F, K, T^*)$ = the price at time t of a European call option written on a futures contract with current price F. The exercise price of the call is equal to K and its expiration date T^* can be shorter than or equal to the expiration date T of the futures contract

F = the futures price at time t of a futures contract for delivery at time T

$$d_1^* = \frac{\ln(F/K) + 1/2\sigma^2(T^* - t)}{\sigma\sqrt{T^* - t}}$$

$$d_2^* = d_1^* - \sigma\sqrt{T^* - t}$$

σ = standard deviation of the relative price changes of the futures contract per unit of time

$N(\cdot)$ = the standard normal cumulative distribution function

Black's formula is closely related to the European call option pricing Eq. (4.18)—presented in Chapter 4—derived by Black and Scholes for stock written options. The main difference is that Black's formula defines the call's price as "the

---

[46] In the section on index futures written options, we use the symbol T^* to denote the expiration date of the option, thereby allowing for the fact that it can differ ($T^* \leq T$) from the expiration date of the underlying futures contract.

present value" of the futures price given that the call expires in-the-money less the present value of the cost of exercising the call at its expiration date, while in the Black and Scholes formula the term "the present value of the underlying asset's price" is simply replaced by the current market value of the asset S. Similarly, in the terms d_1^* and d_2^* the risk-free rate of interest doesn't appear while it did in the Black and Scholes formula's definition of d_1 and d_2 in Eq. (4.18).

The latter difference is due to the fact that the long futures position in the hedge involves no net cost-of-carrying since it doesn't require any initial cash transfer and since even the credited (debited) marked-to-market account for daily settlement bears interest. Clearly, the holding of the underlying stock or commodity to hedge an option written on a spot instrument forces the investor to "immobilize" a cash amount equal to the market value of this instrument as soon as he initiates his hedge. The cost-of-carrying that physical asset or commodity is then—in the absence of interim dividends or convenience yield—at least equal to the interest rate he could have earned by investing an equivalent amount in riskless securities (or loans). This is basically what the comparison of Black and Scholes call option pricing formula with Black's call option pricing formula tells us.

In fact, the Black and Scholes formula can be easily derived from Black's formula. If we assume, for example, that the underlying instrument doesn't make any interim cash payments, then the equilibrium pricing relationship of a futures contract can be invoked.

$$F = S e^{r(T-t)} \tag{7.20}$$

If we then substitute this expression for the futures price in Black's European call pricing Eq. (7.32) and further assume that the option expires on the same date T as the underlying futures contract, we obtain

$$C(S e^{r(T-t)}, K, T) = e^{-r(T-t)}[S e^{r(T-t)} N(d_1) - K N(d_2)] \tag{4.18}$$

$$= S N(d_1) - K e^{-r(T-t)} N(d_2)$$

This is simply the Black and Scholes pricing equation for a European call option written on a nondividend paying security.

This can be easily understood if we remember that the Black and Scholes pricing formula can also be derived in a risk-neutral world where it is assumed that all assets have a rate of return equal to the riskless interest rate r. Accordingly, the expected future spot value of the asset should simply be equal to its current value compounded at the risk-free rate of interest. But this is precisely how the futures price in Eq. (7.20) is defined. Hence, since the option pricing framework is preference-free, we can say that Black's model can be used to value an option on a futures contract or on the underlying security itself assuming that the latter is expected to earn a risk-free rate of return over the option's remaining time to maturity. We can then conclude that if a European option on the spot asset or commodity has the same expiration date as an option written on a futures contract on that same asset or commodity, and if the options and the futures contract expire at the same date, then both options should be priced equally.

Intuitively, it follows that forward and futures prices should be equal if there is not interest rate uncertainty. In addition, we know that the price of a futures contract at its expiration date should be equal to the spot value of the underlying asset at that date. Hence, for options written on the spot and on the futures contract that expire on the same date as the futures contract, they will have the same payoff at maturity, namely for a call option:

$$C(F, K, T) = C(S^*, K, T) = \max(S^* - K, 0)$$

And they should therefore have the same current price—in the absence of interest rate uncertainty—to avoid riskless arbitrage opportunities. This derivation of the Black and Scholes formula from Black's futures option pricing model then simply proves that the latter model is consistent with an arbitrage-free economic setting.

European put options written on futures contracts can also be priced using Black's arbitrage-free pricing framework. It is, however, simpler to derive Black's European put option pricing formula by applying the put-call parity relationship to the previously defined European call option pricing formula Eq. (7.32). The latter procedure is easier to implement, but it requires preliminary knowledge of the put-call parity relationship among European options of identical exercise prices and expiration dates written on futures contracts.

To derive the put-call parity relationship for futures options, let us consider a portfolio created by buying a futures contract and a put on that futures and by selling a call option on that futures that has the same exercise price and maturity date as the put. The payoff structure of this portfolio at the maturity date T of both options can be represented as follows:[47]

	$F^* > K$	$F^* \leq K$
Value of the long put	0	$K - F^*$
+ Value of the long futures contract	$F^* - F$	$F^* - F$
− Value of the short call	$-(F^* - K)$	0
Net result:	$K - F$	$K - F$

Since the final outcome of this portfolio is perfectly riskless and equal to the difference between the exercise price and the initial futures price F in all states of nature prevailing at the expiration date T^* of the option, the current value of this portfolio should be equal to the present value of $K - F^*$ (discounted at the risk-free interest rate) to preclude riskless arbitrage opportunities. Hence, it should be true that:[48]

---

[47] Note that the put-call parity relationship is derived under the assumption that the put option and the call option both expire on the same date T^*. Further, the futures contract is assumed to be priced like a forward contract, for example, as if interest rates were certain and hence its value at time T^* is assumed to be equal to the value of an identical forward contract, namely $F^* - F$.

[48] The zero reminds us that initially the long futures position doesn't lead to any cash inflow or outflow.

$$P(F, K, T^*) + 0 - C(F, K, T^*) = (K - F)e^{-r(T^*-t)}$$

In other words, we obtain

$$P(F, K, T^*) = C(F, K, T^*) + (K - F)e^{-r(T^*-t)} \qquad (7.33)$$

The put-call parity relationship for European options written on a futures contract simply states that the put's price should be equal to the value of an otherwise identical call—with the same exercise price K and expiration date T^*—plus the present value of $(K - F)$.

We see that the put-call parity relationship among European put and call options written on futures contracts does not depend on the current futures price F, contrary to the put-call parity relationship prevailing among European put and call options written on a spot underlying instrument, namely:

$$P(S, K, T^*) = C(S, K, T^*) + Ke^{-r(T^*-t)} - S \qquad (2.26)$$

Rather it depends on the "implied spot price" embedded in the futures price or on the "discounted" futures price: $Fe^{-r(T^*-t)}$.

Indeed, this can be explained by the fact that a futures position involves no cash transfer when it is initially bought or sold. To prove that the put-call parity relationship then holds with respect to the implied spot price, we assume once again that the futures contract expires on the same date T^* as the two options and we substitute the futures price F in Eq. (7.33) by its equilibrium relationship to the spot price defined in Eq. (7.20). We then obtain

$$P(F, K, T^*) = C(F, K, T^*) + (K - \hat{S}e^{r(T^*-t)})e^{-r(T^*-t)}$$

$$P(F, K, T^*) = C(F, K, T^*) + Ke^{-r(T^*-t)} - \hat{S} \qquad (7.34)$$

where

$\hat{S}$ = the spot price of the asset or good implied by the equilibrium futures price relationship Eq. (7.20).

This relationship is almost identical to the classic European put-call parity relationship Eq. (2.26) except that it holds with respect to the spot price $\hat{S}$ currently implied by the futures price, which does not necessarily equal the observed market price S of the underlying asset or good.[49]

We can now use the put-call parity relationship Eq. (7.33) for European options on futures contracts in conjunction with Black's formula Eq. (7.32) to derive the valuation equation of a European put option written on a futures contract. Simply by substituting $C(F, K, T^*)$ in Eq. (7.33) by its expression given in Black's valuation formula Eq. (7.32), we obtain

$$P(F, K, T^*) = e^{-r(T^*-t)}[KN(-d_2^*) - FN(-d_1^*)] \qquad (7.35)$$

---

[49] Essentially because of various market imperfections and restrictions that might not necessarily affect the prices of futures and spot instruments equally and, as we have seen, may actually imply that the futures price equilibrium relationship Eq. (7.20) is violated.

where

$P(F, K, T^*)$ = the price at time t of a European option written on a futures contract for delivery at time T. The exercise price of the put is equal to K, its expiration date T^* can be less than or equal to the expiration date T of the futures contract, and all other symbols are the same as previously defined in Black's call valuation Eq. (7.32).

Hence, if we are willing to assume that the futures price follows a lognormal diffusion process and interest rate uncertainty doesn't matter, the general framework for valuing European call and put options written on stocks can easily be extended to the valuation of European options written on a large variety of futures contracts. The realism of these two hypotheses should obviously be assessed in light of the specific characteristics of each futures contract serving the function of an underlying financial asset. For example, one might ask: Is it true that the price of a futures contract on a stock index or gold follows a lognormal diffusion process? Does the same assumption hold for a futures contract on oil, lumber, or a T-bill? Moreover, in the latter case as well as for all options written on fixed-income futures contracts, the assumption of interest rate certainty is clearly inconsistent since those assets' prices are essentially driven by the stochastic evolution of interest rates over time. Obviously, the consistency and the validity of Black's relative pricing model for options on futures contracts cannot be assessed at that level of generality and globalization. Further empirical studies of Black's pricing performance for each specific type of futures contract written options are necessary to either support or reject this straightforward extension of Black and Scholes model's main assumptions to the pricing of European options written on futures contracts.

For our problem of pricing of options written on stock index futures, the preliminary question we need to solve is whether early exercise of these options is valuable since most of these traded options are in fact of the American type. Since the futures contract does not entitle its owner to any interim cash flows, the problem looks simpler—at least for American call options—if we derive conclusions based on our previous analysis of stock options. Unfortunately, this is a case where intuition is misleading since it can be shown that American call and put options written on futures contracts can be optimally exercised at any time prior to maturity due to the specific nature of a futures contract. This is precisely the feature of American options written on futures contracts we will now analyze to be able to value stock index futures options consistently.

B   The Pricing of American Options Written on Stock Index Futures Contracts

As pointed out by Whaley (1986), a simple way to show that American call and put options written on a futures contract can be exercised prior to maturity is provided by analyzing Black's valuation model for European options on futures contracts. Let us examine the European call's valuation equation, namely:

$$C(F, K, T^*) = e^{-r(T^*-t)}[FN(d_1^*) - KN(d_2^*)] \tag{7.32}$$

Suppose the futures price becomes so large that $N(d_1^*)$ and $N(d_2^*)$ will both tend to unity. In the latter case, Black's theoretical call's price collapses into

$$C_L(F, K, T^*) \simeq e^{-r(T^*-t)}[F - K] \tag{7.36}$$

where

C_L = the fact that this formula is used for large values of F

Moreover, we know from the restrictions to rational option pricing stated in Chapter 2 that an American option should be exercised if its unexercised value is less than or equal to its exercised value, which in the case of a futures contract written call option is equal to $F - K$. Now, clearly if interest rates are positive we see

$$F - K > (F - K)e^{-r(T^*-t)} \tag{7.37}$$

So for large values of F, the American call could be exercised prior to its expiration date T^*.

Note that in deriving this result, we made no assumption about the underlying spot instrument and whether it provides any interim cash flows. It then follows that this result is perfectly general and will apply to American call options written on all types of futures contracts. In other words, there will always exist a sufficiently high value of the futures contract, $\overline{F}$, above which an American call is worth more "dead" than alive. Hence, in the case of futures contracts written options, both American call and put options may be optimally exercised prior to maturity without any further constraint regarding the nature of the futures contract or on the underlying spot instrument. For sufficiently high (low) values of the futures contract early exercise of a call (put) on the futures contract will be optimal and hence Black's European options' pricing model cannot be applied to American options on futures contracts.

Indeed, invoking an argument similar to the one explaining why Black and Scholes model couldn't be used to price American call options on dividend paying stocks or American put options, we can say that Black's model cannot be used to price American call and put options written on futures contracts since those latter options—because their early exercise is valuable—are worth more than their European counterparts.

Before we explain how American futures options should be valued, we provide some useful intuition and theoretical justification to understand why it may be optimal to exercise both types of American calls written on a futures contract prematurely. Let us return to the parity relationship between the futures price and the spot price of an asset supposing that the latter pays no interim dividends or coupons, so that the net cost-of-carrying the spot asset is simply equal to the interest rate. Hence, the futures price then satisfies

$$F = Se^{r(T-t)} \tag{7.20}$$

In addition, we know that as time passes, the futures price will progressively evolve toward the spot value of the asset. Hence, the future's price continuously loses a fraction of its value with respect to the underlying asset spot price. In that respect, Brenner, Courtadon, and Subrahmanyam (1985) defined an option on a futures contract as an option on an asset that pays "dividends" at a continuously compounded constant yield equal to the riskless interest rate. With that analogy, a futures contract can be viewed as a dividend paying asset and we can again rely on the arbitrage restrictions developed in Chapter 2 to see that "early exercise" of the call option may indeed become optimal.

Moreover, we can derive a parallel with our discussion about dividend paying stocks and American call options valuation in Chapter 5, where we proved that under the continuous dividend yield assumption, early exercise of an American call option could never be ruled out if the stock price happened to be sufficiently large.[50] Hence, this result is directly applicable to the previously defined futures price and therefore explains why it may be optimal to exercise an option on a futures contract prematurely.

We can further observe that if the futures contract's underlying physical good or asset bears a dividend payment, a coupon, or a convenience yield, then the futures price is related to the underlying spot instrument according to the following relationship:

$$F = S e^{(r-\delta)(T-t)} \tag{7.30}$$

where

δ = the assumed constant continuously compounded dividend or coupon (or convenience yield) of the underlying instrument

It therefore appears that if the underlying security of the futures contract is paying dividends, this will slow down the rate at which the futures price depreciates over time relative to the price of the physical commodity or asset, and thus implicitly lower[51] from r to $r - \delta$ the continuously compounded dividend yield on the futures contract. Hence, we can see indirectly that—*ceteris paribus*—a call option written on a futures contract is less likely to be exercised before expiration if the underlying physical security pays a dividend than if it doesn't, since in the former case the continuous dividend yield on the futures contract is implicitly lowered by the physical asset or commodity's cash flow payment rate. By a similar argument, we can say that—*ceteris paribus*—an American put written on a futures contract is more likely to be exercised before maturity if the underlying physical security bears positive interim cash flows.

Brenner, Courtadon, and Subrahmanyam (1985) have run simulations showing that indeed futures call (put) options are less (more) likely to be exercised before maturity, the higher the quarterly payout on the underlying spot instrument.

---

[50] See Chapter 5, Section 3B.

[51] We are assuming here that δ is a positive dividend or net convenience yield. Obviously, for those commodities which have a negative net convenience yield, the opposite will be true.

Finally, they have shown—and this can be inferred by looking at Eq. (7.30)—that if the dividend yield on the physical instrument δ is exactly equal to the riskless interest rate, then:

$$F = S$$

The relationship suggests that options on the futures will in this case have the same value as options on the spot and, therefore, should be priced using the same methodology.

However, most of the time this is unlikely either because the underlying physical asset pays no dividends or it pays a discrete dividend flow over time. We would therefore expect to find differences between the prices of American call and put options written on a physical instrument and the prices of other-wise "identical"—as far as their maturity date and exercise price are concerned—American call and put options written on a futures contract.

Since American options written on futures contracts do not a priori follow any particular timing rule as far as their early exercise policy is concerned, they should be valued using a framework similar to the one previously discussed in Chapter 6 Section 3 for American put options written on common stocks, namely by checking at each point in time whether the American call or put's unexercised value is greater than its exercised value.

There has been little theoretical and empirical research dealing with the valuation of American options on futures contracts. Whaley's (1986) study on the pricing of futures options is both a theoretical contribution to and empirical application of the pricing of stock index futures written options. Whaley accepted the assumptions underlying Black's model, namely that markets are frictionless, trading takes place continuously, there is no interest rate uncertainty, and finally the futures price has a lognormal distribution; or in other words, relative futures price changes are normally distributed and obey the stochastic differential Eq. (7.29). Applying the same technique used by Black, we can show that if a perfect hedge can be constructed with a long futures position and a short offsetting position in the American call option that is continuously maintained—through appropriate rebalancing of the long futures position—over time, then the rate of return on this riskless hedge should be equal to the risk-free interest rate to avoid arbitrage opportunities in the markets.

Based on this partial equilibrium condition, we can derive the valuation equation an American call written on a futures contract must satisfy. It can be shown[52] that the price $C\prime$ of an American call written on a futures contract should satisfy the following partial differential equation:

---

[52] See Black (1976) and Whaley (1986). Notice that this partial differential equation differs from the one described in footnote 15 applying to options on a spot underlying asset or index. In the former case, the term involving the first derivative of C with respect to the state variable vanishes since the futures contract can be viewed as a security paying a dividend equal to the riskless rate (i.e., having a zero growth rate in a risk-neutral economy).

$$\frac{1}{2}\sigma^2 F^2 \frac{\partial^2 C'}{\partial F^2} + \frac{\partial C'}{\partial t} - rC' = 0 \tag{7.38}$$

where

σ^2 = the instantaneous variance of the futures price relative changes

C' = the price of an American call written on a futures contract and expiring at date T^*

F = the price at time t of a futures contract for delivery at date T, $T \geq T*$

The American call option's price must in addition satisfy its initial boundary condition, namely:

$$C'[F^*, K, T^*] = \max[F^* - K, 0] \tag{7.39}$$

This simply says that the American call should, at its maturity date T^*, be worth the maximum between its then prevailing exercise value $(F^* - K)$ and zero.

In addition, and unlike for European calls, the American call's price is at each point of time subject to the early exercise condition:

$$C'(F, K, T^*) \geq \max[0, F - K] \qquad \forall t, t < T^* \tag{7.40}$$

Equation (7.40) simply says that if the call's unexercised value—given by the partial differential Eq. (7.38)—happened to be smaller than its exercise value, then the call should be exercised and accordingly be priced at its prevailing exercise value $(F - K)$.

Similarly, based on a perfect hedge and the no-arbitrage restriction, it can be shown that the American put's price will satisfy the same partial differential equation[53] subject to the following boundary conditions, which at maturity is

$$P'[F^*, K, T^*] = \max[0, K - F^*] \tag{7.41}$$

Prior to maturity the put price must satisfy the early exercise condition, namely

$$P'[F, K, T^*] \geq \max[0, K - F] \qquad \forall t, t < T^* \tag{7.42}$$

It should be mentioned that the prices of European calls and puts written on futures contracts satisfy the same partial differential Eq. (7.38) subject to the constraint that at maturity they should be worth the maximum between their exercise value and zero. Under this setting, Black (1976) was able to analytically solve Eq. (7.38) for the prices of both European call and put options and their theoretical values can hence be computed with the resulting analytical formulas Eqs. (7.32) and (7.35) examined in the previous section.

---

[53] The symbol P' will replace the symbol C' to emphasize that we are now referring to the price P' of an American put option. Hence, subject to the boundary conditions Eqs. (7.41) and (7.42), P' will satisfy

$$\frac{1}{2}\sigma^2 F^2 \frac{\partial^2 P'}{\partial F^2} + \frac{\partial P'}{\partial t} - rP' = 0$$

Unfortunately, there is no analytical solution to the partial differential Eq. (7.38) either for American call options prices satisfying the boundary conditions in Eqs. (7.39) and (7.40) or for American put options prices satisfying the boundary conditions in Eqs. (7.41) and (7.42). Hence, the theoretical values of these American options must be computed by relying on numerical approximation techniques. Whaley (1986), however, did rely on an analytic approximation of the values of both put and call stock index futures options that attempts to fit the early exercise premium implicit in American options prices—that is, the difference between the prices of an American option and an otherwise "identical" European option—with a quadratic function.[54] This method has the advantage of being computationally more tractable and efficient if a large number of options have to be valued as was the case for Whaley's empirical study on the Standard & Poor's 500 futures contract written options.

Since we are mainly interested in valuing stock index futures options, a closer look at Whaley's empirical results is in order to determine whether this perfectly general American futures option pricing model—which represents a direct extension of Black's original European futures option pricing model—is appropriate given the nature of the underlying instrument, namely a stock index futures contract.

Whaley's study was based on the observed prices of both call and put options written on the Standard & Poor's 500 futures contract from January 1, 1983, the day these instruments began to trade on the Chicago Mercantile Exchange, through December 30, 1983, hence covering 232 daily observations. He retained transaction prices but excluded all options with a maturity exceeding 26 weeks from his sample since they were thinly traded.

Whaley first examined whether the American futures option pricing model leads to systematic biases when applied to Standard & Poor's 500 futures contracts written options. He found that indeed there was a "moneyness" bias[55] and a "time to maturity" bias over the period analyzed. In particular, comparing the observed option prices to their theoretical values, he concluded

1. The model overpriced out-of-the-money calls and underpriced in-the-money calls. However, for very short-term options, the pricing bias was the strongest for at-the-money calls, which were highly overpriced by the model.
2. In general, the model overpriced short-term calls and underpriced long-term calls. However, the pricing "bias" by maturity segment was less pronounced than the observed "moneyness" bias.

---

[54] This quadratic approximation technique was originally derived by Macmillan (1986) and applied by Barone-Adesi and Whaley (1987) for the pricing of American options on dividend paying stocks. We have already examined how this analytic approximation technique could be implemented to solve for the prices of American options written on stocks in Chapter 6, Section 3.

[55] "Moneyness" refers to the degree to which an option is trading in-the-money.

3. The model underpriced in-the-money put options and overpriced out-of-the-money put options.

4. In general, the model overpriced short-term put options and underpriced long-term put options. For put options, both the maturity and the "moneyness" biases appeared to be serious as far as their magnitude was concerned.

In addition, Whaley explored whether the model's theoretical values could have been used to hedge mispriced futures options against the underlying futures contract. Each day, options were priced using the model and if, for example, the call was undervalued, it was bought and an offsetting short position of $\partial C'/\partial F$ futures was initiated simultaneously. Conversely, if the call was overpriced—its market price was greater than its theoretical price—it was sold short and an offsetting long position in $\partial C'/\partial F$ futures contracts was simultaneously undertaken. Similar strategies were also implemented with put options.

These hedges were either revised each day—involving a rebalancing of the futures position whenever the hedge ratio $\partial C'/\partial F$ or $\partial P'/\partial F$ changed—or kept unrevised until the expiration date of the option. In both cases,[56] however, the hedged position was maintained until the option's expiration date. Both types of hedges resulted in significant excess returns over the risk-free rate of return and even after taking transaction costs into account, Whaley reported evidence that floor traders—not retail customers, however—could have earned significant riskless arbitrage profits by relying on the model's predicted call and put prices.

Hence, as pointed out by Whaley, the joint hypothesis that the American futures option pricing model is correctly specified and the Standard & Poor's 500 futures options market is efficient cannot be supported by the data. This raises several important issues regarding the consistency of applying this very general—by its assumptions—futures option pricing model to stock index futures written American options.

Of course, one might argue that Whaley's results can be partially attributed to the choice of his reference period that started with the introduction of the S&P 500 futures option contracts and hence covered the period where market participants were still "learning" how to deal with or price these new instruments. Unfortunately, he showed that by splitting his period into four subperiods there is no evidence of greater market efficiency at the end of the period (December 1983) than at the introduction of these option contracts (January 1983).

Moreover, since the futures market for the Standard & Poor's 500 is very liquid, there was on average a delay of only 23 seconds between each transaction price for the option and the futures contract, indicating that asynchronous trading should not be regarded as either a problem or a possible explanation for the results.

There is one problem, however, that we have already discussed that may partially explain why this arbitrage based option pricing model may again be

---

[56] The main difference between the two strategies is the net gain or loss on the intermediate futures position which has to be added or subtracted from the rebalanced hedge strategy's profit.

subject to some controversy for stock index futures written options. Indeed, if we compare the features of such an option with those of a stock index option, there is a major difference in their exercise settlement procedure regarding early exercise. Yet, if the stock index futures option owner exercises his call or put prior to maturity, he will receive a long or short position in a *traded* asset, namely the futures contract, whereas the stock index option owner will, of course, receive the cash settlement value based on the difference between the price of the index and the exercise price of the option, hence based on the value of a *nontraded* asset. Therefore, the stock index futures option writer can fully protect himself by taking an offsetting position in the futures contract since prior to maturity his obligations relate to the value of the latter traded asset.

However, at the expiration date of the contract, the hedge's liquidation is slightly different since both the option and the stock index futures contract expire on the same date. The option will have to be exercised as a function of the then prevailing futures price, which is itself equal to the then prevailing closing price of the index. Hence, the stock index futures options owners' or writers' underlying instrument loses its negotiability over time, since the value of their option position at the expiration date actually relates to the spot value of the index and to all the problems the latter value's determination actually implies.

Therefore, the American futures option pricing model, which ignores that the cash settlement of the futures option at expiration depends on the value of a nontraded asset, might actually suffer from an "exercise bias" similar to the one previously discussed for stock index options and stock index futures pricing models. However, since both the futures option and the futures contract will be settled in cash at expiration, this bias is far less important than for stock index options where the hedge had to be closed by liquidating a "physical" portfolio to provide the cash amount necessary to close the stock index written option position.

Since both the short and the long position of stock index futures written options are settled in cash with respect to the closing price of the index, there is no "apparent" exercise loss. Nevertheless, since the hedge ratio has been computed with respect to the futures price while the hedge will be liquidated with respect to the index's spot price, the number of futures contracts bought or sold may actually fail to provide a perfect hedge if the spot and the futures markets are not closely integrated prior to the expiration date.

Finally, Whaley's American futures option pricing model's assumption regarding the stochastic properties of the futures price may also be questioned since recent evidence on the increased volatility in the stock market and in the stock index futures markets strongly contradicts the lognormal distribution of the futures price assumed by the model. If the variance of the stock index futures price is stochastic or if it experiences large infrequent jumps—like on October 19, 1987—then this model will not price stock index futures options consistently.

Ramaswamy and Sundaresan (1985) have proposed a general model that can to some extent address criticisms of the American futures written options model. These authors recognized that the "true" underlying state variable that will affect futures prices and therefore futures options prices too[57] is the market value of the spot or physical underlying instrument. They derived a model in which stock index's price determines the stock index futures price and the influence of the dividend (spot index) can therefore be more directly assessed through the parity futures pricing relationship. Using that latter relationship, the futures price is actually decomposed and expressed in terms of the spot index's price, the interest rate, and the dividend payments. Therefore, all those factors will explain the American futures option prices and explicitly enter into the option valuation model.

Moreover, recognizing the importance of interest rate uncertainty, Ramaswamy and Sundaresan extended their model by allowing both the interest rate and the spot index's price to vary stochastically over time. In their model, the futures price is not priced anymore as a forward contract since interest rate uncertainty matters, and of course, this enables them to account for the marked-to-market procedure and for its impact on futures prices consistently. The stock index futures option is then priced as a function of the stock index's price and the interest rate, relying on an arbitrage-free valuation setting.

This American futures option pricing model is indeed appealing since it satisfactorily deals with the futures price specification and since it relates the futures written option price to its fundamental underlying variables: the spot value of the physical instrument—in our case the stock index—and the interest rate.

Unfortunately, Ramaswamy and Sundaresan's two-factor option pricing model is computationally cumbersome and requires estimating several parameters describing the stochastic process of the interest rate in addition to the variance of the stock index's returns. Moreover, their model has only been used on simulated data for comparative statics purposes, so we have no empirical evidence to compare its pricing performance for American stock index futures options to that of Whaley's model.

Finally, it should be pointed out that specifically for stock index futures options, the model proposed by Ramaswamy and Sundaresan doesn't offer any better solution than Whaley's model to the problem created by the exercise settlement procedure of those contingent claims. The problem is even more delicate in this case, since their two-factor option pricing model is based on the assumption that a perfect hedge can be constructed with a written (purchased) stock index futures option and with an offsetting position in the underlying stock index and in riskless lending (or borrowing).

If the futures market is for some institutional reasons not fully integrated with the spot market, the hedge ratios that will be computed on the basis of the spot index's value will actually deviate from the hedge ratios computed from

---

[57] In fact their model doesn't apply to any specific futures option contract, they simply relate the futures and the option price to the "spot" value of an underlying "unspecified" good. To maintain the coherence with our discussion, we shall in fact discuss their model in a more restrictive context, namely that of stock index futures options.

the index futures' contract market prices, and therefore will not provide a "fully" covered or immunized position. In particular, if the early exercise of the option—involving the transfer of an index futures short or long position—is considered, the hedging strategy underlying their two-factor model may fail to provide full protection whenever basis risk becomes significant.

Hence, as we can see, the theoretically assumed equilibrium link between the values of the futures contract and the spot index is a critical issue that needs further empirical support to warrant option pricing models that rely on such a high degree of integration between the futures and the spot markets.

6 OPTIONS ON THE SPOT INDEX, OPTIONS ON THE FUTURES INDEX, AND MARKET INTEGRATION: CONCLUDING REMARKS

In summary, we can say that the valuation of options on stock index futures contracts is a rather delicate task that depends on the interactions between three markets—the stock market, the index futures market, and the options market. In particular, several theoretical and empirical issues still need to be solved, they relate in particular to the question: Should these options be valued as a function of the stock index futures contract's price or as a function of the underlying stock index's market price? Theoretically, the second solution is more appropriate since we know that the prices of both the futures contract and the futures option contract are in fact driven by the spot value of the index over time. Moreover, this primary relationship enables one to introduce the dividends of the index's component stocks, the interest rate uncertainty, and other determinant factors explicitly in the option pricing model.

However, from an empirical standpoint, if we look at the contractual features of these three distinct markets, the answer might actually be reversed. Since the index futures contract is a traded asset in zero net supply, it is a priori more liquid than a portfolio of stocks—in positive net supply—replicating the index. From that perspective, hedging with an index futures contract is simpler and less risky than hedging with a stock index replicating portfolio.

For the same reason, it is generally easier to take short positions in the futures market than to sell individual stocks short. The transaction costs are also smaller when the offsetting position involves buying or selling a specific index contract rather than a large number of individual stocks to maintain the appropriate hedge ratio.

Moreover, when the option and the futures are both settled in cash at the expiration date of the option, the "exercise bias" is less pronounced than if the hedge were built with a replicating portfolio of stocks that needs to be bought or sold at expiration to allow for the cash settlement of the written option. Finally, to the extent that basis risk exists and that the futures and the spot index are violating an equilibrium relative pricing relationship—due to different margin requirements, transaction costs, asynchronous information, et cetera—the futures price will deviate from its parity relationship with the spot index's value.

Undoubtedly, all these factors make the hedging strategy very sensitive to the choice of the underlying instrument, and in the case of futures options, obviously the offsetting position should be taken in the underlying futures contract and not in a spot index replicating portfolio. Indeed, if basis risk, transaction costs, and "exercise risk" matter, the former strategy will be preferred.

In this respect it is interesting to observe that even options on the spot index tend to be generally[58] hedged by an offsetting position in the futures contract rather than in a replicating stock portfolio. The former offers greater flexibility, liquidity, and certainly allows for a nonnegligible reduction in transaction costs, which will more than compensate for the fact that the futures index is not a perfect surrogate for the underlying spot index.

Indisputably, the fact that the market value of individual stocks is not accurately and immediately reflected in the value of the spot index is the main reason precluding a synchronization of the futures contract price movements with those of the spot index. The former price will, if it is actively traded, actually be more closely related to the market prices of the spot index's component stocks than the spot index value itself.

Hence, should this mean that options on the spot index are actually "redundant" assets and that index futures options should actually be preferred? This is an open empirical issue that is highly related to the efficiency, contractual specifications, and to institutional barriers governing each of these distinct financial assets. In the absence of standardized option contracts with the same features written both on the stock index and on its futures contract, any conclusions are not justified since they will primarily result from the different characteristics of each option contract. For example, the S&P 500 futures option contract is an American type while the S&P 500 spot index option contract can only be exercised at maturity. By a similar argument, options on the spot S&P 100 may actually be preferred to options on the futures S&P 500 contract since the size of the former contract is smaller.

There is enough diversity to provide each market participant with a suited market monitoring strategy that can be implemented with index futures contracts, spot index option contracts, index futures option contracts, and even a combination of these three financial instruments. However, it is important to remember that these instruments trade in different markets and under different regulations, and that their respective efficiency should therefore be further explored to suppress—noncompetitive—or add—more appropriate—market risk-monitoring tools.

Closely related to this subject is the increasing concern among market participants that these futures and options markets have actually contributed to increase

---

[58] This result has been pointed out in an unpublished study by Morse (1988), who pointed out that the prices of options written on the S&P 500 spot index appear to be very closely related to the value of the American Stock Exchange Major Market Index futures contract and attributed this phenomenon to the tight "cash-futures" arbitrage relationship that exists for the latter stock index futures contract.

the volatility of the underlying stock market. There is therefore a "challenge" for the academic community to prove that these instruments can actually improve portfolio management strategies by controlling the degree of market risk exposure and even allowing its absolute reduction. Indisputably, these financial instruments provide protection, flexibility, and innovative portfolio management strategies so that any question raised about their necessity is actually irrelevant. Rather focus should be on their relative performance and effectiveness in fulfilling these objectives. Hence, to provide a solid justification for their existence and further improve the contractual specification of these financial instruments, the following two main objectives should be simultaneously considered.

1. The academic community should be focusing more carefully on market imperfections and specific characteristics of nontraded assets—such as stock indexes—to integrate these features explicitly into futures and options pricing models. Simultaneously, it should encourage empirical studies designed to help portfolio managers discriminate between competing stock index futures and stock index options pricing models as well as between competing market risk-monitoring instruments on the basis of their relative performance and efficiency.

2. The financial community—whose innovative capacity is indeed unlimited—should, however, consider more carefully the long-term needs and objectives of some market participants—such as insurance companies and pension funds—and hence create and standardize short-term as well as long-term futures and options contracts that could enable institutional investors to hedge their market risk exposure over the long run.

   Indeed, it is rather surprising to see the variety of short-term financial instruments that are currently offered to an active portfolio manager compared to the lack of possibilities actually faced by more legally constrained, passive, or long-term goal-oriented portfolio managers. They currently have no other choice than to incur huge transaction and portfolio rebalancing costs associated with rolling over short-term options or futures contracts and to the implementation of "dynamic portfolio insurance" policies. This clearly deters more than one institution from engaging in "market risk" monitoring strategies using short-term stock index futures or stock index option contracts.

To summarize, we can say that stock index related financial instruments are rather complex instruments whose prices depend on the aggregate value of many stocks, the interdependence between many markets—the spot, futures, and option markets—and the institutional imperfections that may alter their trading efficiency. Hence, although these financial instruments do provide a variety of appealing trading strategies, they simultaneously require that portfolio managers have additional technical skills as well as a global view of market interactions. It is therefore essential to understand how these financial assets should be priced and managed to benefit from their main attribute: providing "control" over the market risk exposure of an equity position.

It is also a prerequisite toward improving their economic functions by lengthening their maturities, creating contracts on major stock exchanges outside the United States that would satisfy the needs of internationally diversified investors, and finally reducing the trading barriers that still preclude stock index futures, stock index options, and options on stock index futures contracts from being optimally integrated into the asset mix of portfolio management institutions.

CHAPTER
8

ANALYZING AND PRICING FOREIGN CURRENCY OPTIONS

1 INTRODUCTION

Since the introduction of traded options on common stocks, the financial community has been innovative in creating and developing traded options that help investors, portfolio managers, arbitrageurs, and speculators monitor various sources of uncertainty that could alter their strategies' performance.

As we have already seen, stock index and stock index futures written options have been a major breakthrough in this securitization process, enabling economic agents to speculate or completely eliminate the market or systematic risk exposure of an equity portfolio. Further, we know that in today's portfolio management, the "market" is not limited by national boundaries as we have presented both theoretical and practical evidence supporting the notion that "international diversification" pays. Indeed, as long as domestic markets remain only partially integrated and experience heterogeneous evolution patterns, any investor can only benefit from spreading his assets over different baskets (countries), thereby improving his performance through country-specific risk premiums.

If we believe in the widest "geographical" interpretation of modern portfolio theory and hence admit that the international capital asset pricing model holds, this implies that only international market risk is priced, and we should again diversify since country-specific risk is then viewed as a residual (non-systematic) and therefore unrewarded uncertainty factor. Whatever the opinion, international diversification is an appropriate portfolio management strategy whose essential benefit is to reduce the risk exposure of an existing asset allocation mix.

Unfortunately, although the goal of investing across countries is to reduce the global market risk exposure of a portfolio, it simultaneously leads to an additional uncertainty factor, namely foreign currency risk exposure. Indeed, an American investor investing in Swiss equity, Japanese convertible bonds, and British Gilts may suffer a negative rate of return on his investment simply because these foreign currencies depreciated against the dollar while the global "market" performance of these assets—in local currencies—was insufficient to compensate for the currencies' depreciation.

Hence, foreign currency risk exposure plays an essential role in international portfolio management strategies since it provides an additional factor on which portfolio managers or investors can speculate—by choosing to invest in countries whose currency is expected to increase or at least remain stable against their reference currency—or about which they should "worry" and hence seek protection.

Moreover, if we consider the fact that currency risk is actually affecting a much broader category of economic agents—consumers, producers, traders, etc.—there is no doubt that financial instruments enabling to hedge an exporter's long or an importer's short position in a foreign currency fulfill a key economic function under today's flexible exchange rates regime.

Although it is still true that most currency transactions actually take place in the interbank spot and forward currency markets, the introduction of standardized futures contracts on major currencies by the International Money Market in 1972 has been a major breakthrough. It provided importers, exporters, and investors with negotiability, liquidity, and additional flexibility—of taking delivery or selling the contract prior to expiration—in monitoring their foreign currency risk exposure. For that purpose, the development of standardized foreign currency option contracts appears to be even more suited since it provides—due to the dissymetric payoff structure of both put and call options—even more flexibility in hedging potential—uncertain—foreign currency denominated transactions.

For example, consider a British truck producer who has submitted a competitive bid for the sale of 1000 trucks to an American building company. He is uncertain about the outcome of his bid (i.e., will he be awarded the contract or not) as well as the behavior of the dollar against the British pound at the time the transaction will be settled. Of course, he can hedge his—potential—long dollar position in the forward or futures market but this clearly wouldn't be an optimal solution if he happened to lose the bid. Indeed, since a forward and a futures contract represent firm commitments or obligations, he would still have to buy back the dollars he originally sold in the forward or futures market although he would have no dollars at his disposal. Hence, closing such a position could result in significant losses if the dollar moved adversely against the British pound and if he had simultaneously lost the bid.

Instead, by purchasing a put option to sell dollars denominated in British pounds, the cost of foreign currency risk exposure will be limited for the producer.

Indeed, if he happened to lose the bid, he could simply sell the option or wait—in the worst case—and let it expire worthless. The maximum loss he would incur is limited to the purchase price of the put option. However, had he won the bid, he could still exercise his option in the case where the dollar depreciated against the British pound and sell it—or leave it unexercised—if the dollar actually increased.

A similar "opportunity cost" problem may arise in portfolio management decisions, for example, if a specific country's stock market looks attractive although there is uncertainty about this foreign currency evolution against the portfolio's reference currency. Hence, the investor may still decide to enter that market by buying stocks or convertible bonds denominated in the foreign currency and simultaneously buying a put option allowing him to sell the latter currency. Hence, currency options provide a safe way of protecting internationally diversified portfolios against potential adverse exchange rate movements and therefore enable portfolio managers to stay in or enter equity markets despite the fairly weak and/or volatile nature of their currencies.

Indisputably, today the uncertainty about major currencies co-movements is highly unpredictable and a fortiori out of control for the financial and economic community involved in multi-national transactions for several economic reasons— inflation, large government budget deficits, asynchronous monetary policies, et cetera. There is no doubt that foreign currency options will continue to grow—in terms of both the volume traded in existing contracts and the development of new standardized contracts—and hence their basic characteristics and functions should be understood by their users.

We will therefore describe and examine the specific features of foreign currency options, pointing out the extent to which their underlying "instrument" (i.e., it is the price of a foreign currency and not of one or more securities as for stock and stock index options) allow us to derive analogies with previously studied traded options.

In particular, we will ask whether currently used foreign option pricing models that are de facto simple extensions of the Black and Scholes pricing model can safely and accurately value these claims. We will see that, due to the specific random behavior of foreign exchange rates, this transposition of existing stock option pricing models has critics and weaknesses. This will lead us to analyze recent research on pricing those options not only "by analogy" but through identifying the key parameters that explain the stochastic behavior of exchange rates and hence of their related option contracts' prices.

Finally, we will conclude this overview on foreign currency options by discussing the state of the art in two important related issues. First, we will discuss the main strengths and weaknesses of existing option pricing models and point out some of the still unexplained "puzzles" that require further research to improve the accuracy of theoretically established foreign currency option prices. Second, we will analyze whether, from a practical standpoint, standardized options contracts fulfill the hedging and speculating needs of economic agents or whether their contractual specification could be improved toward providing additional flexibility and variety while fulfilling these objectives.

2 GENERAL CHARACTERISTICS OF A FOREIGN CURRENCY OPTION

Historically, it is on the Philadelphia Stock Exchange that the first foreign currency standardized option contract, which was written on the British pound denominated in U.S. dollars, began trading in 1982. The Philadelphia Stock Exchange then progressively diversified its contracts so that we can today buy or sell put and call options on underlying "assets" such as the Canadian dollar, French franc, Japanese yen, German mark, Swiss franc, and the British pound. In 1984, the International Monetary Market also started trading options on foreign currency futures contracts denominated in dollars. This meant that one could now buy or sell an option that allowed taking long or short positions in major currencies futures contracts. In Europe, the London International Futures Exchange (LIFFE) also started offering foreign currency futures options denominated in British pounds and U.S. dollars while spot foreign currency standardized option contracts were traded in Amsterdam.

In this study, we will analyze spot currency option contracts since they are directly related to the specific nature of the underlying asset (i.e., the exchange rate) while foreign currency futures contracts written options this dependence is only indirect so that most of our discussion would have focused on the particularities of an option written on a futures contract, a subject which we have already examined in the context of stock index futures options in the previous chapter.

To illustrate the characteristics of spot currency options, we will examine how the contracts traded on the Philadelphia Stock Exchange are actually specified, using as an example the German mark (DM) call and put options denominated in U.S. dollars:

Contract	DM/$
Size*	62,500 DM
Expiration months	March, June, September, December
Striking price	U.S. cents per DM
Quotation of the option	U.S. cents per DM
Type of option	American

*Observe that the size of the contract can be different for each currency. For example, French franc/dollar-denominated options contracts have a size of 125,000 French franc, Japanese yen/dollar-denominated options contracts have a size of 6,250,000 yen, and Canadian dollar/U.S. dollar-denominated options have a size of 50,000 Canadian dollars, and so on.

By definition, a foreign currency call (put) option entitles its owner with the right to buy (sell) a specified quantity of the foreign currency at a prespecified exercise price and at any time prior to or at its expiration date.

In this example, we can see that like most traded options, foreign currency options are generally of the American type and hence enable their holder to exercise the call or the put at any time during the option's remaining time to maturity. This will be true for nearly all standardized foreign currency options. It is worthwhile mentioning, however, that over-the-counter traded foreign currency options—mainly through an interbank market—are generally European call and put options.

Now to examine more carefully how standardized options are actually quoted, suppose that on April 26, 1988, we look at *The Wall Street Journal* and observe the following price quotes for some of the DM/U.S. dollars option contracts traded in Philadelphia:

Current spot exchange rate	Exercise price	Call June	Put June
59.69	60	0.65	0.70
59.69	59	1.30	0.40

The put and the call options expiring in June that have an exercise price of .60 dollars are both nearly at-the-money since the spot exchange rate (59.69 U.S. cents per DM) is very close to their striking price. The 59 call and put options are respectively trading in- and out-of-the-money, as can be seen by observing their respective quotes of 1.30 against 0.40.

Now, if we want to compute the price of the 59 June call option, we must take into account the size of the contract, hence:

$$\frac{\text{price of the call}}{\text{call}} = \frac{\text{premium}}{\text{quotation}} \times \text{size of the contract}$$

This implies[1] that in our example, the price of one June 59 call will be equal to:

$$C = \frac{1.30}{100} \times 62,500 = \underline{\$812.5}$$

We can now illustrate how these foreign currency options can be used to hedge a transaction or a position denominated in a foreign currency. Suppose that on April 26, 1988, an American car producer sold 100 cars to Germany and that he will only receive the 1,200,000 DM proceeds at the end of May 1988. Hesitating about the possible evolution of the DM against the dollar, he finally decides to cover his long-DM position by buying put options on the Philadelphia Stock Exchange.

Of course, there is no put option expiring exactly on the same date his transaction ends, but he can nevertheless purchase a put option expiring in June and sell it at the end of May. Hence, he decides to buy the at-the-money 60 June put option. To cover his DM proceeds, he must determine the number of put contracts he should purchase. Considering the size of a unitary contract (62,500 DM),[2] the number n of put options he must buy is equal to:

---

[1] Since the premium quotation is in U.S. cents per unit, we divide by 100 to express it in dollars.

[2] Here, we are focusing on an "imperfect" hedge since it doesn't rely on the put's delta—or hedge ratio—with respect to the foreign currency.

$$n = \frac{1,200,000}{62,500} = 19.2$$

So he finally decides to buy 19 put options at a total price of

$$P = \text{number of puts} \times [\text{premium quotation} \times \text{size of 1 contract}]$$

$$= 19 \times \left[\frac{0.70}{100} \times 62,500 \right]$$

$$= \$8312.5$$

Given the actual exchange rate of 0.5969, the current value of his transaction in U.S. dollars is equal to

$$1,200,000 \times 0.5969 = \$716,280$$

So that the "maximum" cost of his foreign currency risk exposure's hedge is equal to 11.605% of his proceeds' current value in U.S. dollars (i.e., 8312.5/716,280). Of course, this represents a high cost that could be diminished if the producer was willing to accept a lower "insurance" coverage by purchasing either fewer contracts or slightly out-of-the money put options.

However, with his "prudent" choice, the producer knows that the final value of his proceeds cannot be lower than \$712,500 since[3] the purchase of nearly at-the-money puts implies that he has "locked" in the current DM/\$ exchange rate—more precisely an exchange rate of $0,60$ in this example—as the lower bound to his transaction's U.S. dollar denominated value.

Indeed, consider the three possible situations one month later:

1. The German mark/U.S. dollar exchange rate remained stable around 0.60. Hence, the producer receives \$716,280 from his sale and he can still sell his at-the-money put—whose quotation will be below 0.70, however, due to the negative time bias affecting call and put options—thereby reducing the opportunity cost of having hedged his transaction.

2. The German mark appreciated substantially against the dollar. In this case, the dollar proceeds from the sale at the prevailing exchange rate are higher than \$716,280, which implies that the put will not be exercised. Instead, the producer can sell the put—since it still has some positive time value prior to expiration—and thereby slightly decrease his net insurance "premium." In this state of nature, the opportunity cost of being insured still remains the highest, but this is the negative "benefit" associated with any insurance policy.

---

[3] The 19 put contracts bought at an exercise price of \$0.60 per DM will hence cover:

$$19(0.60 \times \$62,500) = \$712,500$$

The hedge is not covering the total portfolio's current value in \$ since only 19—instead of 19.2—puts have been bought.

The advantage is that with an option contract, contrary to a forward position, for example, the producer doesn't need to fulfill any obligation when the German mark moves in the adverse direction. Had he instead hedged his transaction with a forward contract, he would still be committed to sell German marks at a less favorable exchange rate—equal to the forward rate—than the spot exchange rate prevailing at the end of May, and would thereby have borne the cost (through a smaller profit) of this hedging instrument's symmetric payoff structure.

3. Finally, if the German mark dropped against the U.S. dollar, the producer would exercise his option, thereby locking in the minimum dollar proceeds of his sale, namely $712,500 even though the exchange rate may actually stand well below 0.60 cents at the end of May.

This simple example shows how foreign currency options can be used by exporters to hedge transactions. However, as we have already seen, a perfect hedge can be accomplished only by selecting the number of put options as a function of their sensitivity to exchange rate movements, i.e., by pursuing "delta" hedging strategies.[4]

Similarly, we can show that an importer of German goods can cover his purchase by buying German marks/U.S. dollar call options. Moreover, if an individual has slightly bullish or bearish views about the DM/$ exchange rate, feeling however that the latter is most likely to remain stable, he might take more risky short positions by respectively selling a DM/$ put option or a DM/$ call option. If he is right, the option owner will not exercise the option and he shall therefore retain the whole premium. Such short, unlimited downside risk positions, however, shouldn't be undertaken with highly volatile currencies and are obviously more appropriate for speculators.

Finally, a wide diversity of final payoffs can be obtained by combining call or put options with different maturities (horizontal spreads) or with different exercise prices (vertical spreads), by combining call and put options (into straddles, strips, straps, or strangles positions) according to each hedger's or speculator's bearish, bullish, or undeterminate opinion about the exchange rate's evolution in the short run.

Since most standardized foreign currency option contracts are actually denominated in U.S. dollars, it will generally not be easy for most economic agents dealing from outside the United States to cover a position that involves a third currency. For example, a French car producer selling in the United States and Germany will find it easier and less costly—in terms of transaction costs—to cover his U.S. dollar-long position than his DM-long position.

Indeed, in the first case, he may simply buy a French franc/dollar call option since the latter's value increases when the French franc increases, or in other words, when the dollar decreases against the French franc. To cover his long German mark position and since there are neither German mark options denom-

---

[4] The latter have already been described in Chapter 5, Section 4.

inated in French francs nor French franc options denominated in German marks, he will have to engage in a "triangular" exchange rate relationship involving the dollar. Hence, he will have to buy a DM/$ U.S. put option, which in the first step "insures him" against a drop of the German mark, against the dollar, and then he will simultaneously have to buy a French franc/$ U.S. call option to insure the proceeds of his sale, now converted in dollars, against the French franc.

Hence, for investors, traders, producers, and portfolio managers whose reference currency is not the U.S. dollar, hedging by means of buying or selling currency options is not an efficient solution when currencies other than the dollar are involved. Indeed, the trading in "triangular" option strategies involves additional transaction costs, monitoring, difficulties in obtaining an "exact hedge" (i.e., buying or selling the relevant number of contracts that will guarantee that the initial position is perfectly hedged), and will therefore discourage participants from hedging "multi-currencies" transactions and/or positions held in non-dollar denominated currencies.

This is clearly a serious penalty for the performance of diversified portfolios held in European or Japanese reference currencies, which we will address more carefully later in this chapter, asking whether some new or modified standardized option contracts could actually satisfy the demand of a growing international economic community for more efficient foreign currency hedging tools.

3   GENERAL ARBITRAGE RESTRICTIONS APPLYING TO FOREIGN CURRENCY OPTION PRICES

Although foreign currency options do not differ substantially from stock options in their contractual specifications, we will see that due to the particular nature of their underlying instrument—a spot exchange rate—the general arbitrage relationships that apply to those options, which are based on the same "non-dominance argument," will still differ in their formulation from the restrictions on the prices of common stock written options presented in Chapter 2. Hence, it will be much simpler to analyze foreign currency option pricing models once we have identified the "specific boundaries"[5] their prices should satisfy to avoid riskless arbitrage opportunities in the markets.

For that purpose, we will use the following notation:

C = price at time t of a European foreign currency call option expiring at time T and whose exercise price is equal to K

C' = price at time t of an American foreign currency call option expiring at time T and whose exercise price is equal to K

---

[5] We will not go over the common rational boundaries these options share with common stocks written options, which are presented in Chapter 2.

P = price at time t of a European foreign currency put option expiring at time T and whose exercise price is equal to K

P' = price at time t of an American foreign currency put option expiring at time T and whose exercise price is equal to K

S = foreign currency spot price

K = striking price of the option

τ = $(T - t)$ = time to maturity of the option

r = continuously compounded risk-free interest rate in the domestic country

r_f = continuously compounded risk-free interest rate in the foreign country

$B(\tau)$ = $\exp[-r(T - t)]$ = $\exp[-r\tau]$ = price of a default-free discount bond maturing in τ years in the domestic country

$B_f(\tau)$ = $\exp[-r_f(T - t)]$ = $\exp[-r_f\tau]$ = price of a default-free discount bond maturing in τ years in the foreign country

$_tH_T$ = forward price of a forward contract on the foreign currency contracted at time t for delivery at time T

Obviously, since options have limited liability regardless of the nature of their underlying asset, the prices of American and European options are always positive, so Restriction 1 is already well-known:

Restriction 1

$$C \geq 0, C' \geq 0, P \geq 0, \text{ and } P' \geq 0 \qquad (8.1)$$

Restriction 2 relates American options to otherwise identical European foreign currency options. Since an American option can be exercised at any time prior to its expiration date and the latter property only conveys its owner with additional rights—without creating any obligation—it should be true that—to avoid riskless arbitrage opportunities—American foreign currency options are worth at least as much as their European counterparts:

Restriction 2

$$C' \geq C; \qquad P' \geq P \qquad (8.2)$$

The reason we have repeated this well-known identity in the case of foreign currency options will become clear when we show that early exercise may be optimal for both American put and call foreign currency options. This may seem surprising at first since we saw that American call options on nondividend paying stocks are never exercised prior to maturity, and are therefore priced as their European counterparts.

However, foreign currency options differ from common stocks written options in that their "underlying security" "*always makes interim continuous payments.*" Indeed, when we "invest" in a "foreign currency" over a specific horizon we are de facto engaging in two simultaneous operations.

1. We buy the currency, which means we exchange one domestic (reference) currency unit against units of the foreign currency.

2. Then, we invest this foreign currency to earn interest. The safest way is to purchase a foreign default-free discount bond that matures at the end of the desired holding period. Therefore, this strategy of "buying" the foreign currency actually leads to an investment earning the risk-free interest rate r_f in the foreign country's default-free bond over the defined horizon.

Hence, we can say that a foreign currency written option actually behaves like an option written on a security paying a continuously compounded dividend yield that is equal to r_f. Therefore, depending on whether r_f is greater or less than r, the domestic risk-free interest rate we can earn on the striking price, a foreign currency American call may or may not be exercised before its expiration date.

We can validate this statement more formally in two steps as we previously did for American call options written on dividend paying stocks. The first step consists of assessing the lower boundary to the price of a European call prior to maturity, while the second consists of proving that this lower bound can—under some circumstances—lie below the exercise value $(S - K)$ of an immediately exercised otherwise identical American call.

Hence, the first part of the proof consists of showing that the price of a European foreign currency call will always be greater than or equal to the difference between the current value of an "investment" in the foreign currency $SB_f(\tau)$, and the present value of the striking price $KB(\tau)$, or in other words, that Restriction 3 must hold:

Restriction 3

$$C \geq SB_f(\tau) - KB(\tau) \qquad (8.3)$$

To see that this relationship satisfies the no-arbitrage restriction, let us construct and compare the outcomes of two portfolios. The first portfolio consists of a long position in the European foreign currency call and \$K invested in domestic riskless bonds. The second portfolio is made up of an investment in one foreign discount bond maturing at the same date as the option, hence the current value of this second portfolio expressed in the domestic currency is equal to $SB_f(\tau)$.

Now, we can examine what the outcomes of those two portfolios should be for all possible states of nature prevailing at the expiration date (T) of the call by looking at the following payoff table.

	Expiration date T	
	$S^* \le K$	$S^* > K$
Portfolio 1		
• Long call	0	$S^* - K$
• Investment in domestic riskless bond	K	K
Value of Portfolio 1	K	S^*
Portfolio 2		
• Investment in foreign riskless bonds	S^*	S^*
• Value of Portfolio 2	S^*	S^*
Portfolio 1 − Portfolio 2	$K - S^* \ge 0$	0

Since the value of Portfolio 1 is always equal to or greater than the value of Portfolio 2 at maturity, its initial value should always be equal to or greater than that of Portfolio 2 if arbitrage opportunities are to be avoided in the markets. Hence, it must be true that:

$$C + KB(\tau) \ge SB_f(\tau)$$

We then find

$$C \ge SB_f(\tau) - KB(\tau)$$

This proves that Restriction 3 must hold under the no-arbitrage condition.

Note we could compare this lower boundary of the foreign currency call's price to the equivalent boundary stated for a common stock written European call, which was defined in Restriction 10 in Chapter 2, namely:

$$C \ge S - KB(\tau)$$

We see that if—as a purely theoretical example—they had the same exercise prices, current value of the underlying asset, and time to maturity, the call written on the foreign currency would always be worth less[6] than the otherwise identical call written on a non-dividend paying stock. Since the former is actually an option written on a security that pays a continuous dividend yield equal to r_f and we know from our previous discussion that European call options written on dividend

---

[6] As long as interest rates are assumed to be strictly positive—i.e. $r_f > 0$—and as long as the option is not at its expiration date $(\tau > 0)$, it is true that: $SB_f(\tau) < S$ since $B_f(\tau) < 1$.

paying securities are always worth less than their counterparts written on identical non-dividend paying securities, this result is perfectly consistent with the general arbitrage restrictions on dividend paying securities written options discussed in Chapter 2.

The second step of our proof involves comparing the value of an unexercised American call with the value of this same call when exercised. This can be done by first combining Restrictions 2 and 3, which implies that:

$$C' \geq SB_f(\tau) - KB(\tau).$$

Comparing this inequality with the well-known restriction that an American call option should always trade for at least its exercise value, namely:

$$C' \geq S - K$$

We see that there are situations where the American call option should optimally be exercised prior to maturity. Indeed, a necessary condition for early exercise occurs whenever:

$$S - K > SB_f(\tau) - KB(\tau)$$

$$\Leftrightarrow \qquad S(1 - B_f(\tau)) > K(1 - B(\tau)) \tag{8.4}$$

In other words, when the present value of the interest rate that might be earned on the foreign investment is greater than the forgone interest that might be earned on the exercise price until the option's expiration date, it may be optimal to exercise the foreign currency call option prior to maturity. As previously, the "timing" of early exercise will be given by comparing the call's current price to its immediate exercise value. Namely, if $C' > S - K$ is violated, the call should be exercised. Hence, the early exercise feature of foreign currency American calls bears additional value and this shows that Restriction 3 will not collapse into a strict identity for American foreign currency calls.

At this stage, we can state general upper and lower boundaries for the price of an American foreign currency call option by combining Restrictions 1, 2, 3, and the well-known fact that an American call should never be worth more than its underlying instrument (since as we saw in Restriction 7 of Chapter 2, the latter can be viewed as a perpetual ($\tau = \infty$) call option with a zero exercise price). Hence, the following upper and lower boundaries must always hold to preclude the existence of dominant securities as shown in Restriction 4:

Restriction 4

$$S \geq C' \geq \max[0, S - K, SB_f(\tau) - KB(\tau)] \tag{8.5}$$

And similarly, we can show—relying on the no-early exercise feature of European options—that the price of a European call option written on a foreign currency must satisfy Restriction 5 to preclude arbitrage opportunities in the market.

Restriction 5

$$S \geq C' \geq C \geq \max[0, SB_f(\tau) - KB(\tau)] \qquad (8.6)$$

Note that in the case of foreign currency European puts, we can show by an arbitrage argument similar to the one used in Restriction 3 for European calls, namely by comparing the values of two portfolios, one consisting of a long put option and a short position in K riskless bonds and the other consisting of a short position in one foreign bond—whose value in the local currency is hence equal to $SB_f(\tau)$—that since the outcome on the former portfolio at expiration in all states of nature is equal to or greater than the outcome of the second portfolio, the first portfolio's current value must be greater than or equal to that of the second portfolio, hence:

$$P - KB(\tau) \geq -SB_f(\tau)$$

This implies Restriction 6:

Restriction 6

$$P \geq KB(\tau) - SB_f(\tau) \qquad (8.7)$$

In other words, a European put should always be worth at least the present value of its exercise price $KB(\tau)$ less the value of an investment in the foreign currency's riskless bond denominated in the domestic currency $SB_f(\tau)$.

We can then use this restriction in conjunction with the property that an American put must always sell for at least its current exercise value, namely:

$$P' \geq K - S \qquad (8.8)$$

This confirms that, as we know from our discussion on common stocks written options, American puts can indeed be exercised prior to maturity. Combining Restrictions 2 and 6, we find

$$P' \geq KB(\tau) - SB_f(\tau) \qquad (8.9)$$

However, this relationship may not be true since there are cases when the exercised value of the put—given in Eq. (8.8)—will be greater than the lower boundary to its unexercised value, namely whenever:

$$K - S > KB(\tau) - SB_f(\tau) \qquad (8.10)$$

We have a necessary condition for the put to allow for the possibility of being exercised prior to maturity. Rearranging Eq. (8.10), we obtain

$$K(1 - B(\tau)) > S(1 - B_f(\tau)) \qquad (8.11)$$

We can see that for a sufficiently low exchange rate—for example, suppose S tends to zero—it may, of course, pay to exercise the put immediately (since

$K > KB(\tau))$. In addition, we can see that the interest rate on the foreign investment has a negative impact on the put's early exercise policy, which is contrary to the case of American call options, since the higher r_f (i.e., the lower $B_f(\tau)$) and the more difficult it will be *ceteris paribus* to satisfy Eq. (8.10). It then follows that we can never rule out a situation in which the lower bound to the European put option value—given in Eq. (8.7)—is below the one applying to American puts given in Eq. (8.8). Thus early exercise can never be ruled out and will actually occur whenever the latter condition is violated by the American put's price.

Hence, we see that for American put options there will always be a chance of early exercise if *ceteris paribus* either the exchange rate or the foreign interest rate is very low, or if the domestic interest rate is very high. For dividend paying stocks, we can see that the foreign currency's early exercise probability is "attenuated" by the fact that the underlying instrument pays a continuous dividend yield equal to r_f. This continuous dividend yield de facto contributes to decrease the difference in value between American and otherwise identical European put foreign currency options while obviously it increases—by allowing for a higher early exercise probability, the higher the level of r_f—the same price differential between otherwise identical European and American foreign currency call options.

We are now able to combine Restrictions 1, 2, and 6 with the well-known upper boundary to an American put's price (i.e., when the underlying instrument is worthless, the American put's price is equal to the striking price) to provide the general upper and lower boundary setting—the American foreign currency put price must always satisfy in Restriction 7

Restriction 7

$$K \geq P' \geq \max[0, K - S, KB(\tau) - SB_f(\tau)] \qquad (8.12)$$

Whereby it follows from the no-early exercise property of European puts that their prices' upper and lower boundaries can be stated as follows in Restriction 8:

Restriction 8

$$K \geq P' \geq P \geq \max[0, KB(\tau) - SB_f(\tau)] \qquad (8.13)$$

With Restrictions 4, 5, 7, and 8, we have been able to define arbitrage-free limits to the prices of both European and American foreign currency options. In addition, we have been able to show that American foreign currency options may be optimally exercised prior to maturity. The necessary condition under which this may be true for put and call options can be summarized as follows in Restriction 9:

Restriction 9

If at any time t prior to the expiration date, the following relationship holds

$$S(1 - B_f(\tau)) > K(1 - B(\tau)) \qquad (8.4)$$

the American foreign currency call option can be optimally exercised before maturity.

If at any time t prior to the expiration date, the following relationship holds

$$K(1 - B(\tau)) > S(1 - B_f(\tau)) \qquad (8.11)$$

the American foreign currency put option can be optimally exercised before maturity.

The early exercise of these options will then occur whenever the restrictions

$$P' > K - S \qquad \text{and} \qquad C' > S - K$$

are violated.

We still need to define a last set of arbitrage-free relationships that will guarantee that foreign currency call and put options are consistently priced relative to each other. For that purpose, we will refer to the concept of "put-call parity." For European foreign currency options, if we assume that the call and the put are written on the same foreign currency, they have the same exercise prices, expiration dates, and the risk-free domestic and foreign interest rates are constant over time, then the put-call parity relationship can be stated as follows:

Put-Call Parity Relationship for European Foreign Currency Options

$$P = C - SB_f(\tau) + KB(\tau) \qquad (8.14)$$

We can prove that this arbitrage-free restriction on the prices of the European call and the European put must hold by comparing the following two portfolios A and B:

- Portfolio A consists of a long position in a European foreign currency put option.
- Portfolio B consists of a long position in an otherwise identical European foreign currency call option, a long position in K domestic riskless bonds, and a short position in one foreign bond (which implies that $SB_f(\tau)$ represents the amount of the short position expressed in the local currency).

We now compare the value of both portfolios in all possible states of nature prevailing at the expiration date of both options.

	Expiration date	
	$S^* \leq K$	$S^* > K$
Portfolio A		
• Long put option	$K - S^*$	0
Value of A	$K - S^*$	0
Portfolio B		
• Long call option	0	$S^* - K$
• Long position in K domestic bonds	K	K
• Short position in one foreign bond	$-S^*$	$-S^*$
Value of B	$K - S^*$	0

Since Portfolios A and B have the same final outcomes in all possible states of nature prevailing at the expiration date (T) of the options, to avoid the dominance of one portfolio over the other their initial value—or purchase price—must be the same. The latter statement confirms that the put-call parity relationship Eq. (8.14) must hold for European foreign currency options.

Since Portfolios A and B have the same final outcomes in all possible states of nature prevailing at the expiration date (T) of the options, to avoid the dominance of one of the portfolio over the other, their initial value—or purchase price—must be the same. The latter statement confirms that the put-call parity relationship Eq. (8.14) must hold for European foreign currency options.

We can now draw a parallel between this relationship and the previously stated put-call parity relationship for stock index futures written options. We saw in Chapter 7 that[7] the put-call parity for stock index futures written European options can be stated as follows:

$$P_F = C_F + (K - F)e^{-r(T^* - t)} \tag{7.31}$$

In other words, the parity relationship holds with respect to the "implied" value of the spot index, namely $F e^{-r(T^* - t)}$.

If we use the "interest rate parity condition" that implies that the relationship between the forward exchange rate $_tH_T$ and the spot exchange rate is uniquely determined by the interest rate differential between those two countries, namely:

$$\frac{_tH_T}{S} = \frac{B_f(\tau)}{B(\tau)} = \exp[(r - r_f)\tau] \tag{8.15}$$

---

[7] We use C_F, P_F to distinguish between the European call and put options on stock index futures and the call and put options C, P on foreign currencies analyzed in this chapter. Also note that in Chapter 7, T^* defines the expiration date of the futures contract written option while T defines the expiration date of the futures contract.

If we further remember that under interest rate certainty, the forward and the futures price (F) for a given delivery date should be the same, then we can use Eq. (8.15) to define the "implied" spot exchange rate as follows:

$$S = {_tH_T}/\exp[(r - r_f)\tau] = F/\exp[(r - r_f)\tau] \tag{8.16}$$

Plugging this definition of the spot exchange rate into the put-call parity relationship for European foreign currency options Eq. (8.14), we obtain

$$P - C = KB(\tau) - \frac{F}{\exp[(r - r_f)\tau]} \times B_f(\tau)$$

$$= K \exp[-r\tau] - F \times \exp[-r\tau]$$

$$\Rightarrow \quad P - C = (K - F)\exp[-r\tau] \tag{8.17}$$

Equation (8.17) shows that the put-call parity relationship for European foreign currency options can also be stated in terms of the spot exchange rate $Fe^{-r\tau}$ implied by the futures (or forward) exchange rate, providing that the interest rate parity condition Eq. (8.15) holds.

Also, by looking at this latter condition, we see that the futures (or forward) exchange rate for delivery at time T, can be expressed as follows:

$$F = S \exp[(r - r_f)\tau] \tag{8.18}$$

We can then decompose the futures exchange rate[8] as being equal to the spot exchange rate S plus the net cost-of-carrying the exchange rate, or more precisely, "an investment" in the foreign currency over the period $\tau(= T - t)$, namely $S[\exp[(r - r_f)\tau] - 1]$.

Relying on our previous discussion about futures and forward contracts in Chapter 7, we see that such an "investment" has a cost-of-carrying per unit of time that is equal to the risk-free rate (r) minus the "convenience yield" or dividend yield such an investment in the foreign currency actually provides and that is equal to the continuously compounded risk-free rate on the foreign riskless bond (r_f).

Hence, through this derivation of the European put and call parity relationship stated in terms of the spot exchange rate and then in terms of the "implied" spot exchange rate $Fe^{-r\tau}$ we have been able to show once again that an option written on a foreign currency behaves like an option written on a foreign riskless security that pays a continuous dividend yield which is equal to r_f. We will see that such an interpretation of the "underlying" asset of a foreign currency's op-

---

[8] Referring to our discussion on the relationship between forward (or futures) prices and spot prices in Chapter 7, we saw

$$F = Se^{c'(T-t)} \tag{7.18}$$

where c' = the instantaneous net cost-of-carrying the good. Hence, in the case of a futures exchange rate contract the net cost-of-carrying the "investment" in the foreign currency is equal to $F - S = S[\exp[(r - r_f)\tau] - 1]$.

tion contract is crucial for understanding the basic methodology and assumptions required to derive foreign currency option pricing models.

However, before we come to that point, we need to examine the last arbitrage-free pricing restriction that applies to American call and put options. Indeed, since these can in fact be viewed as options "on dividend" paying foreign securities, we will not be surprised to observe, like in the case of dividend paying stock options, that the put-call parity relationship stated for European options does not hold any more. Indeed, since the early exercise feature of foreign currency American options is "valuable," there will be no more identity relationship since the payoff of an American put can no longer be replicated with the payoffs on a portfolio consisting of a long position in an otherwise identical call, a long position in the domestic bond and a short position in the foreign bond.

Rather, as for common stock[9] written options, it can be shown that an upper limit to the price of the American put is given by the following inequality:

$$C' + K - SB_f(\tau) \geq P' \tag{8.19}$$

Indeed, to show that this inequality must hold let us suppose, by contradiction, that it doesn't, or in other words, that we observe

$$C' + K - SB_f(\tau) < P'$$

We could then form a riskless arbitrage position by selling the American put, buying the American call, selling the foreign riskless bond, and investing $K in domestic bonds.

Indeed, if the put isn't exercised prior to maturity, the liquidation of the position at the expiration date of both options will lead to the following possible outcomes:

	Expiration date	
	$S^* < K$	$S^* \geq K$
Buy the put back	$-(K - S^*)$	$- - -$
Sell the call	0	$S^* - K$
Buy the foreign bond back	$-S^*$	$-S^*$
Withdraw the proceeds from the $K invested in domestic bonds	$K/B(\tau)$	$K/B(\tau)$
Final outcome	$K((1/B(\tau)) - 1)$	$K((1/B(\tau)) - 1)$

---

[9] More precisely, in Chapter 2 (Section 4 D) we found that for common stocks that pay dividends, the upper boundary to the American put's price was equal to

$$P' < C' + K + S - D$$

The only difference is that here, the dividend on the foreign security is assumed to be continuous so $SB_f(\tau) = Se^{-r_f \tau}$ replaces $S - D$.

We see that no matter what happens at date T, we end up with a riskless cash inflow equal to the interest rate earned on the $\$K$ invested in domestic riskless bonds. Clearly, since our initial investment involved no cash outflow, this is a pure riskless arbitrage profit.

Following a similar argument, we can show that if the put is exercised before maturity, we would deliver the $\$K$ to fulfill our obligation. In addition, we would use the foreign currency amount we received to buy back the foreign bond and yet would still end up with a net profit since we still own a call option, we earned some interest on the $\$K$ invested in the riskless domestic bonds, and moreover, the amount of foreign currency we took delivery of will exceed the purchase price of the foreign bond (since at any time $t, t \neq T$, we have $S_t > S_t B(\tau)$).

Hence, in this case too, we end up with a riskless positive outcome that becomes an arbitrage profit if that portfolio required no initial cash outflow. Therefore, if the markets are such that arbitrage riskless opportunities are precluded, the following relationship cannot hold.

$$C' + K - SB_f(\tau) < P'$$

This proves, by contradiction, that the upper boundary to the put's price defined in Eq. (8.19) must hold.

By a similar arbitrage argument, it can be shown that the lower boundary to an American put's price is defined as follows:

$$P' \geq C' + KB(\tau) - S \qquad (8.20)$$

If this relationship doesn't hold, we can create a riskless arbitrage strategy by buying the put, selling the call short, taking a long position in the currency, and borrowing the present value of $\$K$ (by selling K domestic riskless bonds). Indeed, this strategy would then imply a positive cash inflow both at its initiation, at the portfolio's liquidation date whether the call be exercised at or before its expiration. This implies, by contradiction, that relationship Eq. (8.20) can't be violated in an arbitrage-free market.

By combining the upper and the lower boundaries defined in Eqs. (8.19) and (8.20), we can state the put-call relationship that must prevail among the prices of American foreign currency options in the absence of arbitrage opportunities:

Put-Call Relationship for American Foreign Currency Options:

$$C' + K - SB_f(\tau) \geq P' \geq C' + KB(\tau) - S \qquad (8.21)$$

This American put-call relationship as well as the restriction that American puts and calls should always sell for at least their exercise value represent the two rational boundaries used by Bodurtha and Courtadon (1987) to test the efficiency of the Philadelphia Stock Exchange foreign currency options markets. Examining all verified trades that occurred from February 28, 1983 (when these options actually started to be traded) to September 14, 1984, the authors found that when simultaneous data for the option and the exchange rate is used, there is very little evidence of put-call relationship Eq. (8.21) violation while the early exercise boundaries'—especially for the German mark and the Swiss franc put options—violation did show some signs of inefficiency.

However, once the two sets of boundaries for early exercise and the put-call relationship were adjusted for both the bid and ask spread and other transaction costs associated to the purchase or the exercise of an option, Bodurtha and Courtadon couldn't reject the hypothesis that the market is efficient and those options were rationally priced. Indeed, out of 52,509 analyzed trades, only 31 violated the early exercise boundary condition and only one put-call pair out of 3,998 violated the put-call relationship Eq. (8.21).

Hence, their study points out how important it is to rely on arbitrage boundaries in conjunction with simultaneous transaction data and transaction costs, to assess whether those "rational" price limits are sustained in the market and can therefore testify of its efficiency. However, such a price boundary setting remains insufficient to determine whether the option's price has indeed been "fairly" set by the market. So far, we can only conclude that it lies within—or violates—a "fair" range, but any conclusion on the precise level of a quoted price—especially when the boundaries are not very tight—might be insufficient for the analysis and management of these options.

This suggests that we must again search for relevant option pricing models that determine the equilibrium option's price and hence provide both practitioners and academics with a precise figure to which the market price of a foreign currency option can be meaningfully compared.

4 THE PRICING OF EUROPEAN FOREIGN CURRENCY OPTIONS

We should not be surprised that the first and most commonly used foreign currency option pricing model can be viewed as an extension of Black and Scholes' option pricing model to the case where the "asset" underlying the option is defined as the spot exchange rate.

The European foreign currency option pricing model was derived by Garman and Kohlhagen (1983) assuming that the main hypotheses underlying the Black and Scholes option pricing model will remain valid for options that entitle owners with the right to buy or sell a foreign currency.

More precisely, Garman and Kohlhagen make the following assumptions:

1. Markets are frictionless, there are no taxes, no transaction costs, no restrictions on short sales, and trading can effectively take place continuously.

2. The spot exchange rate denoted by S is assumed to be lognormally distributed over time or, stated in other words, the relative instantaneous change in the spot exchange rate (dS/S) is assumed to be normally distributed with mean μ and variance σ^2 per unit of time. More formally, this implies that the instantaneous relative change in the spot exchange rate satisfies the following stochastic differential equation:

$$dS/S = \mu dt + \sigma dz \qquad (8.22)$$

where

dS/S = the instantaneous relative change in the exchange rate

μ = the expected relative change in the exchange rate per unit of time; μ is an intertemporal constant

σ = the unexpected relative change in the exchange rate per unit of time. Hence, σ^2 is the instantaneous variance of the relative change in the exchange rate process and it is an intertemporal constant

dz = standard Gauss-Wiener stochastic process that is normally distributed with mean $E[dz] = 0$ and variance $\text{Var}[dz] = dt$.

3. The instantaneous continuously compounded risk-free interest rate (r) in the domestic country is an intertemporal constant.

4. The continuously compounded interest rate on a default-free discount bond issued in the foreign country and maturing in τ years is also assumed to be constant. Stated in other words, the instantaneous risk-free—in terms of default risk—interest rate (r_f) in the foreign country is assumed to behave like the risk-free interest rate in the domestic country and hence is certain.

Under these assumptions, Garman and Kohlhagen showed that it is possible to construct a perfect hedge by taking a short position in the European foreign currency call option and offsetting it with a long position in foreign currency riskless bonds.[10] Providing that this portfolio can be continuously rebalanced to maintain the hedge over the call's remaining time to maturity, it should earn no more than the domestic risk-free interest rate over any instant since it is de facto a perfectly riskless investment.

Using this no-arbitrage condition, Garman and Kohlhagen derived the following partial differential equation the price of a European foreign currency call must satisfy

$$\frac{1}{2}\sigma^2 S^2 \frac{\partial^2 C}{\partial S^2} + (r - r_f)S\frac{\partial C}{\partial S} - rC + \frac{\partial C}{\partial t} = 0 \qquad (8.23)$$

where

$\partial^2 C/\partial S^2$ = the second partial derivative of C with respect to S

$\partial C/\partial S$ = the first partial derivative of C with respect to S

$\partial C/\partial t$ = the first partial derivative of C with respect to t (time)

---

[10] More precisely, in order to construct such a perfectly hedged position, a long position in $N(d_1)$ foreign riskless bonds must be taken to exactly offset any gains or losses on the written call. Note that for foreign currency options, the hedge ratio $(\partial C/\partial S)$ is equal to $N(d_1) \cdot B_f(\tau)$ as we shall see later in this chapter and as is understandable since we must actually buy $N(d_1)$ foreign bonds whose current price in the foreign currency is equal to $B_f(\tau)$.

In addition, the foreign currency call option's price must satisfy the boundary condition prevailing at its expiration date (T), namely:

$$C(S^*, K, 0) = \max[S^* - K, 0]. \tag{8.24}$$

The authors were able to derive an analytical solution to the partial differential Eq. (8.23) subject to the well-known expiration date boundary stated in Eq. (8.24). This solution is, of course, the European call option's theoretical price given by Garman and Kohlhagen's model under the set of previously stated assumptions and providing that there are no arbitrage opportunities available. More formally, it expresses the call's price as follows:

$$C = SB_f(\tau)N(d_1) - KB(\tau)N(d_2)$$

$$\Leftrightarrow$$

$$C = Se^{-r_f\tau}N(d_1) - Ke^{-r\tau}N(d_2) \tag{8.25}$$

where

C = the price at time t of a European call option written on the foreign currency that has an exercise price equal to K and a time to maturity equal to $\tau(= T - t)$.

$$d_1 = [\ln\left(Se^{-r_f\tau}/Ke^{-r\tau}\right) + (\sigma^2\tau/2)]/\sigma\sqrt{\tau}$$

$$d_2 = d_1 - \sigma\sqrt{\tau}$$

$N(\cdot)$ = the standard normal cumulative distribution function.

If we take a closer look at Eq. (8.25), we see that it is very similar to the Black and Scholes European call option pricing formula Eq. (4.18) that applied to calls written on nondividend paying stocks. Actually, the only difference between the two formulas is that here the term $Se^{-r_f\tau}$ replaces the term S that represents the current price of the stock in Black and Scholes valuation model.

To be even more precise, we can return to our discussion in Chapter 5 regarding the extensions of Black and Scholes model to call options written on stocks that pay a continuous dividend over time. We saw that in the latter case, it was sufficient to deduct the continuous dividend flow over the option's remaining lifetime from the stock price (i.e., to replace S by $Se^{-\delta\tau}$) in order to obtain the adjusted Black and Scholes valuation Eq. (5.10) that applies to European call options written on stocks that pay a continuous and constant dividend. But this corresponds exactly to the formulation of the foreign currency European call valuation Eq. (8.25) when we identify $Se^{-r_f\tau}$ with an investment in a foreign (riskless) security that pays a constant continuous dividend at a rate of r_f per unit of time.

Hence, the derivation of the foreign currency call valuation formula can be viewed as an application of Black and Scholes option pricing model to a call on a foreign (riskless) security paying a continuous dividend yield over time. If the assumptions of the Black and Scholes model are consistent with the behavior of the price of the security expressed in the domestic currency—namely $SB_f(\tau)$—

then, we have a valid and simple model to price this specific category of traded European calls.

Before we analyze the relevance of that extension of Black and Scholes model to the pricing of foreign currency calls, we will identify a few basic properties of the Garman and Kohlhagen European call option pricing model and its related valuation Eq. (8.25):

1. The sensitivity of the call's price to an infinitesimal change in the exchange rate is obtained by taking the first derivative of C in Eq. (8.25) with respect to S, which results in

$$\frac{\partial C}{\partial S} = \Delta_C^* = N(d_1)B_f(\tau) > 0 \qquad (8.26)$$

where Δ_C^* denotes the hedge ratio, or in other words, the quantity of spot exchange rate we should "buy" to hedge every written call. Given the expression of $\Delta_C^* = N(d_1)B_f(\tau)$, we see that this hedge is actually accomplished by buying $N(d_1)$ riskless foreign bonds at a price of $B_f(\tau)$.

By looking at Eq. (8.26), we can confirm that the proper hedge to any European written call consists of an investment in $N(d_1)$ riskless foreign bonds or, stated in the local currency, we would invest an amount $SN(d_1)B_f(\tau)$ to exactly offset any gains (losses)—expressed in the local currency—on our short call position.

Furthermore, since the first derivative of the call's price with respect to the exchange rate is positive, we obtain the expected result that the higher the level of the exchange rate the more valuable the call. Moreover, it can be shown that the second derivative of the call's price with respect to the exchange rate is also positive[11]—$\Gamma_C^* > 0$—so that we can state, as in the case of common stock written options, that the European foreign currency call price is an increasing convex function of the exchange rate under the assumptions underlying Garman and Kohlhagen's model.

Since the delta or hedge ratio Δ_C^* depends both on the exchange rate (S) and on the option's time to maturity (τ), it will change with the passage of time and with any change in the spot exchange rate, implying that any "delta-targeted" foreign currency risk-monitoring strategy will have to be revised very frequently.

2. A sensitivity analysis of the European foreign currency call price will lead us to some familiar results as well as others that are specific to that category of

---

[11] The second derivative of the call's price with respect to the exchange rate also called gamma (Γ_C) is equal to:

$$\Gamma_C = \frac{\partial^2 C}{\partial S^2} = \frac{B_f(\tau)}{S\sigma\sqrt{\tau}}N'(d_1) > 0$$

where $N'(x) = (1/2\sqrt{\pi})e^{-x^2/2}$

options, in particular.[12] Several of these results are provided in the following list:

- The European call will be more valuable the higher the domestic interest rate ($\partial C / \partial r > 0$), thereby reflecting that a higher interest rate decreases the cost (i.e., the present value of the exercise price) of exercising the call and hence raises its price.
- The European call will be more valuable the lower the striking price ($\partial C / \partial K < 0$), thereby reflecting that a higher striking price increases the cost of exercising the call at its expiration date and hence makes the right to purchase the currency at a higher unitary "purchase price" equal to K less attractive.
- The European call will be more valuable the higher the standard deviation of the relative spot exchange rate changes ($\partial C / \partial \sigma > 0$) since, as in the case of common stocks written options, we can only benefit from the effects of increased riskiness. Indeed, it increases the dispersion of the final outcomes and hence the range of outcomes where the option will expire in-the-money while leaving us perfectly insensitive—since we are not obliged to exercise the option—to the fact that increased dispersion also results in a broader range of outcomes where the call expires out-of-the-money.
- An additional parameter that didn't appear in the analysis of common stocks written options must also be accounted for since it enters the Garman and Kohlhagen's pricing formula and will therefore affect the foreign currency's call option's price: it is the foreign riskless interest rate r_f.

  Intuitively, since the latter can be identified with a "dividend yield" and we know from our previous discussion about dividend paying stocks written European calls that interim cash flow payments actually decrease their values, we suspect that there will also be a negative relationship between the price of the European foreign currency call and the risk-free interest rate in the foreign country.

  This intuition is indeed correct since the first derivative of the call's price with respect to the foreign riskless interest rate is negative ($\partial C / \partial r_f < 0$). To explain, as the foreign interest rate increases, holding the call option becomes less appealing since we are losing the opportunity of investing "immediately" at a higher interest rate in the foreign country. Given that the call is European and immediate exercise is therefore impossible, an increase in the foreign interest rate can only lower the call's price.

---

[12] The derivatives of the call's price with respect to the parameters r, K, σ and r_f are respectively equal to:

$$\partial C / \partial r = \tau B(\tau) K N(d_2) > 0$$
$$\partial C / \partial K = -B(\tau) N(d_2) < 0$$
$$\partial C / \partial \sigma = B(\tau) K \sqrt{\tau} N'(d_2) > 0$$
$$\partial C / \partial r_f = -\tau B_f(\tau) S N(d_1) < 0.$$

- The last and perhaps most unusual relationship arises from the analysis of the call's price behavior with respect to its time to maturity. For foreign currency call options, it has been shown[13] that the first derivative of the call's price with respect to time to maturity can be of either positive or negative, namely:

$$\frac{\partial C}{\partial \tau} = -r_f B_f(\tau) SN)(d_1) + rB(\tau)KN(d_2)$$

$$+ (B(\tau)\sigma KN'(d_2))/2 \sqrt{\tau} \overset{>}{\underset{<}{=}} 0 \qquad (8.27)$$

Clearly, whenever the first term in Eq. 8.27 is greater than the two last terms, we will observe the unusual situation that the call's price actually decreases when its time to maturity increases. Chesney and Loubergé (1987b) showed that for in-the-money short-term European calls and all very long-term calls, this derivative will indeed be negative. They also pointed out that as r_f tends to zero, this negative relationship will vanish since the foreign currency call then behaves like any other call written on a nondividend paying security, hence being more valuable the longer its remaining time to maturity. We see that it is the existence of "the continuous dividend yield" on the underlying instrument that leads to this unusual pattern since a European call cannot be exercised before maturity and hence, will de facto be losing its value if an immediate investment in the foreign riskless bond proves— due to a high level of r_f—to be more rewarding than the domestic interest rate we can earn until maturity on the exercise price.

For American calls, this situation will not happen since we saw in Chapter 2 that, due to their early exercise feature, these options prices will always have a positive derivative with respect to time to maturity. Hence, this suggests that since the continuous dividend yield may lower a European call's "time value" while this loss in price can be avoided for the American call— by exercising it as soon as its price would drop below its exercise value—we must not expect Garman and Kohlhagen's formula to price American call options consistently.

The situation of foreign currency written options is analogous to the one previously discussed in Chapter 5 where we showed that for a "sufficiently high stock price" (here spot exchange rate), early exercise could never be ruled out for American call options written on common stocks that pay a continuous dividend yield. For that reason, the Black and Scholes formula— even properly adjusted for the continuous dividend yield—did not apply to those American calls. From this discussion it is obvious that the early exercise feature of foreign currency American calls is indeed a "valuable" additional characteristic of these options that precludes us from using Garman and Kohlhagen's model to determine their theoretical prices.

---

[13] See Chesney and Loubergé (1987b).

3. Finally, we can mention that although the European foreign currency call valuation formula does not apply to American options, it can, however, be easily extended to price European foreign currency puts. We accomplish this by simply invoking the put-call parity relationship for European options examined in Chapter 3, namely:

$$P = C - SB_f(\tau) + KB(\tau) \tag{8.14}$$

By replacing the call's price C with its analytical expression in Garman and Kohlhagen's formula Eq. (8.25), we then obtain

$$P = SB_f(\tau)N(d_1) - KB(\tau)N(d_2) - SB_f(\tau) + KB(\tau)$$

$\Leftrightarrow$

$$P = KB(\tau)N(-d_2) - SB_f(\tau)N(-d_1)$$

$\Leftrightarrow$

$$P = Ke^{-r\tau}N(-d_2) - Se^{-r_f\tau}N(-d_1) \tag{8.28}$$

where[14]

P = the price at time t of a European foreign currency put option whose time to maturity is equal to τ, whose exercise price is equal to K, and given that the current value of the exchange rate is equal to S

$$d_1 = (\ln[Se^{-r_f\tau}/Ke^{-r\tau}] + 1/2\sigma^2\tau)/\sigma\sqrt{\tau}$$

$$d_2 = d_1 - \sigma\sqrt{\tau}$$

$N(\cdot)$ = the standard normal cumulative distribution function.

We can define the same set of comparative statics for the European foreign currency put that we previously used for the European call. In particular, it can be shown that:

- The foreign currency put is a decreasing[15] convex function ($\partial P/\partial S < 0$ and $\partial^2 P/\partial S^2 > 0$) of the exchange rate ($S$) or, in other words, its price decreases at an increasing rate when the spot exchange rate increases.
- The foreign currency put price is a decreasing function of the interest rate (r) in the domestic country ($\partial P/\partial r < 0$) since a higher interest rate lowers the present value of the exercise price, thereby lowering the profit we can *ceteris paribus* expect to earn by exercising that put at its expiration date.
- The foreign currency put's price is an increasing function of the exercise price (K) since the latter represents the maximal profit (when $S = 0$) the put may earn when it is exercised at maturity. For any expected value of the exchange rate, a higher exercise price of course increases the chances that the put will expire in-the-money at maturity.

---

[14] Remember that $N(-d) = 1 - N(d_1)$.

[15] The put's price first derivative with respect to S is equal to:

$$\frac{\partial P}{\partial S} = \Delta_P^* = B_f(\tau) \times [N(d_1) - 1] = -B_f(\tau)N(-d_1) < 0$$

- The foreign currency put has *ceteris paribus* a higher price, the higher the standard deviation (σ) of the exchange rate ($\partial P/\partial \sigma > 0$). This relationship stems from the fact that a put has a dissymetric payoff structure and will therefore only benefit from a higher volatility in the underlying instrument. The more risky or volatile the exchange rate the more chances there are to see the put expire in-the-money—which is beneficial to its owner—while the associated higher probability to see it expire out-of-the-money doesn't weaken its owner's position.

- The foreign currency put price is positively related to the foreign interest rate (r_f). This is because a higher interest rate or dividend yield does *ceteris paribus* lower the value of the underlying instrument—$Se^{-r_f\tau}$—thereby making the put option more attractive and more likely to be in-the-money. Indeed, the higher the interest rate in the foreign country and the more we will gain by the delayed (forced) decision to exercise the put at maturity since a higher dividend yield—here r_f—lowers the cost-of-carrying the foreign exchange investment and thereby increases the current value of the put.

  A similar result has already been mentioned for European puts whose underlying stocks pay dividends. Indeed, whenever there are interim cash flows, we know that the stock price will drop by the dividend amount on each ex-dividend date and the latter reduction contributes to raise the current value of the European put option if these dividends will be paid before its expiration date.

- Finally, it can be shown that the put's price first derivative with respect to time to maturity, can be of either sign, namely

$$\frac{\partial P}{\partial \tau} = Sr_f B_f(\tau)N(-d_1) - rB(\tau)KN(-d_2)$$

$$+ (KB(\tau)\sigma N'(d_2))/2\sqrt{\tau} \gtrless 0 \tag{8.29}$$

This suggests that a put's price can—for given values of the other parameters S, σ, r, r_f, and K—actually decrease when its maturity is increased. Note that a similar relationship has already been observed for European options on nondividend paying stocks and that it results in both cases from two antithetic effects related to the passage of time: on one side, an increase in τ decreases the present value of the exercise price, hence suggesting that the relationship between P and τ should be negative. On the other side, an increase in time to maturity raises the chances of observing a favorable outcome (i.e., the put ending in-the-money) thereby suggesting that the longer the time to maturity, the more we may benefit from the exchange rate variability. In the case of the foreign currency written put, there is a third effect associated to the continuous dividend yield on the foreign investment, which suggests that additional time might be valuable since it contributes to a lower value of the foreign investment (i.e. $Se^{-r\tau}$)thereby increasing the put's degree of "moneyness." Hence, the presence of a continuous dividend yield contributes—*ceteris paribus*—to attenuate the negative impact a longer time to maturity can have on a European put's price while exactly the opposite statement was found to be true in the case of European call options.

Since American put options can always be exercised before expiration to avoid the negative "time to maturity effect," it follows that their prices always have a positive derivative with respect to their time to maturity. As previously shown for American calls, through the existence of their early exercise feature, American puts can also avoid such a potential depreciation, and we must therefore recognize that this "additional right" conveys additional value to these options.

Hence, an appropriate model for both American put and call options on foreign currencies should explicitly take into account their early exercise feature and—according to Restriction 2 in Chapter 2—allow them to be priced in excess of their European otherwise "identical" counterparts.

4. It might seem irrelevant to spend such a long time discussing the European foreign currency option pricing model when we know that most traded foreign currency options are actually of the American type, and hence should not be priced with Garman and Kohlhagen's pricing equations. However, this would ignore the existence of an important over-the-counter or interbank currency option market that offers standardized—generally European—option contracts to its customers.

Hence, appropriate tests[16] of this formula can only be conducted on such interbank traded European foreign currency options, which is precisely the data Chesney and Loubergé (1987a) used in their empirical study. Based on historical as well as predicted estimates of the exchange rate volatility, the authors conclude that at least for their sample of U.S. dollar/Swiss franc European options during 1983, Garman and Kohlhagen's formula had a tendency to overprice foreign currency European options.

Of course, we cannot reject the validity of a pricing formula due to the lack of additional tests supporting or rejecting Chesney and Loubergé's results and due to the fact that the quality of the price quotes, the synchronicity of the data, the choice of compatible domestic and foreign interest rates may also partially explain some biases since they preclude us from testing the formula with "clean" market data and reliable estimates of the volatility of the exchange rate. However, we will see that empirical studies of the American option pricing model—based on the same hypotheses underlying Garman

---

[16] It should be noted that some empirical studies (by, for example, Shastri and Tandon (1986)) regarding the efficiency of the Philadelphia Stock Exchange foreign currency market can actually be criticized since they applied Garman and Kohlhagen's option pricing model to value the American foreign currency options traded on this exchange. Hence, the fact that Shastri and Tandon find a significant price discrepancy between the theoretical and market values of these options shouldn't at all be surprising and it doesn't provide either a test of the formula's robustness or a sign of market inefficiency.

and Kohlhagen's European foreign currency pricing model—tend to support the conclusions reported by Chesney and Loubergé's. This suggests that some of the main assumptions in Garman and Kohlhagen's model might actually be inconsistent or too simple to deal with the complex behavior of those options' underlying instrument: the spot exchange rate. We will analyze the latter point after we examine how American foreign currency options should be valued from a theoretical standpoint.

5   THE PRICING OF AMERICAN FOREIGN CURRENCY OPTIONS

The approach generally followed to price foreign currency American options is conceptually similar to previous extensions of either Black and Scholes' model or Black's model to price American common stock and stock index futures written options respectively. The starting point is the same, that is, the European option pricing model is not relevant since it doesn't account for the fact that it might be optimal to exercise American options prior to their expiration date.

Second, the model is derived by assuming that all the relevant hypotheses—except for the early exercise feature—of the European option pricing model remain valid. For foreign currency American options this suggests that we still assume frictionless markets where trading can take place continuously, constant risk-free domestic and foreign interest rates, and, of course, the exchange rate is lognormally distributed so that its relative instantaneous changes still satisfy the stochastic differential equation (8.22).

Under these assumptions, a perfect hedge involving the American option and an offsetting position in the foreign riskless bond can be constructed and continuously rebalanced over time. Since it is perfectly riskless, it should return the instantaneous (domestic) risk-free interest rate per unit of time to avoid arbitrage opportunities in the market. Based on this "nondominance" argument, it can be shown that the price of an American call or put foreign currency option will satisfy the same partial differential previously stated (see Eq. (8.23)) for European options, namely:

$$\frac{1}{2}\sigma^2 S^2 \frac{\partial^2 X}{\partial^2 S} + (r - r_f)S\frac{\partial X}{\partial S} - rX + \frac{\partial X}{\partial t} = 0 \qquad (8.30)$$

where

$$X = C' \text{ if it is an American call option}$$

$$X = P' \text{ if it is an American put option}$$

It is subject to the following boundary conditions if it is a call option:

$$C'[S^*, K, T] = \max[0, S^* - K] \qquad (8.31)$$

$$C'[S, K, T] \geq S - K \text{ for all } t < T \qquad (8.32)$$

The first boundary, at the expiration date of the call, simply says that it should be worth the maximum between its exercise value and zero while the second boundary, which is specific to the American call, requires it to sell for at least its exercise value prior to maturity.

Similarly, the American put option will satisfy the partial differential Eq. ((8.30) with $X = P'$) subject to the following symmetric boundary conditions:

$$C'[S^*, K, T] = \max[0, K - S^*] \tag{8.33}$$

$$C'[S, K, T] \geq K - S \text{ for all } t < T \tag{8.34}$$

There is neither an analytical solution to the partial differential Eq. (8.30) subject to the boundaries in Eqs. (8.31) and (8.32) for the American call nor for the American put under the boundary conditions in Eqs. (8.33) and (8.34).

Such a conclusion has already been reached in the case of American options written on dividend paying stocks or on stock index futures contracts. Hence, the most commonly used approach consists of solving the partial differential Eq. (8.30) numerically to approximate the theoretical prices of American call and put options written on foreign currencies.

This technique has been followed by Bodurtha and Courtadon (1987) to test the performance of the foreign currency American option pricing model on a sample of 20,000 options trades that took place at the Philadelphia Stock Exchange from February 28, 1983 to March 26, 1985. In their study, Bodurtha and Courtadon use the implied standard deviation computed from options prices at date $t - 1$ to price the options on the following day (at date t). They argued that this gives more credibility to the model as a pricing tool since the studies which use the implied standard deviation computed from option trades executed during the same day are de facto using information which is not available to traders until the end of the day. They used the T-bill rate that matures as closely as possible to the option as a proxy of the domestic interest rate (r). However, this leaves them with the problem of finding similar securities that trade at the same time in foreign countries to obtain the proxy for the foreign riskless interest rate (r_f). One solution would have been to use forward foreign exchange contracts and assume that the interest rate parity holds in order to infer r_f from that relationship[17] for observed values of the domestic interest rate, spot exchange rate and the forward price. However, since such data on forward contracts was not available, the authors assumed that the interest rate parity holds with respect to the foreign currency futures contracts traded on the Chicago International Monetary Market to compute the foreign risk-free interest rates (r_f). The bias was not severe since, as we have seen in the previous chapter, the difference between the futures and

---

[17] The interest rate parity implies that:

$$_tH_T = S_t \cdot \frac{B_f(\tau)}{B(\tau)} = S_t e^{(r - r_f)\tau} \tag{8.15}$$

If interest rates are constant, then the same relationship will hold with respect to the futures contract's price (since $F = {}_tH_T$).

the forward price is typically negligible—according to a study by Cornell and Reinganum (1981)—for foreign currencies.

The results obtained when Bodurtha and Courtadon compared the theoretical prices of the foreign currency options to their market prices can be summarized as follows:

- On average, the American option pricing model overprices put options relative to call options.
- The model leads to a "moneyness bias" since it severely overprices in-the-money and slightly overprices at-the-money options on a dollar term basis while it underprices out-of-the-money options.
- The model also shows a "maturity bias" since the overpricing of the options tends to be a decreasing function of their time to maturity, especially for at-the-money options. The effect of maturity is however mixed for in-the-money options, which experience a "humped" pricing bias according to their remaining time to maturity. (Their overpricing first increases with time to maturity, then decreases and finally increases again for options that have more than 180 days until expiration.)

Indisputably, the study of Bodurtha and Courtadon raises several questions about the relevance of the American option pricing model—essentially based on the Black and Scholes model's underlying assumptions—when applied to foreign currency American options. In particular, the fact that the model systematically overprices at-the-money options while it underprices out-of-the-money options may suggest that the distributional properties of the exchange rate differ from those assumed by the model.

Hence, this study's results strongly suggest that the hypothesis of a lognormally distributed exchange rate should be further analyzed and even rejected if it isn't supported by the true stochastic behavior of exchange rates over time. In their concluding remarks Bodurtha and Courtadon suggested that the presence of jumps in the exchange rate process may account for the observed moneyness bias, and recommended further research to more carefully explore this possibility.

However, we must recognize that their study actually tests two hypotheses jointly, namely the relevance of the assumptions underlying the American option pricing model and the validity of the interest rate parity relationship. Unfortunately, since they did not present their results by currency type, we cannot draw any conclusions about whether the observed pricing biases for some currencies have actually been caused by violations of the interest rate parity relationship (with respect to the futures price). In summary, this empirical study as well as the results Chesney and Loubergé (1987a) obtain for European foreign currency options jointly suggest that the straightforward extension of Black and Scholes model's hypotheses to foreign currency options pricing should be examined more closely and even—if necessary—rejected in favor of a more thorough analysis of the pricing mechanisms governing these contingent claims.

6   ANALYZING THE PROBLEMS RELATED TO THE PRICING OF FOREIGN CURRENCY OPTIONS

The two models presented for the pricing of European and American foreign currency options are the most widely used among the financial community. However, recent empirical and theoretical research suggests that these models, which represent a straightforward extension of stock written option pricing models, actually fail to account for the specificities of foreign exchange options and therefore fail to accurately price these financial assets.

The main problem is obviously related to the stochastic properties of the exchange rate, the unique state variable that explains foreign currency prices in this framework. We will therefore consider whether the exchange rate violates the lognormal distribution assumption and examine some recent theoretical option pricing models that explicitly deal with this issue. Finally, we will examine whether other assumptions of Garman and Kohlhagen's model merit further attention to determine if they should be modified or relaxed to more accurately price foreign currency options.

A   The Distributional Properties of the Exchange Rate and the Pricing of Foreign Currency Options

Several empirical studies including McFarland, Richardson, and Sung (1982), and Wasserfallen and Zimmerman (1985, 1986) have indeed shown that the distribution of relative changes in the exchange rates presents fatter tails than for a normal distribution curve and furthermore that it is dissymetric. This implies that Assumption 4 underlying both the European and American foreign currency option pricing models is violated[18] since the latter requires that relative changes in the exchange rate be normally distributed.

Alternate models of the behavior of exchange rates have indeed been proposed (modeling exchange rates with a stable Paretian distribution or with a normal distribution that has time-varying parameters, etc.) but as pointed out by Jorion (1987), these models have never been compared and it is still not clear which one provides the most realistic description of the stochastic behavior of foreign currencies' relative prices.

Wasserfallen and Zimmerman (1986) analyzed the exchange rate's behavior based on intra-daily interbank exchange rate quotes of the U.S. dollar/Swiss franc exchange rate. They found evidence that the distribution of the exchange rate departs from normality since it is indeed leptokurtic (i.e., has fat tails) and dissymetric. In addition, their study suggests that the variance of the relative changes in the exchange rate is neither constant nor deterministically distributed over time.

---

[18] Under Assumption 4 underlying the Garman and Kohlhagen and the American option pricing models, the instantaneous relative changes in the exchange rate are normally distributed with a constant mean and variance per unit of time.

The latter finding has been used by Chesney and Scott (1987) who rejected the assumption that the exchange rate is lognormally distributed and explicitly accounted for the stochastic variance of the exchange rate. Hence, they derived a two-factor option pricing model in which the exchange rate (S) and the volatility (σ) of the exchange rate are assumed to be the two relevant variables that explain foreign currency option prices.

They accepted all other assumptions underlying Garman and Kohlhagen's model to develop their model. However, the assumption that the exchange rate is lognormally distributed was replaced by the following two stochastic differential equations describing the joint behavior of S and σ, the two state variables over time, namely:

$$\frac{dS}{S} = \mu dt + \sigma dz_1 \tag{8.35}$$

and

$$d \ln \sigma = \beta(\alpha - \ln \sigma)dt + \gamma dz_2 \tag{8.36}$$

where

μ = expected relative change in the spot exchange rate per unit of time; μ is an intertemporal constant

σ = unexpected relative change in the spot exchange rate per unit of time; σ is itself a stochastic variable

dz_1 = standard Wiener process associated to the exchange rate process

$\beta(\alpha - \ln \sigma)$ = the expected instantaneous change in the logarithm of the volatility, where β = a constant defining the speed of adjustment and α is a constant defining the long-term mean of the volatility's logarithm

γ = the unexpected change in the logarithm of the exchange rate

dz_2 = standard Wiener process associated to the logarithm of the exchange rate process

Note: dz_1 and dz_2 may actually be correlated, and the correlation coefficient ρ_{12} between these two Wiener processes must then be accounted for in the joint distributional properties of dS/S and $d \ln \sigma$.

Hence, the authors assumed that the volatility of the exchange rate process is stochastic and its logarithm follows a mean-reverting—also called Ornstein-Uhlenbeck—stochastic process over time. In other words, the logarithm of the exchange rate's volatility $(d \ln \sigma)$ is assumed to revert to its long run steady-state mean value α, which it will approach with a speed of adjustment equal to β. Moreover, the logarithm of the volatility evolves erratically—with a standard deviation equal to γ—around this mean-reverting tendency, driven by a standard Wiener process dz_2.

Since the volatility of the exchange rate is not a traded asset, the option pricing model cannot be derived with a simple hedging portfolio and applying the no-arbitrage condition as we previously did when the state variables were traded. This is because the market premium for "stochastic volatility" risk cannot be computed—since it doesn't relate to any traded asset or portfolio—and hedged in the market. Therefore, the authors relied on an equilibrium asset pricing model originally developed by Cox, Ingersoll, and Ross (1981) to derive the partial differential equation that the price of a foreign currency option must satisfy.

However, to solve that partial differential equation and obtain a tractable expression for a European currency option's price, Chesney and Scott made two simplifying assumptions:

1. The market price for stochastic volatility risk is equal to zero.
2. The stochastic processes of the exchange rate and the logarithm of the volatility are uncorrelated ($\rho_{12} = 0$).

Using a Monte Carlo simulation method, the authors were able to solve the valuation equation and obtain the theoretical prices of European call and put options.

Chesney and Scott then applied their "random variance" foreign currency option pricing model using price quotes for the U.S. dollar/Swiss franc European options traded by the Credit Suisse First Boston Futures Trading during the year 1984 and compared its pricing ability to that of Garman and Kohlhagen's European foreign currency option pricing model. This comparison led to the following results:

- The random variance model does indeed outperform (i.e., leads to smaller mean squared error and mean absolute deviations between model and market prices) the Garman and Kohlhagen model when the latter relies on the historical volatility of the exchange rate.
- The random variance model underperforms Garman and Kohlhagen's model when the latter relies on daily updated estimates of the exchange rate volatility (computed, as in the case of stocks written options, using the implied standard deviation method).

Furthermore, Chesney and Scott's study showed that the random variance model still produces pricing biases since it tends to overprice out-of-the-money call options, underprice at-the-money and in-the-money call options, and (strongly) underprice out-of-the-money put options. Hence, the empirical evidence generated from this study only weakly supported the random variance option pricing model as an—efficient and tractable—alternative to the simpler single-factor model proposed by Garman and Kohlhagen.

Indisputably, the random variance model is conceptually very appealing since it attempts to integrate random changes in the volatility of the exchange rate into the option pricing framework. However, this second state variable—which is not traded—adds several theoretical and statistical problems to the derivation of the option pricing model:

1. In particular, the stochastic process of the volatility itself might require further investigation to support the mean-reverting process adopted by the authors.

For example, should we allow for the possibility of jumps in the volatility of the exchange rate?

2. The model requires the estimation of the parameters (α, β, γ, and ρ_{12} when their values aren't arbitrarily assigned) in addition to the estimation of the volatility of the exchange rate (σ), which is the only unknown parameter that needs to be estimated to apply the single-factor foreign currency option pricing model. Hence, the random variance model will be more sensitive to measurement errors and the reliability of the "primary data" (option prices and spot exchange rate quotes) used to estimate this set of parameters.

3. Finally, it is critical to determine whether stochastic volatility is considered a systematic (and hence rewarded) risk component in the market or a diversifiable source of uncertainty that doesn't require any risk premium. As when Chesney and Scott did this pioneering study, there is still no theoretical evidence supporting or contradicting their assumption about a constant "stochastic volatility risk market premium."

We conclude by saying that the random variance model is at an early stage of development and recommend further examination of its potentially meaningful solution to the theoretical weakness of Garman and Kohlhagen's model description of the spot exchange rate process. In particular, additional empirical research on the behavior of the volatility of the exchange rate itself would be very useful to validate and extend the stochastic volatility foreign currency option pricing model, and to distinguish between those currencies for which the volatility really is stochastic and those for which it is more difficult to sustain, and for which alternative assumptions about the stochastic behavior of the exchange rate should be explored.

While Chesney and Scott's random variance option pricing model is essentially based on the non-stationary volatility of the exchange rate over time, some recent research has focused on other characteristics of the exchange rate's distribution and, more precisely, on its leptokurtic shape. Any distribution curve that has heavier tails than the normal distribution could therefore—a priori—provide a better explanation of the exchange rate's stochastic behavior. Further, the presence of discontinuities or "jumps" may well explain this departure from normality of the spot exchange rate.

Bodurtha and Courtadon (1987) suggested that using a mixed jump-diffusion process would certainly attenuate the observed "moneyness bias" induced by the American option pricing model. They based their conjecture on the fact that for common stocks written options, Merton's jump diffusion model corrects for the overpricing of at-the-money options and the underpricing of out-of-the-money options as well as for the time to maturity bias observed when we price those claims assuming that the state variable follows a continuous-time stationary diffusion process.

Jorion (1987) explored this conjecture by addressing whether discontinuities or jumps affect the exchange rate's behavior over time and hence should induce us to reject the stationary stochastic process described in Eq. (8.22) as a valid representation of this state variable's random evolution. He assumed that the exchange rate follows a mixed-jump diffusion process[19] and estimated this process for the U.S. dollar/German mark exchange rate over two distinct periods.[20] Over the fixed exchange rate period using monthly data from January 1959 to May 1971, the author found a significant jump process component, which is not surprising given the regulated exchange rate monitoring—by successive reevaluations of strong currencies—that occurred under this regime. He then proceeded with the same test during the flexible exchange rate regime, analyzing the period from January 1974 to December 1985 using both weekly and monthly data for the U.S. dollar/German mark exchange rate. Based on both types of data and whether the whole period or subperiods (using weekly data only) were used, the author found that the jump component of the process was significant. Jorion's results thus suggest that the distribution of exchange rates does present a strong jump or discontinuous component even under the flexible exchange rate regime.

Finally, Jorion tested whether the peptokurtic exchange rate distribution could be modeled alternatively assuming that the exchange rate follows a diffusion process with time-varying parameters. In particular, he examined whether the exchange rate follows an ARCH-process (for autoregressive conditional heteroskedastic process) of the first order. Under this specification, it is assumed that the conditional variance is a function of the last-squared innovation[21] in the exchange rate process. Jorion found evidence supporting the ARCH-process and since this stochastic process can significantly explain the U.S. dollar/DM exchange

---

[19] This stochastic process has already been discussed in the case of common stocks written options when we examined Merton's jump-diffusion option pricing model in Section 4D of Chapter 6. More formally, if the exchange rate follows a jump-diffusion stochastic process, then it is defined by the following equation:

$$\frac{dS}{S} = \mu dt + \sigma dz + (J - 1)\pi$$

where

μ = the instantaneous expected rate of return of the spot exchange rate; μ is an intertemporal constant

σ = the instantaneous standard deviation of the relative changes in the exchange rate conditional upon there being no jump over the next instant; σ is a constant

π = a continuous-time Poisson process with intensity parameter λ

$J - 1$ = the size of the jump in the exchange rate relative changes. $\log J$ is a normally distributed random variable with $E[\log J] = \alpha$ and $\text{Var}[\log J] = \gamma^2$

[20] The parameters of the stochastic process for dS/S are obtained using a maximum likelihood estimation technique [(see Jorion (1987)].

[21] If we denote by h_t the conditional variance of the logarithm of the exchange rate relatives, then:

$$h_t = a_0 + a_1(x_{t-1} - \mu)^2$$

where

x_{t-1} = the last observation of the exchange rate process (here $\ln(S_{t-1}/S_{t-2})$)

μ = the expected value of the exchange rate process $\ln(S_t/S_{t-1})$

α_0 = a constant

α_1 = the parameter inducing the heteroskedastic component of the variance

rate, it suggests that the volatility of the exchange rate—while not stochastic—does deterministically change over time.

Finally, he found that even after accounting for heteroskedasticity in the variance of the exchange rate process—through an ARCH-process—the jump component remains significant and therefore should definitively not be ignored for the U.S. dollar/German mark exchange rate analyzed in his study.

This led to his proposal of an extension of Merton's jump-diffusion option pricing model to foreign currency options. As in all our previously examined arbitrage-based option pricing models, he assumed that "jump risk is diversifiable," interest rates in both countries are constant, and markets are frictionless and continuously open for trading. The jump-diffusion model was then applied to a sample of "simulated" U.S. dollar/German mark European call options using the parameter estimates for this exchange rate that he had previously computed with weekly data over the period 1974–1985. The resulting "simulated" U.S. dollar/German mark call prices—theoretical call prices—were compared to those obtained by applying the Garman and Kohlhagen European call option pricing model.

Jorion showed that the pricing bias (i.e., the difference between the theoretical option price obtained with Garman and Kohlhagen's model and the assumed "true" price obtained using the foreign currency jump-diffusion foreign currency option pricing model, goes in exactly the same direction as the one previously documented in empirical studies where the former model's theoretical prices were compared to observed option market prices.

In other words, accounting for the jump component and using the jump-diffusion option pricing model should substantially reduce the "moneyness" bias of Garman and Kohlhagen's foreign currency option pricing model, at least as far as European call options written on the U.S. dollar/German mark are concerned. Although this only represents a preliminary result that is not based on traded foreign currency options, it is very promising for further research. Indeed, it clearly suggests that a jump-diffusion foreign currency option pricing model can account for and substantially reduce the "moneyness" bias of the single-factor option pricing model proposed by Garman and Kohlhagen.

Of course, the next step would be to generalize Jorion's results to other currencies, different subperiods, and, of course, "traded" options. At the current stage, however, we find Jorion's methodology very appealing since he starts by asking the relevant question: what is the "true" process underlying the exchange rate behavior over time? He then proceeds to test whether the data really support the jump component in the exchange rate process, and finally proposes a model that is consistent with the observed behavior of the exchange rate.

Further empirical studies would be very helpful to determine the ability of the jump-diffusion model to price options written on various currencies—whose jump component may have different significance levels—and traded in different markets. However, the latter conjecture also suggests that further theoretical research should be concerned with extending the foreign currency jump-diffusion model to American options—since most traded options are of the American type—which appears to be a rather complex but nevertheless challenging research topic.

B Some Other Issues Related to the Pricing of Foreign Currency Options

Thus far we have examined and relaxed only one of the basic assumptions underlying Garman and Kohlhagen's foreign currency model, namely the one that specifies the stochastic behavior of the exchange rate. Since the exchange rate represents—except in the random variance option pricing model—the unique factor which, in addition to time, determines the foreign currency option's price, it is essential to correctly assess its distributional properties before we can accurately price these options.

At the current stage, two directions have been used to relax the normally distributed exchange rate assumption: (1) the introduction of a second state variable to account for the stochastic volatility of the exchange rate and (2) a mixed jump-diffusion process fitted to that state variable's path. Given the observed results from the application of the jump-diffusion option pricing model, the second approach appears to be preferable. However, we are at too early a stage of both theoretical and empirical research to state any irreversible conclusions regarding the most appropriate and reliable specifications for the exchange rate stochastic process and the resulting option pricing model.

Although important, the issue of identifying the spot exchange rate's process should not deter us from examining other problems related to the pricing of foreign currency options. Many of these issues that have received little attention relate to the other assumptions underlying Garman and Kohlhagen's model. The following problems should deserve a more careful examination:

1. Can we assume that the exchange rate (or the exchange rate and its volatility) is (are) the only state variable(s) that contain all the relevant information to price foreign currency options? In particular, for foreign currency options involving the currency of a politically or economically unstable country, it becomes unclear whether the exchange rate will account for this additional uncertainty or, alternatively, whether another state variable related to this country's political risk should be added to the model (to account for restrictions on foreign currency purchases, sales or abnormal spreads between the bid and ask quotes of that currency, etc.). Furthermore, should political risk be treated as a diversifiable source of risk, hence unpriced or—possibly, for some currencies—as a systematic risk component that may lead to an additional risk premium?

   Alternatively, we may think that the discontinuities or jumps in the exchange rate process already reflect (or result from) such unexpected political or economical risks (like an election, a change in the country's monetary policy, etc.). But we still have to determine whether such a jump component in the exchange rate process is indeed diversifiable—in which case Merton's jump-diffusion option pricing model can be extended to foreign currency options—or whether it is a systematic risk component. In the latter case, we can no longer use an arbitrage-based argument to price foreign currency options since the jump risk component is not related to a traded asset or portfolio that can hedge it. Given these rather complex unresolved issues, a closer look at the fundamental mechanisms underlying the exchange rate jumps would certainly be a first step toward improving our knowledge about and identifying the factors that generate this discontinuous risk component of the exchange rate process.

2. A second closely related problem addresses the constant interest rate assumption underlying all the previously examined foreign currency option pricing models. That is, they all assume that the interest rate in both the domestic and the foreign country are constant over the option's remaining time to maturity. Unfortunately, there is no empirical evidence regarding the extent to which foreign currency option mispricing may result from such a simplifying assumption. Especially for American options whose early exercise possibilities are to a great extent determined by the differential between the foreign and the domestic interest rates this question should be addressed in more detail. Indeed, if the interest rates in one or both countries experience wide swings, this may have a nonnegligible influence on the prices of American and—to a lesser degree—European foreign currency options.

Before suggesting that the interest rate in the domestic and/or foreign country should be treated as state variables in the option pricing models, one certainly needs to examine and empirically establish whether and for which countries interest rate uncertainty really matters. This preliminary task is necessary, since there is no need to overspecify a model by adding two—non-traded—state variables, if the latter only negligibly affect some (or all) foreign currency option prices.

Since most traded options have a time to maturity that doesn't exceed a year, we would intuitively expect the bias resulting from the constant domestic and foreign interest rate assumption to be small, and even smaller for short-term options. However, we need empirical evidence to validate or reject this simplifying unrealistic assumption for each type of option—American and European—and for each type of currency.

Moreover, even if we assume that Garman and Kohlhagen's simplifying assumption holds, we still need to value foreign currency options and hence find reliable and mutually consistent proxies of the domestic and foreign interest rates. Most of the time, the securities available in one country—for example, Treasury bills—will not have any exact counterpart in the other country—for example, there are no traded riskless short-term discount instruments in the Swiss money market. Therefore, an interest rate differential may be arbitrarily increased or decreased by the heterogeneous characteristics of the proxies chosen in the two markets. In addition, a given formula's pricing accuracy may be artificially biased by the asynchronous trading problem since interest and option exchange rates are rarely traded or quoted at the same time.

A solution proposed by Bodurtha and Courtadon (1987) consists of inferring the only foreign variable, which is therefore likely to be traded during different time periods, from the futures price quoted for the foreign currency's futures contract trading on a domestic exchange. Although appealing, this procedure of identifying the foreign interest rate implicitly, must be treated carefully since it assumes that the interest rate parity with respect to the futures price is valid.

Finally, this procedure will require "cross currency" interest rate parity relationships to be verified every time a futures contract between the two desired currencies is not traded. Hence, the interest rate parity is then even more solicitated and the problem of asynchronous trading between the two futures contracts, the option, and the exchange rates involved is then likely to reappear.

This points out that we should carefully choose the parameters that enter into the option pricing model, especially when input data—here interest rates—is quoted in two different countries, which will only amplify—mismatching or nonsynchronous trading related—option pricing biases.

3. A third and final issue is related to the institutional barriers and market imperfections each of the previously presented models ignores. As for common stocks or stock index written options, it would be very useful for both academics and practitioners to know how transaction costs, margin requirements, and spot exchange rate bid and ask spreads affect the models' pricing ability.

Finally, we should remember that all the previously examined option pricing models rely on the assumption that a perfect hedge involving the option and an investment in the foreign currency can be maintained over the option's remaining time to maturity. A priori, since we are taking an offsetting position in a foreign riskless bond, which is a "traded" security, we will not be facing the problems such a perfect hedge involved for stock index options (whose underlying "asset" is not traded in the market).

However, another difficulty may arise for foreign currencies since the offsetting position is traded in another country, which may for diverse political or economical reasons, impose restrictions on the transfer of securities to foreign investors. Hence, we see that for politically unstable countries and for otherwise "stable" countries with "temporary" restrictions on capital transfer, the perfect hedge may suffer from occasional rebalancing penalties that may materialize in larger transactions costs, taxes, and, under the worst scenario, an absolute restriction for nonresidents to buy or sell the hedging security. Political risk should not be neglected since it can seriously affect an investor's ability to hedge a foreign currency option position, and therefore preclude existing option pricing models from providing accurate theoretical values.

Hence, we see that the fundamental assumption underlying all the previously examined arbitrage-based option pricing models (i.e., the maintenance of a perfect hedge) is itself contingent upon the irrelevance of political risk. While we may argue that this assumption holds for currently traded options on major currencies—such as the yen/dollar, the German mark/dollar, the pound/dollar, et cetera—this doesn't mean that the problem should be neglected for more "unstable" countries' currencies used in standardized option contracts or more simply because of the discontinuous but nevertheless underlying nature of political risk in all countries. In this perspective, we must assess this uncertainty's component relative importance in each country and ascertain whether it is priced or simply treated as (internationally) diversifiable and, therefore, not bearing any risk premium.

Hence, we see that in addition to the fundamental issue related to the specification of the spot exchange rate, some new problems arise when we value options that have an international dimension. In particular, identifying the factors that generate jumps in the exchange rate process, specifying their nature as being systematic (or not), verifying if the interest rate parity holds, and finally assessing whether interest rate uncertainty in both countries really matters represent some of the challenging research areas to determine if this more careful integration of the "international dimension" can improve the performance of existing foreign currency option pricing models.

7   Conclusion

As a final comment, we conclude that the theoretical models available to price foreign currency options are still at the developmental stage of identifying the relevant factors affecting these contingent claims' prices. Currently, Garman and Kohlhagen's model for European foreign currency options and its extension to the pricing of American options represent the most widely used approaches to value and design strategies with these financial instruments. Although, the application of a model by a large category of market participants may lead to a self-fulfilling prophecy (i.e., prices will to some extent be set according to the model) such a "simple" argument shouldn't preclude us from searching for more appropriate solutions through research and extensions of the proposed alternatives, namely a random variance option pricing model or a jump-diffusion option pricing model. Indeed, the development of more reliable and accurate foreign currency option pricing models can only improve and reinforce the efficiency of the foreign currency option markets and optimize the foreign currency risk-management strategies undertaken in these markets.

Indisputably, academic research can play a substantial role in achieving these objectives, but it cannot offer solutions to some major practical problems that the financial community must recognize; that is, whether the currently proposed standardized option contracts optimally respond to the variety of risk-monitoring strategies participants in these markets are willing to undertake. Indeed, we have seen that the dissymetric payoff structure of option contracts is particularly useful in the foreign exchange market since it enables producers, consumers, and portfolio managers to hedge a foreign currency denominated transaction whose realization is uncertain. From that perspective, option markets clearly have the advantage of offering more flexibility than the futures or the forward foreign exchange markets.

However, some features of existing foreign currency standardized option contracts could be improved to give even more flexibility to market participants without falling into the other extreme of providing them with "tailored," and there-fore, also illiquid financial instruments. In particular, the following characteristics of standardized option contracts deserve some comments:

1. The time to maturity of most traded foreign currency options doesn't exceed twelve months and hence precludes investors or portfolio managers with long-term horizons—such as mutual funds, for example—to hedge their interna-tionally diversified equity or fixed-income securities positions. Indeed, the al-ternative of rolling over short-term currency options doesn't allow for a perfect hedge and, furthermore, it leads to an increased "insurance premium" attributed to additional transaction costs.

2. Most actively traded foreign currency options use the dollar as the reference currency. Although investors in Amsterdam and London can find foreign cur-rency options denominated in guilders or pounds, the volume and the number of these contracts are far less than those of dollar denominated foreign currency options traded on the Philadelphia Stock Exchange, for example.

   Obviously, the cost of hedging is increased—via triangular option sales and purchases—for market participants whose reference currency is not the dollar. In Europe, trading on one or several exchanges of options denominated in a stable European currency such as the German mark or the European Community Unit (ECU) may prove to be useful in light of the European community's proposed economic and financial integration projects of the 90s.

3. Most actively traded foreign currency options are of the American type while clearly some market participants would like to have "fixed" maturity hedging or speculative tools. We can draw a parallel with a car insurance policy contracted for x years; clearly the owner wouldn't be satisfied if the policy could be redeemed by the insurance company at any time before the x years actually expired. Confirming this type of argument, we saw that American exchanges have recently introduced European stock index options—like options on the S&P 500 Index and the XII Index—to respond to the perfect hedge strategies required by many institutional investors. However, while they can now monitor or hedge their market risk exposure over a fixed horizon, the same isn't true for their currency risk exposure unless they engage in the buying and selling of over-the-counter traded European foreign currency options.

   Hence, we see that there are several possibilities that can be explored to improve the flexibility of existing traded foreign currency options and maintain the competition and efficiency of the standardized markets where they trade. This problem should be addressed since there is an increasing variety of traded or "implicitly" traded foreign currency options an investor may select to fulfill his objectives. Among these alternative instruments, we can quote the following:

- Over-the-counter traded foreign currency options
- "Implicit" foreign currency options embedded in the specification of many new forward contracts like the "range forward" contract or the "tunnel" forward con-tract, et cetera, whose popularity in the interbank community steadily increases

- "Implicit" foreign currency options embedded in the structure of several newly issued fixed-income securities. For example, recently in the Swiss bond market, several foreign borrowers issued bonds that offer put and call options on a foreign currency to either themselves and/or the lenders. These are typically long-term European and American options, which are found in ALPS (Adjustable Loan Perpetual Securities), FIPS (Fixed Interest Payable Securities), and other types of debt issues.
- "Implicit" foreign currency options embedded in convertible fixed-income issues that allow the bondholder to convert his fixed-income security into the issuer's equity, which is denominated in a currency other than the bond itself.

All these coexisting foreign currency options are typically longer lived than standardized option contracts. Further, they are often denominated in currencies other than the U.S. dollar and may hence partially respond to the unfulfilled objectives of standardized traded foreign currency options.

These "hybrid" instruments, however, are even more complicated to value than "straight" standardized foreign currency options since they do not trade separately from the asset—a bond, or a forward contract, for example—to which they are associated. Indisputably, since such "hybrid" foreign currency options as well as existing over-the-counter or exchange traded foreign currency options have dramatically expanded—both in volume and in variety—as a response to the increased volatility in the exchange rates observed during the last fifteen years, it is essential that the financial community understands how to use and to value such instruments.

In addition, the analysis of foreign currency options is important since no investor or manager can deny that diversification pays, but that international diversification pays even more. The main advantage of the latter strategy is, of course, that it reduces investment risk to its systematic (rewarded component). However, to offset its undesirable "secondary"—but not through its resulting impact on a portfolio's performance—effect, it is universally acknowledged that the foreign currency risk exposure of a portfolio cannot be left unmanaged.

From that perspective, it is certainly more efficient in the long-run to learn how foreign currency options should be priced and introduced in a portfolio management strategic plan—for hedging or speculating purposes—than to limit investments to simple but sometimes costly "bets" on cross-currency future relationships.

CHAPTER

9

CONCLUSION

In this study, we have presented a detailed analysis of standardized traded options, focusing on two topics in particular, the economic justification of contingent claims and the examination of option pricing models that have been developed to assess their "fair" value.

As far as the first subject is concerned, no one today would deny that options have an essential financial function, namely that of providing various categories of economic agents with dissymetric payoff structures, and thereby offering a concrete means of monitoring their exposure to heterogeneous sources of uncertainty. The growth—both in terms of volume and geographical expansion—and innovation observed in traded option markets reflect the increasing popularity of these instruments in the financial community.

We analyzed the following four categories of standardized option contracts and emphasized their importance in the context of today's internationally diversified portfolio management.

- Stock written options
- Stock index written options
- Stock index futures written options
- Foreign currency written options

From a conceptual standpoint, the initial analysis was achieved through an in-depth examination of stock written options. In a second stage, we extended the presentation to options written on a "basket" of stocks (i.e., a stock index), a futures contract (more precisely, a stock index futures contract), and finally options written on a foreign currency. Our purpose was to show the possible diversity in the underlying assets as well as the specific problems associated with the analysis and pricing of each newly created category of traded options.

Although these four categories of options offer by far the most direct responses to the monitoring of portfolio management's main risk exposures, they are only part of the vast population of options currently available. Indeed, options are "everywhere" and one strategy for assessing their diversity is by lengthening the "list" of standardized traded options to include

- Fixed-income securities written options
- Commodities written options
- Precious metals written options
- Agricultural products written options

Another approach is by examining the variety of nontraded options such as

- The option feature embedded in callable bonds
- The option feature embedded in convertible bonds
- The option feature embedded in stock right issues
- The caps, collars, and floors often accompanying floating rate debt issues

We could go even further by showing that many classical "assets" or "concepts" in finance can actually be viewed, analyzed, and priced as an option (or a combination of options).

The most widely recognized extension of the option pricing theory to "indirect" options is Merton's (1973) application to the pricing of the capital structure of the firm. He showed that under some specific assumptions, the equity (or the stock) of the firm can be viewed as a call option on the value of the corporation owned by its shareholders. Indeed, if we suppose that a corporation has only one debt issue and equity, then clearly at the expiration date of the debt issue, the stockholder will experience one of two possible results:

- receive nothing in the case of bankruptcy or in other words if the value of the firm (V^*) is equal to or less than the face value of the debt (B)
- be entitled to the difference between the value of the firm (V^*) and the face value of the debt (B) if the former is greater than the latter

Therefore, at the maturity date of the bond issue, the value of the stock of the company is equal to $S = \max[0, V^* - B]$, a payoff structure we are already familiar with and that shows that the shareholders are *de facto* holding a European call on the value of the firm that expires at the redemption date of the debt issue and whose exercise price is equal to the face value (B) of the debt.

Similarly, the debt issue, or in some more complex situations, the junior, senior, and subordinated debt issues of a corporation can also be analyzed and priced using the option pricing theory. Although we will not explore this subject further, it is important to know that even in corporate finance, capital budgeting decision, mergers and acquisitions strategies' evaluation, et cetera, the option theory does apply because there are so many real and financial assets involved, so many decisions that actually generate optional rights and hence dissymmetric payoffs to their owners and issuers.

Hence, the conceptual dimension of an option extends far beyond standardized option contracts traded in the markets. This suggests that the analysis of the latter represents the cornerstone to understanding and evaluating the "cost" of a large variety of financial decisions we make everyday without even realizing the additional value they have stemming from their "hidden" option property(ies).

For all these reasons, an in-depth analysis of existing option pricing models was necessary to identify and summarize the key parameters underlying an option's fair "value." Indeed, whatever the type of option we are valuing, we have seen that it was essential to

- Identify the relevant state variable(s) that explain the option's price behavior over time
- Specify the stochastic process of these state variable(s) consistently
- Determine whether option exchanges are indeed compatible with the "perfect market" paradigm and the continuous trading assumption
- Examine whether all the state variables used to price the option contract are traded assets or, alternately, whether replicating portfolios exist that can perfectly hedge unexpected shifts in these state variables. If neither of these two conditions is met, we have seen that the market price of these "unhedgeable" uncertainty factors must be estimated before we can actually price the contingent claims.

Furthermore, since nearly all option pricing models examined in this study are partial equilibrium models derived under the assumption that there are no arbitrage opportunities in the market, they will be highly sensitive to any incorrect specification of the underlying state variable(s) that are suppose to capture "all" the relevant information to price the option.

Finally, these models are also highly vulnerable to any market imperfection that could preclude the feasibility of the perfect hedge under which theoretical option prices are actually derived (using the no-arbitrage condition). We, therefore, emphasized for each type of option—especially stock index written options—how departures from the perfect market paradigm in terms of transaction costs, short selling restrictions, infrequent trading, illiquidity, capital transfer restrictions, et cetera, could alter the pricing ability of existing option pricing models.

In this respect, we have deplored the frequent lack of originality characterizing option pricing models, which partially explains some of their limits. Indeed, the Black and Scholes option pricing model has often been inappropriately extended to the pricing of other traded options although its underlying assumptions are inconsistent with the environment in which those options actually trade and/or with the true distributional "properties" of their underlying instrument. This situation is improving due to the tremendous research effort to focus more carefully on the main weaknesses of the Black and Scholes option pricing model to create models that match the reality of financial markets more closely. As a result, today we have at our disposal a large variety of existing option pricing models that can be used to price standardized stock option contracts, foreign currency option contracts, stock index option contracts, et cetera, and which can also provide the necessary risk-monitoring parameters that enable us to build strategies involving these same option contracts.

To summarize, we can say that options already instigated an "innovative" asset pricing theory whose applicability domain has over the past fifteen years been extended to a variety of traded, nontraded, and even only indirectly "option-like" financial instruments or decisions. Nevertheless, we still require an active academic involvement to provide more powerful option pricing models that accurately represent the characteristics of each specific type of contingent claim being valued, and that can be used simultaneously as efficient portfolio management decision-making tools.

However, an "active" involvement of the financial community is equally desirable and becomes a "must" given that options have literally transformed the "art" of management over the past decade. By active involvement, we essentially mean that students and professionals should make the necessary pedagogical effort that will enable them to understand the very nature of options, price them accurately, and use them effectively in a variety of risk-monitoring strategies.

Indisputably, this "educational option" is currently deeply in-the-money and should not be left unexercised since options are "everywhere" and understanding them conceptually is necessary at both individual and corporate levels to stay active and competitive for future investment and portfolio management challenges.

REFERENCES AND FURTHER READING

Ball, Clifford A., and Walter N. Torous (1985). "On Jumps in Common Stock Prices and Their Impact on Call Option Pricing." *Journal of Finance*, 40, 155–74.

Barone-Adesi, G., and R. E. Whaley (1987). "Efficient Analytic Approximation of American Option Values." *Journal of Finance*, 42, 301–20.

Beckers, Stan (1981). "Standard Deviations Implied in Option Prices as Predictors of Future Stock Price Variability." *Journal of Banking and Finance*, 5, 363–82.

Black, Fisher (1975). "Fact and Fantasy in the Use of Options." *Financial Analysts Journal*, 31, 36–41, 61–72.

Black, Fisher (1976a). "Studies of Stock Price Volatility Changes." *Proceedings of the 1976 Meetings of the American Statistical Association, Business and Economic Statistics Section*, 177–81.

Black, Fisher (1976b). "The Pricing of Commodity Contracts." *Journal of Financial Economics*, 3, 167–79.

Black, Fisher, and Myron Scholes (1972). "The Valuation of Option Contracts and a Test of Market Efficiency." *Journal of Finance*, 27, 399–418.

Black, Fisher, and Myron Scholes (1973). "The Pricing of Options and Corporate Liabilities." *Journal of Political Economy*, 81, 637–59.

Blattberg, Robert C., and Nicholas J. Gonedes (1974). "A Comparison of Stable and Student Distribution of Statistical Models for Stock Prices." *Journal of Business*, 47, 244–80.

Bodurtha, J., and G. Courtadon (1987). "Tests of an American Option Pricing Model on the Foreign Currency Options Market." *Journal of Financial and Quantitative Analysis*, 22, 153–67.

Bookstaber, Richard M. (1987). *Option Pricing and Investment Strategies*, rev. ed. Chicago: Probus.

Brennan, Michael (1986). "The Cost of Convenience and the Pricing of Commodity Contingent Claims." Unpublished paper, University of British Columbia.

Brennan, Michael, and Eduardo S. Schwartz (1977). "The Valuation of American Put Options." *Journal of Finance*, 32, 449–62.

Brennan, Michael, and Eduardo S. Schwartz (1978). "Finite Difference Methods and Jump Processes Arising in the Pricing of Contingent Claims: A Synthesis." *Journal of Financial and Quantitative Analysis*, 13, 461–74.

Brenner, Menachem, Georges Courtadon, and Marti Subrahmanyam (1985). "Options on the Spot and Options on Futures." *Journal of Finance*, 40, 1303–17.

Brenner, Menachem, Georges Courtadon, and Marti Subrahmanyam (1987). "The Valuation of Stock Index Options." Unpublished paper.

Capozza, D., and B. Cornell (1979). "Treasury Bill Pricing in the Spot and Futures Market." *Review of Economics and Statistics*, 61, 513–20.

Chesney, Marc, and Henri Loubergé (1987a). "The Pricing of European Currency Options: Empirical Tests on Swiss Data." *Aussenwirtschaft*, II/III, 213–28.

Chesney, Marc, and Henri Loubergé (1987b). "L'Evaluation des Options sur Devises: Que Faut-il Retenir des Recherches Récentes?" Unpublished working paper, University of Geneva.

Chesney, Marc, and Louis Scott (1987). "An Empirical Analysis of European Currency Options: A Comparison of the Modified Black-Scholes Model and a Random Variance Model." Unpublished paper, University of Illinois.

Chiras, Donald P., and Steven Manaster (1978). "The Information Content of Option Prices and a Test of Market Efficiency." *Journal of Financial Economics*, 6, 213–34.

Christie, Andrew A. (1982). "The Stochastic Behaviour of Common Stock Variances." *Journal of Financial Economics*, 10, 407–32.

Copeland, Thomas E., and J. Fred Weston (1988). *Financial Theory and Corporate Policy*, 3rd ed. Reading, MA: Addison-Wesley.

Cordero, Ricardo, and Walter Wasserfallen (1986/87). "Options und Futures in der Schweiz." *Finanzmarkt und Portfolio Management*, 10, 23–27.

Cornell, B., and K. French (1983). "Taxes and the Pricing of Stock Index Futures." *Journal of Finance*, 38, 675–94.

Cornell, B., and M. R. Reinganum (1981). "Forward and Futures Prices: Evidence from the Foreign Exchange Markets." *Journal of Finance*, 36, 1035–45.

Cox, John C. (1975). "Notes on Option Pricing 1: Constant Elasticity of Variance Diffusions." Working paper, Stanford University.

Cox, John C., Jonathan E. Ingersoll, and Stephen A. Ross (1981). "The Relationship between Forward Prices and Futures Prices." *Journal of Financial Economics*, 9, 321–46.

Cox, John C., and Stephen A. Ross (1976a). "The Valuation of Options for Alternative Stochastic Processes." *Journal of Financial Economics*, 3, 145–66.

Cox, John C., and Stephen A. Ross (1976b). "A Survey of Some New Results in Financial Option Pricing Theory." *Journal of Finance*, 31, 383–402.

Cox, John C., Stephen A. Ross, and Mark Rubinstein (1979). "Option Pricing: A Simplified Approach." *Journal of Financial Economics*, 7, 229–63.

Cox, John C., and Mark Rubinstein (1985). *Option Markets*. Englewood Cliffs, NJ: Prentice Hall.

Elton, E. J., M. J. Gruber, and J. Rentzler (1984). "Intra-Day Tests of the Efficiency of the Treasury Bill Futures Market." *Review of Economics and Statistics*, 66, 129–41.

Emanuel, David C., and James D. Macbeth (1982). "Further Results on the Constant Elasticity of Variance Call Option Pricing Models." *Journal of Financial and Quantitative Analysis*, 17, 533–54.

Engle, Robert (1982). "Autoregressive Conditional Heteroscedacity with Estimates of the Variance of United Kingdom Inflation." *Econometrica*, 50, 987–1007.

Evnine, Jeremy, and Andrew Rudd (1984). "Option Portfolio Risk Analysis." *Journal of Portfolio Management*, 10, 23–27.

Fama, Eugene F. (1965). "The Behavior of Stock Market Prices." *Journal of Business*, 38, 34–105.

Fama, E. F., and G. W. Schwert (1977). "Asset Returns and Inflation." *Journal of Financial Economics*, 5, 115–46.

Figlewski, S., with J. Kose and J. Merrick (1986). *Hedging with Financial Futures for Institutional Investors: From Theory to Practice*. New York: Ballinger.

Galai, Dan (1977). "Characterization of Options." *Journal of Banking and Finance*, I (December).

Galai, Dan (1978). "Empirical Tests of Boundary Conditions for CBOE Options." *Journal of Financial Economics*, 6,187–211.

Galai, Dan (1983). "A Survey of Empirical Tests of Option Pricing Models," in *Option Pricing*, ed. Menachem Brenner, pp. 45–80. Lexington, MA: D.C. Heath.

Garman, M., and S. Kohlhagen (1983). "Foreign Currency Option Values." *Journal of International Money and Finance* (December), 231–37.

Geske, Robert (1978). "Pricing of Options with Stochastic Dividend Yield." *Journal of Finance*, 33, 617–25.

Geske, Robert (1979). "A Note on an Analytical Formula for Unprotected American Call Options on Stocks with Known Dividends." *Journal of Financial Economics*, 7, 375–80.

Geske, Robert, and H. E. Johnson (1984). "The American Put Valued Analytically." *Journal of Finance*, 39, 1511–24.

Geske, Robert, and Richard Roll (1984). "On Valuing American Call Options with the Black-Scholes European Formula." *Journal of Finance*, 39, 443–55.

Geske, Robert, and Kuldeep Shastri (1985). "Valuation by Approximation: A Comparison of Alternative Option Valuation Techniques." *Journal of Financial and Quantitative Analysis*, 20 (March).

Grabbe, J. (1983). "The Pricing of Call and Put Options on Foreign Exchange." *Journal of International Money and Finance* (December), 239–54.

Haugen, Robert A. (1986). *Modern Investment Theory*. Englewood Cliffs, NJ: Prentice Hall.

Hull, J. (1989). *Options, Futures, and Other Derivative Securities*, Prentice Hall. Englewood Cliffs, NJ.

Hull, J., and A. White (1987). "The Pricing of Options on Assets with Stochastic Volatilities." *Journal of Finance*, 42, 281–300.

Ingersoll, Jonathan E., Jr. (1987). *Theory of Financial Decision Making*. Totowa, NJ: Rowman & Littlefield.

Jarrow, Robert A., and G. S. Oldfield (1981). "Forward Contracts and Futures Contracts." *Journal of Financial Economics*, 9, 373–82.

Jarrow, Robert A., and Andrew T. Rudd (1983). *Option Pricing*. Homewood, IL: Dow Jones Irwin.

Johnson, H. E. (1983). "An Analytic Approximation of the American Put Price." *Journal of Financial and Quantitative Analysis*, 18, 141–48.

Jorion, Phillipe (1987). "On Jump Processes in the Foreign Exchange and in the Stock Market." Unpublished paper, Columbia University.

Klemkowsky, Robert C., and Bruce G. Resnick (1979). "Put-Call Parity and Market Efficiency." *Journal of Finance*, 34, 1141–55.

Kon, Stanley J. (1984). "Models of Stock Returns: A Comparison." *Journal of Finance*, 39, 147–65.

Latané, Henry A., and Richard J. Rendleman, Jr. (1976). "Standard Deviations of Stock Price Ratios Implied in Option Prices." *Journal of Finance*, 31, 369–82.

Leland, Hayne E. (1980). "Who Should Buy Portfolio Insurance?" *Journal of Finance*, 35, 581–94.

Leland, Hayne E., and Mark Rubinstein (1981). "Replicating Options with Positions in Stock and Cash."*Financial Analysis Journal*, 37, 63–72.

Macbeth, James D., and Larry J. Merville (1979). "An Empirical Evaluation of the Black-Scholes Call Option Pricing Model." *Journal of Finance*, 34, 1173–86.

Macbeth, James D., and Larry J. Merville (1980). "Tests of the Black-Scholes and Cox Call Option Valuation Models." *Journal of Finance*, 35, 285–300.

McFarland, James, Pettit Richardson, and Sam Sung (1982). "The Distribution of Foreign Exchange Price Changes: Trading Day Effects and Risk Measurement." *Journal of Finance*, 37, 693–715.

Macmillan, L. W. (1986). "Analytic Approximation for the American Put Option." *Advances in Futures and Options Research*, 1.

Merton, Robert C. (1973). "Theory of Rational Option Pricing." *Bell Journal of Economics and Management Science*, 4, 141–83.

Merton, Robert C. (1976). "Option Pricing When Underlying Stock Returns Are Discontinuous." *Journal of Financial Economics*, 3, 125–44.

Merton, Robert C. (1977). "On the Pricing of Contingent Claims and the Modigliani-Miller Theorem." *Journal of Financial Economics*, 5, 241–50.

Merton, Robert C., Myron Scholes, and Mathew L. Gladstein (1978). "The Returns and Risks of Alternative Call-Option Portfolio Investment Strategies." *Journal of Business*, 51, 183–242.

Modest, David M., and Suresh M. Sundaresan (1983). "The Relationship between Spot and Futures Prices in Stock Index Futures Markets: Some Preliminary Evidence." *Journal of Futures Markets*, 3, 15–41.

Morse, J. N. (1988). "Index Futures and the Implied Volatility of Options." Unpublished paper.

Parkinson, Michael (1980). "The Extreme Value Method for Estimating the Variance of the Rate of Return." *Journal of Business*, 53, 61–65.

Ramaswamy, Krishna, and Suresh M. Sundaresan (1985). "The Valuation of Options on Futures Contracts." *Journal of Finance*, 40, 1319–40.

Rendleman, R. J., and C. F. Carabini (1979). "The Efficiency of the Treasury Bill Futures Market." *Journal of Finance*, 34, 895–914.

Ritchken, Peter (1987). *Options: Theory, Strategy and Applications*. Glenview, IL: Scott, Foresman.

Roll, Richard (1977). "An Analytic Valuation Formula for Unprotected American Call Options on Stocks with Known Dividends." *Journal of Financial Economics*, 5, 251–58.

Schmalensee, Richard, and Robert R. Trippi (1978). "Common Stock Volatility Expectations Implied by Option Premia." *Journal of Finance*, 33, 129–47.

Schwartz, Eduardo S. (1977). "The Valuation of Warrants: Implementing a New Approach." *Journal of Financial Economics*, 4 (January).

Scott, Louis O. (1987). "Option Pricing When the Variance Changes Randomly: Theory, Estimation and an Application." *Journal of Financial and Quantitative Analysis*, 22 (December).

Shastri, K., and D. Tandon (1986). "Valuation of Foreign Currency Options: Some Empirical Tests." *Journal of Financial and Quantitative Analysis*, 145–60.

Smith, Clifford W., Jr. (1976). "Option Pricing: A Review." *Journal of Financial Economics*, 3, 3–51.

Stapleton, R. C., and M. G. Subrahmanyam (1984). "The Valuation of Options When Asset Returns are Generated by a Binomial Process." *Journal of Finance*, 39, 1525–39.

Sterk, William E. (1982). "Tests of Two Models for Valuing Call Options on Stocks with Dividends." *Journal of Finance*, 37, 1229–38.

Sterk, William E. (1983). "Comparative Performance of the Black-Scholes and Roll-Geske-Whaley Option Pricing Models." *Journal of Financial and Quantitative Analysis*, 18, 345–54.

Wasserfallen, Walter, and Heinz Zimmerman (1985). "The Behavior of Intra-Daily Exchange Rates." *Journal of Banking and Finance*, 9, 55–72.

Wasserfallen, Walter, and Heinz Zimmerman (1986). "The Wiener Process, Variance Measurement and Option Pricing—Evidence from Intra-Daily Data on Foreign Exchange." Working paper, University of Bern and Hochschule St-Gallen.

Whaley, Robert E. (1979). "A Note on an Analytical Formula for Unprotected American Call Options on Stocks with Known Dividends." *Journal of Financial Economics,* 7, 375–80.

Whaley, Robert E. (1981). "On the Valuation of American Call Options on Stocks with Known Dividends." *Journal of Financial Economics*, 9, 207–12.

Whaley, Robert E. (1982). "Valuation of American Call Options on Dividend Paying Stocks: Empirical Tests." *Journal of Financial Economics*, 10, 29–58.

Whaley, Robert E. (1986). "Valuation of American Futures Options: Theory and Empirical Tests." *Journal of Finance*, 41, 127–50.

Wiggins, James B. (1986). "Stochastic Volatility Option Valuation: Theory and Empirical Estimates." Working Paper, Cornell University.

INDEX

Adjustment procedure, 193
Agricultural products options, 290
ALPS (Adjustable Loan Perpetual
    Securities), 287
American option(s):
  binomial approach to, 150–156
  Black and Scholes model in pricing,
    127–133
  defined, 4
  early exercise feature of, 6, 13n,
    37–38, 150–161
  exercise value of, 12n, 46
  flexibility of, 29
  on foreign currency, 248–249, 263,
    273–276
  on futures contracts, 232–241
  intrinsic value of, 12n, 27–28
  on nondividend- vs. dividend-paying
    stocks, 34, 86, 150–161
  put-call parity relationships for, 42–46,
    263
  relationship between price and time to
    maturity, 91
  relative pricing of, 46–47
  restrictions on pricing of, 26–32
  solutions to the pricing of,
    156–161
  on a stock index, 189, 196–198
  stock prices and, 96–97
American Stock Exchange, 1, 4, 182
American Stock Exchange Institutional
    Investor Index (XII), 189–190, 191,
    193, 196, 199, 286

Apparent arbitrage opportunity, 222, 223
Approximation technique, 160, 237n
Arbitrage portfolio, 147
Arbitrage restrictions:
  on common stock written option prices,
    26–32, 49, 86–87, 91, 93, 96,
    98n, 127n, 128, 196, 201, 234
  on foreign currency option prices,
    252–263
ARCH-process (autoregressive conditional
    heteroskedastic process), 280
Asynchronous trading, 223, 241, 283
At-the-money options, 12, 135
Autoregressive, 280

Bankruptcy, 290
Basis, 206–207, 208
Basis risk, 222, 241, 242
Beta coefficient, 140–141
Beta of a portfolio, 217n, 218
Bid/ask spreads, 178, 179
Binomial multiplicative process, 52–55,
    72
  convergence of, 76–77, 102–104
  criticisms of, 74–75
Binomial option pricing model, 19n
  advantages of, 50
  analyzing, 55–61, 66–71
  applying, 61–65
  assumptions underlying, 51–55
  equilibrium pricing constraint
    imposed by, 71–72

Binomial option pricing model (*Cont.*)
  hedging and, 123
  perfect hedge in, 68–70
  in pricing American options, 150–156
  recursive replication technique, 61–64
  relative pricing characteristic of, 70–71
  risk-neutralized probabilities of, 71, 72
Black and Scholes Formula:
  computation of, 108–122
  dividends and, 122–127
Black and Scholes option pricing model,
    2, 19n, 39n, 72
  advantages of, 88
  area under the normal curve, 105
  assumptions underlying, 77–78, 83–84,
    101, 146, 163–168, 226–227, 275
  compared to Black's option pricing
    model, 228–230
  consistent performance of, 145–146
  criticism of constant variance
    assumption in, 163–168
  dividends and, 122–127
  as a European call valuation formula,
    80
  examples using, 81–83, 120–122
  foreign currency option pricing models,
    as an extension of, 247, 264, 266,
    273 fundamental characteristics of,
    84–88
  hedging and, 123
  implied standard deviation from 118n
  interest rates and, 91–92, 112–113,
    146–149
  as an investment decision-making tool,
    107–143
  limitations of, 122, 143, 146, 291–292
  measuring risk exposure with, 133–143
  Merton's expansion of, 147–148,
    171–172, 173
  perfect hedge in, 83–84
  in pricing American options, 127–133
  pricing methodology of, 101
  problems in applying, 107–108
  relation to the binomial option pricing
    model, 74–81
  significance of, 73–74
  and standard deviation of stock returns,
    97–98
  stock prices and, 92, 93–94, 109
  stock return variance and, 113–120
  striking price and, 89, 109–111
  technical considerations in computing,
    108–122
  time to maturity and, 89–91, 111–112
  weaknesses of, 176

Black's option pricing model, 227–229, 273
  assumptions underlying, 235
  compared to Black and Scholes option
    pricing model, 228–230
  Whaley's study of, 237–238
Bodurtha and Courtadon's foreign currency
    option pricing model, 274–275
Bottom straddle, 21
Butterfly spread, 20

Call option:
  defined, 4
  impact of dividends on, 35–36
  modified, 110
Capital budgeting, 291
Cash delivery, 215
Cash settlement, 189, 200, 201, 216
Center for Research in Security Prices
    (CRSP), 185n
Central Limit Theorem, 103–104
Characteristics of options, 1–24
Chesney and Scott's foreign currency
    option pricing model, *see* Random
    variance foreign currency option
    pricing model
Chicago Board of Options Exchange,
    1, 5, 181, 182
Chicago Mercantile Exchange, 237
Clearing Corporation, 22
Commodity futures, 182
Commodity options, 2, 290
Compound call option, 158–159
Constant elasticity of variance, 163–165,
    166
Constant risk-free interest rate assumption,
    146–149
Continuous dividend yield, 269
Continuous-time perfect hedge, 85
Continuous-time state variable, 75, 87
Convenience yield, 261
Convexity, 93, 94, 96
Cost of carrying model, 206–207
Covariance, 214–215
Covered call position, 17
Cox's call option pricing model, 163–166
Cross-currency interest rate parity, 284
Currency risk exposure, 24, 182
  in international portfolio
    management strategies, 246–247

Daily settlement procedure, 212
Default-free bond, 229
Deferred right, 109n

Delivery date, 225
Delivery risk, 224
Delta, 92, 100, 135
Delta hedge, 137, 138, 251, 267
Diagonal spread, 20
Diffusion process, 161, 163
Dilution factor, 110
Discounted futures prices, 231
Discounting function, 111
Dissymetric payoff structure, 246, 285
Diversification, 181, 184, 245–246, 287
Dividends:
    and the Binomial option pricing model,
        150–156
    and the Black and Scholes option
        pricing model, 122–127
    impact on option prices, 32–38
    and the pricing of American options,
        156–161
    and put-call parity relationships, 41–46
Dow Jones Composite Average, 184
Dow Jones Industrial Average, 186
Dynamic asset allocation strategy,
    178–179
Dynamic portfolio insurance policies, 243

Early exercise feature, 37, 46, 86
    binomial approach to, 150–156
Elasticity, *see* Constant elasticity of
        variance; Price elasticity of variance
Embedded options, 2, 3
Equally weighted stock indexes, 184–185
Equilibrium price, 219, 222
European Community Unit (ECU), 286
European option(s):
    defined, 4
    exercise value of, 12n
    on foreign currency, 249, 264–273
    foreign currency option pricing model,
        264–268
    on a futures contract, 226–232
    implied standard deviations from, 118n
    interest rates and, 91–92
    intrinsic value of, 12n
    maturity of, 89–91
    on nondividend- vs. dividend-paying
        stocks, 33, 87
    price behavior of, 98–100
    pricing on a nondividend-paying stock,
        49–72 put-call parity relationships
        for, 38–41, 66
    relative pricing of, 46–47
    restrictions on pricing of, 26–32

    on a stock index, 188, 192–195
    stock prices and, 92, 92–97
    value at expiration date, 26–27
European Stock Index, 198
Exact hedge, 252
Exchange rate, 248
    in determining a foreign currency
        option's price, 282–284
    volatility of, 278, 279
Exercise bias, 241
Exercise price, 5, 109–111. *See also*
        Striking price
Exercise risk, 200, 201
Exercise rule, 201
Exercise values, 12, 201, 225
Exercising an option, 4, 9
Expiration cycle, 6, 225
Expiration date, value of options at,
    26–27
Extreme values variance, 116–117

Fat tails, 276
Financial futures contracts, 211–215
Financial Times Stock Exchange Index,
    188
Finite difference numerical approach,
    160n
FIPS (Fixed Interest Payable Securities),
    287
Fixed-income securities written options,
    2, 290
Fixed maturity hedging, 286
Foreign currency options, 2, 182
    arbitrage restrictions on prices of,
        252–264
    defined, 248
    dollar as reference currency, 286
    embedded, 287
    fixed maturity hedging, 286
    flexibility of, 286
    general characteristics of, 248–252
    hedging and, 249–251, 265, 273, 284,
        286
    historical background on, 248
    hybrid instruments, 286–287
    institutional barriers and market
        imperfections in, 284
    interest rates and, 268, 283
    problems related to pricing of, 276–287
    risk-monitoring, 267
    role of exchange rate in determining
        price of, 282–284
    stable vs. unstable countries, 284

Foreign currency options (*Cont.*)
   time to maturity of, 286
   underlying security for, 253–254, 261
Forward contracts
   basic properties of, 202–211
   cost-of-carry model, 206–207
   defined, 202
   vs. options contracts, 202–203
   on precious metals, 208
   price of, 203–205
   value of, 205–206, 208
Futures contracts, 202
   basic properties of financial, 211–215
   basic properties of stock index,
      215–219
   defined, 211
   vs. forward contracts, 212
   marked-to-market, 212, 213–214
   pricing of, 219–224
Futures price, 212–215

Gamma, 93, 100, 135, 137
Garman and Kohlhagen's foreign currency
    option pricing model, 264–268, 278,
    281, 285
   basic properties of, 267–269
   weaknesses of, 279, 282
Gauss-Wiener process, 264
Geske's compound call option pricing
    model, 158–159
Global market risk exposure, 246. *See
    also* Currency risk exposure
Gold futures, 182

Heating oil futures, 182
Hedge(s):
   in the binomial option pricing model,
     123n
   in the Black and Scholes option pricing
     model, 123
   defined, 17
   and foreign currency options, 249–251,
     286
   and stock index futures, 217–219,
     241–242
   types of, 18–19
   See also Perfect hedge
Hedge ratio, 18, 134, 173n, 178, 179,
    198, 239, 241, 265, 267
Hidden options, 291
Horizontal spread, 19, 251
Humped pricing, 274
Hybrid foreign currency options, 286–287

Identical option, 42, 214
Immobilization, 229
Immunization, 68, 134, 137, 217
Implicit foreign currency options, 286
Implicit position, 39
Implied standard deviation (ISD),
    117–120
Indice CAC, 188
Inflation, 247
Institutional Index option contract, 4
Integer rule, 5
Interbank markets for futures contracts,
    212
Interbank-traded foreign currency options,
    4, 272
Interest rate parity condition, 260, 284
Interest rates, 91–92, 112–113, 209, 268,
    283
International capital asset pricing model,
    245
International diversification, 245–246, 287
International Monetary Market, 182, 246,
    248, 274
In-the-money options, 12, 89, 135, 166
Intrinsic value, 12, 27–28
Investment horizon, 14n

Jump-diffusion stochastic process, 77n,
    171, 172, 173–174, 175n, 176, 279,
    281
Jump process option pricing formula, 169
Jump risk, 173, 174

Known dividends, 123–125

Leptourtic, 276
Limited position, 39
Liquidity, 22, 86, 177, 178, 179, 182,
    200
Lognormal distribution, 76, 77, 83, 161
London International Futures Exchange
    (LIFE), 248
Long position, 8, 16, 17, 18, 19, 39, 43,
    134, 138, 157, 173, 178, 182, 198,
    199, 200, 201, 214, 220, 226, 227,
    238, 239, 241, 251, 254, 259, 262,
    263, 265
Long straddle, 21

Major Market Index, 216
Margin requirements, 22, 179, 241

Market imperfection, 214, 284
Market manipulation, 22
Market-oriented portfolio, 202
Market risk exposure, 190, 243
Market risk monitoring strategies, 243
Market-weighted stock indexes, 187–188
Marking-to-market procedure, 212,
    213–214
Mathematical symbols, defined, 26,
    252–253
Maturity, 6, 49, 89–91, 111, 237
Maturity bias, 275
Mean-reverting stochastic process, 277
Mergers and acquisitions strategies, 291
Merton's option pricing model, 147–148,
    171–172, 173, 290
Mispricing, 36, 40, 86, 146, 217, 283
Mixed jump-diffusion process, *see*
    Jump-diffusion stochastic process
Modified call option, 110
Monetary policies, 247
Moneyness bias, 166, 237, 275, 279, 281
Multi-currency transactions, 252
Multiplicative binomial process, 52, 54,
    55, 74

Negative basis, 208
Net carrying cost, 206, 207, 229
New York Stock Exchange (NYSE), 2,
    174, 181, 184
New York Stock Exchange Composite
    Index, 183, 188, 193, 199, 216,
    225
No arbitrage restriction, 198
Nondominance, 25, 273
Nonlinear payoff structure, 16, 20
Nonnegativity condition, 26
Nontraded assets, 183, 239, 243, 290
Normal distribution, 76, 79, 102, 270
NYSE Financial Subindex, 184
NYSE Industrial Subindex, 184
NYSE Transportation Subindex, 184
NYSE Utilities Subindex, 184

Offsetting transactions, 9, 200
Oil futures, 2, 182
Open interest, 7, 8
Opening position, 8
Opportunity costs, 247
Option(s):
    bearish views and, 16
    bullish views and, 14
    defined, 3–4, 26

dynamics of, 6–8
essential financial function of,
    289
on a foreign currency, 247–287
on a futures contract, 224–226, 234
vs. futures and forward contracts, 3,
    16
gains and losses on, 13n
historical background on, 1–3,
    181–182
key parameter to value, 72
maturity, 6, 49, 89–91, 111, 237
payoffs, 16
standardized, 21–24
strategies for, 13–21
types of, 3
unit size, 225
value of, 12
written on a stock, 5–6
written on a stock index, 188–190
See also American option; Call option;
    European option
Option Clearing Corporation, 22
Option premium, 4
Option price:
    basic properties of, 9–12
    determinants of, 88–98
        interest rate, 91–92
        standard deviation of stock returns,
            97–98
        stock price, 92–97
        striking price, 89
        time to maturity, 89–91
    differences between theoretical and
        actual, 177
    factors influencing, 46
    relationship between striking price and,
        28, 46
    role of arbitrageurs in, 9, 10–11
    stock riskiness and, 97–98
Option price sensitivity:
    defining and using, 133–136
    numerical example of, 136–139
    price elasticity and, 139–143
Option pricing:
    arbitrage-free approach to, 181–244
    discrepancies in, 176–177
    impact of dividends on, 32–38
    partial equilibrium models for, 176–177
    rational boundaries to, 25–47
    restrictions that apply to, 23, 26–32
    restrictions to rational, 233
    single-factor models, 177
    two-factor models, 240
    See also Binomial option pricing model;

Option pricing (*Cont.*)
    Black and Scholes option
    pricing model; Black's option
    pricing model; Merton's option
    pricing model; Whaley's option
    pricing model
Option pricing theory:
  analyzing, 290–291
  extensions of, 290
  limitations of, 179
Option strategies:
  analyzing, 13–21
  hedges, 18–19
  spread positions, 19–20
  straddles, 20–21
Option trading:
  regulation of, 1–2
  risks in, 22–23
  secondary market for, 22
  strategies associated with, 8–9
Ornstein-Uhlenbeck stochastic process,
  277
Out-of-the-money options, 12, 89, 135,
  140, 166
Overpricing, 275, 278, 279
Over-the-counter markets for futures
  contracts, 212
Over-the-counter-traded foreign currency
  options, 249, 272, 286, 287
Over-the-counter-traded stock options, 4,
  184

Pacific Stock Exchange, 2
Panic decline, 199
Parity futures price, 219, 220, 221–222,
  223
Parkinson's extreme values variance
  measurement procedure, 116–117
Parsimony principle, 112
Partial differential equation, 235n, 278
Partial equilibrium option pricing models,
  176, 235
Payoff redistribution, 14
Payout-protected options, 122n
Payout-protection rule, 6
Perfect forecast ability, 98
Perfect hedge, 17, 18, 134–135, 137,
  138, 164n, 172–173, 177, 178, 179,
  235
  in the binomial option pricing model,
    68–70
  in the Black and Scholes option pricing
    model, 83–84

  continuous-time, 85–86
  on foreign currency options, 252, 264,
    265, 273, 284, 286
  and stock index options, 191, 198–200
Perfect market, 179
Philadelphia Stock Exchange, 2, 182,
  248, 263, 272n, 274, 286
Poisson stochastic process, 77n, 169, 172
Political risk, 284
Portfolio insurance strategy, 178, 179
Portfolio management strategy:
  currency risk exposure in, 246–247
  stock index futures and, 243
  stock index options and, 190–192
Portfolio rebalancing, 86, 135, 178, 199,
  235, 238, 243
Precious metals forward contracts, 208
Precious metals written options, 290
Preference-free pricing formula, 84, 167
Price elasticity, 92n, 119n, 139–143
  of variance, 164
Price-weighted stock indexes, 185–186
Pricing bias, 237, 281
Protective put strategy, 18
Pseudo-American call valuation, 129–133
Pseudo hedged position, 199
Pure diffusion stochastic process, 172
Pure jump stochastic process, 77n,
  168–169, 171
Put-call parity relationship, 17n, 19,
  38–46, 66, 125, 230–231, 259–260
  for American foreign currency options,
    263
  for American options on
    dividend-paying stocks, 44–46
  for American options on
    nondividend-paying stocks, 42–44,
    101
  for European options on
    dividend-paying stocks, 41
  for European options on
    nondividend-paying stocks, 38–40,
    87
Put option, defined, 4

Quadratic approximation technique, 237n

Random variable, 53, 76
Random variance foreign currency option
  pricing model, 278–280
Range forward contracts, 286
Recursive replication technique, 61–64

Redundant assets, 242
Relative pricing, 46–47, 70–71, 84
Replicating portfolio, 50–51
Reverse hedges, 19
Right issues, 110–111
Risk, 70 ,71, 88, 133–142
Risk-averse economy, 84
Riskless arbitrage, 29, 33, 36, 50, 177n, 201, 207–208, 252
Risk-monitoring strategies, 285
Risk-neutral economy, 72, 84, 85, 88, 101, 229
Risk-neutralized probabilities, 71, 72
Risk premium, 149, 168
Roll's American call valuation model, 157–158, 159

SBS Swiss Index, 188
Securities and Exchange Commission (SEC), 5
Selection bias, 217
Short position, 8, 13, 14, 16, 19, 22, 39, 41, 43, 152, 158, 178, 182, 199, 201, 204, 217, 223, 224, 225, 227, 238, 239, 241, 246, 248, 251, 257, 259, 262, 265
Short straddle, 21n
Silver futures, 182
Simple jump process, 169–170
Single contract, 5
Single-factor option pricing models, 177
Spot exchange rate, 252, 260, 261
Spot index, 215, 216
Spread positions, 19–20
Standard & Poor's (S&P) 100 Index, 181, 188, 189, 199, 242
Standard & Poor's (S&P) 500 Index, 181, 183, 188, 196, 199, 216, 217, 218, 221, 222, 225, 237, 242, 286
Standard deviation of stock returns, 97–98
Standard Wiener process, 277
Standardized option contracts:
    additions to the list of, 290
    categories of, 289–290
    evolution of, 1–2
    reasons for, 21–22
Stochastic process, 161–163, 171, 291
Stochastic volatility, 176, 278
Stock index futures, 2, 24, 183, 215–219
    analyzing options written on, 224–241
    complexity of, 241–244
    defined, 215

    hedging and, 217–219
    valuing, 219–224
Stock index options, 2, 24
    vs. common stocks, 183
    description of a contract, 188–190
    equally weighted, 184–185
    general characteristics of, 183–188
    market-weighted, 187–188
    as nontraded assets, 183
    perfect hedges in, 198–200
    and portfolio management strategies, 190–192
    price-weighted, 185–186
    problems related to the pricing of, 198–202
    valuing American options, 196–198
    valuing European options, 192–195
Stock market crash of 1987, 146, 162, 171, 175, 179, 199, 239
Stock prices:
    in the Black and Scholes option pricing model, 92, 93–94, 109
    discontinuities in the sample path, 168–175
    distributional properties of, 161–175
Stock return variance, 113–120
    historical, 114–117
    implied standard deviation method, 117–120
    nonstationarity of, 163–168
    technique used to compute, 116n
Stock splits, 5, 6, 110
Stock written options, 2
Straddles, 20–21, 251
Strangles, 251
Straps, 251
Striking price, 5, 28, 89. *See also* Exercise price
Strips, 251
Supershares, 192
Sure profit investment strategy, 40, 43, 46, 86
Swiss Option Exchange, 111
Synthetic positions, 18, 178

Tax considerations, 51, 179
Term structure of interest rates, 147
Theta, 90, 99
Time bias, 138, 237
Time value, 12, 138, 269
Top straddle, 21n
Traded assets, 239, 241
Trading barriers, 86

Transaction costs, 22, 51, 177, 178, 179, 198, 241, 242
Treasury bill written options, 182
Treasury bond futures written options, 2
Treasury bond written options, 2, 182
Treasury note written options, 182
Triangular option strategies, 252, 286
Tunnel forward contracts, 286
Two-factor option pricing models, 240

Underlying asset diversification, 181
Underlying instruments, 5, 6, 198n
Underpricing, 86, 87, 166, 275, 278, 279
Unknown lividend payments, 126–127
Unitary period, 74

Value Line Composite Stock Index, 183, 216, 222–223, 225
Vertical spreads, 19, 251

Volatility of stock price, 116, 122, 167
Volume, 8

Wall Street Journal, The 6, 7, 225
Whaley's option pricing model, 237–239
Written option, 1, 2, 3, 5, 17, 24, 29, 33, 134, 139, 183, 202, 224, 225, 228, 232, 233, 235, 237, 239, 240, 241, 248, 252, 254, 256, 257, 260, 262, 267, 268, 269, 273, 276, 278, 279, 280, 284

XII Index, *see* American Stock Exchange Institutional Investor Index

Yield to Maturity, 113

Zero-sum game, 14, 16